A Finger Pointing from the Grave

The shock of Sara's death had driven her sister Krissy to her knees. Still clutching the phone, she had convulsed in wrenching sobs, as the grieving voice of her mother echoed softly in her ear. Finally, exhausted, she had collapsed into a fitful sleep. The telephone's insistent ring awakened her. Still dazed, Krissy picked up the receiver. Her cousin's voice was low and urgent. Had Sara ever given to her for safekeeping the documents she copied from Fred's safe?

"What documents?" Krissy asked. She couldn't remember that summer day in 1989 when Sara had rifled her husband's files, found the combination to the safe, and, frightened by her own temerity, called her sister from Fred's basement office as she thumbed through a sheaf of documents she had taken. Forgotten or dismissed as too dramatic was Sara's admonition to take copies of the documents to police should anything ever happen to her.

Secrets
Never Lie

The Death of Sara Tokars—
A Southern Tragedy
of Money, Murder and
Innocence Betrayed

R. ROBIN McDONALD

AVON BOOKS ◆ NEW YORK

SECRETS NEVER LIE is a journalistic account of the actual investigation and conviction of Fred Tokars in 1997 for the murder of Sara Tokars in Cobb County, Georgia. The events recounted in this book are true. Scenes and dialogue have been reconstructed based on formal interviews, local and federal law enforcement records, court transcripts, and published news stories. Quoted testimony and other court-related statements from before, during, and after trial have been taken verbatim from transcripts.

AVON BOOKS, INC.
1350 Avenue of the Americas
New York, New York 10019

Copyright © 1998 by R. Robin McDonald
Published by arrangement with the author
Library of Congress Catalog Card Number: 97-94864
ISBN: 0-380-77752-5
www.avonbooks.com

First Avon Books Printing: June 1998

AVON TRADEMARK REG. U.S. PAT. OFF. AND IN OTHER COUNTRIES, MARCA REGISTRADA, HECHO EN U.S.A.

Printed in the U.S.A.

WCD 10 9 8 7 6 5 4

For Sara

A person commits the offense of murder when he unlawfully and with malice aforethought, either express or implied, caused the death of another human being. . . . Malice shall be implied where no considerable provocation appears and where all the circumstances of the killing show an abandoned and malignant heart.

From the Georgia Criminal Code

ACKNOWLEDGMENTS

The story of the murder of Sara Tokars has been carefully reconstructed using material from four criminal trials, numerous court hearings and court filings, personal letters and correspondence, police reports and transcripts of police interviews, corporate records, civil trial records, dozens of news stories and television accounts, and multiple interviews with people associated with the case that took place over five years, beginning in December 1992 shortly after Sara Tokars was slain.

The dialogue appearing throughout the narrative has been drawn directly from those highly detailed court and interview transcripts, and augmented, when necessary, by personal interviews with the participants. Many of those conversations were recounted again and again in court hearings, a number of which I personally attended and covered as a reporter during the four years between Sara Tokars's death and her husband's conviction for her murder in March 1997.

I extend my special thanks to court reporters Patti Allen, Rufus Hixson, and Judy Pulliam as well as my close friends Paige Love and Michael Smith for their invaluable help in providing me with court transcripts of the trials.

I also owe a debt of gratitude to my colleagues in the news media who worked alongside me—among them Don Plummer, Bill Rankin, Emma Edmunds, Ann Woolner, Lolita Browning, Leigh Green, Keith Williams, Lynn Harasin, Don Johnson, Jim Kaiserski, Paul Crawley, Al Ashe, and Michael Marsh—who offered me their invaluable insights, their anecdotes, their encouragement, and their help whenever I needed it.

I am also grateful to my editor at Avon Books, Stephen S.

Power, who always believed in this story, that it needed to be told, and that I was the one to do it. His encouragement, his thoughtful edits, and his suggestions have helped to shape this book and always made it better.

I would like to thank the many people associated with the murder case who appear throughout the narrative—those who knew Sara Tokars, who participated in the hunt for and the prosecution of her killers, or who ardently defended them— for their patience, and their willingness to spend hours upon hours of their time talking with me, both on and off the record, as they shared with me their honest impressions, their insights, their anger, and their grief.

Finally, I want to express my admiration for the Ambrusko family. Sara's six surviving sisters and her parents endured not only their deep grief at Sara's death but also the intense and continuing scrutiny of the news media in one of this state's most sensational and highly publicized murders. They submitted to public hearings in which their character and motives were repeatedly called into question in an orchestrated effort to defend Sara's husband by attacking them. Yet they remained dedicated to their sister's memory and to her two children who had watched their mother die. They are, and always will be, among the bravest people that I know.

Prologue

The Secrets in the Safe

HE CAME, IN THE END, FOR THE MONEY.

The sweet-faced woman's low, urgent voice on the telephone had left the detective curiously unmoved. But Sara Tokars owed him nearly a thousand dollars although her pearls and an engagement ring were still secure in his safe. Ralph Perdomo hoped to persuade her that cash was still the currency he preferred.

A small, compact man with thinning gray hair he swept back in a modified pompadour, Perdomo was a former New Jersey police officer. His nasal tenor, his oversized spectacles, and his office in the remodeled basement of a spacious suburban ranch defied the stereotype of a broke, belligerent, back-alley private investigator. Yet, for more than thirty years, Perdomo had depended for his living on the sordid revelations that accompany divorce. He hired out as an investigator primarily to Atlanta's attorneys, who counted among their ranks Sara's husband, Fredric Tokars.

Sara had hired Perdomo to follow Fred—an action that, in a marriage as desperate as Sara's, bordered on sedition. Her husband, she said, was having an affair. The woman lived in an elegant row of apartments in one of Atlanta's most expensive and desirable neighborhoods. She was a boutique sales clerk at nearby Lenox Square, one of Atlanta's most affluent malls. Neither Sara nor Perdomo knew that the woman's

1

roommate was a drug dealer or that he was one of Tokars's clients. Not that it would have mattered to Perdomo.

He had listened with growing impatience as Sara told him she suspected her husband associated too freely with his drug-dealer clients and that he might be abusing drugs himself. He was skeptical when she told him that her husband "shoved her around" and threatened her, promising that if she didn't do what he wanted, "he knew people who knew what had to be done."

And the private detective, for all his years of experience, had no concept of the angry inquisition Sara faced if Fred suspected she was spying on him, or the trembling irrepressible panic that threatened to swallow her when she considered what her husband might do. The detective didn't understand that Sara's actions were those of a small, hunted animal, and that she truly feared a man who won his way by bullying and belittling her.

In fact, Perdomo suspected Sara was being melodramatic, that she was just another betrayed and wounded housewife willing to say whatever was necessary to pursue a lucrative divorce. He simply didn't believe her. Sara's hesitant story was too bizarre, a product of a wild and wounded imagination, not an accelerating desperation. And Fred Tokars was a divorce attorney, a member of the clubby profession upon which Perdomo depended for his trade.

As a result, he had not taken to heart Sara's urgent warnings to be cautious as he trailed her husband. He had been spotted by Fred, a former assistant district attorney who promptly reported him to Atlanta police.

The encounter with police, though embarrassing, had told Perdomo what he needed to know. He was unwilling to do more than confirm Fred's affair until Sara matched the thousand-dollar retainer she had already paid him by redeeming her jewelry from his safe for cash. He hoped his visit to the Tokars's home in response to Sara's agonized call would persuade her.

The Tokars's home was in one of Atlanta's more exclusive, predominantly white northern suburbs in a county, that despite a pretense of refinement, cultivated a reputation for intolerance. In 1989, when Perdomo met Sara at her home,

Newt Gingrich had not yet moved to Cobb County, and his thunderous election as Speaker of the U.S. House of Representatives was still no more than an ambitious dream. The Cobb County Commission had yet to pass its resolution that praised family values by rejecting gays and lesbians such as Gingrich's half-sister and the commission chairman's youngest daughter.

But the seeds that secured Gingrich's political future were clearly there, sown among Cobb County's fashionable subdivisions by families who had fled from the city's desegregated schools and forced busing, its escalating poverty, decay, and crime, and nurtured by northern Republicans attracted to Atlanta's booming economy. Atlanta residents would have once referred to them derisively as Yankees, but the word in Henry Grady's New South city had become increasingly irrelevant and lost its power to sting.

The Tokars's home, built of gray wood and trimmed in stone, was nestled at the crest of a wooded lot in one of those east Cobb subdivisions, on a secluded street of spacious three-hundred-thousand-dollar homes. As Perdomo stepped from the air-cooled car's comfortable chill, the July heat enveloped him like a second breath. It was the miserable heat of a Georgia summer—a pitiless swelter that settles in the body's swampy hollows and makes even the glasses sweat. Unlike the flat malevolent radiance of the western plains, Georgia's heat has heft and breadth. It registers breath, sucks away strength, and, with nightfall, exhales a palpable damp.

Sara met the detective in the driveway. She stood there, guileless and unvarnished, her toddler sons commandeering her knees. Hair the color of high noon clung damply to her neck and forehead in the simple style she had worn since high school. Worry betrayed her. She was neither as young nor as carefree as she first appeared.

"Please come in," she urged Perdomo. "I have something to show you."

As Sara opened the door, the detective was shocked to find the house was as stifling as a tenement. Sara apologized profusely.

"There is no air-conditioning," she explained. "My husband pays all the bills in cash, and he won't get the air conditioner repaired until he has more cash available.''

As Sara's youngest sister, Krissy, hustled Sara's tiny sons upstairs, Sara led Perdomo to the basement where Fred Tokars kept an office. The Tokars's home was sparsely furnished, Perdomo noted. The furniture was, for the most part, cheap and worn, the kind most often found at thrift stores or in motels that had seen better days. Given Fred's growing visibility in Atlanta's legal community and the Tokars's smart address, Perdomo was taken aback. He had not expected to find so little in a home that, based on appearances, should have housed far more.

"My husband is out of town," Sara said, as much to reassure herself as the detective. Fred had long forbidden Sara to enter the basement, declaring it his personal sanctuary from both her and the children. In a room where Fred had established a private office, Sara pointed out several wires dangling from the junction box near the ceiling. The ends of the wires were wrapped in black electrician's tape.

"Could someone be tapping the phones?" Sara asked.

Perdomo was noncommittal. "They are telephone wires," he acknowledged. "And they're attached to the main system. It's possible that a telephone could have been hooked on to them." He dismissed her concerns that her telephone conversations might be monitored. "If you think there might be a wiretap on the phone, you need to call the telephone company."

The curt advice offered Sara neither reassurance nor relief. Her husband had worked for the Southern Bell Telephone Company before he passed the bar. He still had friends who worked there. And if he had installed a listening device on the telephone, Sara did not want to risk his wrath by revealing she had discovered it. Her husband was already monitoring her actions. She simply wanted to know how far he had been willing to go.

Perdomo was equally dismissive when Sara directed him to a safe that sat in her husband's office.

"Fred doesn't know I have the combination," she told Perdomo as she knelt, spun the dial, and swung open the door. Inside the safe, Perdomo eyed a stack of manila folders as

well as several unmarked vials of white pills. Sara scooped
up a handful of pills.

"Do you know what these are?" she asked.

"No," Perdomo said, shying away from vials she offered.
"I have no idea what they are. There's no way I can identify
them. If you take them to your family doctor, he can probably
tell you what they are."

But Sara wasn't finished. She began pulling files from the
safe that she had thumbed through on an earlier foray into
the basement. Prominent among them were folders marked
with the names of Caribbean islands, small commonwealths
where banking laws made illicit money-laundering and tax
evasion an easy proposition.

In calling Perdomo to the house, Sara was seeking answers
to questions that she almost feared to ask. "I think my husband may be involved in illegal activities," she whispered.
"I want you to look at these files."

Perdomo barely glanced at them. She was married to a man
he viewed as a "very prominent attorney." She was behind
on her bills and, although she still owed the private detective
nearly a thousand dollars, she could offer no more than a
promise to pay as collateral.

When she hired Perdomo, Sara's suspicions hadn't strayed
beyond the possibility that her husband was having an affair.
And it was no surprise that when Perdomo confirmed that
Fredric Tokars was unfaithful, his distraught and angry wife
would have little good to say. But suggesting that a former
assistant district attorney was consorting with drug dealers
and indulging in criminal behavior seemed ludicrous.

"I doubted her at the time because of Mr. Tokars's reputation in the community," Perdomo said. "I thought she was
just another injured spouse who was making wild accusations
against her husband."

Perdomo refused to take the files Sara offered him. "Your
husband is an attorney," he said. "That's his safe. If I touch
anything in that safe, I am invading his privacy."

The detective knew that Sara, as Fred's wife, had legal
access to the safe and, legally, he was free to peruse the documents she offered. But Perdomo had no intention of pursuing the investigation unless Sara paid him an additional fee.

Besides, his specialty was surveillance of suspected adulter-
ers, not financial fraud. He wanted no part of any criminal
investigation, particularly of an Atlanta attorney who was beginning to contribute heavily to local political campaigns.
And there was the economic stability of his agency to consider. Perdomo relied primarily on attorneys like Fred, not
clients like Sara, for the bulk of his income.

"Copy everything you think is valuable," he finally advised her. "Then give the copies to your attorney or someone
you trust. I won't be able to help you."

I won't be able to help you. Hard words for a woman who
had to swallow her fear before she could hire Perdomo and
pay him to follow her husband. Now, that same fear rattled
in her throat. She and her sons were hostages in a loveless,
faithless, and increasingly sinister marriage. Looking at Perdomo she realized that, regardless of her husband's sins, she
still needed money to ransom her way out.

"Please," she begged the detective. "Fred has told me that
he has all kinds of political connections and contacts, and he
can have us taken care of any time he wants to."

But Perdomo was unsympathetic as well as single-minded.
Sara owed him money. He was suspending his services until
he was paid. As they left the basement, Perdomo brushed
aside her final question.

"Ralph, if anything ever happens to me, will you give your
surveillance file to the police?"

"Yes," Perdomo said with a sigh, certain that he was simply indulging a spiteful delusion. He would.

He could not know, as he backed away from the Tokars's
home that day and abandoned his own investigation, that
Sara's desperate quest for information and her dalliance with
divorce would make her someone to be reckoned with in the
gritty, dim-lit world of nightclubs, drug deals, and dirty
money that had ensnared her husband. He never guessed that
the files Sara had thrust at him from the safe would later
follow her killer like the echoes of an unfinished prayer.

Part I

═══

SARA

One

A Fatal Phone Call

WHEN SARA FIRST SAW HIM ON THE EVENING NEWS, FREDRIC Tokars was a junior prosecutor assisting in a murder trial downtown—the gruesome slaying of an Atlanta attorney by his lover.

Despite the grim tableau on the television screen, she recognized him as a fellow Yankee in a southern city, someone from her hometown high school, someone who had grown up in the same comfortable, white-bread suburb of Buffalo, New York. Sara was reassured by the image of the slender, awkward man. He reminded her of her childhood, and she had always felt safe as a child.

On impulse, Sara called him. A friend of hers was looking for a lawyer, and she thought that Fred could help. They hadn't spoken for years, but Fred's younger brother had dated Sara's younger sister in high school. His father had been one of her own father's students at the University of Buffalo's School of Medicine before he, too, became a doctor.

At that point in her life, Sara was hungry for familiarity and the easy comfort it engendered. She was thirty-one, attractive and outgoing, with a wide, white smile and blonde hair falling below her shoulders just as it had in high school. But a recent divorce had left her bruised, although she rarely showed it, and insecure about her future and her faith.

She was separated from her close-knit family, except for

9

her youngest sister and living in a city that became her home only because she had followed her former husband there. She was anxious that the Catholic Church and her parents would frown on her divorce, and she still wrestled with the agonizing insecurity that often accompanies the dissolution of a marriage. Sara gravitated easily to anyone who reminded her of home, so when Fred asked her for a date, she accepted.

That single phone call altered her future as surely as a weathervane marks the wind. It would become for Sara Ambrusko a collision course with darkness.

To understand Sara, one has only to know her family. She was the middle daughter in a family of seven girls—all of them blonde, all of them taught from childhood to be unfailingly polite. Her father, John Ambrusko, was a prominent Buffalo surgeon; her tiny mother, Phyllis, a gentle woman who never raised her voice.

Sara's father was the youngest of eleven children born to an immigrant Hungarian couple. His father had worked for a dollar a day in the foundries north of Buffalo while his mother ran a boarding house and took in washing to support the family.

Devoted to hard work, Sara's paternal grandmother was also devoted to God. Every Sunday, she would march her children off to church in their worn but freshly patched clothes. No challenge, she told Sara's father as a boy, was too great with hard work and prayer.

It was, in many ways, a hard life. Sara's father was born above an old saloon the family operated before Prohibition. One sister was blind. Another had been crippled by polio. As a youngster, Ambrusko worked to supplement the family's meager income, peddling newspapers and selling milk from the family cow. By the time he was fourteen, he was working after school and on Saturdays at a market willing to wink at child labor laws, hauling fruit and vegetables and sweeping floors for $3.50 a day.

Every Saturday, a doctor driving an elegant automobile would stop by the market. "He always had a linen suit," Ambrusko remembered. "He always looked immaculate. He would always buy his fruits and vegetables from me. I used to think, 'Geez, what do I have to do to get a job like that?' ''

For the remainder of his life, Ambrusko would be governed by a resolute determination to succeed so he could provide amply for his family. He would pass that sense of familial devotion on to his daughters, especially to Sara.

In high school, Ambrusko befriended a prominent Buffalo doctor's son which, in turn, led to "an amazing friendship" with his friend's father, a Buffalo surgeon. The older man soon became Ambrusko's mentor. He encouraged him to go to medical school, influenced him to become a surgeon like himself, and, in later years, helped propel the talented younger physician to prominence through personal recommendations and referrals as the surgeon of Buffalo's elite.

Ambrusko met Sara's mother while he was a surgical fellow at the Mayo Clinic in Rochester, Minnesota at the end of World War II. He had just returned from active duty in the South Pacific, where he had spent one year as the only doctor on a destroyer and another in a field hospital in the New Hebrides Islands.

"All I want is a real nice girl," he told friends eager to find him a date. "Are there any nice girls left in this world?"

Phyllis Eusterman, a dentist's daughter and the niece of the Mayo Clinic's prominent chief of medicine, was, according to Ambrusko's friends, the nicest girl in town.

Within a year, the couple were married. In 1948, Ambrusko returned with his new wife to Buffalo where he joined the surgical faculty at the University of Buffalo's medical school and opened a general surgical practice. In 1950, he became chief surgeon at Kenmore Mercy Hospital in one of Buffalo's northern suburbs, a post he would hold for the next twenty years.

A brilliant, determined, and opinionated man with a blunt, honest manner, Sara's father challenged death daily in hospital operating rooms with a fearlessness born of prayer.

"I had to be fearless when a patient came to me, because, more often than not, I was their last hope," he said. "I needed to be brave for them. I was fearless because I had a deep belief in the power of prayer, and I believed the Blessed Mother would help me if she felt I was worthy."

He worked long, grueling hours, often donating his services

to patients who couldn't afford to pay him. But he created for his wife and daughters a charmed world, at least as the sisters now remember it.

"We were always the good girls," said Krissy Ambrusko, Sara's youngest sister. "We ate our vegetables, said our prayers, crossed our legs at the ankle, and always said 'please' and 'thank you.' "

Devout Catholics, they attended parochial school as children. And, as a family, they said prayers on their knees every night to the Virgin Mary.

The seven sisters were—and remained throughout their lives—each other's best and closest friends.

Sara and her sisters grew up in a spacious, six-bedroom home Ambrusko built for his family in Amherst, a Buffalo suburb, on a street where Ambrusko said, "I was the only one who had a mortgage." In the winter, the children skated on a lake in front of the house. In summer, they built tree houses on the property, which sprawled over two acres, dallied in small rowboats on the lake, or swarmed around the pool, where they played host to a growing coterie of neighborhood youngsters and beaux.

As the middle child, Sara was at the center of her family. But more than that, she was their heart.

If her older sisters were more practical, more serious about the world, Sara was all sun and silver linings. She was an athlete—a cheerleader captain, an accomplished skier who rode horses and played tennis with abandon. She was the family organizer, their one-woman booster club, the one who took care of everyone, who seemed capable of fixing anything.

"What was most important to Sara as we were growing up was that we all be together," said her younger sister, Joni Ambrusko. "Trimming the Christmas tree, going to the drive-in in our pajamas, the Saturday afternoon hot dog cookouts were heaven to her. It was Sara who thought that going to the Buffalo Bills games in a blizzard—and lugging blankets and thermoses of hot chocolate and Dad's battery-powered hot socks—was just the greatest because, as she said when one of us tried to get out of it, 'It's always best when we're all together.' "

It was Sara who cajoled her father into buying a twelve-year-old cabin cruiser so the family could spend Sundays together on the Niagara River whenever he wasn't on call. Whenever the motor failed to start, it was Sara who climbed into the hold to tinker with the engine. And when a sailboat filled with children capsized, Sara swam to shore for help. As her younger sisters followed in her effervescent wake, Sara taught them how to drive, how to ski, how to ride, how to do all those things that she loved doing.

"I think you're getting it!" she crowed when Joni stalled for the tenth time on the expressway as Sara was teaching her to drive an old Toyota with a manual transmission.

"You're doing great, Karen," she yelled encouragingly when her younger sister made her first tentative run on snow skis, then hoisted her on her back and piggy-backed her down the slope.

Sara, Joni said, "was the brave one. She told us to try."

By the time Sara was a teenager, the Ambrusko home had become a gathering place for scores of young people drawn to weekend cookouts and the camaraderie of the seven sisters. Fred Tokars was one of them.

The Tokars family lived just two blocks from the Ambruskos, and for more than two years, Andy Tokars, Fred's younger brother, dated Karen Ambrusko, Sara's sister.

In fact, Andy was nearly a fixture in that openly affectionate household. He often joined Dr. Ambrusko in his den for Saturday football games. He was the grateful recipient of warm plates of food that Karen's mother prepared for him to eat after workouts with the high school rowing team.

Karen doted on him. But, throughout the years they dated, Karen said Andy could never bring himself to say, "I love you," in return.

Fred had the same lanky build as his younger brother, unruly brown hair, and the same plain but intelligent face. He was Sara's age and was a member of her class at Amherst High School. But although he drifted through the sisters' parties from time to time, Fred remained throughout their adolescence at the edge of Sara's life.

More than her other sisters, Sara aspired to be like her mother—by nature an utterly selfless woman, who, according to her youngest daughter, "cares about other people so much she feels what other people feel." But she idolized her prominent and politically connected father—a talented practitioner in a profession that brooked no error yet granted him the grace of saving lives, a generous father who lavished his daughters with comforts and sought to shelter them from the casual and reckless vagaries of life. Throughout her life, Sara would strive to please him.

If the Ambruskos were strict about anything it was their daughters' safety. They were not allowed to drive alone, especially at night. When they reached their teens and began dating, the sisters occasionally bridled at those rules. "But it got drilled into us," said Sara's sister, Karen Wilcox, "and we'd always take precautions about things."

But Sara always seemed invincible, one of her sisters wrote years later. "If we got caught in a thunderstorm, she managed to run between the raindrops. Sunshine always followed her. She could do anything and do it well. Nothing was too great a challenge."

Sara was also the one daughter who insisted that, as she and her sisters departed for college and began building lives far from Buffalo, that they continue to return home for holidays and reunions. Her love of skiing had lured her from Buffalo in 1971 to the University of Colorado at Boulder. While there, she became her now scattered family's anchor, planning birthday celebrations, marking anniversaries, orchestrating holidays, making certain that at least one daughter would be home for Mother's Day to weave the flowers with which, as children, they had always crowned their mother.

"We always tried to go home for Christmas, even when we were grown up," Joni Ambrusko remembered. "It was a tradition. I don't remember Sara ever missing one."

Sara's older sister, Therese, still remembers reuniting with her sister at an airport en route to Buffalo for a family reunion only to learn their flight had been canceled. "Sara explained that we had to get home, it was our mom's birthday, and then burst into tears," Therese said.

Sara reveled in those holidays and surprises. There was about her a radiant innocence, and she nurtured an implicit faith in human nature that her childhood had done nothing to discourage.

But that trusting, generous nature made her vulnerable to men attracted by her vitality and beauty. Like many women of her baby-boomer generation who grew up in sheltered, suburban homes, her self-worth still hinged, to no small degree, on the approval and attentions of men, on when and whether she would marry. The sometimes shallow, self-absorbed young men who strolled through Sara's life sometimes took advantage of her gentle nature, her youngest sister said years later, while offering her little or nothing in return.

After she graduated from the University of Colorado with a degree in education, a family crisis drew Sara home. Plagued by cataracts, her father was surrendering a surgical career that spanned nearly five decades. Still energetic and unwilling to retire, he accepted an appointment as Manatee County's public health director in Bradenton, Florida, near Sarasota. At age sixty-four, he was embarking on a new career in a rural town where the median age was sixty-eight.

While her mother remained behind to sell the family home, Sara moved to Bradenton with her father where she became his rock. She cooked his meals. She helped him study for the Florida Medical Board exam. She buoyed his spirits as he struggled to accept the fact that he would never operate again.

"In that little town," Sara's sister, Joni, wrote years later, "a tremendous bond between father and daughter was born. She pulled him through. Dad adored Sara's enthusiasm for life. She loved his dedication to healing the sick."

"Sara's zest for life was contagious," said her father. "She showed me how to find complete joy in the simplest things. She told me I could accomplish anything. Her energy propelled all of us."

Once in Bradenton, Sara began teaching fourth grade at the local elementary school. She had always loved children—perhaps because she had three younger sisters and there were always children in the Ambrusko house, perhaps because a child's unabashed delight in simple things remained unadulterated in Sara. Said her sister, Krissy, "It never took much to make her happy."

By all accounts, Sara was a memorable teacher. She was

as devoted to her students as she was her family. Some were from poor homes. Sara wanted to give them a future. She called them, "my kids," as she confided to her sister, "If I can find one thing that each child is interested in, I can use it to give them some confidence. If they like planes, maybe, with my help, they can become pilots. If they like to draw, I'll give them the confidence to be commercial artists."

In a farewell poem Sara wrote for her children in 1978, she praised each child, as she noted:

> There was a whole variety in this fourth grade crew
> And each one was different in the things he'd do
> So, I'll mention each one in part of this poem
> I'll never forget you because this room was our home.

Fifteen years later, her students were still writing her letters, saying that they remembered her.

"Sara's special quality of love and giving of her self will always be remembered," wrote the mother of one student. "Especially for our son, Daniel, who was first inspired by Sara's excellent caring talents as a teacher."

Still an athlete, the young schoolteacher also taught aerobics to Bradenton's seniors. In those weekly classes, she offered encouragement to many of them who had retired to Florida only to find themselves lonely and depressed.

Sara met her first husband on the beach near her father's Bradenton home. Steve Wiegand was brazenly handsome, an Illinois resident who had come to Sarasota on vacation to visit his parents. After Wiegand left Florida, he and Sara cultivated a long-distance romance. When he moved to Atlanta and became an instructor at a health club just north of the city, the couple decided to marry.

They were wed in St. Martha's Catholic Church in Sarasota in 1981. Sara, the third of the sisters to marry, wore her younger sister's wedding dress, her veil, and an elegant train. Her sisters were her bridesmaids—a family tradition. The reception was pure Florida—catered at poolside with shrimp, lobster, and a steel-drum band.

The union may not have been all that her father envisioned.

"He was a nice fellow, but he just seemed like he was, well, in a fog all the time," Dr. Ambrusko reflected. "He was a nice-looking guy, but he always seemed to be half-asleep or something."

John Ambrusko wanted for his daughters husbands who would provide for them as well as love them, just as he had. The man he hoped would marry his ebullient Sara was a professional, a lawyer or a doctor like himself, with a career that would support what Sara most desired.

"All she ever really wanted was a family like ours," her sister Krissy said, "to have kids and stay home," to be just like her mom.

Dr. Ambrusko may have worried about the kind of future Sara's first husband could provide. He was a racquetball instructor and a partner in the health club where he taught. "Hell," her father remembered ruefully, "there's no future in that."

But Sara was clearly delighted. The vibrant optimism that had always been her hallmark only deepened after her engagement. Small doubts that had nibbled at the core of her self-confidence as, still single, she moved toward thirty, disappeared. Generous and open-hearted, she no longer feared living the balance of her life alone. She moved with Wiegand to Atlanta and quickly adapted to her husband's life.

And for southerners Sara's age, if not for Sara, Atlanta rose like Oz on the horizon. Dominating its skyline were dual beacons—the alien blue dome of the Hyatt Regency and the state capitol dome sheathed in gold. They promised wealth wedded to the future in those excessive, hedonistic years.

The couple settled in a condominium near Wiegand's club just north of the city in a suburb skewed toward youth and money. Sara began teaching aerobics classes at the club, which catered to a clientele that included young nightclub investors and professional football players with the Atlanta Falcons. Savvy about fashion and still imbued with the optimistic spirit that had characterized her adolescence, Sara also managed the club's accessories shop and began marketing its merchandise.

It may not have been the career that she envisioned, if she contemplated one at all. Missing from it were the children that she had doted on as a teacher. But she had willingly traded that life for a marriage with the promise of children of her own. She had left her close-knit family and moved to a southern city that may have radiated her own bright energy but was far less tradition-bound.

Her marriage was not an easy one. Like so many health clubs, Wiegand's soon developed financial difficulties, and the partnership that operated it dissolved. By then, Wiegand and Sara were both friendly with a young nightclub manager named Jim Killeen. Killeen had moved to Atlanta from Miami as an employee of Playboy Clubs International. By the time he began frequenting the health club, he was managing Elan, the trendiest of the city's northside nightclubs. Killeen hired Wiegand as a front desk manager and doorman. A short time later, he hired Sara to supervise the desk and promote the club.

Neither her sheltered Amherst childhood nor her Bradenton elementary school classroom prepared her for Elan. There, Sara's life became an endless string of glittery, indulgent nights among people glistening with drink, coarse with pleasure, and animated by desire or drugs. And Sara soon feared that for her husband, cocaine had become as much of a temptation as the lithe, wistful women drenched with scent who flourished at Elan like hothouse flowers.

Her marriage to Wiegand couldn't survive his infidelities or indulgences. And Sara watched her dreams dissolve amid the nightclub's smoky pallor of excess.

Sara didn't ask for much—a simple, swift divorce with no strings or consequences. She would pay her own way. If she couldn't sidestep heartbreak, she could still avoid a scene. When she left him, she broke all ties with hope. Then she turned to the Catholic Church to make amends.

Shaken by what she saw as her own failures, Sara's confidence was crushed. But true to form, she worried less about herself than she did about her family. Her parents' disappointment was what Sara feared the most. Devout as her family— and Sara—remained, divorce was not supposed to be an option. A marriage before God was final. In divorce, Sara was unraveling a blessing. Anxious to assuage their fears that her divorce would sunder her from her faith and God, Sara sought to have her first marriage annulled. It mattered to her that she should be free to marry again in a union that could be blessed.

Sara turned thirty the year she left Wiegand—an unsettling, lonely crossroad that her marriage should have spared her. For the next two years, she shared a suburban condominium with her youngest sister, Krissy—who had been so smitten with Atlanta that she abandoned the Florida college where she was first enrolled. When he separated from his first wife, Jim Killeen rented the sisters' spare bedroom, where he lived until his second marriage.

By offering Killeen a place to live, "Sara was trying to help him out," her sister said. He was Sara's closest friend. He had hired her when the health club failed and promoted her career even as her marriage foundered. She owed him. She understood the pain of a divorce. She also admired him as an honest man who frowned on alcohol and drugs and boasted that he was "clean" in a business that was easily sullied. They used to joke, somewhat ruefully, that they should have built a life together, Krissy recalled, not with the spouses they eventually married.

Throughout that time, Sara remained at Elan, eventually moving to its corporate offices where she became marketing director for several nightclubs and restaurants, including one called Sneakers in which Killeen had invested. Sara handled the clubs' promotions and charity events, and, with Killeen, designed a number of advertising campaigns. Krissy became her assistant, and elan sponsored splashy swimsuit contests and lingerie fashion shows in which Sara's youngest sister modeled.

If indeed she thought about it, Sara may have regarded herself with rueful amusement—a woman who drank only occasionally and rarely dated—creating campaigns intended to attract more people to a nightclub that had contributed to the disintegration of her marriage. But it provided her with a modicum of security and a very generous salary. "She really excelled at it," said her sister. "But it was not really her goal in life."

Soon after her divorce, Sara reverted to her maiden name— Sara Ambrusko—still quietly harboring her dream of a marriage with sweet-faced children and a house that rang with their voices. In a city where so many were on the make or on the go, in a profession that was often fast and loose, Sara remained, at heart, traditional. And in the youth-driven culture that defined Atlanta in the eighties, she was beginning to feel old.

So, when Fredric Tokars materialized on the television news, she was cheered by his familiar face. When she called him and he asked her out, she said yes with pleasure. Said her sister, "She just sort of assumed they'd be the same."

Fred was then a junior staff member in the downtown Atlanta offices of the county district attorney. He was tall and slender, with an intellectual rather than a handsome face. He wore tortoise-shell glasses and combed his unruly light brown hair behind protruding ears. He looked a little like Clark Kent and a lot like an accountant, which is what he had been before he earned his law degree in night school. She heard in his flat, familiar upstate accent the normalcy of her childhood. Growing up as physicians' children, they had once shared a neighborhood, common friends, a high school graduation. He was a sturdy link to a life that Sara sorely missed.

He was also "a guy in a white hat," Krissy said, someone who enforced rather than broke the law, who prosecuted drug dealers rather than dallying with them, a man who made Sara, stripped of her marriage and her dreams, feel secure once more.

"He was a good guy," Krissy would earnestly explain years later. "That was part of his appeal."

As Fred became Sara's frequent companion, he would enthrall the sisters with stories of criminal cases where, in his accounts, he frequently took center stage. For Sara, he was a window on a grim and brutal world from which she had been insulated all her life. But safe in their sunny condominium, secure in jobs comfortably north of the city limits, the sisters were fascinated rather than afraid.

Sara knew that, because he was a prosecutor, Fred made less money than his counterparts in private practice. But that only enhanced his image as far as Sara was concerned. Said her sister, "We felt it reflected a certain amount of character."

"Do you think I should marry him?" Sara asked her

younger sister, Karen, the first Christmas that she and Fred spent together as a couple.

"Sara, do you think you should get to know him better?" Karen answered. "You know, date him at least a full year before you marry him?"

By then, the Ambrusko family knew that Sara and Fred were "very serious." And of utmost importance to Sara, her father was impressed. Dr. Ambrusko didn't remember Fred. "I didn't know the boys although they lived in our neighborhood," he said. But when Fred reminded Sara's father that his own father had been Dr. Ambrusko's student, the elderly gentleman was pleased.

He remembered Fred's father as "brilliant, a really fine gentleman. When he graduated, he was a very fine physician. . . . He was always very highly thought of in medical circles."

Fred, a certified public accountant with a law degree, appealed to Dr. Ambrusko as "an aggressive, hard-working young man."

"He had a double degree in two fields I felt were very aggressive fields," Sara's father explained. "I was always impressed with someone who was a hard worker and trying to get ahead."

And Fred was ambitious. He explained to John Ambrusko that his dual standing as a certified public accountant and a lawyer gave him entree to a wealthy clientele in need of tax shelters and financial advice—a far more safe and lucrative profession than his job as a public prosecutor. Dr. Ambrusko approved. If Sara were to marry him, Fred Tokars would provide well for Ambrusko's middle child.

Sara was clearly taken with Fred, as much for who she thought he was as for whom he claimed to be. On his careful surface, he was everything she had been taught to want in a husband. And he promised the kind of future that her first husband had either never intended or abandoned.

Fred was "the knight on the shining white horse," Sara confided to her cousin, Mary Rose Taylor. "In her point of view, Fred was not unlike her father," Taylor said. "Her father helped fight disease in people, and Fred helped fight the bad guys, as she put it, and she saw tremendous parallels between her father and Fred."

"Maybe she wasn't so much in love with him as she was with his image," Krissy once suggested of her sister's growing attachment to Fred. "She was getting older. She wanted to have kids. That was the most important thing. She wanted to believe in what she thought was there."

But neither Krissy nor her sisters are certain that Sara and Fred ever discussed those eager dreams to duplicate her parents' marriage and recreate her childhood for children of her own.

"I don't know if they talked about it, or if Sara assumed it. I don't remember her saying, 'Fred wants these things, too,' " Krissy said. "But they were the same age. If I were her, I would assume that if someone wanted to marry me, they were ready to settle down."

Months later, Sara called her sisters to tell them she and Fred had married. The couple had eloped in a simple civil ceremony in the courtroom where Fred prosecuted felony cases. They said their vows before the superior court judge to whom Fred's cases were assigned.

"They just showed up one morning," remembered Fulton Superior Court Judge John Lankford. "They were just a typical, joyful couple who were ready and eager to get married."

Sara didn't even tell her youngest sister, who was still living in Atlanta, until after the wedding. Their sudden marriage, without family or friends, had been her husband's idea.

But in a family as close as the Ambruskos, where weddings were a charming excuse to reunite, Sara's private ceremony was a stunning aberration. It was not like Sara to exclude her family from what should have been a celebration.

Sara gently brushed aside their questions. She had already had a traditional Catholic wedding with her sisters standing by her like the Graces while her marriage was blessed by a priest. She had already worn a white gown and a veil and been feted at a poolside reception. She didn't want her father to finance even part of a second wedding just because her first had failed. After all, there were still other daughters who deserved their formal weddings, too. And, although she was legally divorced from Wiegand, the Catholic Church had not yet annulled that marriage.

"She was a little concerned that her parents might not understand that she hadn't had her first marriage annulled," her new husband would later explain.

And so, the family was assuaged. Sara, as always, had taken someone else's interests to heart. And, thus, no one suspected that Fred's surprise proposal might have been borne, not of spontaneity, but of a darker need.

If Sara at that moment sensed a subtle shift in her relationship or shivered at the airless touch of some unseen web, she dismissed it. She reassured her family she was happy. And, during those first new months of marriage, she appeared to be. How could she know that, seven years later, in the final desperate moments of her life, the hero she had admired and married would have become inextricably entangled in her death.

Two

A Matter of Control

FRED WAS NOT THE MOST ATTENTIVE OF YOUNG HUSBANDS. Almost as soon as the couple married, and Sara moved into Fred's condominium, he began spending far less time with her. He rarely ate dinner at home, choosing to dine, instead, with his "business associates."

His excuses seemed legitimate. He was a prosecutor in one of the country's most violent districts. He aspired to be a judge. He had established his own accounting firm through which he also sold insurance. He was still hosting weekend seminars and teaching night school classes.

In fact, Fred treated Sara as if she were an afterthought in his highly scheduled, upwardly mobile life. Their hasty, undistinguished wedding marked the channel of their marriage. And Sara, who had for most of her life shared a home with family or friends, experienced the first thin chill of isolation, a nagging emptiness that wasn't quite hunger and wasn't yet heartbreak.

"I thought it was sort of unusual," Sara's father said. "He hardly ever had dinner at home. He was always working late at night. . . . Sara used to be discouraged about the fact that he was never home."

But when Sara's sisters began raising small alarms about Fred's apparent indifference toward his wife, Dr. Ambrusko defended him.

"He's a young guy trying to get ahead," he would gently chide his daughters. "He's working hard. It's very difficult for him. He's in a highly competitive field."

In fact, Dr. Ambrusko admired Fred, seeing in his ambitious son-in-law a younger reflection of himself. He remembered the arduous, exhausting hours and the unyielding drive that propelled him to the chief surgeon's post at Kenmore Mercy Hospital. He encouraged his son-in-law: "You just have to keep plugging away to try to get ahead just like I had to in my business." And he deflected his daughters' worried criticisms, secure in his belief that Fred was truly providing for his Sara.

Indeed, aside from the fact that her husband was rarely home, Sara did seem happy. Within five months, she was pregnant with the couple's first child, an event that coincided with the annulment of her first marriage and her second wedding to Fred, on December 14, 1985, by a priest in a Catholic church. But her church wedding was as unremarkable as the civil ceremony that had preceded it. There were no guests, no family, no reception. Only Jim Killeen and his wife were invited, and stood beside Fred and Sara as a priest blessed their union. Not even Sara's sister Krissy was there.

Shortly before the baby's birth, Fred and Sara bought their suburban home near one of Atlanta's most exclusive country clubs. Its price tag may well have stretched the couple's finances. Fred told a colleague that "creative financing" had enabled him to buy it.

The house, with its wooded lot and large backyard, reminded Sara of her childhood home in Amherst. But Fred soon used the purchase to try to drive a wedge between his wife and her youngest sister, with whom she was especially close. Before the couple married, Fred had promised his wife that they would look after Krissy—the youngest, least conventional, and most headstrong of the Ambrusko daughters—until she finished college. But when Krissy asked Fred if she might rent the basement of the three-story home—an arrangement that would have eased the couple's burden of debt, allowed Krissy to help Sara with the baby and keep her lonely sister company while Fred worked late and traveled—his response was emphatic and succinct.

"I'm newly married," he told his sister-in-law abruptly. "I want to be with my wife, and I don't want you to live here." Instead, the basement would become the sanctuary from which he would eventually ban his wife.

Throughout her pregnancy, Sara worked. As the advertising and promotions manager for Sneakers and Elan, she earned about forty thousand dollars a year, far more than her ambitious husband earned as an assistant district attorney. But Sara anticipated the day when she could leave her job to become a full-time mother.

It was surprising then that Fred, having just assumed a hefty mortgage on a new home, would decide in August 1986—one month before their baby was born—to quit his job at the Fulton County district attorney's office and open his own law practice. His decision may well have been triggered by the couple's mounting financial obligations and Fred's own certainty that, as a private tax and criminal defense attorney, he could easily surpass his modest prosecutor's salary. According to Murray Silver, the attorney from whom Fred rented an office in the CNN Center, "He wanted to make money fast."

"It takes a long time to develop a law practice. You just can't do it overnight," Silver said. "Sure, you get to the point where you command large fees. That only comes after you have a track record. . . . I don't see how you can come into the practice of law and say, 'I'm going to get rich quick.' But that was his attitude: 'I'm going to get rich quick.' "

On September 23, 1986, the couple's first child was born. They named him Fredric William, Jr., after his father but soon began calling him Ricky. For Sara, the baby's birth should have engendered the deep contentment of knowing that she and Fred were now a family, that she was neither alone nor too old to bear children. Instead, as Tokars began defending clients he had once sought to jail, financial pressures ballooned, and the marriage began showing signs of wear.

"I remember Sara telling me that when Fred went from working at the district attorney's office to starting his own private practice, he seemed to change," Krissy recalled later. "And I remember her telling me that she thought it might have been because of the stress of starting his own practice."

It was as if, Sara confided to her sister, she had married one person only to discover that she was, in fact, married to someone else—a man who, rather than loving her, treated her with indifference or indulged in petty cruelties.

"He was no longer the kindly, giving person that she thought she married," said her cousin, Mary Rose Taylor, with whom Sara was very close. "She was puzzled by the change in his personality."

As they shared lunch, or chatted by telephone, the cousins wondered whether Fred's cold metamorphosis was simply an unpleasant side-effect of his drive to nurture his struggling practice through its infancy. If that was the case, Sara wanted to support him.

Sara had always assumed that once the baby was born, she would leave her job. Grounded in tradition and devoted to family, she had made no secret of that desire, but when she broached the subject with her husband after Ricky's birth, he objected angrily.

Sara was stunned. Staying home to raise her children was not an option. It was supposed to be a given. But she also couldn't afford to watch a second marriage dissolve, and she had always been the peacemaker in her family. So, Sara continued to work, trying when she could to leave her office early to be with her baby and finish the remainder of her work at home. There were still evening promotional events that required her presence at the nightclubs. And Sara's absence from home during one of those events led to a bitter argument between her sister and her husband that ended in their angry estrangement.

Krissy was babysitting Ricky that night. Sara was orchestrating a promotional event at Sneakers, a high-energy nightclub for young adults between eighteen and twenty-five. Fred, as usual, was working late. Sometime during the evening, Ricky became ill. He began crying, and, unsure what to do, Krissy called her sister at the club. Sara immediately headed home. She and her husband arrived almost simultaneously.

"Sara, I'm here. You can go back to work now," Fred informed his wife.

"That's okay," Sara answered. "I got things started so I don't have to go back. I can stay home."

"No." Fred was insistent. "No, you need to go back. You need to make sure you do your job. I can handle Rick."

But something in his tone angered Sara's younger sister. The hour was late, and Krissy had privately shared Sara's growing hurt at her husband's thoughtless slights and the rattling disappointment that followed Fred's angry refusal to allow her to remain home with Ricky. Fred was bullying her gentle, accommodating sibling. And Sara wasn't fighting back.

Krissy stepped to her older sister's defense.

"Look, Fred, Sara's been doing this a long time. If she doesn't have to go back, she doesn't have to go back," Krissy challenged.

Fred's anger was absolute. "You're just a spoiled brat. You don't know the value of a dollar," he shouted. "You don't understand how it is to work."

"Look, Sara knows her job," Krissy retaliated. "If she doesn't have to go back, she doesn't have to go back. Just leave her alone."

And so it went. It was a wild and brutal argument, teeming with blunt accusations, belittling rejoinders, and ugly distortions. Krissy was no match for him. He took her apart. It ended only when Krissy, strangling on tears of rage, screamed at her brother-in-law, "Fuck off. Leave my sister alone," and ran from the house.

Sara called her later to apologize for her husband and the icy efficiency with which he had savaged Krissy.

"I think I'll divorce him," she told her sister quietly, "because this is a reflection of what he is really like. He's not the man I thought I married."

Her carefully nurtured dreams were beginning to unravel.

For months after Ricky's birth, Sara continued to work. Yet, she soon began to feel she was failing at both tasks. She wasn't giving either her job or her baby her full attention, and, as a result, she feared both were suffering.

By then, Atlanta's booming nightclub business was experiencing a decline. Drink-and-drive laws had acquired stiffer penalties. Two-for-one happy hours were outlawed in the state. And AIDS was becoming a fierce, final reality. The nightclubs Sara promoted began losing money. When Sara approached her employer, Doug McKendrick, about working at home so she could care for her son, he told her bluntly, "It's not going to work."

"I either fired her or asked her to resign," he said, and Sara's wish finally was granted by default.

But before she lost her job, Sara provided her husband an entree into the nightclub business. Fred had, through Sara, become acquainted socially with her bosses and cultivated a friendship with Killeen. He had begun doing some of their legal work. Eventually, he would capitalize on those connections.

When Sara lost her job, her husband seized the opportunity to assume complete control of the couple's finances. "Fred used to tell her she didn't know the value of a dollar," Sara's sister remembered. "He had the attitude that she couldn't control her spending. That's what he used to say to her. That's why he put her on a strict budget."

He refused to permit her to have a checking account or credit cards in her name. He balked about buying furniture or making repairs. He insisted that she pay their bills by money order or in cash. He told Sara he never used credit cards or checks because the payments could be traced and serve as an indicator of his income. He insisted that his clients, whenever possible, pay his fees in cash. In that way, he told Sara, he could sidestep state and federal taxes whenever he thought they were excessive.

But he also told Sara—and her family—that she was irresponsible with money. During her previous marriage and while she was single, Sara had acquired a number of credit cards. She had brought that credit debt to her marriage with Fred, and he told her repeatedly that she relied on credit and spent money far too freely.

Instead of a checking account, Fred gave Sara a weekly three-hundred-dollar cash allowance. To many, Sara's budget might not have seemed overly penurious. By 1992, it had risen to four hundred a week. From that cash allowance, Sara was expected to buy groceries, household supplies and sundries, keep her small children in clothes and diapers, buy her own clothes and cosmetics, pay the family's medical bills, cover the costs associated with the children's dog, and pay for household repairs, cleaning, and maintenance. If she needed additional money for a child's birthday or an unanticipated expense, Fred might give his wife some additional cash. But, more often than not, the extra cash Fred reluctantly gave Sara was not enough to cover the cost. If she protested that she didn't know how much she would need to cover an expense, Fred would tell her bluntly, "Then you'll just have to make another trip."

Sometimes he would simply tell her he had no money, that he had not found time "to make his collections." Even when the children were ill, Fred was rarely persuaded to augment her weekly budget and give Sara money for a doctor. Instead, he would tell her she would have to wait until the following Monday when he doled out her weekly allowance.

"She would have to do things like cancel the cleaning lady for that week and try to save up that way," remembered Sara's sister, Karen, with whom Sara often talked. "She was good at saving money. She could save it, if there was a reason."

But Fred also required his wife to itemize all her expenses and present him with receipts. He would raise questions about why she made a particular purchase or spent a certain sum of money as if her own ability to make decisions was somehow flawed. And obtaining money, over time, became a struggle in which Sara was always the supplicant and her husband was always the final authority.

"She told me Fred really resented her spending his money, and that he really wanted her to go back to work and put the kids in day care," Krissy said.

Sara tried, according to her sister, who watched with growing frustration as the woman she idolized was forced into a subservient role. She established a small promotions company, Sara Ambrusko Productions, and began soliciting small contracts in the suburbs and designing ad campaigns for small retail stores. Her prominent cousin also capitalized on Sara's marketing talent, occasionally hiring Sara to promote her charity fund-raisers, including the Swan House Ball at an historic Buckhead mansion that attracted national attention for the Atlanta History Center.

Sara also submitted budgets to her husband. He routinely rejected her requests or only gave her part of what she asked.

"It wasn't that he didn't have it," Krissy bitterly recalled. "He would just make her fight for it."

Sara didn't understand, her sister said. She was married to an attorney, a man who had convinced her father that his accounting and law degrees coupled with the tax seminars he taught gave him access to a lucrative clientele. Sara had always assumed that attorneys made a more than comfortable living, and, until their marriage, Fred had done nothing to disabuse her of the notion. But whenever she asked about the family's financial situation, Fred refused to discuss it.

Over time, Sara began to rebel in small ways. Using her sister's address, she quietly obtained credit cards in her own name, which she used whenever her husband either refused to give her money or was away from home. But the resulting monthly payments made her financial difficulties even more acute. And gradually, the attractive woman who had, before her marriage, been a fashionable dresser, found she could no longer afford to buy clothes of her own. Instead, she wore her youngest sister's hand-me-downs.

"Sara was not good with money," Fred would say later. "When I married her, she was sort of living life in the fast lane. She'd just bought this Mercedes-Benz from Larry Csonka, the football player. She would hang around with people who had money. And she had like three, four, five, six credit cards, and she was barely making the payments on them."

Of the allowance he gave her, Fred acknowledged, "She didn't like it. But she got more cash than most other women. . . . Every bill in our house was always paid—everything. She had a new car, a fairly new house. She had money for hairdressers, money for the kids to go to private schools, and I'd give her cash. I didn't want her to use credit cards, but she'd get a credit card anyway, and she'd use it.

"She worked some part-time, and she may have been making some money there, but I would assume that most of the money that she had I was giving to her.

"I used to call her a brat sometimes, or her sister a brat," he explained. Her family had always had money, and Dr. Ambrusko had spent it freely on his daughters. The sisters, as youngsters, had access not only to their parents' credit cards but also to "a cookie jar full of money" into which they dipped at will, he said.

He had warned her about spending excessively on their two sons. "They're going to turn out to be little brats," he said, ignoring Sara's pleas not to label his sons so coldly.

"She was just never disciplined enough," he complained. "She had a bank account if she needed it. She knew where it was. I had a safe with usually enough money in it to buy anything. She knew how to get in the safe. I gave her money when she wanted it. She had a credit card. She had rich parents. I don't think she was ever deprived of anything."

As Sara became dependent on her husband for money, he began using the family purse strings to limit Sara's access to her family. He began raising objections whenever she wanted to visit her aging parents in Florida or attend family gatherings with the baby. He told her she could spend either Thanksgiving or Christmas, but not both, with her family in Florida, although the couple rarely spent a holiday with Fred's parents, whom Sara didn't meet until after Ricky was born. If Sara defied her husband, he would refuse to give her money for gas or a hotel room. Yet, despite his objections, when Sara resolutely made the nine-hour drive from Atlanta to her parents' home near Sarasota, Fred would usually join his wife in Florida, as if he were compelled to monitor his young wife once she asserted her own will. But the demands of his legal practice and the residual pain of an old injury always dictated that he travel by air. When Sara drove to Florida with her baby, she did so alone.

"Her one joy in life was bringing the kids down here to Florida," her sister said. "It was always a battle."

Whenever Sara visited, her father, out of habit, would often ask her if she had enough money to make the return trip home. Sara always assured him that she did. But if he pressed her, which he generally did, John Ambrusko would invariably discover that his daughter had no more than twenty dollars in her wallet.

That troubled him. So did whispers he heard from Sara's sisters that Fred would not give her the money to pay for some needed dental work. A forthright man, Dr. Ambrusko raised the matter with his son-in-law on more than one occasion.

"You know, Fred, my wife and I always had a basic rule," he chided his son-in-law during one of those private discussions. "We never had a lot, but we had enough. And she always knew what I had, and I always knew what she had, and if money was needed, why, there wasn't any question about it. I didn't try to limit her.

"My impression is that things aren't going to go well unless you have a marriage with Sara where she has what she needs, and you know what she has and what she needs, and you have a better understanding about finances. I don't think it is fair for Sara to have to come down here without any money. I don't think it is fair for her not to have the things she should have because you don't want to help her financially."

But Fred insisted he had placed Sara on an allowance because of the credit debts she had brought to the marriage. Now that he had paid those debts, he was simply asking Sara to be more disciplined about her spending.

"Is this true?" Dr. Ambrusko asked his daughter later.

"It's a lie," she responded hotly. "He never paid anything of mine."

Sometime after her son Ricky's birth, Fred's growing control escalated into physical abuse. Sara kept it from her family. But on rare occasions, her resolve to remain silent faltered as she sought comfort or reassurance from anyone who spoke to her in kindness.

Like many of the people Sara met, Murray Silver—who shared a law office with Fred—was taken not only with her beauty but with her gentle charm. So, he has never forgotten what Sara told him in a quiet telephone call she placed to him before her second child was born—the first and only time she ever talked to him by phone. Silver had invited Tokars and his wife to a party he was hosting. Sara had called him at the office to express her regrets. She and her husband would not be able to attend.

"I feel so bad that we're not able to come to your party," Sara said. "I'm not well."

Silver promptly expressed his sympathy and his best wishes

for her recovery. The invitation remained open, he said, if her health improved.

There was a small silence at the other end of the line. Then Sara said softly, "I can't come because I have bruises on my left arm and side where Fred beat me."

Silver was stunned. But as he struggled to find something appropriate to say, Sara suddenly asked, "You wouldn't say anything about this, would you?"

In a voice shaky with panic, she began begging the attorney, "Please don't say anything about this. Don't even tell Fred I called."

And before she rang off, she urgently repeated, "I've got your word now? You won't mention this?"

Sara's sisters never knew their brother-in-law's treatment of Sara had escalated to physical abuse. As much as Sara shared with them on an almost daily basis, she always withheld from them that one terrifying, intimate detail. She held her tongue, hid her bruises, and pretended that although Fred was difficult and occasionally unkind, he was not a brutal man. Only the two women whom Sara hired to clean the house ever saw the bruises, or the occasional black eye. But Sara never volunteered an explanation, and they never asked for one. To broach the subject would have been to interfere, despite their silent compassion for the slight, soft-spoken woman and her sweet-faced child.

It was during those early years of her marriage to Fred that Sara renewed her friendship with her cousin, Mary Rose Taylor, a former television anchorwoman who had married a wealthy Atlanta developer and become a prominent fundraiser for a number of the city's charities and politicians. Taylor had been aware that, since Ricky's birth, Sara's marriage to Fred was growing more tenuous and troubled.

Taylor had been the first member of their extended family to divorce, despite her Catholic faith. Sara had been the second, and the residual guilt they both shared drew them closer together. Over occasional lunches at Taylor's house, or during their frequent telephone conversations, Sara confided to her cousin some of the details of a marriage, less than two years old, that was already beginning to fray. Although Sara was devoted to her son, and wanted other children, she told her cousin she felt powerless to do anything to make the marriage better. So Taylor was unprepared when, in 1987, Sara announced she was pregnant with her second child.

"I can remember being quite surprised when I found out that Sara was pregnant again, that she would choose to get pregnant again when her marriage was perhaps a little tenuous," Taylor recalled. "But Sara was determined. She was a person of enormous commitment, and she was determined to make this marriage work, and she wanted to be a wife and mother more than anything in the world."

In a wistful conversation with her younger sister, Sara told Krissy, "I don't want Ricky to be an only child. I want the two of them to have each other no matter what."

Three months before Sara became pregnant with her second child, her husband, who by then had added insurance agent to the list of his credentials, bought a $250,000 life insurance policy on his wife's life, naming himself as beneficiary in the event of her death. In her small, elegant hand, Sara signed the policy application.

If she privately questioned why her husband would buy such a generous policy on her life at a time when her marriage was faltering, his earlier purchase of a policy insuring his own life and his explanation that the policies were a form of investment that promised high returns, may have mollified her. Her son, Ricky, was named as a secondary beneficiary which may have also offered reassurance.

Michael Philip Tokars was born by Caesarian section on April 20, 1988. But Fred's reaction to his second son's birth was one of decided indifference. Sara's mother, Phyllis Ambrusko, traveled to Atlanta to see her newborn grandson and help her daughter with both children. She was troubled enough by her son-in-law's reaction to discuss the matter with Sara's older sister, Gretchen.

Although Sara was exhausted from the surgery, the birth, and the disruption of sleep that comes with caring for a newborn, her husband found little time to care for his oldest son— now a nineteen-month-old toddler, the new baby, or help with the household chores. Instead, he lived his life as if he had no other responsibilities but those bred by his career, and obligations that extended only to his business associates, his clientele, and friends whose social or political standing had proven beneficial.

When he was at home, which was infrequently, he spent his time working out in the basement where he kept an office and his exercise equipment.

"He's just very selfish, very into himself," Phyllis Ambrusko told her older daughter at the time.

So, Sara turned to her own close-knit family for solace and affection. She insisted on traveling to Florida when Mike was just two weeks old for her father's seventy-fifth birthday, a celebration she had arranged during the final months of her pregnancy.

"I remember arriving late at night," her sister Therese recalled. "Sara grabbed my hand and said, 'Theresie, you have to see Mike.' And she pulled me into the bedroom where Mike was sleeping and said, 'Isn't he beautiful, Theresie?' "

Shortly after Mike's birth, Fred assumed another responsibility that kept him away from his family. He took a two-month sabbatical from his law practice to become campaign treasurer for Leah Sears, a Fulton County state court judge and the wife of Love Collins, with whom Fred had worked at Southern Bell.

That summer, Tokars immersed himself in Sears's campaign for a Fulton Superior Court judgeship, much as he had immersed himself in his new law practice in the months following his first son's birth. In both cases, his actions surely generated additional strain on an increasingly tenuous marriage and placed the burden of caring for the couple's children solely on Sara. It was almost as if—when his sons were born—Fred was driven to draw attention away from the new baby and Sara to focus it once more on himself. His timing was clearly impractical. His decision to open his own law practice when Ricky was born and assume the responsibility of helping to orchestrate a political campaign shortly after Mikey's birth generated tremendous financial and time pressures that enhanced the stress of adjusting to a newborn in the house. In both cases, Fred's actions could be explained as seizing an opportunity that would enhance his career. They could also be described as self-absorbed.

So, it should have come as no surprise that, after Mikey's

birth, Fred had a vasectomy. He made the decision alone. He never consulted Sara or even informed her that he had scheduled the minor operation until after it had been performed. Any dreams Sara may still have harbored of raising a large family were gone.

Four months after her second son's birth, Sara penned her own hand-written will. Scribbled on a yellow legal pad in a hasty hand, Sara revoked all prior wills that she had signed jointly with her husband—wills that left everything to him in the event of her death and placed their children in his brother's care if both Fred and Sara were to die.

"I remember her calling me because Fred wanted her to sign a will, but she wasn't allowed to have a say in who was named as the guardian for her sons," Therese said. "He told her the financial matters of their family were none of her business."

After her children were born, Sara always believed that, if anything were to happen to the couple, her own family, not Fred's, should become the boys' guardians. Fred had eventually acquiesced and promised to change the couple's will. He never found the time.

In her own will, Sara bequeathed all her belongings and her income to her children. She named her sister, Therese, a San Francisco attorney, as her executor and the boys' trustee. She appointed her sister, Karen, and Karen's husband, Neal—who still lived in Buffalo—as guardians for her sons "if my husband does not survive me," her only reference in the will to Fred.

Her two housekeepers, Retta Shaw and Retta's sister, Ronda Bedgood, signed the will as her only witnesses. The day they signed it, Sara filed the will in the Cobb County probate judge's office.

The sisters, both motherly women, were more than Sara's housekeepers. They were also occasional babysitters, sometime confidants, and friends. When they arrived that August day to clean the house, Sara asked them simply, "Would you sign a paper for me? It's my will."

It was the first sign Sara was worried about the welfare of her children should anything happen to her. It was also an indication that her marriage was falling apart.

Sara didn't volunteer her reasons for drawing up her own will without hiring an attorney, a will that barely mentioned her husband and seemed clearly designed to circumvent any benefits he might accrue if she were to die. But Ronda and Retta were certain that Sara had asked them to witness it because she trusted them not to let Fred or anyone else know of the document's existence. By then, they knew that Fred rarely gave Sara money for herself, the children, or the household and that she was constantly having to ask him for money for unforseen expenses. They knew she had a bank account she kept secret from her husband where she kept what little she could save. They had seen, but never discussed, Sara's occasional black eye. They had noted silently Fred's utter indifference to his wife and children whenever he came home, how he would enter the house without speaking or otherwise acknowledging his family's presence. They knew that he never hugged his sons or lifted them in his arms. And they knew that, even if Sara never said so, she was clearly afraid of her husband.

By then, Sara's family was keenly aware that their daughter was being slighted. After the birth of his second son, Fred was almost never home. He would rise early in the morning, sometimes before dawn, to leave the house. He arrived long after dinner was done and the children were in bed. When Fred did call to say that he'd be working late, Sara would often hear chatter in the background, as if he were calling from a restaurant or bar.

Used to staying in close touch, her parents would call their daughter in Atlanta two or three times a week. They generally called around 8 p.m., but whenever Dr. Ambrusko would inquire, "How is Fred?", his daughter usually responded, "He isn't home yet."

"I don't think he ever had dinner at night with the family," Sara's father said. "We just accepted the fact that Fred wasn't home."

"Where does the guy have dinner?" he finally inquired of his daughter.

"He stops with one of his business associates someplace and has something to eat on the way home," she said.

Fred's long absences from home made his continued control over the couple's finances even more difficult for Sara. She needed dental work that he would not finance. The deck of the house had rotted and needed to be rebuilt. The downstairs toilet leaked and had rotted the floor around it. The skylight needed repair. And, although by then Fred claimed his income exceeded one hundred thousand dollars annually, the sparse and shabby household furnishings did not reflect it. A masculine black couch and chairs that apparently had furnished his apartment as a bachelor dominated the living room. At the dining room table were canvas director's chairs. There were no curtains in the house, and no framed pictures on the spare, white walls.

Fred, pleading a weak and injured back, refused to do any housework, yardwork, or minor repairs. When repairs became imperative, Sara hired someone from the finite supply of cash that Fred gave her every week. Occasionally, her sister's boyfriend would drop by to make some minor repair.

"I know Sara didn't have very much money, and that she was always trying to make ends meet with regard to looking after the health and welfare of her children," said her cousin. "When you saw Sara, it was obvious she didn't have much money to spend on herself."

Fred's attitude toward his wife only worsened when he drank and enhanced the alcohol's effect with prescription pain relievers. "Sara knew he was an alcoholic, and she couldn't get him to stop," her older sister, a nurse, once noted.

Once, she surprised Fred in his basement office snorting a line of white powder that Sara immediately suspected was cocaine. But when she demanded to know what he was doing, he explained the powder was merely a "special sinus medication."

"You should know better than to ask me questions like that," he challenged her. His back injury required medication for the constant pain, he said. And the drug he was sniffing, while not for his back, was prescribed medication, he insisted. "You should know better," he repeated, and Sara never mentioned it again.

But if Fred's drinking, his apparent drug use, and the constant stream of belittling remarks he directed at his wife wore Sara down, his private legal practice and his clientele clearly frightened her. He refused to discuss his clients, his business associates, or his practice with Sara, and banned her from his basement office. He hid from her the fact that throughout much of their marriage he reported to the Internal Revenue Service an annual income ranging from two to three hundred thousand dollars, although he sometimes made Sara sign their joint returns, and occasionally signed her name to the returns himself. When jailed hotel magnate Leona Helmsley protested that she was jailed for tax evasion when she had simply signed her husband's tax returns, Sara told her sister, Krissy, "If that's the case, I'm in big trouble because Fred makes me sign stuff all the time. But I can never read it, and I don't know what it is. He won't let me look at it."

She knew her husband now counted criminals among his clients. And because Fred insisted that he be paid in cash, Sara suspected a number of the men and women he defended were drug dealers. She worried that their money might be tainted by the illicit sales they made. He always carried a gun in his right-hand coat pocket. He kept several more in the house, and slept with a gun on the bedstand at night. Sara grew afraid of what she didn't know about her husband and the seedy, street-lit world where he often sought his clients. She was also disappointed. Her husband was no longer someone she could rely on to make her world a safer place. Her insistence that Fred install an alarm system in their home was a measure of that fear.

Since Fred rarely cared for his children, Sara hired a babysitter to watch her sons while she was away, even if Fred were home. For the truth was that, even when Fred volunteered to take care of the boys, Sara didn't want her husband watching them. She feared her husband would expose the children to his clients or associates—people about whom she knew little but whom she instinctively distrusted.

One day, she called her older sister, Gretchen, nearly frantic with fear. Fred was defending a client who had admitted he sexually abused small children. Fred had gone to his client's house and had taken his two sons with him.

"I'm so upset," Sara confided to her sister. "Why would he take our children to see some slimy person like that?"

But if Sara was anxious about leaving her children in her

husband's care, her sons only intensified her fears. Both boys disliked being left alone with their father. They wanted Sara with them all the time, and were desperate to go with her whenever she tried to leave them.

When the couple spent time in Florida with Sara's family or at the Tokars's vacation home in Canada, Sara's sister Karen noticed that, despite Fred's efforts to treat his wife and children with affection, there was only a veneer of warmth. He attempted to play with his sons, but his efforts were as awkward as the occasional kiss on the cheek he would bestow upon his wife. The boys were reluctant to play with a father who rarely played with them at home. Fred had too little practice. He simply didn't know how.

Once, when Karen observed, "Sara, you know, Fred seems kind of nice," her younger sister responded, "Oh, Karen, he's just faking it in front of you guys so it will look like he's a good father."

There were times when Fred treated his wife more kindly, and Sara would tell her sisters with relief, "Well, you know, Fred's been okay, lately." But those good times never lasted, and Sara was never sure what governed those seismic shifts in her husband's temperament that left her so unbalanced. Sara was, at heart, nonconfrontational, a woman who would do anything she could to sidestep an argument or avoid an ugly confrontation. She had always been the peacemaker in a family whose members rarely raised their voices. She was unused to her husband's unpredictable temper, and his obvious disdain as he accused her of being spoiled, selfish, or irresponsible. Yet she found herself swept into terrible arguments with him, and would later tell her sisters, "I just don't know what would make him so mad."

"She would be so bewildered," her sister Joni recalled. "She was having the hardest time trying to figure out what was causing these fights. . . . They would be out somewhere, and, on the way home he would start screaming at her. She didn't realize she had done anything wrong."

Sara did everything she could to avoid those inevitable exhausting battles with her husband. "Sometimes she would just try to listen," Joni said, "but he would just keep yelling at her, berating her. Sometimes, she would yell back at him. That didn't work either.''

At times, Sara was certain there was nothing she could do to satisfy him or redeem herself. When she saw herself reflected in her husband's eyes, she saw the distortions of a circus hall of mirrors—a demanding, dwarfish woman that Sara didn't recognize and couldn't defend. "Mean" was the word Sara used when she discussed it with her family. Fred was mean.

But believing it was another matter. Over time, Sara began to doubt her judgment as her own image of who she was eroded. Relief gave way to wary exhaustion whenever her husband was affectionate. She grew terrified of displeasing him, and her ability to make decisions gradually evaporated until Sara seemed incapable of handling even the smallest chores. She complained that Fred wouldn't repair the lock on the kitchen's sliding glass door, but, in spite of easy advice from her sister, seemed helpless to take care of it herself.

She grew hesitant and guarded whenever her husband was around. "She reminded me of a little puppy," Joni said, "who would just look up like she got kicked a lot."

Three

A Deepening Suspicion

ON MOTHER'S DAY 1989, SHORTLY AFTER HER YOUNGEST son's first birthday, Sara discovered that Fred was having an affair. What made her suspicious wasn't her husband's frequent absences from home, or the corrosion of trust, or the lies, which after Fred's quiet vasectomy, Sara was finally beginning to discern. It was, rather, the contempt that accompanied lies so obviously thin and poorly crafted that it no longer mattered to her husband whether she believed them or not.

He left for Bermuda on Mother's Day weekend without her. Although she had given birth to their two sons, there would be no Mother's Day cards, no breakfast in bed, no crown of flowers, no honorary luncheon at an Atlanta restaurant. He told her tersely he was traveling on business to the islands, and the fact that he could abandon Sara so casually on a day that honored her scalded her more deeply than his impulsive anger, his jealousy, or his other casual slights. She determined to learn what business was of such import that it demanded her husband's presence in the Caribbean on a weekend when he should have been at home. Instinctively, she knew it was another woman.

Sara discovered the woman's name in a business diary that Fred had left behind. It was a plain, sturdy name with a hint of decorous spelling. Sara was desperate to know who she was, certain now that her second husband had become as faithless as her first. Deeply hurt but still proud enough to be angry, she consulted her youngest sister. They agreed to hire a private detective to determine if Sara's anguished suspicions were correct. She asked her cousin for the name of a detective. But fearing Fred would discover she was making an inquiry, Sara begged Mary Taylor not to mention her by name. Fred was, by then, a traffic court judge in Atlanta—a part-time, patronage post bestowed on him by Atlanta Mayor Andrew Young at the request of Leah Sears, whose post as a Fulton Superior Court judge Fred had helped achieve. To Sara—unfamiliar with Atlanta politics—her husband was as politically connected as he boasted. She was terrified someone in Atlanta might alert him.

Taylor promptly called her own attorney for advice. Armed with the names of three private detectives, she called her distraught cousin back.

"Why don't you talk with an attorney about this?" Taylor urged Sara. But Sara refused. She wanted to know whether her husband was having an affair, but she couldn't bring herself to think about the consequences should her suspicions be confirmed. She had no money, she told her cousin. But once she hired a private investigator, she would find a way to pay him. Taylor immediately offered to help. Sara turned her down.

"Sara had a lot of pride," Taylor said. "She wanted to do this on her own, and she would never take money from me."

When Sara hired private investigator Ralph Perdomo on May 26, 1989, she gave him one thousand dollars. She later gave him, as collateral, her engagement ring and pearls. She didn't know that Perdomo had worked for lawyers who were colleagues of her husband, including a former law school classmate who would soon become Fred's partner.

When Sara hired him, she warned Perdomo and his assistant that her husband was a former assistant district attorney in Atlanta, that he knew many of the city police and wouldn't hesitate to call them if he suspected he was being followed. Then she gave the detective the address of an upscale apartment in Buckhead, one of Atlanta's premier neighborhoods, that her husband might be using for his trysts. Sara didn't know the apartment was home to one of her husband's clients, a drug dealer who shared it with Fred's paramour, with whom he had been sleeping until he went to jail.

Sara was right to warn the detectives. Her husband was a naturally cautious and somewhat suspicious man. One evening, Perdomo's assistant, Mike Gibson, spotted Tokars enter the apartment Sara had described, followed a short time later by a woman. Within minutes a police patrol car appeared, and, although its occupants never spoke to Gibson, they carefully noted his license plates as they swung behind his car. Spooked and determined to avoid a confrontation, Gibson hurriedly left.

The next time, Perdomo staked out the apartment himself, waiting patiently in a car he had parked, not in the lot, but on the street. Like Gibson, Perdomo soon spotted Fred. Minutes later, Perdomo noticed the curtains shielding the window move slightly. A short time later, an unmarked police car pulled alongside him. On the police scanner in his car, Perdomo heard them say, "Yeah, that's the guy's car."

The police officers told Perdomo they had received a complaint. Who was he and what was he doing?

Perdomo admitted he was a private investigator, but told the officers he was seeking a runaway child who he believed had sought shelter in an apartment at the end of the street. His explanation appeared to satisfy them. They wished him a nice day and left. Perdomo remained another hour but abandoned his surveillance before Fred left. When he called Sara to report what he had seen, she assumed from their conversation that Atlanta police were conducting their own surveillance, and that Perdomo's presence was hindering their investigation. It was a simple but significant misunderstanding that would lead Sara's cousin to suspect Fred was a criminal and repeatedly to urge Sara to prove it.

Now that Sara knew with reasonable certainty that Fred was having an affair, she was shaken by another kind of fear—that she might have been exposed to a sexually transmitted disease or infected with HIV, the precursor to AIDS. A visit to her gynecologist did little to reassure her. He diagnosed a cervical dysplasia—a smattering of abnormal cells indicative of a chronic inflammation. At Sara's insistence, he also administered an AIDS test. She was clear.

But even the possibility of exposure horrified her. Not only had her husband betrayed her, he had risked exposing her to a deadly disease. On this point she was certain. She would never sleep with him again. Much later, Fred would say that Sara had told him she had hired a detective to follow him and that the episode had spurred the couple to seek counseling.

"She said she was worried about the kids, and that I was drinking too much and she wanted it to stop," he said. "We used to joke about it sometimes. I'd say I'd want to fool around, and she'd say, 'Oh, why don't you just go get your girlfriend?' It was a joke between us."

But Sara's sisters were repulsed by Fred's crude attempts to persuade them. They knew Sara too well. She had been betrayed by faithless men before. Adultery was not amusing. It was shattering a sacrament.

At some point that wretched summer, Sara did ask for a divorce. But if she thought her wayward husband would be relieved, she was mistaken. It was a fling, no more, he said. Despite what his girlfriend might choose to believe, he had never intended to marry her. Divorce, he told his wife angrily, was utterly out of the question. If she insisted on leaving him, Fred informed her bluntly he would challenge her for sole custody of their children. And, he said, he would certainly win. Among the judges, he had powerful friends. As a former assistant district attorney, he still knew county prosecutors and police. He would not hesitate to call upon those political connections if she forced his hand. And, once he had won sole custody, he would make certain that Sara would rarely, if ever, see her boys.

What Sara didn't realize is that Fred had far fewer connections than he boasted. And it is highly doubtful that those few he numbered among his friends would have interfered if Sara had sued for a divorce. But Sara, politically naive and isolated in her marriage, had no way of knowing whether her husband's threats were real. And if he was willing to use the sons he rarely saw as bartering chips, Sara had to believe he might successfully carry out his threat. It became the linchpin in every subsequent conversation about a possible divorce. It was the rock she could not get around—the thought that she might lose her children to such a casually brutal man.

"We were afraid of him and what he would do," her sister, Gretchen said.

"But he's liable to make me look like an unfit mother," Sara would wail whenever Gretchen urged her to leave him.

"How could he ever do that?" Gretchen answered.

"He's smart enough to pay people to say something about me or to plant something in my car to make me look like a bad person," Sara said.

Amid her growing fears, Sara had detected the first faint scent of corruption.

She was not the only one. A short time after Perdomo was confronted by undercover police at the apartment where Fred met his mistress, Sara's cousin also began asking about Fred's business associates. She was puzzled as to why undercover police would be watching the same townhouse Fred had chanced to visit. She wondered whether someone other than his wife had raised questions about the people with whom he surrounded himself.

"Sara, do you know what Fred is involved in?" Taylor asked her cousin one day. "Do you know what his business dealings are, or who he has business dealings with?"

"No," Sara replied. Her husband had made a point of guarding his business, refusing to share even the most general details.

"Does he keep any of his records around the house? Does he have an office in the house?" Taylor pressed.

"Yes, he does in the basement."

"Well, Sara, why don't you check his desk or his files and see if you can find any indication of what Fred's professional life might involve."

It was a suggestion, in a marriage such as Sara's, that bordered on sedition. But it was one that might provide Sara with the means of divorcing her husband and retaining sole custody of her sons.

Within days, Sara called her cousin from the basement of her house—a room Fred had forbidden her to enter. She was sitting at her husband's desk. When her cousin answered, Sara had already found the key, unlocked the desk, and searched it. In a file drawer, under S, she had discovered the combination to her husband's safe. Nearly breathless at her temerity, she asked Taylor what she should do.

"Go over and open the safe," Taylor said. There was a pause while Sara left the phone. Then she was back.

"I've found several folders. One is marked Montserrat."

Montserrat was a Caribbean island, one of several small island commonwealths where banking laws made money laundering and tax evasion an easy proposition. Taylor was suddenly alarmed. As a journalist, she had reported on stories involving drug smuggling and money laundering, all of which involved shell corporations and offshore bank accounts. She recognized Montserrat as one of those havens that shrouded bank accounts in secrecy and shielded people and companies desiring to hide their earnings from the government, disaffected partners, their spouses, or police. If Fred was involved in illicit activities, she reasoned, his telephone might be monitored and any conversation overheard.

"Sara," she said firmly, "call me when you get to Krissy's." And she abruptly hung up the telephone, hoping her cousin would understand.

Sara did understand. Later that day, she called Taylor from her sister's home. As she described the documents in greater detail, Taylor warned her, "I think it is evidence of money laundering."

"This may be your only chance of having access to any of Fred's business records," she continued. "You ought to begin copying them immediately."

But she insisted that her cousin take precautions. "Go to a place where you can copy the documents. Do it someplace that is not near the house or that Fred might frequent. Make sure you do the xeroxing. Do not turn it over to anyone else."

Then, still worried that any telephone conversation might be intercepted and unwilling to discuss the documents in detail, she urged Sara, "Please come see me."

But Sara did not immediately act on her cousin's advice. Perhaps she was frightened by her own audacity. Perhaps she had exhausted her reserves of stamina in hiring a detective, asking for a divorce, then surreptitiously rifling through her husband's papers. Perhaps she sank into a numb depression,

unwilling or unable to believe that the man she had married
might be engaging in criminal behavior. Instead of making
her own copies, Sara turned to Ralph Perdomo for help. In a
guarded telephone call, she asked him to come to the house.

"I have something to show you," she said.

It was in July or August—both miserably hot, damp
months in Georgia—when Perdomo made his first and only
visit to the Tokars's suburban home. Her husband was out of
town and, by then, Sara owed Perdomo "a considerable
amount of money." Sara met him in the driveway and escorted the private detective to her husband's basement office.
She apologized for the oppressive heat. The air conditioning
was broken, and her husband, as always, had refused to give
her the money to repair it. Once in the basement, Sara opened
the safe as she confided that her husband was not aware she
had acquired the combination.

"I want you to look at something," she said.

When she had first hired Perdomo, Sara wanted only to
confirm her suspicions that Fred was having an affair. Now,
after conversations with her cousin, she wanted to know if
her husband had descended into crime. She was a smart
woman, but knew little of the intricate financial transactions
that might mask the illegal acquisition of money or the ways
in which income could be hidden from the IRS or a suspicious
spouse. Because Perdomo was a professional investigator who
marketed his police experience and a law degree, she had
turned to him in desperation, convinced that he must have the
expertise to determine whether her husband was simply hiding money from her or whether Fred's associations with his
criminal clientele had crossed some legal line. If she could
prove her husband's legal practice had become unsavory and
stained, she could take her children and leave him, certain
that, even with the political clout Fred boasted, no judge
would give him custody of their sons.

Sara began pulling files from the safe as she spilled out her
suspicions. Fred's clients were drug dealers, and he, too,
might be entangled in the trade.

But Perdomo refused the files she offered. He distrusted
her "because of Mr. Tokars's reputation in the community,"
he said later. Because he depended on attorneys such as Fred

for his wages, and counted among his clients other lawyers who knew him, Perdomo had handled the investigation for Sara more gingerly than he normally would.

"She was married to what we considered at the time a very prominent attorney," he explained much later. "I understand that, because she had access to the safe, I could have looked at the documents, but I didn't want to take that kind of chance."

Besides, Sara owed him money. He had no intention of pursuing the investigation unless he received additional funds.

"I won't be able to help you," he said curtly.

Crestfallen, Sara appealed to him. "Fred told me that he has all kinds of political connections and contacts, and he can have us taken care of any time he wants to."

But the detective was unmoved. As she escorted him to his car, Sara made one final urgent plea.

"If anything ever happens to me, will you turn my files over to the police?"

The detective curtly agreed. But, by then, Sara was no more than an uncomfortable financial liability. She appeared to him as one more overwrought and vengeful wife with insufficient financial resources. He said as much to Steven Labovitz, the lawyer who had recommended the detective to Sara's cousin. The two men privately agreed that Sara's anger at Fred for indulging in adultery had surely bred more irresponsible and unfounded accusations.

But if Perdomo summarily dismissed his client's fears, Mary Rose Taylor did not. Over a period of months, she chided her cousin, "Sara, have you finished copying the documents?"

"No, not yet," Sara always answered.

Sara had reason to worry. After she first asked her husband for a divorce, Fred wrote a will, established his brother, Andy, as trustee, gave him absolute control over Fred's estate, and made him guardian, in the event of Fred and Sara's death, of the Tokars boys.

In the will, Fred left to his wife their worn and tattered household furnishings "if she survives me." He also left the house to Sara but suggested that his trustee not use his estate's income to pay the mortgage. The will also gave Andy Tokars, as trustee, sole authority to invest the assets and income of the Tokars's estate, out of which he could, but was not required, to pay money to either Sara or the children. If Andy elected to pay Fred's survivors any income, the will specified that he could "refrain from paying any amounts whatsoever" and that any stipend "need not be made equally to said beneficiaries."

"This trust is set up for the primary benefit of my wife," Fred stated in the will, "and I intend my trustee to be liberal in this regard to her, but I do not restrict in any way his absolute discretion."

It was, in short, a punitive document that denied Sara any say in the distribution of her husband's estate if he should die, and made her and the children beholden to her brother-in-law for any inheritance or income. It also tacitly reinforced Fred's threat to take the children from her if she left him. Fred signed it on July 19, 1989.

"Sara didn't want the trust to begin with," Andy Tokars explained later. "If Fred had to have a trust, she didn't want me to be the trustee. If the trust had to be set up, she wanted one of her sisters to be the trustee."

Sara was concerned most about the guardianship of the Tokars boys. In her own earlier will, she had appointed her sister Karen and Karen's husband Neal as guardians of her sons in the event of her death. But Fred, Andy said, "trusted me, that I could better take care of them. Sara thought her sisters knew them better, knew their wants."

Sara was upset about the will, Andy conceded. She didn't understand why Fred would place all of his estate in a trust that guaranteed her neither the assets nor income she would need to support her sons if her husband died. "She preferred to have the money herself," Andy insisted.

Five weeks after he penned the new will, Fred insured Sara's life for another $1.5 million.

Although Fred had insured Sara's life for $250,000 in 1987, on August 24, 1989 he purchased a second life insurance policy on her life—this one for five hundred thousand dollars. Again, he named himself as Sara's beneficiary.

At the time that he insured Sara's life, Fred did buy mirror life insurance policies on himself, purchases that he later singled out as proof of his innocent intentions, despite the phenomenal sums. But the policies insuring Sara's life and those that insured Fred's differed in one highly significant way. While Fred was the beneficiary if Sara died, Sara was not the reciprocal beneficiary of her husband's policies. Andy Tokars, as the trustee of his brother's estate, was also its sole beneficiary.

No independent insurance agent raised alarms about the phenomenal sums of insurance bought on the life of a housewife who had no independent businesses or corporate partnerships to secure. By then, Fred had also become an insurance agent, and he sold the policies to himself.

Sara, who signed the policy applications, couldn't help but recognize the brazen implications. Followed by detectives that Sara had hired, caught in an illicit sexual liaison, her husband had threatened her if she ever left him, then promptly raised the ante on her life.

The next day, Sara called her cousin's lawyer, Steven Labovitz. He agreed to meet with her on August thirtieth. Two days before that meeting, on August twenty-eight, Fred insured Sara's life a third time for an additional $1 million. When Sara walked into Labovitz's office to discuss a possible divorce, she was worth $1.75 million to her husband dead.

Sara didn't know it, but Labovitz's law firm was grounded far more deeply than her husband in Atlanta city politics. Labovitz's law partner and close friend was an Atlanta city councilman who within five years would become the city's mayor. Labovitz himself would run Bill Campbell's successful mayoral campaign and become his chief of staff after Campbell's inauguration. Those political connections meant Sara was consulting attorneys closely tied to the very people her husband knew and sought to influence.

When Sara met Labovitz, she impressed the attorney—as she did most men—as attractive. But despite her beauty and her resume, Labovitz found her timid and lacking in confidence. She told him hesitantly that her marriage was one of emotional abuse that often strayed into physical violence. She said she feared her husband was either an alcoholic or addicted to drugs. She had come to him on the advice of her cousin because she was seeking a way out.

That day in Labovitz's office, Sara faced one of the blunt realities of divorce—that it would cost money. Labovitz required a substantial payment in advance. She would also need a nest egg to support herself and the children if the court delayed in ordering alimony and child support. To proceed, she needed to establish her financial independence—the one thing she clearly did not have.

It was a sobering conversation. And, at the time, Sara faced more pressing financial problems. She still owed Perdomo money, but she worried that Fred would discover she no longer had the engagement ring and pearls she had left with the detective as collateral. She had substituted an inexpensive ring for her engagement diamond, knowing it would not withstand more than cursory scrutiny. Faced with that terrifying dilemma, Sara made a desperate visit to the private investigator.

She began crying as she pleaded with Perdomo. She had no money and no way to pay the balance of his fee. But she was truly frightened that her husband would find the jewelry missing. The detective was unmoved. The solution was simple. As soon as she paid him the eight hundred dollars she owed him, he would return her ring and pearls. Until then, they would remain in his safe.

Sara panicked. She was too insecure to remind the detective that, despite her urgent warnings to take precautions as he trailed her husband, he and his partner had been spotted. And Perdomo clearly didn't understand the risk Sara had taken when she hired him.

"I doubted it at the time, because of Mr. Tokars's reputation in the community," he said.

Unable to persuade Perdomo, and now frantic with worry, Sara again sought help from her cousin.

"Can you help me get my pearls back?" Sara begged.

"I will do anything to help you," Taylor answered.

At first, Taylor offered a second time to pay Perdomo's bill, but Sara again refused. Desperate as she was to reclaim her jewelry, Sara didn't want to rely on anyone to rescue her from a marriage she had freely chosen. She wanted no one to assume her debts.

So Taylor contacted Labovitz a second time.

"She's just scared of Fred's temper and what he might do if he found out the pearls were gone," Taylor told Labovitz.

"My God, Mary," he answered. "Why didn't you tell me?"

Labovitz did talk with Perdomo, and the private detective eventually agreed that, as a goodwill gesture, he would simply "write the money off." But he balked at doing so without a legal release that he required Sara to sign. Sara told her cousin later that the private investigator also asked her to sign a notarized statement swearing that she had never had a relationship with him, a request Perdomo denies ever making. Appalled at the suggestion, Sara refused to sign, and her jewelry remained in the detective's safe.

That October, Taylor invited Sara to lunch, deeply worried about her cousin's well-being. She feared Sara did not fully understand the sinister implications of marriage to a man aligned with the underworld of drugs. She had bridled all summer at Sara's seeming inability to copy the documents she had discovered in her husband's safe. Taylor determined "to put the fear of God" in her.

That day, she interviewed Sara as if she were a source and Sara's husband a suspect in a criminal investigation. "It was," she said later, "a natural instinct. But I almost couldn't believe I was doing it."

And in response to Taylor's persistent questions, Sara's story spilled out. In that lengthy conversation, Sara told her cousin that Fred had begun taking occasional trips to the Bahamas on business. The one time she accompanied him, he spent all day in town on business, explaining later he had gone to a bank to open offshore accounts for clients.

What Taylor learned from her cousin during that luncheon alarmed her—from his small deceptions before their marriage to his almost rabid insistence on conducting their household affairs in cash. Everything that Sara told her suggested Fred might be involved in illegal activities. According to Sara, he consorted with "shady characters." There was every indication Fred was involved in laundering money and that he was opening accounts for himself or his clients to avoid paying taxes.

But when she tried to explain the risks to her cousin, Sara

replied, "Mary, I don't think Fred is involved in stuff like that. I think he's really just trying to hide money from me."

"Sara," Mary forcefully insisted, "based on everything I know, based on all my years of investigative reporting, every inkling tells me that Fred is involved in a dangerous business and that your life may be in jeopardy. How can you, Sara, as concerned as you are about the children's safety, raise them in this kind of atmosphere?"

Sara began to cry. "I can't leave Fred," she replied. "He's threatened to take the children away."

"I loved Sara like a sister," Taylor said. "And there was every indication that Fred was involved in illegal activity that could potentially harm her. But Sara was more afraid of losing her boys. Sara didn't buy into what I was telling her. She felt that if anything was going on, that Fred was trying to hide money from her. She did not understand. Even after my conversation with her, I do not believe she fully grasped the implications of what I was talking about and what Fred was involved in."

In the end, it all became too much for Sara. She had to regroup and calm Fred's suspicions as she quietly built a case against him that would keep her children in her care. In a letter to Labovitz, Sara outlined the course she intended to follow.

> *The welfare of my sons has been the most important factor to consider. Your advice gave me the direction I need in order to make the objective decisions that would be the most beneficial for all of us. Therefore, it will be necessary for me to postpone a divorce for a few years so I may take the time to establish as much independence as possible.*

But Sara's willingess to contemplate divorce and the new urgency she applied to her quest for information on her husband made her someone to be reckoned with in the murky world of nightclubs, politics, and drugs to which her husband was attracted.

At some deep level, Sara suspected that path was treacherous. When Perdomo finally relinquished her rings, her necklaces, and pearls in November 1989, she asked him, "Ralph, will you still turn my files over to the police if anything ever happens to me?"

"Yes," Perdomo sighed. He would.

Four

Of Documents and Divorce

"SARA, HAVE YOU COPIED THE DOCUMENTS YET?"

It was a question that, for Mary Taylor, became a kind of rosary in those months following Sara's furtive opening of her husband's safe. Born of suspicion, fed by worry, the question opened every conversation and closed every farewell.

"Oh no, Mary," Sara would respond with cheery distraction. "But I'm getting to it. You know I'm so busy with the boys."

"Sara," Mary would insist firmly. "Given the circumstances, I think it is very important that you copy those documents as quickly as possible. It may be your only chance at ever having access to any of Fred's business materials, if you should ever need them."

Then she would patiently repeat the instructions she had given to Sara the day her cousin had first pulled the sheaf of files and papers from Fred's basement safe. Go to a copy shop. Avoid nearby businesses that Fred might frequent. Don't let anyone else handle the documents. Be careful.

On their face, the documents told Sara little about her secretive husband's business enterprises. Yet, if the documents did provide clues to what Mary suspected was a deepening history of criminal activity, Sara could divorce Fred easily without risking custody of her two sons. His cold threats would become idle and empty when matched against a record of financial crimes.

But if Fred were to learn Sara had secured such evidence, Mary feared for her cousin in the havoc that Fred, in his anger, might wreak. So, she persisted every time she talked with her cousin, or invited her to lunch. "Sara, you must copy the documents."

Months passed, as Sara demurred. It was hard to know whether she simply didn't understand the potential significance of the papers in the safe or whether she just didn't believe it. Or whether she was quietly terrified that somehow Fred would know she had removed them and made copies, that somehow—even if he were out of town on business— she would certainly be caught.

So Mary breathed deeply with relief when Sara finally answered, "Yes." Over time, Sara had summoned the will and copied everything in the safe.

"Are they in a safe place?" Mary asked her cousin.

"Yes," Sara answered. She just didn't tell her cousin where.

Sara had taken the copied documents to Krissy's.

In Krissy's Buckhead apartment, the two sisters sat down on the floor and spread Sara's copies of Fred's files, bills, and diaries in front of them.

"They're Fred's," Sara told her youngest sister. "They were in the basement. I've made copies." Facing each other, as if they were teenagers culling through the stuff of scrapbooks, Sara and Krissy began sifting through the documents, trying to guess at their significance.

What they found was evidence that Fred had bank accounts scattered from Georgia to the Caribbean. Sara was stunned to find accounts in the Bahamas that had been opened under what appeared to be derivative names. Her youngest son's name was Michael Philip, and Sara soon discovered an account in the name of Philip Michaels. A second account had been opened in the name of Andrew Fredericks, apparently derived from her husband's first name and that of his younger brother, Andy. There were corporate papers for exotic-sounding companies—among them Arabian-European Enterprises and Stoltz-Lindeman Investments Inc. that Sara knew nothing about. There were unsigned letters to a Florida bank that had been investigated by federal authorities for laundering drug dealers' money in south Florida, and a Caribbean bank charter. Scattered amid the appointment diaries, calendars, bank statements, and telephone bills she had copied, Sara also found receipts for a hundred-thousand-dollar certificate of deposit, and a second one worth two hundred thousand.

"Krissy, I think Fred is hiding money from me," Sara breathed.

She was both angry and afraid. During the four years since their marriage, as Fred had grown tight-fisted and harsh whenever she spent money on herself or on the boys, his own lifestyle had remained one of constant travel, drinking and dining with business associates, nightclubs, limousines, and expensive covert liaisons with other women.

For Sara, the evidence that her husband had banked vast sums of money on several Caribbean islands also confirmed her growing suspicion that he was sidestepping federal taxes.

"He never uses credit cards or checks because he says it could be traced," Sara told her sister. "That's why we pay for everything in cash. He doesn't want to have to pay taxes on it.

"I'm in big trouble," she continued. "Fred makes me sign stuff all the time, and I can never read it. I don't know what it is. I've signed our tax returns, but he won't let me look at them."

Her thoughts turned immediately to her children, then ages three and one. If anything were to happen to her—an accident, an illness—she wanted them to benefit from the funds Fred had apparently stashed away. Penned the previous year in secret, Sara's handwritten will, naming her sister Karen and Karen's husband Neal as her son's guardians, remained unchanged. Sara was suddenly determined that her sons would have access to what she viewed as a hidden inheritance.

"Krissy," she said urgently, as she scooped up the documents and thrust them at her sister, "put these in a safe place. . . . If anything ever happens to me, take them to the police."

Initially shaken by the suggestion that anything untoward

could ever happen to Sara, Krissy placed the copied documents in a filing cabinet together with her sister's will. But the youngest Ambrusko daughter soon dismissed any thought that something disastrous might happen to her older sister, or that Sara's life might become forfeit, not to chance or illness, but to a simmering evil and design. The documents Sara copied remained in the filing cabinet. When Krissy moved to a house north of Atlanta the following year, the documents were dumped unceremoniously in a box, where they languished forgotten in the basement until November 30, 1992, when Sara's cousin Mary urgently unearthed them.

Over the course of 1990, Mary talked with Sara often, more worried than her cousin that Sara's marriage was charting sinister waters.

"Sara, has anything changed?" she asked whenever the cousins talked.

"Oh Mary, nothing has changed," Sara always replied.

But since she had written her note to attorney Steven Labovitz, thoughts of divorce circled Sara like rapacious crows.

"It was a constant decision-making process," her sister Krissy remembered. "We talked about it all the time—what could happen, how to do it, how she and the boys would live. She was always trying to figure it out."

Sara had hoped somewhat distractedly that Fred would leave her after she confronted him with his affair. Instead, Fred had insisted the affair meant nothing to him and that divorce was not a card he cared to play. If Sara persisted in leaving him, he warned, he would fight her with every weapon he could muster in his legal and political arsenals.

That was enough to dissuade Sara. Unlike her husband, she had spent her life avoiding confrontations. At times, at least at home, Fred actually appeared to draw strength from them, while anger simply sapped Sara, leaving her heavy with exhaustion. And there were her boys, still toddlers, to think about. Leaving Fred would disrupt their lives, not so much because they would no longer see their father—they rarely saw him as it was—but because Sara would have no choice but to return to work and leave her children in someone else's care. Even then, no attorney would assure Sara that Fred could never take the children from her. To leave Fred would disrupt a life that, while unhappy, was not yet unbearable.

And truth to tell, Sara's own will had fled like some lost shadow at dusk. She who had always been the venturesome child for whom courage was an afterthought now seemed timid and unsure. The athlete who once challenged the wind on the ski slopes of the Rockies and New England now found herself struggling against emotional exhaustion to guide her children through each day. The woman who had successfully marketed two of Atlanta's most fashionable nightclubs could no longer summon the ingenuity to secure a sliding back door.

"Sara, just saw off the end of a broomstick," Krissy urged her when Sara complained that Fred wouldn't give her the money to buy a locking metal bar for doors that were easily jimmied.

"I tried," Sara answered. "But I can't."

And for much of 1990, Sara appeared to resign herself to her by then loveless marriage. She had sworn off sex with Fred after his affair and refused to resume it in spite of his occasional overtures. Eventually, she abandoned the master bedroom, choosing to sleep with her sons instead of her wayward husband. "He's lied to me too many times," she explained to her sister.

"Your girlfriend called," she bitterly informed her husband after she began receiving occasional hang-up calls.

To temper the hurt, Sara sought solace in her boys. "I think she really loved our childhood," said her sister. "I think she wanted to give those kids the same kind of childhood that we had."

And Sara had a knack with children. She wore easy holes in the knees of her jeans playing on the floor with her sons. She would laugh and say her knowledge of the world was limited to what appeared on the Disney Channel. Her generosity of spirit extended to the neighborhood youngsters. As they barreled through the yard with her sons or tromped cheerily through the house, Sara would drink in their innocence and glee like an elixir.

The neighborhood children called her "Miss Sara." Whenever the younger boys rode their toy cars into the cul-de-sac with a child's reckless abandon, "Miss Sara could whistle very loud to warn us if a car was coming," one of her sons' playmates remembered. The older children who gravitated to the Tokars's home after school before their parents returned from work organized "The Jake Rescue Squad" to hunt down the Tokars's tiny spaniel whenever he escaped from his backyard pen.

She praised them all, infusing the older ones with the self-esteem she lacked as she encouraged them not "to settle" when they dreamed. "Sara was the angel of the neighborhood," one friend recalled. "Like the Pied Piper, Sara always had a trail of children following her."

"Just sit in a comfortable chair and hold him all night long," she told one friend whose tiny son had a cough and couldn't sleep.

"Patsy, Paul is perfect, the perfect role model," she told another neighbor of her son. "I want Rick and Mike to grow up to be just like him."

Sara's slender, tow-headed sons responded to that devotion. "It was a bond like nothing I've seen," Krissy said. "My dad used to say, 'They are so close to her. What would they do without her?' "

Over her husband's escalating and contentious objections, Sara resolutely continued to visit her parents in Florida every few months. By then, Fred no longer gave Sara or the boys presents on holidays or their birthdays. He complained loudly that she bought the boys too many toys—indulgences he insisted would turn them into "little brats." But Sara had always loved holidays. If her husband were too busy, miserly, or callous to celebrate, Sara would organize holidays for her parents that would bring her sisters home. She planned them all—Thanksgiving, Christmas, Mother's Day, Father's Day, anniversaries, birthdays, family vacations. She would cook the holiday dinners, buy the tree, hang the ornaments, distribute handmade Christmas cards. She insisted they all come home to Bradenton.

"Her one joy in life was bringing the kids down to Florida," Krissy said. "That was the only thing she did to spend money." When her husband refused to let her fly with their small sons, she outfitted the car with a tiny, battery-powered television and a VCR to keep them occupied during the nine-hour drive. When he refused to give her money, she traveled with as little as twenty dollars and a prayer. And when he found he couldn't stop his normally pliant wife from loading the car every few months and heading south like an uncaged bird, Fred would reluctantly follow, flying into Tampa where he would join Sara and the boys for the last leg of the trip as if he were compelled to monitor his wife during every absence he didn't govern. "It was always a battle," Krissy sighed. But in that struggle for dominance that surfaced whenever Sara headed home lay the seeds and strength of her growing rebellion. And Fred's struggle to govern her stiffened, like a salt-soaked rope in the sun.

Over time, the changes in the couple's life that Fred contemplated would make a divorce even more difficult, or at least convince Sara that was the case. They would also insure that his wife was always being watched and that nothing would happen at their house without his knowledge. His actions meshed conveniently with what Fred hoped was a budding political career.

By 1989, Fred was a part-time traffic court judge in Atlanta. He soon realized that to qualify for the higher judicial posts he coveted, he needed a Fulton County address.

During his first year as a part-time judge, the solution was a simple one. He signed a joint lease with Sara's sister, Krissy, for a Buckhead apartment in north Atlanta that gave him a nominal city residency. But in 1990, Krissy moved to a house in Woodstock in Cherokee County north of the city. At first, Fred simply rented another apartment, this one on Roswell Road. Using that address, he registered to vote and acquired a Fulton County license plate. He insisted that the apartment was never a love nest for his illicit liaisons. It contained no furniture and he said he never paid to connect the utilities. It was, in fact, a shell address, a minor ruse to safeguard his political appointment. But it was, at best, a temporary fix for an ambitious man who was accumulating a surplus of political debts in Fulton County, where he worked, not Cobb County where he lived. He began talking to Sara about moving to north Fulton County, or even into Atlanta. He soon acquired a $190,000 lot in Sandy Springs and told his wife they should begin making plans to build and enroll the boys, now nearly school age, in the north Fulton public school system. The move, he insisted, would solve the residential requirements attached to both appointed and elected office.

And as the Tokars marriage foundered, Fred, perhaps intentionally, again raised the ante. He formed a partnership with divorce attorney Emily Sherwinter, a former law school classmate. Together, Tokars and Sherwinter embarked on an aggressive advertising campaign that attracted celebrities such as Paulette Holyfield, wife of World Heavyweight Boxing Champion Evander Holyfield.

Their highly publicized representation of Holyfield showed the unorthodox lengths to which Fred was willing to go to win. When Fred and his partner were hired, Paulette Holyfield had already signed a settlement agreement with her husband. But before it was approved by a judge, Holyfield won the world boxing championship and a purse worth millions, and his estranged wife traveled to Houston where she slept with him. Sherwinter and Tokars immediately declared the settlement agreement void, and demanded on Paulette's behalf a new agreement to include a generous share of the boxer's winnings. Georgia law allowed them to do it, but it was an extreme and vituperative form of legal hardball that Sara, cognizant of her husband's legal skills, could not have failed to recognize.

Just a few months later, Sherwinter dissolved the partnership, although, for a time, she and Fred continued jointly to advertise their services. Colleagues suggested that Sherwinter did most of the work, while Fred publicly claimed the credit. But Sherwinter said Fred's secrecy, his "mercenary attitude," and her nagging doubts about his legal ethics persuaded her to dissolve the partnership.

By then, Sherwinter had also learned, to her dismay, that the law partner and former classmate she had known for a decade wanted to insure her life for as much as $2 million and list himself as her beneficiary. She dismissed the suggestion at the time, although it returned to haunt her later, telling Fred plainly, "The firm wasn't where we wanted it to be" to justify the expense.

That same year, Fred's father died. After his devastated, lonely mother, Norma, began calling her son every morning at 5 a.m. to talk, he began urging her to move from Buffalo to Atlanta. She could work part-time in his law office and occasionally babysit for her grandsons. When they built the house in Sandy Springs, Tokars informed his wife that they would include in the plans an apartment for his mother. But Sara knew that Norma Tokars, who was deeply devoted to her son, would also be his eyes and ears.

Not that much about Sara escaped her husband's notice or his scrutiny. Fred had, by then, become fanatical about the mail. He erupted in anger if Sara looked at the mail, or even attempted to bring it in the house. He insisted on reviewing all the mail, even his wife's. Under those circumstances, acquiring a credit card, with its monthly statements, was impossible. But when Krissy moved to Woodstock, Sara applied for and received a card at her younger sister's new address.

Her husband's tight-fisted grasp on household finances made Sara a beggar. Every request for funds she made precipitated a fight. As the Tokars boys grew old enough for preschool, Sara wanted to enroll them in a Catholic day school where she knew they would be nurtured in her faith, as she and her sisters had been. Fred wouldn't agree to pay the tuition of both children.

Sara had chosen St. Jude the Apostle, where many of the neighborhood children were enrolled, and where Sara and the boys also attended mass. But because the school is small and intimate, Ricky, the oldest child, was placed on a waiting list before he was admitted to preschool.

Sara bartered for her younger son's tuition. She agreed to teach two days a week and substitute occasionally, arrangements the school often made with families for whom tuition was a financial hardship.

"I remember her trying to convince me how dedicated she was, how important it was to her and to her husband to have them here," remembered Principal Ron Svoboda. "She was willing to teach for nothing to get the boys in."

Having Ricky on a waiting list unnerved Sara. When both sons were finally accepted, she cried with relief. Inseparable and extremely attached to Sara, Ricky and Mike attended prekindergarten together their first year at St. Jude. Trained as a teacher, with a degree in elementary education, Sara volunteered in her sons' classrooms.

The school children responded to Sara just as the neighborhood youngsters had. Always cheerful, "She was one of those people who never seemed to be worried or bothered by anything," Svoboda said. "If she was, she didn't let it show. That's why the children responded to her so well."

The children trailed Sara. She was at ease on the floor or in the dirt, comfortable with the child's-eye view of the world it afforded her. "That's a God-given talent," Svoboda said. "I don't think you can teach people to do that."

But the teachers at St. Jude's who soon became her friends knew that Sara's marriage was unhappy. "I remember Sara asking how it was to be a single mother," Jean Robinson recalled. "I encouraged her to work on her marriage for her boys and because of our religion. I wish I had told her to leave, be strong, be safe, pray to God, and know she had help from all who loved her."

Yet the response of her own sons and their small companions to Sara's presence in their classroom clearly energized her. So did the admiration of the teachers she assisted. No longer isolated in King's Cove where her critical husband was her only mirror, Sara's confidence slowly revived. With the boys happily settled in school, Sara, for the first time, began talking about going back to work.

But if Sara's decision to enroll the boys in prekindergarten classes at St. Jude's was a subtle attempt to sidestep a threatened move to Fulton County, it failed. Now that his sons were in private school, Fred suggested that it didn't really matter where the family lived. School districts were no longer a factor. The family could move inside the city limits, where Fred could qualify for a city judgeship as well as a county post. As for returning to work, why Sara could work for him. He needed someone to collect overdue bills from a clientele that still skewed toward criminals and drug dealers. But Sara had something else in mind. She wanted her own independence that a job outside her husband's purview would afford. She wanted her own money. And she still wanted a divorce.

On April 17, 1991—a year after she had written a note to attorney Steven Labovitz postponing a divorce—Sara met with him again. It was an extended conversation which convinced the attorney that, this time, Sara really intended to pursue divorce. The discovery of the documents in Fred's safe, her extended conversations with her determined cousin, Mary, and a newfound confidence derived from teaching had made Sara more certain of her circumstances. She was beginning to recognize her husband for what he was and had let him know she knew it.

That day, Sara told the attorney she had asked Fred for a divorce. Then, for ninety minutes, she spilled out all of her frustrations, suspicions, and her fears. She told him everything. "He's a control freak," she insisted bitterly, a man who abused, manhandled, and belittled her. He had acknowledged he was laundering money for his clients. He was investing their money secretly offshore and some of his own as well.

Sara told Labovitz how she had accompanied her husband on one of those business trips to the Bahamas in 1988 where he was scouting for offshore banks. He had spent an entire afternoon opening bank accounts for American clients, she recalled.

Now, she feared that if she left him, his political associates might help him make good on his threats to take the boys.

Labovitz sought to reassure her. "Based on what you're telling me about his lack of interest in the children, I think there would be very little chance for him to get custody," he said. Besides, Sara would file for divorce in Cobb County, where the couple lived, not in Fulton County where Fred claimed to be so politically influential. He sidestepped all suggestion that Fred was engaging in financial fraud. He wasn't sure he believed her. Sara was clearly naive about the complexities of high finance and banking; her impressions of her husband's profession were colored by her chronic lack of money and Fred's overbearing behavior. And Ralph Perdomo had already warned him that he thought Sara's allegations were as empty as they were bitter.

But Labovitz's reassurances about a possible custody fight meant little to Sara. Her boys were as dear to her as breath. She could not comprehend a life without them.

So Labovitz moved on to more utilitarian matters. "Sara,"

he said, "I want you to write a marital history listing everything—the good, the bad, and the ugly. Tell me how you met,
when you married. Discuss all the things you've told me"—a
record of neglect that skewed into abuse. "It's very important
for you to get organized if you want to move forward."

Labovitz also asked Sara to compile a household budget
on which a judge could base temporary alimony and child
support, and list any assets she had, assets she knew or suspected Fred had, and assets the couple shared. In 1989, Sara
had begun reading her husband's appointment diaries. Now,
Labovitz asked her to begin keeping a marital diary of her
own.

Two months later, on June twenty-eighth, Sara again
sought a conference with Labovitz. The custody question still
distressed her.

Again, Labovitz urged Sara, "If you're really worried
about custody, you should be keeping a detailed diary of
when Fred sees the children. I also want you to keep in that
diary everything he says to you."

Again, he tried to reassure her. "Based on what you have
told me, Fred isn't home that much and doesn't spend much
time with the children. No judge is going to award him custody."

But custody wasn't Sara's only worry. Money and her lack
of it were clearly troubling her as well. Labovitz required a
$2,500 retainer fee to initiate divorce proceedings. He billed
$175 an hour. Meanwhile, Fred had begun requiring his wife
to itemize her weekly household expenses and purchases, including every bra and every pair of panties, before he would
turn over Sara's weekly cash allowance. He would quibble
with her over nearly every purchase, asking why she hadn't
found a cheaper buy. Now determined to return to work, Sara
had asked Fred for money to purchase a wardrobe—something more professional than the jeans and pullovers she had
worn since Ricky was born. Fred promised her the money,
but never followed through.

Labovitz warned Sara that, if she wanted a divorce, she
must have money to retain him, then pay for food, lodgings,

and other household necessities until he could schedule a hearing.

"If you can get that, there's a possibility we can get a hearing very quickly, that the court will award you monthly support," he said. He encouraged her to seek help from her parents or from her cousin, Mary, who was happily married to a wealthy Atlanta developer.

"I'm certain that Mary wouldn't mind giving you money if you needed it," the attorney suggested.

"My father is well-to-do," Sara acknowledged hesitantly. "But I'm reluctant to ask him for help. I try not to bring my problems home to my parents. Let me see what I can do."

She never followed through.

"Steve could not guarantee that she would get possession of the children," her cousin, Mary, said later. "And with no guarantee, she was not willing to move ahead."

Again, Sara refused to ask her cousin or her parents for the money she had to have before she could leave her husband. "Sara had a lot of pride," Taylor said. "She wanted to do this on her own, and she would never take money from me."

Instead, Sara asked Mary for help in finding a job. Mary promptly enlisted her cousin's help in arranging a fund-raising benefit to restore "The Dump," Atlanta author Margaret Mitchell's derisive name for the old Peachtree Street apartment building where she had penned *Gone With the Wind*.

At that benefit, which Mary Taylor hosted in the fall of 1991, Labovitz spotted Fred and Sara from a distance. He waved at Sara, but they never spoke. It was left to Sara to explain to her husband how she had come to know a fellow divorce attorney who came so highly recommended by her cousin.

Some time later, Sara again called Labovitz at his office. Things were no better. She was still considering divorce. But Sara could offer him nothing more definitive. Labovitz never saw or spoke to her again.

What the attorney did not know was that a divorce and bitter custody battle with the requisite examination of Tokars's assets would surely have brought to light the fact that, by March 1990, Fred was not only representing drug dealers, he was doing business with them. And the more seriously Sara dallied with divorce, the more certain it became that her sunny, east Cobb world and her husband's street-lit world of drug dealers, city politics, and crime would inevitably collide.

Part II

===

FRED

Five

Fred

FRED TOKARS HAD ALWAYS BEEN AMBITIOUS. THAT WAS how his high school friends described him—as a hard working, self-contained young man eager to amass his own credentials and win recognition for his accomplishments. Calculating rather than animated, and remarkably even-tempered, he was a member of the high school swim team, a long-distance competitor whose forte was endurance and control rather than speed. Schooled in that rebellious, idealistic decade that fostered the civil rights struggle, student militancy, race riots, and the Vietnam War; Fred's classmates remember that he waxed passionate about only one thing. He was preoccupied with making money.

Like Sara, Fred was the grandchild of immigrants who, like Sara's own grandparents, had settled in Buffalo, New York. Fred was born in Hot Springs, Arkansas, while his father, Jerome Tokars, was still in the United States Army. His mother, Norma, was a U.S. Army nurse who had served in the Philippine Islands. The G.I. bill paid his father's way through medical school at the University of Buffalo where Sara's own father had matriculated and taught. For forty years, his father was a family physician in Buffalo. And for much of that time, Norma, a registered nurse, assisted her husband in his medical practice.

Like the Ambruskos, the Tokars family lived in wealthy

73

suburban Amherst. Like Sara, Fred was the family's middle child. Both were children of privilege. When Fred was still a boy, his father bought a large summer cottage on the banks of Lake Erie in nearby Ontario, Canada. Every year, he and his four siblings, two brothers and two sisters, would spend idyllic summers with their mother at the beach while Dr. Tokars commuted to his Buffalo office.

"We were pretty close in age," Andy said of the Tokars children. "We played together a lot when we were young." Jerome, Jr., the oldest child, was the scholar who eventually followed their father into medicine, Andy said. Fred, according to his younger sister, was always the family comedian, whose stunts could send the younger children into gales of giggles. He was also his younger brother's mentor and his chief protector, a relationship that would continue throughout their lives.

In Amherst, the Ambruskos and the Tokars lived just two blocks apart. And, as teenagers, Fred and Andy were usually invited to the Ambrusko sisters' parties. As a high school sophomore, Andy moved to the heart of Sara's family when he began dating Karen Ambrusko.

Extremely proud and highly competitive, Fred made no real impression on any of the popular Ambrusko sisters, including his classmate, Sara. They moved in different social circles. She counted among her closest friends the cheerleaders, the majorettes, the high school queens and athletes who are every high school's royalty. Although Fred did play football as a freshman—and was, according to his sister, "a real good blocker"—as he grew to gangling manhood, he traded his football jersey for swim trunks and a sport that better suited his lean, rangy frame and where he could excel. He was, his brother said, a talented swimmer with the will and the endurance to medal in grueling, long-distance events.

Yet something of the free-wheeling, undisciplined discontent of the sixties appealed to Fred. By then, the film *Easy Rider* had become synonymous with the decade, and Fred bought a motorcycle that he rode with abandon until he wrecked it. He idolized the Beatles, particularly the owlish antics and socially conscious poesy of John Lennon. While Sara and her friends ignored the Beatles and danced instead to Motown melodies, Fred became a guitarist in a rock-'n-roll garage band that favored Beatles tunes. His most cherished gift from his father was an electric guitar like Lennon's that he kept for years after he traded music for more serious and lucrative pursuits.

In 1971, after he and Sara graduated, Fred left Buffalo for a more tropical clime—the sweltering, exotic damp of the University of Miami in Florida. There, he majored in accounting. He was, as always, a hard worker. His sophomore year, he won a one-year tuition scholarship. And early in his college career, he began moving into the ranks of student government, acquiring political offices with which he would later enhance his resume.

"We were surprised that he was such a good student," his mother Norma Tokars said years later.

That sophomore year, Fred met Alan Bell, a year younger than Fred and much like his brother, Andy; a young man whose life would intersect Fred's more than once and whose career eventually, would parallel Fred's own. Bell was then a drummer contemplating a music major, a self-described shy underachiever who had struggled through high school with barely adequate grades.

They met in Math 101 and quickly became friends. Bell idolized Fred. And Fred, in turn, became the impressionable younger man's mentor. He persuaded Bell to pledge his fraternity and became his big brother. He urged him to abandon his music major in favor of business administration, Fred's own major, take accounting courses, and join the professional business fraternity to which Fred also belonged.

He molded and sculpted Bell in his own image, and Bell, in turn, became his surrogate brother. A more disciplined student than Bell, Fred studied six hours a day and often urged the younger man to accompany him to the library instead of drifting into a weekend party or a bar.

"He introduced me to a world," Bell said, "that better prepared me for life."

Even though Fred's family in Buffalo was well-to-do, Bell remembers that, as college students, "We were so poor. We didn't have any money. Fred didn't even have an allowance."

Bell remembers Fred as being popular in college. He

wasn't a jock, but he was athletic. He had an easy smile and manner, a shock of thick, curly, sun-bleached hair, and an indelible tan. Women were attracted to him. He flattered and charmed them. One sorority chose him as their "Dream Man." "He was All-American, very nice," Bell said. "I wanted to package that."

He was also politically ambitious, astute enough to join the organizations and cultivate friendships with the people who would vote him into the offices for which he diligently campaigned. As a sophomore, Fred held the post of student supreme court justice. By his junior year, he was the treasurer of his fraternity and a campus honor society. His senior year he was elected president of both organizations and treasurer of Miami University's student government association. He was also tapped to join the Iron Arrow, which numbered among its members the most elite, popular, and powerful students on the University of Miami campus. When he graduated in 1975 with a bachelor's degree in business administration with a specialty in accounting, he had a 3.7 average.

On his last day in Miami, after he had packed his bags and loaded a rental car with gear, Fred embraced Bell as he said farewell. "If there's anything you ever want or need from me," the younger man promised, "no matter when, where, or how, I'll be there."

That fall, Fred enrolled at the University of Georgia in Athens an hour northeast of Atlanta, and, after a year of intensive accounting courses, he earned an advanced degree in accounting. He became a master of money.

His grades and the political skills he had acquired running for political office at the University of Miami served him well. In 1976, shortly after Fred earned his graduate degree, Price Waterhouse—one of the "Big Eight" accounting firms— hired him as a junior accountant in Atlanta. At the beginning of his career, Fred Tokars had seemingly hit the jackpot.

While at UGA, he had formed a fast and lasting friendship with an undergraduate accounting major named Ruth Bartlett, a platonic bond that, at times, appeared stronger than the bond he had with his own family.

"Our family kind of adopted Fred," Bartlett recalled. "Often, he wouldn't go home for Christmas or Thanksgiving. He would spend Thanksgiving or Christmas with us.''

Bartlett, whose family lived in Atlanta, was one of three daughters. "I always felt like Fred was the brother I never had,'' she said. "He kind of looked on my family and me in the same light.'' Her father, Bartlett recalled, "always treated Fred like the son he never had.''

As students, Fred and Bartlett studied together. They took the certified public accountants examination together, and, after they were both hired by Price Waterhouse, moved to the same Atlanta apartment complex. Fred, she remembered, was smart, diligent, and driven. He was also, she said, "a good friend and someone I could rely on.''

When Andy Tokars graduated from college and called his brother with only ten dollars in his pocket, Fred persuaded him to come to Atlanta to find a job and share his apartment. And it was Fred who, after the advent of Atlanta's ten-kilometer Peachtree Road Race, persuaded both Andy and Bartlett to begin running and became their unofficial coach and trainer. Fred, Andy said, "was always concerned about staying in shape.''

Fred spent two years as an auditor at Price Waterhouse. In 1978—"a little disenchanted with all the traveling,'' according to his brother—he left the accounting firm to become a salesman with the National Cash Register Corporation. His success in selling computerized cash register and inventory systems and software to large department stores such as Rich's and Macy's led to his membership in the company's salesman of the year club. He also began delving avidly into computer programming.

"He was kind of like one of my right arms,'' said his supervisor, Hosea Batton. "He was always punctual, very aggressive, really wanted to get ahead. I had a feeling we didn't really offer as much for him as he really wanted.''

It was during his tenure at NCR that Fred first began participating in seminars. To market the corporation's computer equipment and software, Fred planned seminars and live demonstrations to boost his sales. He would use those skills in the years that followed to augment both his status and his income.

"Fred was an achiever,'' Bartlett remembered. Active since

his graduation in the Georgia Society of CPAs, Fred sponsored continuing education courses on behalf of the society, whose members he often joined for beach trips to Hilton Head and ski trips to Vail.

But somewhere during those early years of Fred's career, the laudable ambition that had defined him in high school began degenerating into disingenuity and self-promotion. Fred began inflating his credentials. He said he had a master's in business administration with an accounting specialty, a three-year course of study. In fact, he had a master's in accounting, a one-year vocational degree. On one resume, he elevated his post as a junior auditor at Price Waterhouse to one that combined the skills of an investment counselor with those of a tax attorney. He had no law degree, yet he claimed to have interpreted major tax court decisions for clients, advised and counseled clients on tax law and investments, and even represented a client on a tax litigation matter in court. The discrepancies weren't indefensible lies as much as they were subtle exaggerations. Individually, they seemed somewhat insignificant. Taken together, they revealed a man increasingly enamored with his own importance, someone willing to dissemble to achieve his goals.

He was also dissatisfied with his career. Since their graduation from the University of Miami, he and Alan Bell had remained in touch. Although Bell had also majored in business and accounting, he had then gone on to law school. By 1979, Bell was a young prosecutor. He had interned with now U.S. Attorney General Janet Reno, then Dade County's district attorney, and had begun assisting in the prosecution of racketeering cases that targeted organized criminal enterprises and required an accountant's wizardry to unravel.

"I could tell Fred was becoming intrigued with the lawyering business," Bell recalled. "I was then moving up in the ranks with the tools that, as a student, he had given me."

"This is cool," Fred confided to his old fraternity brother as he listened to Bell's accounts of his cases. "I want to go to law school, too." That year, while still employed at NCR, Fred enrolled at the Woodrow Wilson College of Law, an unaccredited and now defunct night law school in Atlanta.

For Bell, who had always looked up to Fred, it was a startling role reversal. "He was the one I followed, the one I looked up to," Bell recalled. "Now, I'm moving up in my career, and suddenly, he's following me."

Despite high grade point averages in college and in graduate school, Tokars's record at Woodrow Wilson was undistinguished. He was, according to his classmates, a voluble man, increasingly impressed with the importance of his own ideas. He was attracted to power, liked being at the center of the circle, and he left in his wake an impression that he was one of the brighter students in the Woodrow Wilson firmament. "He was," according to one former classmate, "always in charge of any situation."

During the four years he attended night school, he also acquired a reputation as a party boy that contrasted with his disciplined approach to his career and studies. He was drawn to the restaurants and nightclubs favored by Atlanta's young, upwardly mobile attorneys, investors, developers, and politicos. He would drink beer for hours, making contacts and basking in the mock intimacy that sprang from the heat and the din of too many people in too little space.

While he was in law school, Tokars changed jobs again, joining the staff of Southern Bell in 1981. According to his resume, he counseled and provided legal advice to the company's data processing procurement department, arbitrated contract disputes, drafted and negotiated procurement and financial agreements, and participated in "a computer-related" lawsuit for one of the largest of the country's "Baby Bells"—all without a law degree or a license to practice law.

In fact, he was just one member of a staff that reviewed and managed computer leasing contracts for the Atlanta-based regional telephone company. He had an interest, but no real expertise, in the growing field of computer law.

But it was at Southern Bell that Tokars first became friends with Love Collins. Collins was a political activist; his young wife Leah Sears was a lawyer who worked for Alston and Bird, a prominent Atlanta law firm. The couple were friends and political allies of Andrew Young, a lieutenant of Martin Luther King's whom President Jimmy Carter had appointed as U.S. Ambassador to the United Nations. When Young became Atlanta's mayor, he appointed Leah Sears as a city traffic court judge, a post generally awarded by the city's mayors to return political favors.

For Fred, that friendship with Sears and Collins would become a stepping stone to Atlanta's political establishment.

In May 1982, while still employed at Southern Bell, Tokars graduated from law school. But in a city that easily attracted the best of the graduates from the South's private and state law schools as well as the native sons and daughters who earned their degrees in the Ivy Leagues, Fred's nondescript record at an unaccredited night law school was anything but a calling card at Atlanta's prominent law firms with their generous salaries and their access to the power elite.

So he took another route. He parlayed a friendship with a fellow college graduate into a job as a junior assistant district attorney in the office of Fulton County District Attorney Lewis Slaton, who presided over Atlanta's criminal prosecutions.

Fred was, as always, a hard worker, willing to learn, and eager to get as much trial experience as quickly as he could. "Fred was a go-getter," said Fulton Assistant District Attorney John Turner, who shared a tiny office with him. "If he was interested in something, he pursued it."

His cases were primarily smaller felonies—thefts, drugs, burglaries, and an occasional assault. He never handled any major cases. Computer crime was then in its infancy and few laws existed to address it. Nor did the district attorney's office, overwhelmed with a ballooning number of felony drug cases in a city that would soon become the violent crime capital of the country, prosecute white-collar crime. But that didn't stop Fred—with his degree in accounting, his background in data processing, and a brand new law degree—from marketing himself as an expert in both fields.

"Like Topsy," Turner said, "it built upon itself." Soon, Fred returned to his night school alma mater to teach. He began lecturing at several local colleges, and organized or appeared as a guest speaker at what seemed to his colleagues to be an endless series of professional tax, accounting, and law enforcement seminars. He even taught occasionally at the federal government's law enforcement academy on Georgia's coast where federal agents trained.

And other assistant district attorneys began taking note of the small, imprecise vanities that Fred affected to bolster his position in the marketplace. In Slaton's office, all the stationery bore the district attorney's letterhead in keeping with his position as an elected official by whose grace the others served. Soon after joining the district attorney's staff, however, Fred ordered his own letterhead stationery. "It wasn't a big deal. It was just a little added vanity," said Jack Boyle, who then managed Slaton's office. "The stationery was delivered, and he was told he couldn't use it."

Then Fred acquired a doctorate from an unaccredited West Coast correspondence school and began referring to himself in his correspondence and seminar brochures as "Dr. Fredric Tokars." The conceit alarmed several of the assistant district attorneys who feared it might border on fraud.

Fred's small conceits never quite strayed into deception. But their occasionally misleading nature, coupled with his predilection for Atlanta's night life and his obvious attraction to the women in his office, prompted his colleagues to dub him "Fast Fred." He would occasionally laugh about the nickname as he dated his way through the district attorney's cadre of female attorneys, including the daughter of a federal judge. And he made no secret of his attraction to Atlanta's glittery nightclubs or his willingness to indulge in the city's unbridled night life.

"Some of the assistants didn't like him," Turner said. "He was a northerner. They were good old boys. They looked at him as a strange pariah. He never made any inroads. He didn't try."

During his three years as an assistant district attorney, Tokars was never assigned to a single judge's courtroom as some of the more senior assistant attorneys were. But he did become friendly with Fulton Superior Court Judge John Lankford, in whose court he most often appeared to plead or argue cases. Lankford was impressed with the congenial, energetic junior prosecutor. "He was a good courtroom man," the judge recalled. "He was a vigorous trial lawyer and did an excellent job." And Tokars, cognizant of the benefits of a judge's beneficence, soon began using Lankford as a reference.

What Fred seemed to covet was both experience and exposure. In an office with a reputation for avoiding all but the most inevitable of trials, and one that rarely prosecuted a death penalty case, he sought to try as many cases as quickly as he could. In 1985, when Turner sought the death penalty for an Atlanta man who had stabbed his lover, a prominent doctor, to death, Fred volunteered to help his colleague with the case.

"Fred came and sat at the table and assisted me throughout that entire trial," Turner said. When jury deliberations extended through the weekend, Tokars joined Turner on Saturday morning to await the verdict in what was then one of the city's more highly publicized crimes.

But despite his colleague's eagerness to offer help in a death penalty prosecution, Turner knew that Fred was not enamored of a career spent prosecuting criminals. "He was more interested in politics," Turner said. "At that time, his interest seemed to be in terms of getting involved and working in the inner circle." What Tokars really wanted, Turner said, was to become a judge.

Like the seminars, lectures, memberships, and occasional honors that somehow always found their way into Fred's promotional pamphlets, his participation, however marginal, in the highly publicized murder trial gave him a certain credibility. In an office with nearly fifty other assistant district attorneys, the case offered something else. It gave Fred visibility. And it reintroduced him to Sara Ambrusko.

There is, of course, no record of that first telephone call the former high school cheerleader made to the promotion-minded prosecutor who had once attended her sisters' summer parties. He was surely flattered when she called. Fantasies are built on such encounters. Sara's sister, with whom Sara shared a condominium, knows only that before the call ended, Fred had asked Sara out for drinks. And Sara, still fragile from the dissolution of her marriage, had accepted.

"Sara's in town. Can you believe it?" Fred told his brother, Andy, after his first date with Sara. "We met, and we seemed to really like each other a lot."

It was, Andy recalled, "just kind of fate."

Sara never knew before she married him that Fred was

immutably drawn to women or that, among his colleagues, he was known as "fast." If she had, all too familiar with infidelity, she surely would have shied away. But Fred appealed to her, not only because she saw in him the aura of her youth, but also because he was so different from her first husband in both manner and appearance. His still boyish face was framed by heavy, dark glasses that made him look, not handsome, but steady and responsible. He was disciplined, earnest, and self-confident—traits of which Sara's father approved. He could also wax expansive, particularly when there was someone to impress. But there was about him an air of genuine sincerity, or so it appeared to most people with whom he came in contact.

In fact, Fred possessed a trait common to politicians and chameleons—an easy ability to reflect what he most wanted other people to see. He had by no means perfected the art when he met Sara. Some of his colleagues, with whom he shared close quarters at the district attorney's office, weren't fooled by an overly ambitious man who was willing to say whatever he needed to get what he wanted. But to Sara, Fred seemed an honest man. He was clearly one of the city's protectors, and Sara admired him for that.

But just as Fred exaggerated his resume and inflated his credentials, he may also have exaggerated the qualities that Sara was seeking in a husband. "Sara thought, here's a guy, a lawyer, from the same neighborhood," her sister said later. "He seemed to be everything we thought we were supposed to marry when we grew up." To Sara, her high school classmate was as smooth and opaque as a mirror. She knew nothing of his excesses or his predilections. And as he regaled the sisters with tales of inner city justice or the laughable incompetence of the people he prosecuted and their sad efforts to hoodwink the system, Sara saw what she wanted to see.

For Tokars, who had political aspirations and made no secret of his desire to someday open a private practice and cultivate a wealthy clientele, Sara was the perfect accessory. She was attractive, personable, and poised. And, as the marketing director for several of Atlanta's most lucrative nightclubs, Sara had desirable contacts in a business to which her new husband was increasingly attracted.

Six

"I'm Going to Get Rich Quick"

AT FIRST, CHOOSING TO SHARE AN OFFICE AT THE CNN CEN-
ter with Atlanta attorney Murray Silver may have seemed an
odd choice for a man such as Fred who aspired to enter Atlanta's social and political arenas. In 1986, the CNN Center
was hardly a prestigious Atlanta address. Sandwiched between a hotel and a sports arena amid a sea of deteriorating
parking lots and abandoned buildings, CNN was still four
years away from discarding its reputation as an upstart television network with a tenuous future.

And Silver—rotund, prone to perspiration, with a voice
that registered a perpetual quaver—had, at best, a tenuous
past.

A University of Georgia graduate, Silver had opened his
own law practice in his native Savannah in 1953 "to anything
that walked in the door." Seven years later, he was disbarred
for deceiving a client and stripped of his license to practice.

Since that time, he had proven, on occasion, to be a careless
attorney, expansive to the point of misdirection—flaws that
not only had led to his disbarment but also made him the
object of at least one civil lawsuit brought by an angry former
client.

Silver coveted the wealth of and access to the corrupt but
charming men he circled like a queasy moth. He gambled in
Las Vegas, playing for high stakes he couldn't quite afford.

He bought thoroughbred race horses. When he traveled, he stayed at the most expensive hotels, occasionally refusing to pay what he couldn't bill his clients. He sidestepped civil judgments by twice declaring bankruptcy and was subsequently investigated, at the recommendation of the bankruptcy judge, on suspicion of fraud.

He fluttered at the fringes of Georgia's conservative but colorful political establishment, seeking to peddle influence where he had none by laying claim to friendships with President Jimmy Carter, banker and former budget director Bert Lance, and former U.S. Attorney General Griffin Bell.

"I'm a very famous lawyer from Atlanta," he would later tell one of the foremost criminal defense attorneys in the nation. "I just like people to know who I am."

But Silver's political connections, such as they were, had less to do with any long-standing participation in Georgia politics than with a penchant for trading testimony—in return for leniency regarding his own transgressions—against clients who were under federal investigation.

Beginning in 1964, when Silver's license to practice law was restored, he began a series of associations with flamboyant men who demonstrated an unfortunate attraction to financial fraud.

There was Sam Caldwell, Georgia's labor commissioner, who appointed Silver general counsel of the scandal-ridden Labor Department in 1964. Silver held that post when, three years later, Caldwell fell on hard times and sank his boat off the Georgia coast in a misguided effort to collect on an insurance policy. Caldwell was caught and convicted of fraud.

And there was Michael Thevis, one of the most successful pornography distributors in the nation. In 1975, as I.R.S. agents sought to unravel the complex web of Thevis's corporations with a mind to shutting his operations down, they stumbled upon Silver—the attorney of record for one of Thevis's Atlanta companies. They also discovered that for three years, Silver had been filing what appeared to be fraudulent personal tax returns. Federal prosecutors agreed not to pursue an indictment against Silver only after the attorney agreed to testify against Thevis as a federal witness.

And, finally, there was Ed Joiner, a self-described "Alabama redneck with balls" who loved football, nightclubs, women, money, and the lure of a fast sale. Silver had known Joiner for fifteen years and described himself as Joiner's "agent and friend."

Joiner was, he acknowledged more than once, a hustler at heart, a charlatan and ne'er-do-well who moved easily from promoting college rock concerts and sports events to selling stock at a New York brokerage and more elaborate, riskier schemes long on creativity but woefully short on collateral. But whether he was promoting concerts or tax shelters, Joiner could be counted on to do one thing—take the money and run.

By 1983, he had driven himself blithely into bankruptcy, trailing in his wake nearly $1 million in empty promises, bad checks, overdue bills, and federal fines. When I.R.S. agents ordered Joiner to abandon his highly lucrative but financially suspect investments in energy-related tax shelters, he ignored them. Within a year, state auditors in Georgia were investigating Joiner for raiding his investors' escrow accounts and the I.R.S. slapped him with a bill for $2 million in penalties and back taxes for what federal prosecutors later described as "a series of fraudulent tax shelters and phony investment opportunities promoted by the defendant . . . [in which] either the defendant or companies controlled by him always ended up with investors' funds."

In 1984, just twenty minutes ahead of I.R.S. agents, Joiner drove his Mercedes to an Atlanta bank where he emptied his accounts to secure a $1.1 million Federal Reserve check. Then he fled to the Caribbean island of Barbuda.

It was while Joiner was in the Caribbean that he reached out to Silver. Taken by Joiner's grandiose plans to turn Barbuda into an exclusive international playground and tax shelter for rich aristocrats, Silver became Joiner's attorney, then his business partner, and, when it warranted, his front man.

And Joiner's Caribbean enterprise became the catalyst that ultimately brought Silver and Tokars together and prompted Fred's departure from the Fulton County district attorney's office.

Both men remember they first discussed sharing an office after Silver convinced a jury to acquit his client on two of three drug charges that had been pending against him. After the trial, Tokars "came over, shook hands with me, and told me that he thought I was as good an attorney as he had ever faced," Silver said. "And he said, 'You know, it may be that I'm going to be leaving here. If I do, can I call you?' "

Several months later, Silver said Tokars did call him.

"I'm going to be leaving the district attorney's office," he said. "I would like to come meet with you and see if there's something we can do to work out a deal."

Tokars insists Silver approached him.

"I was handling a case in the D.A.'s office, and he was representing one of the defendants, and we just got to talking, and he offered me the opportunity to rent an office from him if I was interested," he explained. "He told me that he had a client by the name of Ed Joiner who had a pretty bad tax problem, and Murray Silver knew I was a C.P.A., and so he asked me if I was interested in renting space from him, and that I would also be able to have a client right from the start."

How much Fred knew of Silver's questionable professional associations at that time is debatable, although such colorful tales circulate easily within the confines of Atlanta's notoriously gossipy legal community. But Fred couldn't have failed to notice the publicity generated—not just in Atlanta but nationwide—by Joiner's increasingly outlandish financial exploits. Politically ambitious, eager to distinguish himself from a faceless sea of attorneys, hungry to promote himself as a legal master of tax fraud, and possessed of a confidence borne of arrogance, Fred couldn't help but consider that handling Joiner's case could catapult his nondescript career into the rarified and pricey reaches of taxation law.

But more than that, the prospect of representing Joiner and the avenues such an association promised to open into the lucrative, tumultuous realm of high finance precipitated Fred's entry into the secretive, sometimes suspect realm of offshore banking.

Caribbean tax laws have always made islands such as the Caymans, the Bahamas, the Turks and Caicos, Antigua, and Barbuda attractive to American businesses and partnerships seeking to reduce their corporate tax burdens. But island banking laws with little or no reporting requirements that place few, if any, restrictions on deposits and withdrawals and shroud bank accounts in secrecy have long made the islands havens for individuals and corporations desiring to hide their earnings from the government, disaffected spouses or partners, federal investigations or police.

By 1986, Fred had developed an abiding fascination with offshore banking and the opportunities such enterprises presented for laundering money—hiding its often criminal origins, usually through a maze of foreign banks and corporations that existed only on paper—so that it could be spent legitimately without arousing the suspicions of the I.R.S.

A self-styled expert without portfolio, Fred, despite his lack of prosecutorial experience in white-collar crime, was, nonetheless, teaching money-laundering seminars at the Georgia Police Academy and the Federal Law Enforcement Training Center near Brunswick, Georgia.

But there was more to his initial conversation with Silver than discussing a Joiner challenge in U.S. Tax Court to more than $1 million in taxes, penalties, and interest. Silver himself needed Fred's accounting expertise.

By 1986, Joiner's Caribbean venture, which included two offshore banks that made sweetheart loans with investors' money to Joiner's own shell companies, had become mired in island politics. And Joiner's loose association with a curious cabal of wealthy internationalists known as the Knights of the Sovereign Order of New Aragon, his own well-publicized description of himself as a Caribbean Robin Hood who was the "key to Barbuda's independence," and his brazen attempts first to bribe Caribbean politicians then, using Silver as his intermediary, reclaim the money when no political payoff was forthcoming, had won him the emnity of the men who governed the islands of Barbuda and nearby Antigua. They stymied Joiner's development efforts.

His plans thwarted by Caribbean officials, Joiner suggested that Silver might succeed where he had failed. He proposed to loan Silver the money to buy majority interest in his bank, the First Bank of Barbuda. In return, Silver would give Joiner the bank stock as collateral for the loan and his proxy to vote on bank matters. Joiner would still control the bank, although Silver's name would appear as owner.

In short, it was a charade. But despite Joiner's historically lax treatment of his investors, Silver became convinced that the illusory investment would generate a fortune if he only had someone well-versed in both accounting and the law to help him navigate the intricacies of such an arrangement.

And there was the nagging but dicey matter of Silver's ongoing bankruptcy that he had instigated to avoid civil judgments against him, some twenty thousand dollars in legal fees from Joiner that he had deposited in the Caribbean but neglected to mention to the bankruptcy judge, and the very nature of the Barbuda bank deal which, at least on paper, provided him with substantial assets that were subject to his creditors' claims if they ever discovered their existence.

As a prosecutor and as an accountant with a self-professed expertise in white-collar theft, the nature of the Caribbean venture with Joiner and Silver should have been clear to Tokars. The legal work required meandered from unethical to criminal, shielded only by attorney-client privilege and the subtleties of Caribbean law. It was, at best, a hazardous choice for someone eying entry into the political arena, where one's associations are subject to heightened scrutiny.

But Fred was a clever accountant for whom lawyering was the art, not of upholding justice but of mastering an illusion. Soliciting individuals such as Joiner and Silver either as clients or as partners was, as it always is, about money. With an enterprise borne of greed and calcuation, Fred quickly recognized the opportunities inherent in the deal. Lured by Silver's promise of thousands of dollars in legal fees perpetually generated by Joiner's offshore banks and Caribbean corporations, as well as the chance to argue Joiner's case in U.S. Tax Court, Fred approached the challenge with alacrity.

On August 29, 1986—just two days after Silver and Joiner transacted the Barbuda bank deal—Fred opened his own law practice in an office adjoining Silver's. Silver was generous. He gave Fred a private office rent free and unlimited access to his law library.

"Murray had purchased a bank from Ed Joiner, and he wanted me to learn as much as I could about it so I could earn legal fees handling some of the matters for him," Fred said later.

And Tokars, Silver recalled, "wanted to make money fast."

As Silver had promised, Fred also appeared in U.S. Tax Court on Joiner's behalf, seeking to reduce more than $1 million in tax liabilities I.R.S. agents had secured against his client. It was heady stuff for a man only four years out of an unaccredited night law school.

But the two attorneys had, like too many investors, placed too much faith in Joiner. And Joiner, true to form, duped them as he had duped so many other partners and investors. Within months, he owed Fred ten thousand dollars in legal fees. But the checks he proffered bounced. And he had compounded the insult by draining funds from Caribbean accounts Silver had established at Joiner's banks. Fred, in turn, dunned Silver for his legal fees, insisting that he had begun representing Joiner after Silver had, in essence, guaranteed payment.

Silver was nearly apoplectic with anger. As Joiner's Caribbean venture collapsed and the island government began threatening to deport him, Silver refused to respond to increasingly urgent calls from Joiner. On November 18, 1986, he wrote Joiner an angry demand letter.

Dear Mr. Joiner:

My office has advised me that you have called frequently in the past few weeks to speak with me, and on at least one occasion you told Fred Tokars that it was urgent that you speak to me because everything was falling apart, and that the bank was being raped by the government agents. I feel quite certain that you received my telegram several days ago wherein I requested that you send me the money you have taken out of the account I had in your bank (Royal Bank of North America in Antigua). You have removed approximately $18,000 U.S. from my account without my knowledge, permission or consent. You lied to me repeatedly and to my son's business associate when you stated that you had paid that $18,000 check, and you maintained that story *for almost two months, and then have the audacity to send the check back saying "refer to maker."*

You told Tokars that you may repay the money if I would talk to you. Why should I talk to you at all? You promised on at least five occasions that money was on the way to Tokars for his legal representation, and you owe him over $10,000. And you lied about that. You haven't caused me nothing but expense, embarrassment, and problems. In case you haven't figured it out yet, Tokars and myself was your last real hope. I remember those nice meetings wherein you stated that God must have sent me to save you and to help you, and then what do you do to me the first opportunity that you had? You ripped me off. You even told your closest friends here in Atlanta that you could not have done anything in your project without me, and you really showed me how much you appreciate everything that I did for you.

I have received information that you cannot own shares in any business in Antigua, that your project will never be approved, and that you face deportation. You can't return to the United States. So, I just don't know what in hell you are thinking about.

If there is one shred of decency left in you, I think you should wire me the money you took out of my account and the money you owe Tokars. If you don't, shame on you, friend. Time is short.

> *Very truly yours,*
> *Murray M. Silver*

But if Silver was enraged, Tokars—intrigued by the possibilities presented by Caribbean bank secrecy laws—was still playing all the angles.

That fall, he called Nicholas Kish, who was living with Sara's younger sister, Joni, in Florida at the time. Kish had been vice president and director of football operations for the Jacksonville Bulls. When the football league collapsed in 1986, he became a sports agent representing several football players. Kish had mentioned that several of his players had substantial sums of money accumulating little more than dust.

Fred was peddling the virtues of an offshore bank.

"But how would a Caribbean investment benefit my players?" Kish wanted to know, not quite understanding the implications of what Fred was suggesting. "Is there a higher rate of interest?"

"No," Fred answered. "It's basically to shelter or hide money, particularly from a spouse. The money would be where somebody couldn't find it."

Three months later, in February 1987, Tokars's Iranian brother-in-law—a commercial pilot with a small private plane—told the U.S. Immigration and Naturalization Service he lived at Fred and Sara's home in Marietta. In fact, he lived on the Florida coast, just a thirty-minute plane ride from the Bahamas and had, for several years, made occasional chartered flights to the Caribbean.

Federal authorities never uncovered any evidence that he ever violated any laws, or that Fred employed him to do so. But they were aware that small private aircraft had for years offered an easy way to smuggle valises of cash out of the United States to Caribbean islands without detection where the money could be deposited without a trace.

Private aircraft are subject to far less scrutiny by U.S. Customs agents than commercial aircraft because the government simply does not have the manpower to monitor the flights of every Cessna or Piper hopping from Florida to a Caribbean island.

Perhaps Fred's brother-in-law had a perfectly harmless reason for misleading the I.N.S. But the potential that Fred could have employed him to carry out such an arrangement—with or without the pilot's knowledge of his cargo—clearly existed according to federal investigators, and would have been a service Joiner might have happily employed.

The island government that ruled Antigua and Barbuda saw through Joiner's ruses. In April 1987, deported from the Caribbean, Joiner slunk home to Atlanta, where federal agents arrested him at his young son's Little League game, leaving Silver and Tokars adrift in the financial flotsam Joiner had characteristically left behind.

The financial debacle he faced surely agitated the young

attorney who had since childhood been driven by a keen desire to accumulate wealth. But instead of blaming himself for succumbing to the sweet but shallow promises of a con man, Fred vented his anger on his unsuspecting wife. Joiner was paying his fees with bogus checks, but it was Sara's plan to leave her lucrative marketing job to stay at home with their first child that infuriated him. He couldn't afford to explain his grave miscalculations or admit that Joiner had simply outsmarted him. If the family was financially strapped, it was Sara, not he, who was at fault. She had lost her nightclub marketing job the month that Joiner was arrested. Within weeks, Fred made what appeared to be an ill-timed purchase for a family strapped for funds. He insured Sara's life for $250,000 and named himself as the beneficiary—a policy which cost him $7,200 a year in premiums. By naming himself as Sara's sole beneficiary, Fred insured that his wife's death would be his ticket to financial security.

After Joiner's deportation and arrest, it was left to Fred to salvage what he could from their "get rich quick" scheme gone awry. Silver was still nominally the owner of the First Bank of Barbuda, a paper bank that held no deposits, and had neither assets nor a fiduciary relationship with any large commercial bank in either the Americas or Europe. Silver also had at least one offshore corporation that he intended to use to house his offshore funds. Vague about the finer points of corporate and tax law, Silver asked Fred to manage his offshore affairs.

As Fred began delving into the arcane science of creating offshore tax havens, he began attending seminars and acquiring manuals from attorneys that advertised and sold their expertise. Still an entrepreneur who maintained a busy schedule of teaching and speaking engagements at conferences and seminars, Fred began compiling his own manual, *Tax Havens and Offshore Investment Opportunities*, which he shamelessly plagiarized from the other manuals he had purchased.

Fred described the manual as "a reference guide" and "an educational tool," acknowledging it described in detail how to utilize offshore banks and offshore corporations "both legally and illegally."

Because the manual detailed both legal and illegal applications, instructions Fred labeled "hypotheticals," the attorney shrewdly included a warning that the manual was not to be used outside a classroom.

"It's a teaching tool. It's hypothetical in nature," he protested. "And it's not to be used in the real world."

It was, in fact, a blueprint for hiding assets and laundering money. And for those inclined toward criminal activities, it was remarkably sympathetic in tone.

Under the chapter heading, "Criminals and Money Laundering," Tokars wrote,

> Criminals of every type, each with the aim of illegal earnings and escape from prosecution, they are all haunted by the same fears, by the same sleepless nights until they discover tax havenry can solve the problems that plague them most. They discover that past experience of being denied the opportunities to enjoy their ill-gotten gains are not as insoluble as they once thought. Being prevented from investing in gainful businesses, from purchasing automobiles, real estate, personal property, because the tax man demands an explanation of the source of the funds is now for many no more than a small inconvenience. This small minority of outside-the-law individuals has constant need for legal money, money they can spend without fear of unpleasantness resulting. They require a means of turning their illegal revenues into acceptable, legal money. Those that engage in this practice refer to the act as laundering.
>
> Unable to share the facilities of offshore banks with the honest element, criminals have quickly come to the conclusion that laundering and other illegal activities are best kept from the light of day. Thus, the underworld never seeks to affiliate with offshore bank owners of integrity, but instead, chooses to operate alone or in connection with other criminals when conducting the affairs of an offshore bank.

Affixed to each manual mailed out was a sticker, "For more information, contact Fred Tokars," and his telephone number.

It sounded like promotional copy.

There was another reason—besides his own involvement,

through Silver and Joiner, with offshore banks and companies—that may have prompted Fred to proclaim his offshore expertise. One month before Fred opened his law practice in the office adjoining Silver's, the U.S. Congress passed sweeping revisions that strengthened federal money-laundering laws designed to trace the movement of large sums of cash generated by illicit drug sales. And the Caribbean islands—with no restrictions on cash deposits and bank secrecy laws that permitted clients to hide behind false names, shell corporations, or blind account numbers—became even more important to those seeking to secrete money or prevent it from being traced.

Through his own limited involvement with Joiner, Fred had quickly learned that to secure ill-gotten wealth while avoiding arrest and jail, a drug dealer would need a savvy lawyer to navigate the maze.

"These money-laundering and cash transaction requirement laws became so complex," Fred would later write in the *Atlanta Business Chronicle*, "drug dealers ultimately need to hire attorneys to explain how to circumvent this new system. . . . For the most part, these professional services are no different than those rendered to legitimate clients."

It is no surprise, then, that after Joiner was arrested, Fred asked Silver to recommend him to his drug-dealer clientele. The former prosecutor recognized that the individuals who distributed or trafficked in drugs could easily generate obscene amounts of money. He was contemptuous of them, but not their cash.

Most of the drug dealers he knew were stupid, Fred told Silver. They did not know what to do with the money they made "with the exception of buying big cars and gold necklaces." He intended to offer them an opportunity to place their money in offshore companies and bank accounts.

"He was," Silver remembered wryly, "trying to get me to get people to bring him money."

Fred may never have uttered the words "money laundering" in discussing the matter with Silver. But Murray knew exactly what he had in mind.

With the Joiner debacle still fresh in his mind, and wary of I.R.S. agents who kept reeling him in for questioning about both his clients and his own finances, Silver told Fred he wanted nothing to do with any scheme involving drug dealers and offshore banks.

"I'm not concerned about the I.R.S.," Fred answered. "I'm not going to leave a paper trail. And without that trail, they cannot follow me. They can't find me. And they can't find the money."

Despite Silver's initial refusal, Fred was persistent. Several weeks later, Fred stopped by Silver's office.

"Have you got a minute?" he asked.

"Sure Fred."

"Can I come talk to you?"

"Certainly."

Fred entered Silver's office and closed the door. "You know this thing is going to work out pretty good," he said.

"What are you talking about?" Silver responded.

Possessed of an overweaning pride in his own abilities, Fred was only too happy to explain. He was representing a wealthy corporate executive who had enjoyed a long career with a Fortune 500 company before he became embroiled in an increasingly nasty divorce. His client had recently entrusted him with $150,000 to deposit offshore and, in so doing, hide it from his estranged wife and the I.R.S.

The fees were substantial. He just thought Silver would want to know. The offer was still open if Silver recommended any of his own clients to Fred for similar tax advice, the attorney said as he left the office.

Several weeks later, Fred stopped by again. His corporate client had entrusted him with another hundred thousand dollars which, in defiance of U.S. currency laws, he had transported to a bank in the Bahamas. He was still soliciting clients. He would gratefully accept any client referrals Silver might care to offer.

Sometime later, Fred again stopped by the older attorney's office. It was late on a Friday, and he entered carrying a large black valise. He opened the satchel conspiratorily. Inside was fifty thousand dollars in cash destined for a Caribbean bank. Either he or a bonded courier would transport the money to the islands, he explained.

But Fred never relied on Silver for referrals, although he

certainly encouraged it. Throughout 1987, Fred actively solicited civil legal work from drug dealers who hired him to
defend them in criminal matters. What Fred offered them was
legitimacy. He told them he had devised ways to transform
the currency tainted with residue of the cocaine that was their
livelihood into what appeared to be the business income of a
small entrepreneur.

Marvin Baynard was one of the first drug dealers Fred approached. A heavy-set man prone to loud clothes and temperamental outbursts, Baynard, using a pager and a network
of runners, sold about a pound of cocaine a week. He generally cleared between five and ten thousand dollars a week.
Like most drug dealers, he had found no way to invest legitimately or deposit his drug profits without attracting the attention of the I.R.S. So he spent it lavishly on nightclubs and
travel, jewelry and clothes. Because the I.R.S. requires U.S.
banks to keep records of all deposits of ten thousand dollars
or more, Baynard hid his drug profits in his bedroom.

Baynard first met Fred in 1987 when he hired him to represent a drug runner who had been arrested—a way of insuring that the man would not trade his name to county
prosecutors in return for a lighter sentence.

During their first meeting, Fred was blunt. "He asked me
how much did I sell in a month," Baynard said, "and he
offered me a little advice, and things he could do for me."

Fred's proposal was simple. He would incorporate a business for Baynard, secure a business license for him, and use
that business as a funnel for his drug profits. For a ten-
thousand-dollar fee, he would establish an offshore bank account for Baynard's Atlanta business in a Caribbean bank he
controlled. When Baynard wanted to buy a car, or a house,
or establish a business, he would take the cash proceeds from
his illegal drug sales and give it to Fred who would then
transport it to the Caribbean for deposit. Once the money was
deposited offshore, Fred's bank would then create fictitious
loan documents and "loan" Baynard his own drug money.
The bank would send the money, in the form of a wire transfer, to Baynard.

The drug dealer would never actually repay the sham loans.
But Caribbean bank secrecy laws would shield his offshore

accounts and the bank, preventing police investigators or the
federal government from retrieving bank records that might
reveal the loan agreement was a fraud.

The offer was an attractive one. Before he began selling
drugs, Baynard had attended college in Atlanta. He majored
in business administration, with an emphasis on marketing,
although he never graduated. He told Fred he wanted to open
his own advertising firm, using drug money as capital. Fred
assured the drug dealer he could advise him on how to inte-
grate those profits into the business, using a network of offshore accounts to legitimize, or launder, the money.

Baynard did hire Fred to incorporate a business, MB Advertising, and paid him one thousand dollars in cash. But he
carefully secured the lease in the name of his personal driver,
who was also one of his drug runners. By then, the attorney
had advised him if drugs were ever found in either his apartment or business, Baynard could sidestep the charges with his
help as long as the place was not in Baynard's name.

Baynard also introduced a business associate in the drug
trade to Fred who had complained he was having tax trouble
and "needed to launder his money and legitimize himself."

But Baynard never would entrust Fred with the profits of
his own weekly drug sales. He found Fred's suggestion that
he invest in a city nightclub "shaky." And, he said, "I didn't
believe he was sending no money offshore and sending it
back over here. That didn't make sense to me, that he could
just shoot it back in here in a different name or something."

To Baynard, the entire scheme envisioned by Tokars
smelled. It was, he said, "one of those lawyer tricks."

But by early 1988, Fred could clearly deliver exactly what
he had promised. Beginning in March 1988, Fred established
at least three offshore corporations, including an insurance
company, in the Caribbean. He opened corresponding corporate bank accounts at the Gulf Union Bank in the Bahamas.
He chartered an offshore bank with the grandiose name, the
Grand Duchy of Luxembourg Bank and Trust Co., Ltd. In
every case, he used an alias.

When he incorporated Arabian-European Enterprises—
whimsically selecting the name because Murray Silver raised
thoroughbreds and an Arabian is a breed of horse—he mas-

queraded as Andrew Fredericks, a combination of his first name and his younger brother's.

When he created Stoltz-Lindeman Investments Inc., he signed his name as William Weitz, his middle name and a last name he simply invented.

When he established the Atlas Insurance Co., he did so as Philip Michaels, the inverse of Michael Philip, the name of his one-month-old second son.

"It was to conceal the fact that I owned the corporations," he explained later. "I didn't want anyone to associate me with owning them."

What few records he retained linking him to the shell companies, the Grand Duchy bank, and the Bahamian bank accounts he secured in his safe or noted in cryptic references in his daily calendars. He was slowly but diligently weaving a web of financial lies.

By then, Fred had also manifested a curious predilection for an attorney—he occasionally hired convicted felons he had defended. Two of those men were Barry Slay and Billy Carter. Slay was a state narcotics agent when he hired Fred to defend him. He had been charged with skimming several thousand dollars during a drug raid from a dealer's illegal stash. Although he always insisted he was innocent of the theft, he eventually pleaded guilty. The state fired him and Fred paid him from time to time as a private investigator.

The attorney had a similar arrangement with Billy Carter. Carter, a former Atlanta police officer, like Slay, had been a narcotics agent with the Georgia Bureau of Investigation. He had lost his job after he attacked his girlfriend, a federal marshal in Savannah, and was convicted of assault.

Although Carter did some private investigations for Fred, he would soon play a far more significant role that placed him in business with the drug dealers he had once pursued.

In the meantime, Fred made use of the two former drug agents' resumes to enforce the notion among his drug-dealer clientele that he was a man of consequence with significant influence and connections. The midlevel dealers to whom he made overtures as an investment counselor often traveled with armed drivers or personal bodyguards whose presence substantiated the occasional veiled threats they issued.

Fred grew accustomed to such blunt methods, and began to employ them himself. And he seemed more than willing to foment suspicion and discord among his clients and their cronies if anyone crossed or angered him.

Once, after the volatile Baynard demanded that Fred sue the drug runner who was his driver for stealing a stash of cocaine, Fred met with the driver, Alex Yancey, who previously had consulted the attorney about his own brush with the law. Fred warned Yancey that Baynard suspected him of the theft, then ridiculed the absent Baynard for even suggesting that one might sue to recover illegal merchandise in a court of law.

"Fred told him that he was crazy," Yancey said later. "Marvin became irate and demanded that he do as he, Marvin, was telling him to do. Fred said he told Marvin, 'Get the hell out of my office or I'll call downstairs and get my G.B.I. buddies and make you disappear.' "

But if Fred did not have bodyguards willing to carry out his threats, he was more than willing to leak damaging information to men who had no qualms about retaliating against a suspected informant or thief with violence.

"He would go to my sources behind my back telling them I was a snitch," Baynard said. "You know, if I'm buying half-keys and keys from a person, and you tell them I'm a snitch, that can cause me to get killed. So I'm going to my sources and they're looking, checking to see if I'm recording the conversation. He had people not trusting me, and it was putting my life in danger. Things he would say behind my back was putting my life in danger.

"I would go back to people and explain what kind of person he is, but eventually, I just decided this way of life wasn't for me. And I left the drug game."

At the time, Baynard's major supplier to whom Fred was apparently passing information was a cocaine distributor from Detroit named Julius Cline. Perhaps Fred liked the illusion of power, the notion that he could jeopardize clients with whom he was at odds simply by cultivating the natural suspicions that ran rife among the street-slick drug networks to which his job exposed him, that misinformation alone could kill them—an old prosecutor's trick. And his willingness to do so reflected his transparent contempt for his clients, if not their money. But it was tradecraft that, while it may have initially accomplished his own vindictive whims, marked him as an untrustworthy man in a realm dominated by black "homeboys" from Detroit who had reason to suspect him simply because of his skin color.

It was a dangerous game for a man with a young wife, a small child, and a baby.

Fred wasn't only cultivating drug dealers. He was also avidly courting Atlanta's African-American political establishment. He was charming and apparently sincere—a sharp accountant, a generous donor, and a tireless volunteer, all traits that made him attractive to anyone launching a political campaign. And, like everyone else noteworthy with whom he came in contact in even the most casual fashion, the candidates he supported and the politicians he met as a result became fodder for his personal publicity mill.

One of those candidates was the wife of his former Southern Bell colleague Love Collins. By 1988, Leah Sears was seeking to trade her traffic court judge's robes for a higher ranking post on the superior court bench in a criminal justice system still largely dominated by white men. Shortly after the birth of his son, Michael, Fred joined Sears's campaign. But equally important to Fred was her husband's rising political prominence. Two years earlier, Love Collins had orchestrated the successful Congressional campaign of U.S. Representative John Lewis. Lewis, then an Atlanta city council member, was a deeply admired civil rights veteran scarred in Selma who, under the leadership of Dr. Martin Luther King, had founded the Student Nonviolent Coordinating Committee.

Fred, then an assistant district attorney, had frequently talked with Collins, offering advice about the strengths and weaknesses of Lewis's fierce and ultimately successful campaign against another civil rights veteran, Julian Bond.

Fred's post as Sears's campaign treasurer gave him an entree he otherwise would have lacked to well-heeled donors in the city's white and black communities, many of them with national reputations as veterans of the civil rights movement and Jimmy Carter's presidential campaigns. Fred hung photos of himself with them on his office walls where his clients would be sure to notice.

When Sears won the election, she introduced Fred to one of Mayor Andrew Young's staff with a recommendation that he be given a patronage appointment as a *pro hac vice*, or part-time judge, on the city's traffic court. Fred, typically, inflated the position on his resume, listing himself as a state court judge. He bought nameplates for the desks at his home and at his office that said officiously "Judge Fredric W. Tokars."

Over time, he touted those sometimes tenuous connections, occasionally suggesting to the clients he defended that for a generous fee he could use his influence to guarantee a lighter sentence or a successful criminal appeal. The felons who hired him believed it, and he took from them exorbitant fees for promises he never intended to deliver.

Fred took advantage of his expanding access to solicit business for his infant Caribbean enterprises, although he had little luck in doing so. He also began soliciting business from friends of Sara's family.

The summer after his son, Mike, was born, a roommate of Sara's sister, Krissy, sought Fred's legal counsel. At the time, Jennifer Lowrey owned a small accessory shop. Short of cash, she was seeking a private investor.

Lowrey met with Fred nearly a dozen times that summer. By that time, Fred had placed his own wife on a strict, cash-only budget and denied her the use of a checking account and credit cards. But whenever Lowrey needed a loan, Fred's reaction was far different, driven by an easily triggered desire to preen and an urgent attraction to young women that had earned him a reputation in the Fulton County district attorney's office. Rather than recommend an investor or a bank, in a show of ostentatious generosity he pulled a heavy roll of cash from his own pocket, peeled away five hundred dollars and presented it to the wide-eyed woman. A second time, he simply left the money in her car. When, astonished by the unorthodox loan, she questioned him, Fred explained that he conducted all his business in cash.

Fred's campaign work for the Sears campaign soon led to a rift between the attorney and Murray Silver. Silver was backing Sears's opponent in the race. At first, their obvious political differences did not cause any overt problems. But then, one of the secretaries complained to Silver that Fred was ordering them to work after hours, but refusing to pay them overtime.

Silver promptly raised the matter with Fred, who claimed that mail-outs of his tax haven manual were occupying the secretaries' time. But Silver soon discovered that Fred was using the office secretaries as an unofficial and unwilling support staff for the Sears campaign.

"He was using the help to send out mailings and requests for contributions and every other damn thing," Silver recalled, "and I finally told him, 'Hey, man, look, that's got to stop.' I felt like then, and I feel now if he wanted to back Leah Sears in a campaign, he had every right to do so, but he ought to pay for it. He shouldn't ask me to pay for it."

Not long after that confrontation, as Silver was returning to the office from a trial, Fred stopped him in the hall and shook his hand.

"I guess you heard that I'm leaving," he said.

"Leaving? No, I didn't hear you were leaving, Fred," Silver replied.

"You know, Murray, I'm just not making money fast enough here," Fred continued. "So, I'm leaving. I'm opening my own private practice."

Months later, Silver bumped into Fred at the Fulton County Courthouse in downtown Atlanta where both men were defending clients. Fred chatted briefly with the older man about the offshore investments he was apparently handling.

"He told me at that time that he had done quite well with it," Silver recalled much later, "and that he had accumulated up to a million dollars."

"The deal is still open to you," Fred reminded Silver as they parted company. "You know, send me somebody."

Seven

The Detroit Connection

WHILE FRED SHARED MURRAY SILVER'S OFFICES, MANY OF the men he counseled were frauds, street corner drug dealers, and thieves. By the time he moved his law office to a more prestigious Peachtree Street address in November 1988, he was casting for clients in far more shadowy circles.

He found there brutal men with a glamorous veneer bought with the illegal millions they earned trading cocaine like commodities. They used their money to buy legitimacy and access to the men and women they had always hungered to be—the professional athletes, film stars, and pop singers whose successes they had coveted from homes in Detroit's dank, squalid urban neighborhoods that made them dangerous with envy.

They were killers and chameleons who believed that, disenfranchised, the world owed them whatever they could take. Beneath the lifestyles of the athletes and pop stars they mimicked they harbored a hard rage—chiseled from Detroit's abrasive, gritty pavements—against white people, the wealthy, and the law.

Their partnership with Tokars was uneasy. They were bright, suspicious men who easily detected the contempt in which Fred held them. Yet, he offered them what they wanted most—a way to convert their illegitimate fortunes into legitimate business enterprises. Using the contacts and acquaintances he had first made through his wife, Fred offered them

104

partnerships in what would become Atlanta's most expensive, flamboyant, and desirable nightclubs.

Their names were Julius Cline, Jessie Ferguson, and Al Brown. And their front man, who grew up in Detroit and Cleveland, was a small, delicately built African-American homosexual who favored costly cars he couldn't afford, oversized designer suits, and the frenetic, cocaine-fueled environment of Atlanta's downtown nightclubs.

Ambitious, heartless, but unfailingly polite, James Mason had a knack for attaching himself to drug dealers like remora to a shark. His business was managing nightclubs, although he had little head for money, and no scruples at all governing its use. Over time, the three Detroit drug dealers, who resettled in Atlanta, became Mason's financial foundation. Ferguson and Cline, in particular, became the mainstays of almost every nightclub that Mason managed or claimed to own.

Sara Tokars never met these men. They were one more aspect of her husband's life that he hid from her with threats, deception, and indifference. But she intuited their existence.

And Sara, if they knew about her at all, held no interest for them, another white woman who feared the heart of Atlanta and made her home in the city's suburban enclaves. Still, they were predators, casually ruthless in protecting their drug enterprise. If Fred were to rouse their ire through carelessness, deception, or a simple trick of fate, they would have few qualms about exacting retribution. Fred's dalliance with them and the dim-lit arenas of drugs and dirty money where they plied their trade left Sara and her sons perilously exposed to the cruel whimsy of violence.

Jessie Ferguson had fled Detroit in July 1985—the crack of gunfire, a dead man, a wounded woman, and the account of a surviving witness driving him southward to Atlanta. On July 26, 1985, a running gun battle had erupted in one of northwest Detroit's grimier neighborhoods. More than two dozen shots were fired as a blue van pursuing a car careened along the city's sweaty, oil-stained streets. The van's occupants were seeking retribution, convinced they had been cheated in a drug deal.

One of the car's three passengers, a drug dealer named

Donte Snowdon, was shot to death that night. The driver, a woman, was wounded, just before she slammed into a parked car. A second man leaped from the wreckage and fled, but not before he saw Snowdon's killer—a man he later identified as Jessie Ferguson.

Ferguson had arranged his first drug deal when he was eighteen, trading a car for a pound of marijuana. At $100 an ounce, the cash the eleventh-grade dropout made from selling weed was quick, easy, and abundant. If he sold just a pound a week, he could clear seventy-eight thousand dollars a year— more than the net income, after taxes, of a corporate executive or a lawyer.

Ferguson's partner was a neighborhood friend, a boy who had grown up across the street and run with Ferguson since the two attended elementary school together in the tense and troubled sixties. His name in Detroit was Lucius Marvin Cleveland. He would make his reputation as a drug dealer and nightclub operator in Atlanta under the alias Julius Cline.

As teenagers, the two young men began making day trips to Jamaica and Barbados, smuggling marijuana back in juice cans. They adopted a handful of aliases to avoid detection— Mitch Love, Mitchell Lovett, Todd Mitchell, and, in a bit of fancy that mirrored their hunger for recognition, the name of Olympic gold medalist Carl Lewis.

Smuggling marijuana through U.S. Customs was a gamble. "Sometimes we made it. Sometimes we didn't," Ferguson said. Occasionally, they lost a drug shipment. In 1980, Ferguson was arrested at the Atlanta airport, caught with a pound of marijuana as he was changing planes, en route from Jamaica to Detroit. He pleaded "no contest" to the charge and was given two years probation. But his arrest didn't curtail his drug smuggling operation. Instead, it made him bolder. Soon, he and Cline were smuggling in forty pounds of marijuana every trip, and clearing sixty thousand dollars in profits.

But the lightweight marijuana leaf makes smuggling in bulk a logistical hazard. So when a supplier in Barbados suggested to the Detroit drug dealers that they graduate from marijuana to cocaine, they eagerly obliged.

Four pounds of cocaine—sold in one kilo (or two-pound)

bricks, was worth more than forty pounds of marijuana and, because of its weight, was far easier to conceal. Ferguson and Cline bought the cocaine wholesale for twenty thousand dollars a kilo. They made a 100 percent profit by repackaging the narcotic and reselling it in Detroit. They were clearing twenty thousand dollars a kilo when the late-night gun battle snuffed out Donte Snowdon's life and sent Ferguson barreling south to Atlanta where the illegal cocaine trade was still in its infancy. Cline soon followed. The two men had nearly three hundred thousand in cash between them, drug profits they could not safely bank or spend and still evade detection.

Shortly after arriving in Atlanta, Ferguson began circulating among the city's African-American nightclubs, quietly evaluating the market for cocaine and seeking a way to invest his illegal profits or convert them to legitimate businesses where infusions of drug money were not easily detected. Ferguson soon became a regular customer at Club 131, a North Avenue nightclub near the Georgia Tech campus, the international headquarters of Coca-Cola, and two of the city's oldest and most violent public housing projects.

Ferguson soon attracted the attention of James Mason, who managed Club 131 and had a preternatural instinct for men with money. He was a man whose ambitions far outweighed both his scruples and his business acumen, and he was hungry to operate a nightclub of his own. He could run a nightclub better than Club 131's owner, Mason boasted. He was scouting for investors willing to float him seventy-five thousand dollars to do it.

The idea appealed to Ferguson, a dark, taciturn man eager to buy himself legitimacy and an expensive lifestyle far removed from the Detroit streets where he was now being sought for murder. When Cline arrived in Atlanta a short time later, Mason easily persuaded Ferguson and his loquacious business partner to invest.

On paper, the financing that allowed Cline and Ferguson to open VIP Atlanta, a nightclub on the city's West End appeared to be legitimate—Cline, Ferguson, and a Detroit trust they shared bought stock in the nightclub. But in reality, the club's financial foundation was laced with drug money. Although the stocks and sales receipts suggested that Cline and

Ferguson had invested sixty-three thousand dollars individually and through their trust, and a Detroit acquaintance had invested sixty-five thousand dollars, the two drug dealers actually invested more than one hundred thousand dollars in the VIP. Their Detroit partner only invested eight thousand. Construction workers, designers, suppliers—secured through Mason's recommendation, all were paid in cash.

The stock transactions masked the infusion of illegal drug profits, cash that could not be deposited in a bank without alerting the I.R.S. The process by which dirty money obtained through criminal activities becomes the foundation of a legitimate business, such as the VIP, is known as money laundering.

Neither Ferguson nor Cline had any public ties to the club. Because they both had felony criminal records, and Ferguson was a fugitive wanted for murder, neither could legally own and operate a Georgia bar. Mason became their front man, the nominal president and owner of the VIP who secured the club's liquor license in his name.

Mason never asked where the money came from, even after Ferguson and Cline began refurbishing the VIP and passing along cash payments that soared as high as fifty thousand dollars. "We didn't come here telling anyone that we were drug dealers," Ferguson said, "but I'm sure he knew from the amount of money."

Mason had underestimated the cost of opening a nightclub. By the time the VIP opened in September 1986, both Cline and Ferguson had spent all the money they had brought with them from Detroit, and Cline had borrowed from his father, who owned a Detroit landscaping business. With no money left to install an adequate sound system, the very heart of a dance club, the two men relied on their disc jockey—a young Detroit "homeboy" who wanted to be an F.B.I. agent—to supply his own equipment. For their own transportation, the two drug dealers depended on dilapidated Volkswagens.

All that began to change when the VIP Club opened in October 1986. The club catered to patrons twenty-five and over, up-and-coming African-Americans who had that decade assumed the reins of Atlanta's city government. It was a dance club, leaning heavily to disco, that served a great martini and occasionally showcased local bands and singers on the verge of stardom.

By any measure, the VIP was an immediate success. The club was packed every night from Wednesday through Saturday, often with as many as six hundred patrons willing to pay five dollars each just to get in the door. It grossed as much as twenty thousand dollars in weekend admissions. An alumni party during a football game between Florida A&M University and Tennessee State drew two thousand people eager to pay a ten-dollar cover charge.

On Atlanta's West End—within minutes of the state capitol, City Hall, the Fulton County seat, Atlanta's police department, and the Atlanta University Center, a consortium of African-American colleges that included Morehouse and Spelman—the VIP Club drew the city's black urban professionals, many of them rapidly rising in position and power. City police provided off-duty security at the VIP, and sponsored benefits at the club for the Police Athletic League, the Afro-American Patrolmen's League, and the family of an officer shot to death while working as an off-duty security guard. Atlanta Mayor Maynard Jackson's campaign staff held a birthday party for Jackson's campaign manager at the club.

The club attracted Atlanta's black athletes as well. Dominique Wilkins, then star center for the Atlanta Hawks, frequented the VIP. John Sally, a Georgia Tech basketball star who was drafted by the Detroit Pistons, hosted his birthday party there.

Julius Cline greeted them all.

Always particular about money, the drug dealer insisted that everyone, even his most faithful customers, pay the cover at the door. As the club's chief backers, Cline and Ferguson intended quickly to recoup their covert investments. But despite the club's obvious popularity, it rarely registered a profit. Instead, the drug dealers received less than a dozen checks during the club's lifetime, none for more than $1,400—less than 10 percent of the initial investment that had so depleted their drug capital. At the same time, Mason was asking them for more money to repair a sound system jury-rigged with used speakers and amplifiers that couldn't survive the pounding disco bass.

"We were just trying to keep it afloat," Ferguson said. "We didn't have any money."

By then, Cline had met another drug dealer at the VIP. Cline began buying cocaine from the dealer, who eventually introduced him to a fair-skinned Jamaican living in Miami known only as Andrew. Andrew had a stable of couriers who carried cocaine for him along the silver interstate stretching from Miami to Atlanta. He was already the main source of cocaine for an immensely popular downtown strip club, Magic City. Cline and Ferguson began buying cocaine from Andrew, as much as fifty pounds a week. Reticent with strangers, Ferguson simply reactivated his former drug network in Detroit. But Cline began selling heavily in Atlanta.

Perhaps it was merely coincidence, but Cline's entry into Atlanta's cocaine market coincided with a skyrocketing crime rate, fueled largely by cocaine, that before the decade ended, propelled Atlanta to its foremost place among the most violent cities in the nation. By mid-1987, Cline was recruiting lieutenants through the city's nightclub network and stashing cocaine at a suburban storage warehouse for distribution in Atlanta, Detroit, New Orleans, and Chattanooga.

And Cline, who once posed for a photo clad in jeans and a black leather jacket as he brandished a gun, began wearing silk shirts and gold chains, then graduated to expensive tailored suits and ties. He traded in his battered Volkswagen for a Jetta, then acquired a BMW and a Porche. He exchanged his Timex for a Rolex and won a listing in Dun and Bradstreet as the VIP Club's vice president.

But Ferguson and Cline knew nothing about running a nightclub. They left the VIP's management to Mason. During the club's two years in operation, the VIP failed to pay state and federal taxes, bounced checks to club suppliers, and was threatened with the suspension of its liquor license for non-payment of sales and federal withholding taxes.

"We're struggling to make ends meet," Mason protested to state liquor agents. "I know of nightclubs in Atlanta where people who sell drugs are offering to invest money. I'm trying to hold on and keep from doing that."

"Do what you can do to keep the business legitimate," one agent told him. "And try to keep the taxes up to date and you won't have much of a problem from us."

Mason's personal affairs were no better. He had declared bankruptcy even before the VIP opened its doors.

On New Year's Day 1988 the VIP Club closed. Several months later, Cline sold the nightclub to a Florida drug dealer and began supplying the club's manager, a former employee, with "eight balls," an eighth ounce of cocaine, to broker to club patrons. That manager, Willie Harris, quickly became one of Cline's trusted lieutenants.

Shortly after the VIP closed, Mason was hired to manage another Atlanta nightclub. He then leased the club owner's Buckhead condominium in north Atlanta, although the rent surely would have taxed his thirty-five-thousand-dollar manager's salary. He drove a new white BMW.

Once established in Buckhead, a highly desirable district of nightclubs, restaurants, and elegant stores, Mason became the bank for Ferguson and Cline. For the next year, the Detroit dealers secreted tens of thousands of dollars in an elaborate town home furnished with antiques that Mason could barely afford. Several days before New Year's Eve in 1988, thirty thousand dollars—cash from Ferguson's drug sales that was locked discreetly in a briefcase—disappeared from Mason's bedroom closet.

The loss cracked the sophisticated facade that Ferguson and Cline had fashioned as nightclub owners. They might introduce themselves as investors and venture capitalists, but their reaction to the money's disappearance smelled of the streets. If necessary, they would kill to reclaim it.

Although the missing money was drug profits and subject to seizure, Mason reported its disappearance to police as a burglary. He claimed he had forgotten to set the house alarm, and someone had broken out the back window. He told police the cash was revenue from the Park Place Salon, a hair styling shop in downtown Atlanta that Cline established using Mason, whom corporate papers identified as the owner, as his cover. Cline laundered drug money through the shop, directing Mason to deposit sacks of cash into salon bank accounts as if they were sales receipts.

Mason told police that he owned the Park Place Salon. He insisted the remainder of the money was receipts from the

VIP Club that he had been unable to deposit in the bank before it closed that day. Mason failed to mention that the VIP was now owned by someone else.

Mason told Ferguson a somewhat different story. To deflect Ferguson's wrath and his scowling suspicion that the diminutive "banker" had absconded with the money and invented the burglary as a ruse, Mason suggested two other suspects— a neighbor with a felony drug conviction and Mason's current companion, a young Atlanta police recruit who worked as the salon's receptionist and, like Ferguson, had a key to Mason's townhouse.

Ferguson responded to Mason's somewhat cavalier suggestions with brutal efficiency. On New Year's Eve, Mason lured the unsuspecting police recruit, Michael Jones, into a liaison with wolves. On some forgotten pretext, Mason asked Jones to meet with Ferguson and Cline at his townhouse. He would join him there later.

As Jones entered the door, Cline closed and locked it. Ferguson sat at the dining room table. Jones took a seat across from him. Ferguson took a 9-millimeter handgun from his pocket and laid it on the table.

"Do you know where my money is?" he asked.

"I don't know, man," Jones, now badly frightened, responded.

Ferguson left his seat and moved toward Jones, asking a second time, "Do you know where my money is?"

"I don't know," Jones chattered.

With the instant, evil movement of a rattler, Ferguson seized Jones and slammed him to the floor. Grabbing the gun, he made Jones swallow the barrel and cocked the hammer of the loaded gun as he demanded, "Do you know where my money is? Tell me or I'll pull the trigger."

Horrified and trembling, Jones shook his head as he gagged on the gun. He knew Mason kept neat stacks of bills secreted in the townhouse, but didn't know where they were or how the money had disappeared.

"I didn't steal it, man. I didn't steal it," he protested in horror.

Twenty seconds later, Ferguson pulled the gun from Jones's mouth. When Mason returned a short time later, Ferguson and Cline left, enraged that the money was still missing, deeply suspicious of Jones, but harboring thoughts that their business partner Mason might well have stolen their cache.

As soon as Ferguson and Cline left, a badly frightened Jones told Mason what had happened. So he was understandably shocked when, later that night at a New Year's Eve party at the VIP Club, Mason insisted on joining Ferguson, Cline, and their dates. When, anxious and clearly uncomfortable, Jones tried to leave, Mason urged him to stay.

Jones didn't consider, as Ferguson and Cline clearly did, that Mason orchestrated the burglary to hide his own theft of the money. Nor did it occur to him that Mason was shiftily depicting him as the real thief, that in casting suspicion from himself, Mason had made Jones the goat.

In fact, Mason informed Ferguson he intended to hire a private investigator to follow Jones and obtained from Ferguson the investigator's fee. Ferguson never met the detective Mason said he hired, but several weeks later, Mason did present the drug dealer with a report.

Jones had been seen in an Atlanta mall, inquiring of a furrier about the purchase of a twenty-five-thousand-dollar fur jacket. He had been followed to Portland where he bought and paid cash for a new car. Ferguson was incensed. If Jones didn't return the stolen thirty thousand dollars, his life was forfeit.

But it was Mason who lured Jones back to the townhouse. On February 2, 1989, Mason asked Jones to come by the Park Place Salon. After leaving the salon, the two men stopped by Mason's residence. Shortly after they walked in the door, the phone rang. Ten minutes later, Ferguson and a friend arrived.

Ferguson immediately ordered Mason to leave. "Get out," he commanded. As Mason hesitated, Ferguson bellowed, "Get out. Get out now, James." Mason abandoned Jones and fled as Ferguson locked the door behind him.

What happened next was baldly brutal. It marked Ferguson, already accustomed to violence, as a sadistic player in the drug game who had long since traded his humanity for cocaine-scented cash.

As the bolt slid into place, Jones felt Ferguson's hand on

his shoulder. At that instant, a stunning shock of electricity coursed through him as Ferguson tagged him with a taser gun, a high-voltage weapon also known as a cattle prod. Jones collapsed writhing on the floor. Ferguson bound him with duct tape, stripped him of his clothes, then dragged him to the kitchen. For the next two hours, the furious drug dealer and his heavyweight companion kicked and battered Jones. As Ferguson read to Jones from the detective's report Mason had given him, he struck Jones viciously with a hammer.

"You took the money, man."

A new car was sitting in the garage of Jones's parents. Ferguson was certain Jones had bought it with the stolen drug money.

"You have a choice," he warned. "Either tell me where my money is or I'll finish with you and start on your parents. I don't care who I have to hurt to get my money back."

Jones, in growing agony and terrified that Ferguson's wrath would soon turn on his family, was powerless to answer. There was no fur coat, no new car. He knew nothing about the money or the allegations made by Mason's anonymous detective.

"I don't know where the money is," Jones screamed as Ferguson began slashing him with a knife and rubbing salt into the deep, raw wounds. He babbled repeated denials as Ferguson let the knife point hover at his genitals and promised to castrate him if he didn't confess.

Nothing assuaged the enraged drug dealer. Nothing convinced him that Jones was innocent. He stunned Jones repeatedly with the taser, burning great patches of skin away until the batteries were depleted. And the exertion of Jones's prolonged torture didn't appease Ferguson's anger. It simply made him hungry.

Thrusting Jones—still naked, bound, and bleeding—into the bathroom, Ferguson sent his pal for hamburgers. Then, while the kitchen floor was still wet with blood, the two men sat down to eat. Through carelessness or sheer arrogance, Ferguson had left the knife in the bathroom.

Terrified that he was dying, frantic that his parents were next, Jones picked up the knife with his mouth, dropped it to the floor, and desperately cut the tape that shackled his legs.

His arms still bound, Jones wrestled open the bathroom door. Dazed, he hesitated, seeking an escape route. At that moment, Ferguson spotted him. In utter desperation, Jones vaulted into the living room and plunged through the bay window into the courtyard. He scrambled to his feet and began to run. Ferguson raced from the apartment, but as horrified neighbors spilled into the yard, Ferguson turned and fled.

Hospitalized with his injuries, Jones never reported to the city police department, where he had intended to begin training the day after he was accosted and tortured. He did identify Ferguson, whom he knew only as Mitch Love, as his attacker. Ferguson was arrested under his alias and was released after he posted a seventy-five-thousand-dollar bond. Even though he was fingerprinted, Atlanta police never checked to see if Ferguson had a criminal record, or they would have discovered that the convicted drug dealer was also wanted for murder in Detroit.

Jones left Atlanta shortly after he was released from the hospital. By then, Mason had sent his apologies. He told Jones, "No way I knew this would happen."

One of the neighbors drawn outside by the uproar that day was Russell Martin, a friend of Mason's and the other suspect whose name, along with Michael Jones, Mason had originally given to Ferguson to deflect his suspicion and his anger. Fred Tokars was Martin's attorney, and Martin was then free on an appeal bond while his conviction was appealed. A woman in a nearby condominium from whom Martin occasionally bought cocaine had also sold cocaine to Mason. And Martin's roommate was Tokars's lover, the one whose name Sara would soon discover in her husband's diary.

Six weeks after Jones landed, bound and bleeding, on the lawn outside Mason's residence, Mason's name and telephone number appeared in Tokars's daily calendar in a notation next to Martin's name—as if, as prosecutors now believe, Martin had passed on word that Mason needed legal help. Fred cared too much about money and was too meticulous not to have returned the call.

At the time, Mason did need help. Atlanta police detectives had questioned him, and considered him as a possible accomplice in the attack on Jones. In his statement to police, Mason had denied inviting Jones to his house just prior to that attack. He claimed that he, not Ferguson, had locked the door. He was vague about the drug dealer, whom he identified as his business partner. He denied that Ferguson lived in Atlanta and insisted that he had no way of contacting him by telephone. During the interview, Mason expressed shock that Ferguson would harm anyone. When he was questioned about the reported burglary, Mason once again suggested Jones was the culprit. A private detective he never would identify had administered polygraphs to Mason, Mason's roommate, and Jones, Mason claimed. Jones alone had been deceptive, he insisted.

In the end, Mason didn't need a lawyer. After Ferguson's arrest, Jones shied away from prosecuting Ferguson, although the drug dealer had nearly killed him. His career in ruins, he simply left Atlanta. When he failed to appear in court, the assault charges were dropped, and the case against Ferguson was closed. A short time later, Ferguson moved to New Orleans where he and Cline were trafficking in cocaine and had opened the first of four nightclubs with their ill-gotten gains. Mason began looking for another nightclub in Atlanta.

Within weeks, he found it—Sneakers of Cobb County, the club that Sara had marketed until her first child was born and was still owned by her former boss, Doug McKendrick. McKendrick's former lieutenant, Jim Killeen, a man who remained Fred's friend as well as Sara's confidant, was managing Sneakers for a consortium of investors who had leased the building from McKendrick.

Again, mere coincidence may have been at play. Mason, who had never worked in a nightclub north of Midtown, may have decided independently of Tokars to buy into a Cobb County club that had always catered to a white clientele. Sheer serendipity may have led Mason to Sneakers, the nightclub most familiar to Fred, the club where his wife had worked, the only one in town where the attorney was acquainted with the owner.

But it would have been like Fred to suggest a deal that would link him inextricably with Sara's former employers. In May 1989, when Mason first approached McKendrick, Sara was having her husband followed. Fred had spotted the private investigator from his mistress's apartment, just two doors away from Mason. Sara had told Fred she wanted a divorce and he, in turn, had threatened to take the children.

Securing Sneakers would seal off one escape route. Sara would have to look elsewhere for work or accept a job with men who were always in contact with her husband. Fred wouldn't let her circumnavigate his growing sphere of control so easily.

But if Sneakers proved convenient in Fred's more cunning efforts to dominate his wife, it also slaked his personal thirst for a nightclub's brazen gaiety. The business lured him like a succubus. As his mousy looks were refracted by the haze of perfume, smoke, and mirrors, he donned an air of expansive urbanity.

In the city's most elite clubs, Fred could seek the clients he coveted most, those who would pay extravagant fees to cloak their illegal profits in legitimacy. By then, Fred had an offshore bank, the Grand Duchy of Luxembourg Bank and Trust Co., Ltd. He had offshore corporations he had acquired from Murray Silver in the Turks and Caicos islands. He had more accounts in the Bahamas, an utter contempt for U.S. law and the Internal Revenue Service, and a scheme to launder money.

The nightclubs generated cash receipts that served as a legitimate cover for infusions of drug money. Drug profits could be combined easily with a club's nightly receipts and deposited without attracting suspicion. More drug money could be smuggled to the Caribbean in suitcases during apparently legitimate business trips where, unlike the United States, sacks of cash could be deposited in numbered corporate accounts held, as Fred's were, under aliases. When James Mason's name first surfaced in Fred's personal calendar, the mechanism for a money laundry was in place. All Fred needed was a wealthy client.

Although he knew the key players, Fred was not initially involved in leasing Sneakers and converting it to a discotheque named Dominique's Club 21 after one-time Atlanta Hawks basketball star Dominique Wilkins. Mason approached McKendrick himself, saying he had secured Wilkins's permission to attach his name to a nightclub. Wilkins and his teammates had frequented the VIP Club when Mason managed it. The basketball player, like other Atlanta sports professionals, had his hair styled at the Park Place Salon. For four thousand dollars a month and a promise to patronize the club, Dominique had agreed to lend the nightclub his name.

"It sounded like fun," he explained.

At the time, Sneakers was sliding into obscurity, its once explosive success diminished and dull. McKendrick was eager to salvage the nightclub, and Mason's promise of an Atlanta sports superstar pleased him. He sent Mason to Killeen. By the end of that summer, Killeen's investors had formed a partnership with Mason and Julius Cline, Zebra, Inc. It was a black and white partnership for a club designed to appeal to suburban whites and well-to-do African-Americans. Cline and Mason lent the new corporation twenty thousand dollars, and Mason began managing the club.

Dominique's was a smash. The flashy disco attracted major sports stars, actors, the lords of Atlanta hip-hop, people who simply "wanted to be seen." Singer Bobby Brown and actors Wesley Snipes and Eddie Murphy patronized the club. Heavyweight boxing champion Evander Holyfield and basketball greats Magic Johnson and Michael Jordan held court there. All of them, the great and the near-great, were featured in photos displayed prominently on the club's walls. Most of them had their snapshots taken with the club's doorman, Willie Harris. Harris was a cocaine broker. His supplier was Julius Cline.

Within weeks of the club's opening, word had spread that cocaine was easily available if a patron requested "something stronger" than a drink and nodded in the right direction. Wilkins's brother, John, first heard the rumors, and fingered Cline and Mason as the culprits. Afraid of jeopardizing his N.B.A. contract and his endorsements, Wilkins promptly called his attorney who, on October nineteenth, fired off a blunt letter to Cline that accused him of dealing drugs. Wilkins wanted out of the deal and his name removed from the club.

Cline, although he was, by then, one of the city's larger cocaine dealers, was enraged. His attorney soon drafted a letter threatening to sue Wilkins for slander and libel. Cline demanded that Wilkins stop repeating the allegations or risk punitive legal action. During a Hawks game, the two men angrily sent word to Wilkins that they had stripped the club of his memorabilia and set it on the curb outside.

But by then, Wilkins and his brother had outlined their suspicions about both Cline and Mason to Killeen. Cline and Mason adamantly denied the charges. They accused their white partners of racism, saying the consortium of white investors was trying to muscle in on the club's black management, force them out of the business with false allegations, and steal their twenty-thousand-dollar investment in the lucrative nightclub, which was then pulling in two hundred thousand a month in revenues.

At a November meeting with Wilkins and the club's white investors, Cline denied using drugs, insisted that he didn't sell them, and boldly announced he would take a polygraph test as proof of his veracity. It was a cold, bitter bluff, and it failed. The investors severed their partnership with Mason and Cline, removed Mason as the club's manager, and installed Killeen in his place.

On the Detroit streets where Cline and Ferguson had first peddled their illegal wares, such disrespect, regardless of its veracity, and the loss of twenty thousand dollars might easily have led to murder. This time, Cline restrained his fury while his attorney called in the infant nightclub's loan and demanded a hefty percentage of its revenues. And, in the midst of the uproar, Willie Harris remained at his post at the nightclub door, where he quietly continued to broker Cline's cocaine.

Masked by the furor was Mason's management of Dominique's, one that mirrored his earlier management of the VIP. Despite tremendous revenues and a celebrity clientele, the nightclub under Mason's watch had already fallen behind in its taxes and never managed a single timely rent payment.

Ousted from Dominique's, Cline and Mason that same month acquired the lease for an abandoned club less than a mile from downtown in the heart of Atlanta's then decaying warehouse district. Called Traxx, the new nightclub catered to older gay men. Mason managed it and, on occasion, made cocaine available to club patrons. Within two months, the club—successful by Atlanta standards—had fallen behind on the rent.

Against that backdrop, in the fall of 1989, Tokars determined to go into business with Mason and Cline.

Tokars insists that, although his client Russell Martin had given him Mason's name the previous spring, he and Mason had yet to meet. That changed, Fred said, after he and Sara—out for a rare familial stroll with their toddlers along the banks of the Chattahoochee River—bumped into Killeen. During that desultory conversation, Fred said he learned from Killeen that Mason was seeking investors in a third club, one with a jazz motif on Peachtree Street in Midtown. Fred soon contacted the diminutive nightclub operator. He wanted a piece of what would eventually become the Parrot Club. He offered both financial support and his services as an attorney, an accountant, and, federal prosecutors say, a money launderer for men who smelled of drug money and neglected to pay their bills.

The gambit was also a way of intimidating Sara. Fred was moving aggressively into a business where she had, before their marriage, made a successful living at a time when she had informed him she wanted a divorce and clearly needed money and a means of support.

With that single phone call to James Mason, Tokars embarked on a whirlwind series of nightclub purchases with Mason, Cline, and, occasionally, Ferguson. First as their partner, then as their attorney, he incorporated the shell companies that owned and managed each club. He used those corporate entities to shield investors with criminal records, and thus sidestep Georgia laws forbidding felons to hold liquor licenses or own and operate a nightclub. For exorbitant fees, he negotiated contracts on behalf of the drug dealers, their cronies, and himself. And, when needed, he represented those same clients and associates in civil and criminal litigation. Their associations with the nightclubs gave them, at least on the surface, a means of legitimate income that could then be used to obtain credit to buy homes and cars.

In short, the former assistant district attorney embraced Mason and his questionable Detroit financiers even as Killeen, still troubled by the persistent allegations of drug use that percolated around Dominique's Club 21, took steps to divorce himself from the club and from Mason, who had remained on the payroll as a marketing consultant.

Just days before Tokars signed on as the Parrot's corporate attorney, corporate secretary, and board director of a corporation that would run the Parrot, Killeen abruptly left Dominique's and asked the state to pull his name from the nightclub's liquor license. In Killeen's place, the remaining investors reinstalled Mason, and raised his salary from five hundred to $750 a week.

Mason and Cline were not the only men of questionable reputation whom Fred solicited. By then, he had placed on his occasional payroll a former drug agent with a criminal record who had become a private investigator. That investigator, former state narcotics agent Billy Carter, reeled in Rocky McDougall as a partner in the Parrot. McDougall, a habitual offender with a felony record of drug distribution and interstate transport of stolen goods, had a propensity for flashy clothes, expensive cars, and diamond jewelry. He masqueraded as a "high roller." He intentionally "dressed like a drug dealer," he would later tell one federal investigator. He was, in reality, an alcoholic who lived off the considerable largesse of an older, well-to-do widow.

When Tokars incorporated the Parrot, Julius Cline's name did not appear either on the nightclub's articles of incorporation or the liquor license. It was the first time since Cline had begun investing in Atlanta clubs in 1986 that his name was not associated publicly with a club he financed. But his growing notoriety as a drug dealer and his forced departure from Dominique's, as well as a felony record under a Detroit alias, might easily have jeopardized the club and attracted the attention of federal drug agents and police.

Nor did McDougall's name appear on any official documents. Instead, Tokars buried investments by Cline and McDougall behind Carter and Mason, who were publicly identified as the principal owners. In a fit of vanity he would later regret, Fred listed himself as a corporate officer and member of the nightclub's governing board. His name also appeared on the club's liquor license application.

It was an elaborate deception, the first move in an intricate game that pitted Fred against the federal government. Through the nightclub, Fred hoped to enlist the drug dealers in his offshore money-laundering scheme, one that would earn him tremendous fees to hide drug profits in offshore accounts and then filter the money, now disguised as legitimate income, back to the state through a series of false loans and deposits.

But Cline never truly trusted Tokars and didn't really like him. He asked another attorney to review the legal documents Fred had prepared, and asked the lawyer to draw up a private partnership agreement with Mason that secured his interest in the Parrot.

And he remained more comfortable storing his drug cash in cardboard boxes in rental warehouses around Atlanta, or spending it on designer cars and clothes than in sending it offshore in the custody of a white man who seemed just a little too slick. Cash that wasn't easily accessible was of no real use to Cline, regardless of Fred's expansive promises.

Almost immediately, Fred was confronted with the vagaries of doing business with criminals. Both Carter and Mason had been lax about filing or paying their taxes, and both still owed money to the government—difficulties that delayed the approval of the Parrot's liquor license.

After the club opened, Cline bragged publicly that he owned the club and kept an office in the basement. And he and Mason adopted the same negligent accounting practices that had characterized and ultimately ruined their other clubs. They didn't pay their taxes or the bills.

McDougall and his widow companion never received more than a few hundred dollars in return for their thirty-thousand-dollar investment. Certain that the Parrot, teeming with patrons, must surely be making money, McDougall eventually confronted Tokars in his office.

"I know they're making money. I don't know why we ain't getting our money," he demanded.

Tokars directed McDougall to Cline. When McDougall found Cline in the nightclub's basement office, Cline arrogantly dismissed him.

"I ain't got time for this small talk with small-time little shits."

McDougall promptly pulled a gun and drew down on the tall, slender drug dealer. "I ain't going to have that shit," he told him coldly. "You're ripping my lady off, and you're ripping me off. My lady is going to get her money one way or the other."

Billy Carter, who witnessed the confrontation, grabbed McDougall, trying to calm him as he escorted him from the club. McDougall returned only once. He couldn't get inside. The nightclub was packed.

The Parrot had only been open a month when Mason attacked one of his employees at the Park Place Salon. For some time, Linda Goodwin, on Mason's instructions, had taken grocery bags of cash, usually small bills no larger than a ten, and had converted them at a revolving list of nearby banks to large bills. Those large bills were later deposited with salon revenues in still another bank. Whether or not she was aware the money in those grocery bags had been generated by drug sales, Goodwin complained loudly and frequently. In April 1990, Mason fired her. But that final, acrimonious discussion rapidly escalated to a physical attack. Mason beat Goodwin savagely, fracturing bones in her face and biting off her ear.

Goodwin pressed criminal charges against Mason and then sued him. With Tokars's help, Mason was able to negotiate a settlement with Goodwin. He agreed to pay her seventeen thousand dollars in monthly installments, the approximate cost of her hospital stay. She dropped the charges. Mason offered his stock in the Parrot as collateral, even though he couldn't do so without Carter's approval, which he never obtained.

For Mason, it was a sweetheart deal orchestrated by Tokars, who had worked with Goodwin's attorney, Paul Howard, when both were assistant district attorneys. No felony charges. A cash settlement that was only a fraction of what a jury might well have awarded. All Mason had to do was meet his monthly payment. But true to form, Mason didn't do it. He made few payments, and those he did deliver typically were late. That cavalier manner would eventually cost him and his partners the nightclub. And, it eventually linked Fred's name publicly, for the first and only time, with that of drug dealer Julius Cline.

But in the meantime, the Parrot functioned as an ad-hoc power base for Fred. A jazz cafe and dinner club, it catered to businessmen and a conservative legal and judicial clientele. The club had live music but no dance floor, no mirrored disco balls. The club had class, which made it an ideal choice for more elegant political fund-raisers. One superior court judge celebrated her victory party at the Parrot. Two other judges, both of whom ascended to federal judgeships, held fund-raisers there. So did Goodwin's accomodating attorney, who would, with Tokars's generous financial support, eventually win his campaign for Fulton County Solicitor General. Press notices hailed it as "a place to be seen" among Atlanta's smarter set.

Fred was, by then, a part-time city traffic court judge who openly aspired to higher office and willingly bought goodwill with loans and $2,500 campaign contributions he made in both his name and that of his unsuspecting wife.

His eagerness to do favors for the politically connected was no more evident than in 1990, the year the Parrot opened, when Fred testified as an expert defense witness on behalf of then Fulton County Sheriff Richard Lankford. Lankford was then on trial for tax evasion—charges stemming from allegations that he used his office to extort money from a county vendor, then failed to report the alleged payoff on his income taxes.

Tokars testified that he had analyzed the sheriff's finances and found that the income reflected on Lankford's tax returns was consistent with his known expenses.

In addition to his job as sheriff, Lankford was also a minister. Payoffs made to him by at least one jail inmate were not bribes, Tokars insisted, but were legitimate "love offerings." Saying he had handled the finances of a number of Atlanta's African-American ministers, Tokars explained that "love offerings" were a tradition in southern African-American churches. Because they were gifts to ministers made in thanks for spiritual comfort and prayer, those offerings were not taxable, Tokars said.

Federal prosecutors insisted Tokars's testimony was fanciful and irrelevant. Extortionists generally don't deposit their ill-gotten gains in their personal bank accounts. And U.S. District Court Judge Harold Freeman called Tokars's testimony "a bunch of malarkey."

Lankford was convicted. But the conviction was later overturned, in part because the jury was never allowed to hear Tokars's "love offering" testimony. Federal prosecutors eventually dropped the tax evasion charges in return for Lankford's assurance that he would never run for public office, a promise he broke in October 1995.

Lankford's highly publicized trial and Fred's own small role became fodder for the attorney's publicity machine.

Soon after the Parrot opened, Mason, Tokars, and Cline seized an opportunity to regain control of Dominique's Club 21. Under Mason's management, the club had seldom paid its bills or its $31,000 monthly rent. On Memorial Day, 1989, Doug McKendrick—who still held the lease—entered the club with sheriff's deputies, seized control, and collected the weekend revenues, some thirty-five thousand dollars. By then, Willie Harris—the doorman who brokered cocaine—had been promoted to club manager. McKendrick kept Harris on the payroll as general manager.

For three months, McKendrick struggled to keep the club operating, pay the bills, and mollify Dominique Wilkins so that the club could remain open under his name. But Dominique's domineering mother and his brother, John, began demanding a say in the club's operation. John wanted a management position. And Wilkins, who was earning four thousand dollars a month to loan his name to the club, soon more than doubled his fee—to ten thousand dollars.

It was at that point that Mason went to McKendrick with a second proposition. He and Harris had cut a deal with star athlete Deion Sanders. Neon Deion, a flamboyant two-sport athlete built for speed, then spent his springs and summers as an Atlanta Braves outfielder and the fall and winter months as a corner back for the Atlanta Falcons. He was a regular at Dominique's, where he had first met Willie Harris. In September 1990, Sanders had agreed, for a fee, to lend the club his name, but only if Harris continued to manage the club and signed the endorsement contract as president of the club's new management firm. Drug dealers Cline and Harris were corporate officers and entitled to hefty management fees.

James Mason was the third member of the board. Fred Tokars was their attorney.

When Dominique's reopened as Deion's Club 21, Tokars attended opening night, where the flamboyant ballplayer and his teammates had gathered. Hanging with the Falcons and the Braves was heady stuff for a night school graduate who had always thought a little too highly of himself. But it wasn't just their fame that attracted him. It was their money, what he could help them do with it, and where, if they were so inclined, he might help them hide it. He offered services to fit their needs—as an attorney, an accountant, or a money launderer. And he owed it all to James Mason and Julius Cline.

The month that Dominique's became Deion's, Tokars helped Mason and Cline buy a fourth Atlanta nightclub, this one in Buckhead with a desirable Peachtree Road address. Zazu's was a restaurant and piano bar. It appealed to an older, well-heeled prominent clientele that favored late, dimly lit nights and slow, smoky jazz. Atlanta Police Chief Eldrin Bell frequented the club, where he occasionally noodled by the piano in a surprisingly gentle tenor. Cline, with Mason as his front man, bought the bar with drug money for fifty thousand down. Again, Tokars negotiated the deal.

But even though Mason and Cline invested and operated legitimate businesses, they were far from legitimate men. They were criminals and swindlers who believed in taking all that they could get. Paying bills or taxes and retiring their debts was never in their game plan, especially if doing so would generate insufficient profits to support their lavish lifestyles.

But their proclivities made little difference to Fred. In fact, they were a windfall.

Each civil lien or lawsuit stemming from an unpaid bill and every criminal defense simply generated more legal fees for the attorney. From the same small core of men, Tokars eventually collected legal fees for civil and criminal defense work, corporate fees, club management fees, accounting fees, and covert fees for the use of his Caribbean money laundry. Those expenses, like the drug dealers' own fees, always came off the top.

One month after Deion's opened, McKendrick began sending Mason notices of default for nonpayment of rent. Mason and company might be collecting management fees, but they neglected to pay Sanders's monthly endorsement fees and failed to pay club taxes.

The story was no different at Zazu's. Although they owed the club's former owner fifty thousand dollars, they never made a single payment. "We're just not doing well. We don't have the money," Mason told Russ Dalba, who held the promissory note.

The club didn't pay taxes, and it didn't pay A.S.C.A.P. for songs performed by club musicians.

In June 1991, just eight months after Mason and Cline bought the club, Mason locked the doors and returned the keys. "We're not making it. I'm going to turn over the keys to you, and you can take the club back over. We don't have any money. We can't pay you. There is nothing here."

But he promised Dalba, "When I get the money, you'll get it." He was lying.

Only once did Mason's intransigence about paying his debts suck Fred into a lawsuit. With his stock in the Parrot at stake, Mason still couldn't bring himself to honor his settlement agreement with Linda Goodwin, the woman he had beaten so badly. Incensed, Goodwin decided she wanted the popular club. On January 14, 1991, she notified Mason through her attorney that he was in default, and she was taking possession of his nightclub shares.

Tokars and his partners had no intention of surrendering Mason's majority ownership in the Parrot without a legal fight. But Goodwin's default demand and the implicit threat of a civil suit precipitated a series of oily legal maneuvers by Tokars, who quickly sought to sever his ties to his business partners while he continued to represent them and the corporation through which they jointly owned the Parrot.

Within weeks of Goodwin's first demand, Tokars quietly resigned as the Parrot's corporate secretary and substituted Julius Cline in his place, despite Cline's felony record under his alias, Lucius Marvin Cleveland. The move put the club's liquor license and Cline at risk.

Tokars later insisted he had resigned his post because Mason had refused to buy liability insurance for the club. But if that was his reason, he waited a full year after the Parrot opened to do it.

Meanwhile, with Mason's Parrot stock in growing jeopardy, Tokars importuned Mason to begin paying Goodwin every month as he had originally agreed to do. But Goodwin wanted none of it. And when her attorney, Tokars's old friend Paul Howard, accepted Mason's payments anyway, she fired him, hired another lawyer, and sued for Mason's majority interest in the nightclub.

She named all the Parrot's corporate officers, including Tokars, in the suit. Tokars, using the law as a blunt instrument, sought to bludgeon Goodwin into submission. He quickly countersued both Goodwin and her attorney—an aggressive, and highly unusual if not improper response. He then petitioned the court to remove his name from the suit and replace it with Julius Cline's. Then he began filing responses on Cline's behalf as his attorney.

It was the first and only time Tokars's name ever appeared on a corporate document tied to Cline or Mason as a partner rather than as a hired gun.

Goodwin's civil suit would drag through the courts for the next eighteen months and would eventually cost Cline and his partners the nightclub. It was the wedge that sundered the silent partnership between Cline and Mason. Cline blamed both Mason and Tokars for pledging stock he had bought in Mason's name, and then losing it. He began to pull away from the nightclub operator and his lawyer. But he harbored an icy rage against both men. Banned from Dominique's, uncomfortable with the gay clientele at Traxx, Cline considered the Parrot his club and kept his office there. In losing the Parrot, he was losing not only a significant investment, but also his position. Until he was reimbursed, he wouldn't ante up again.

Perhaps that is why Mason walked away from Zazu's as soon as Goodwin sued. But it is certainly why he soon cozied up to another Detroit drug dealer who competed with Cline for Atlanta's cocaine trade.

Anthony "Al" Brown had made an impression the first night he waltzed into Dominique's. The club had a strict dress code. Suits and ties were required unless a patron was a recognized celebrity. Brown came to the door wearing sneakers, a sweat suit, and looking "like one of the typical dope boys."

The bouncers turned him away at the door. Brown demanded to speak with the manager. When Harris came to the door, Brown flashed a roll of cash, peeled off one hundred dollars for Harris, and promised to buy the club's most expensive champagne. Harris escorted him to the VIP lounge where the celebrities and big spenders mingled, and Brown began ordering $125 bottles of Dom Perignon.

Mason met Brown for the first time that night, after distastefully noticing his sweats. He didn't like anybody slouching through in sweat suits, even if they were stars. But Brown was spending a lot of money and that, as always, impressed Mason. At odds with Cline, who by then had stopped lending him money and buying him expensive cars, Mason was seeking another shark.

And Brown liked what Cline had—his nightclubs, his cocaine network, his access to the athletes, the politicians, and the stars. He coveted it. And he began cultivating the men closest to Cline, men like Mason and Tokars, who were for sale to the highest bidder.

On June 24, 1991, federal drug agents finally caught up with Willie Harris. He was caught in a drug sting accepting nearly thirty pounds of cocaine from some drug runners with whom he did occasional business. Business at Deion's plummeted.

Harris hired one attorney who wasn't able to free him on bond. Afraid Harris might bring down their drug-financed fiefdom of nightclubs, Mason went, not to Cline, but to Al Brown, for help. With five thousand dollars from Brown, Mason hired Tokars to defend Harris.

By that time, Brown, Mason, and Tokars all had clear reasons to isolate and silence Cline. The drug dealer had always distrusted Tokars, a circumstance that the loss of the Parrot only exacerbated. For his money laundry to succeed, Tokars needed to do business with a drug dealer who trusted him with his cash.

Cline also was angry at Mason and unwilling to bankroll any longer a man whose arrogant mismanagement had already cost him three clubs. He was beginning to talk about thousands of dollars Mason owed him—money he had fronted for the Parrot and cocaine, or simply lent Mason when he asked—that he now expected to collect.

And Brown saw Cline as a competitor.

When Tokars met with Harris in jail, he hinted broadly— as he always did—that he held undue sway over anonymous federal judges and that he could exert that illicit influence on Harris's behalf. He obtained sworn statements from Cline, for whom Harris sold cocaine, and Mason, whom he had occasionally supplied with the illegal drug, affirming that Harris was not a drug dealer—a particularly cynical maneuver.

Then he recommended that Harris become a government witness in return for a lighter sentence and set up Julius Cline.

"Hey, you're cool with Julius," Tokars told Harris as they sat in his office discussing the government's case. "Could you do Julius?"

Harris was startled that Tokars knew Cline was a drug dealer.

"Julius didn't do anything to me," he replied. "Julius didn't get me in the trouble I'm in. You know, he's been pretty good to me. He's been real good to me, and I'm not going to do it."

"Okay," Tokars agreed. "If you do Julius, it will roll down and get Mason because everybody knows James doesn't have any money. He gets his money from Julius."

Instead, Harris began fingering other Atlanta drug dealers.

Meanwhile, Mason was arranging to buy still another Atlanta nightclub, this time for Al Brown, his new money man and mentor. The Cheshire Bridge Road establishment that Mason selected housed two clubs, one for lesbians and one for transvestites. Financed by Brown with fifty thousand in drug money, the $250,000 clubs became known as Diamonds and Pearls, Mason's most expensive purchase. Brown was eager to flex his financial muscle. He spent between three and four hundred thousand to renovate both clubs, more than Cline had ever been able to muster.

"He was spending unnecessary money" just to show he could spend it, Harris noted after Mason hired him to work there while federal charges were still pending and Harris, with Fred's help was free on bond.

Tokars was the club's attorney. He incorporated it, negotiated its purchase, sought to protect it from Mason's other creditors, and brushed by the velvet ropes at the entrance as long lines of patrons eagerly waited long past midnight to party amid the trappings of money and fame.

Bouncers frisked patrons for weapons at the door. The sports stars such as Atlanta Falcons wide receiver Andre Rison, and the hip-hop stars such as his companion, Lisa "Left Eye" Lopes of TLC, were escorted upstairs to the VIP lounge where the champagne and lobster were free, and the women were both exquisite and expensive. Diamonds, with its dance floor and disco music, mirrored Deion's Club 21—tainted now by Harris's arrest—and lured former namesakes Deion Sanders and Dominique Wilkins.

Next door, the bartenders wore tuxedos as Pearls sought to duplicate the Parrot's ambiance and clientele with a classy understated appeal and a motif that revolved around intimate cocktails and jazz.

Julius Cline must have noticed that Diamonds and Pearls seemed designed to siphon his celebrity clientele from both Deion's and the Parrot.

Shortly after Diamonds and Pearls opened, Mason walked away from Deion's, where he had sidestepped paying the bills and the rent for nearly a year, cavalierly abandoning Cline and his investments as he had done every previous club.

With the Parrot in jeopardy, Cline clearly resented Mason's new partnership with Brown and the fact that, for the first time in nearly a decade, the most desirable nightclub in Atlanta did not belong to him.

"Julius was pretty upset that James had did a club with Al rather than him because they had always done clubs together," Harris noted later.

And drug dealer Andre Willis recalled Cline telling him, "I'm going to get James just as soon as everything dies down."

Cline began reminding his lieutenants that Mason owed him money, between fifty and seventy-five thousand dollars.

In a conversation with Tokars, Mason set the figure even higher, at three hundred thousand dollars.

"Don't worry," an amiable Tokars had answered as they sat at the Diamonds bar. "It will be taken care of." As if he had a reason to know.

Eight

Eddie Lawrence

SITTING AT THE BAR THAT NIGHT WAS A SOMETIME DRUG dealer, thief, and counterfeiter named Eddie Lawrence. He was Fred Tokars's newest shadow—a front man who, unlike Mason and his cronies, Tokars could manipulate and control.

Like many of the attorney's seamier associates, Eddie Lawrence was a former client. He had come to Fred by way of Marvin Baynard, one of the first drug dealers Fred had solicited for his Caribbean money laundry. Baynard bought his cocaine from Julius Cline.

Two of Baynard's young lieutenants—Dexter Askew and Alex Yancey—were Eddie's friends and former schoolmates. Like Baynard, both of them were drug dealers. But, like many others who sold drugs on Atlanta's streets, both had spent little time in prison for their crimes.

Yancey, in particular, was bright. For two years he had attended Clark College, one of a city consortium of colleges that included Spelman and Morehouse, where he had majored in mechanical engineering. It was on the city streets that wound through the Atlanta University Center campus that Yancey first met Marvin Baynard. He soon became Baynard's driver and one of his drug delivery men.

Yancey worked for Baynard less than a year before he was arrested while delivering cocaine in Cobb County. But his five-year sentence on that charge was probated, and Yancey spent just four months in a halfway house before he was released.

Almost immediately, Yancey returned to Baynard's payroll.

It was Baynard who first introduced Yancey to Fred Tokars. And while Baynard and Tokars spoke about laundering Baynard's drug profits through a small advertising company, Yancey listened intently.

As Tokars explained it, he was soliciting ten-thousand-dollar "investments" from interested individuals who needed to mask their illegal earnings. In return, each "investor" would receive loan documents from Tokars's Caribbean bank. Those loan documents could then be used to purchase property, automobiles, or establish legitimate businesses. Of course, those faux loans would never be repaid. But the paperwork Tokars generated would reflect that they had been. At least, that was the scheme Fred was marketing so aggressively.

Instinctively, Baynard never completely trusted Fred. With good reason. Those ten-thousand-dollar "investments" were secreted in bank accounts identified only by number or by confidential aliases Fred established. Only Fred knew how to identify those accounts. His signature was the one required to authorize a transfer of funds.

No matter what he promised the drug dealers he tried to lure into his schemes, Fred alone controlled their Caribbean funds. Because the lawyer would hold apparently legal loan documents issued by his own shell bank in the islands, he was poised to sue for the funds he was shepherding if the men who entrusted him with them were arrested, killed, or sent to jail.

Default was his ace. The truth was that his Caribbean bank could sue the drug dealers for whom he fabricated loans at any time for nonpayment, even though the money in the bank was theirs.

In 1988, while he was still on probation, Yancey was arrested again, this time for violating state gun laws. Having met Fred through Baynard, he went to him for advice only to find he couldn't afford him. But he soon found it hardly mattered. In return for his guilty plea for carrying a gun as a convicted felon, he was once more placed on probation and asked to pay a thousand-dollar fine.

Three years later, Yancey would again find himself in legal trouble. Once more, he would turn to Tokars for help. But this time, he brought Eddie Lawrence with him.

Lawrence was, at heart, a pretender and a thief. He had first met Yancey when the two were in the eighth grade. The two had gone to high school together. After they graduated in 1982, Lawrence began a somewhat aimless and ultimately short-lived pursuit of an advanced degree. He spent a year at the Academy of Professional Drafting. He enrolled at Alabama State University in Montgomery and took classes at Atlanta Metropolitan College. He never graduated. Instead, he drifted into house painting and minor remodeling, hiring family and friends like Yancey whenever he needed a crew.

He was a little man with big ideas about his own importance. In 1988, he named his unincorporated, one-man operation Lawrence Industries, as if he were a booming enterprise ready to assume his position in the ranks of Atlanta's foremost corporations.

Lawrence built his jack-leg business by buying dilapidated houses priced at less than fifty thousand dollars that he would then renovate and rent. But Lawrence had no credit and no cash. Bad checks were his stock in trade. More than one seller was stung after accepting a check for the full value of the property from Lawrence Industries, only to find that it wouldn't clear the bank.

Meanwhile, Lawrence—with deeds in hand—would renovate those houses, lease them, and pocket the monthly rents. Several sellers sued him civilly and eventually won judgments that Lawrence pointedly ignored. He lacked any concept of honesty. His word on any given day meant nothing. His workmanship was often faulty and frequently incomplete. He did as little as necessary to earn his fees, then vanished without completing a job. But Lawrence's cavalier willingness to cheat the people on whom he built his business would eventually contribute to his downfall. Faced with criminal charges that he had passed worthless checks, deeply in debt, the target of a federal counterfeiting investigation, Lawrence began his descent down the cellar stairs of crime to murder.

Lawrence had always been lured by easy money. So, in the summer of 1991, when Yancey proposed that his friend invest in a scheme to buy and sell cocaine that would double his investment, Lawrence readily agreed. With six thousand dollars he borrowed from Eddie, Yancey bought a half-pound of cocaine wholesale. He promised that its subsequent street sale would garner the pair twenty thousand dollars.

But Yancey never repaid the borrowed money. Instead, he told Eddie he had fronted the drugs to another dealer, who was supposed to repay him with proceeds from illegal sales. Instead, Yancey claimed his contact stole the drugs and kept the money for himself—a story reminiscent of one he had offered to Baynard five years earlier when some of Baynard's cocaine stash had disappeared after he entrusted it to Yancey.

Lawrence was furious. But unlike Julius Cline or Jessie Ferguson, whom he had yet to meet, Lawrence was not an instinctive killer. Still, he insisted Yancey was going to have to find the money somehow.

A news report on CNN offered Yancey a solution. The story reported on the newest tool of counterfeiters—a specific brand of color copier. The report intrigued Yancey, who soon located several books on counterfeiting currency. Obtaining a color copier posed little problem.

"I had a couple of gentlemen and myself steal it," Yancey said.

Lawrence didn't help Yancey steal the copier, but he did help him case several copy shops before Yancey spotted the one he wanted.

Yancey was meticulous. "He would go in and take a picture with a lot of different colors in it, and see which copier was the best one," Lawrence said.

After burglarizing a shop north of Atlanta, Yancey and four cohorts hauled the five-hundred-pound copier to his suburban home in a stolen van. By November 1991, Yancey was printing counterfeit twenty- and fifty-dollar bills. He became an amateur artisan, carefully selecting copy paper and ink, then using floor wax and various dyes to make the counterfeit bills appear more real. United States Secret Service agents would later say Yancey was "a natural."

Yancey's girlfriend eventually threw him out, and Yancey

moved, with his stolen copier, into a back bedroom of Eddie Lawrence's home in town. The duo soon began passing the counterfeit bills at nightclubs and using them to buy cocaine from other dealers. Yancey also enlisted several of his less savory friends to distribute the counterfeit bills, fellow drug dealers to whom he sold the money for circulation or resale.

But Yancey soon grew dissatisfied with the color copier's reproduction. After cutting a deal with a small offset press to use copying equipment at night for what they claimed was a commercial printing contract with Lockheed, Yancey and Lawrence hauled the stolen copier to a deserted dirt road and burned it.

Then they began manufacturing money at night in twenty-, fifty-, and hundred-dollar denominations—until they had printed $2 million in worthless currency. The duo never passed more than a fraction of that sum. Within weeks, the phony money had attracted the attention of the U.S. Secret Service, who traced it to Yancey's drug-dealer friends. Secret Service agents soon targeted Yancey and Lawrence. And the counterfeiters' friends began warning the two men that federal agents were looking for them.

Terrified, Yancey turned to Fred Tokars for help.

On January 20, 1992, Yancey and Lawrence met with Fred in his Peachtree Street office downtown. During that meeting, they told the attorney they had been counterfeiting money and that the Secret Service was closing in. It was only a matter of time before they would be arrested. They wanted advice as to what they should do.

That advice would cost them each twenty-five thousand dollars, Fred told the two men. He needed ten thousand cash or collateral from each man up front before he could do anything to help them.

Fred neglected to mention that he was already representing a drug dealer they had supplied with counterfeit bills, a man who had already given their names to the Secret Service.

Lawrence offered the buyer the deed to a rental house near the Atlanta University Center as payment. Yancey assumed that the proffer covered his legal fees as well.

"Meanwhile," Fred warned them, "stop making money, and don't talk to anyone by phone."

Near the end of the meeting, Fred expressed a particular curiosity about the counterfeit bills Yancey had printed.

"Can you get me some counterfeit money?" he asked. "I've never seen counterfeit before. I could probably distribute some of it in the Bahamas," he mused.

Yancey was aghast. Fearing arrest, he and Lawrence had already stopped distributing the phony bills. "No," he told the attorney tersely. "I can't."

The following day, Lawrence deeded to Fred one of his rental houses in lieu of a twenty-five-thousand-dollar fee. Yancey witnessed the exchange, confident that the deed, worth nearly fifty thousand dollars, included his own legal fees as well as his companion's.

Within days, Yancey was shocked to find he was mistaken. He arrived home to find Secret Service agents in Crown Victorias parked outside the house he shared with Eddie and on parallel streets nearby. Yancey spotted them before they saw him. He fled and placed a panicky phone call to Tokars.

"Fred, these guys are following me. They're swarming all over me. Is there anything you can do to stop them from following me?"

"Get me some money down here," Fred coolly responded. "If you haven't been arrested yet, don't worry about it. Call me when you get arrested."

And the attorney hung up the phone.

It was the second time Fred had cut Yancey loose. This time, Yancey knew he couldn't cut his own sweet deal with prosecutors. This time he faced federal charges and a stiff sentence he couldn't renegotiate without a lawyer. Desperately, he burned the bulk of the money in Lawrence's fireplace, pocketed the remainder, then fled Atlanta—a two-year journey that took him first to Macon, then to New Orleans, Houston, Dallas, Fort Worth, St. Louis, Phoenix, Las Vegas, Palm Beach, and San Francisco. On the run, Yancey lived on counterfeit, until his face and his biography surfaced on "America's Most Wanted."

Meanwhile, the Secret Service began questioning Lawrence. Lawrence told the agents curtly they could talk to his attorney. Within days, Fred had scheduled a meeting between Lawrence and the federal agents, one the lawyer ne-

glected to attend. Lawrence agreed to cooperate and help
them find and prosecute Alex Yancey. Before he left, he
agreed to be polygraphed. He lied during the examination,
although Fred told him later that he passed—a lie that
Lawrence cheekily believed.

U.S. Secret Service Agent Mike Davis said he told Fred
that Lawrence's polygraph suggested he had been deceptive
when answering questions about his role in Yancey's counterfeiting operation—which flatly contradicted the lawyer's
assurances that Lawrence had only been minimally involved.

Less than two weeks after their first meeting, in spite of
the Secret Service agent's warning, Fred made his counterfeiter client his business partner.

Fred's explanation as to why he chose a petty criminal to
manage four real estate, mortgage, and construction concerns
was smooth and disingenuous. Lawrence, he insisted, had
never suggested he was a counterfeit thief. Instead, he had
accompanied Yancey, looking for a lawyer to help him evict
a recalcitrant tenant. Only after Yancey fled did Lawrence
approach Fred about the Secret Service investigation, saying
agents were harassing him because he was Yancey's friend.

Fred eventually acknowledged that Eddie had been deceptive on his polygraph but insisted Eddie had resolved the matter by providing agents with additional information. He
claimed he had always told Lawrence to tell the truth. And
eventually, the lawyer insisted, the Secret Service cleared his
client as a suspect, an assertion that Secret Service agents say
is patently untrue.

Fred insisted that he never billed Eddie more than five
thousand dollars in fees. It was Eddie, he insisted, who asked
him for a loan, using the rental house as collateral.

Forming a construction company, a mortgage company, a
real estate firm, and a real estate sales firm was Eddie's idea,
the lawyer would later claim. It was Eddie who suggested
that each business would feed the other, and someone who
owned them all could easily collect multiple fees from a single customer.

"I saw it as an entry into the black business in southwest
Atlanta," Fred insisted. "It was a unique opportunity. The
plan made sense to me."

In return for his investment, Fred established a holding company—Tokars Contract Management, Inc.—that controlled the four companies he created for Lawrence. Tokars was the majority shareholder. Eddie contributed ''sweat equity.'' Just twenty-five, he also assumed the heady presidential title of Eddie Lawrence Industries, a construction company; Southwest Mortgage and Finance Corp., a mortgage firm; Eddie Lawrence Realty; and Eddie Lawrence Homes, Inc.

Fred rented a suite of seven offices on Greenbriar Parkway near a south Atlanta mall for Eddie that he soon filled with office furniture, computers, and a staff. The suite also boasted a large conference room, two bathrooms, and a waiting area. Eddie had his own airy, private office.

Soon, Eddie was seeing his face on billboards, bus bench advertisements, and on the cover of Atlanta's *Black Pages* as a businessman to know.

''When Eddie Lawrence started his business seven years ago, he did so without a budget,'' his biography in the *Black Pages* boasted.

> Lawrence recalled the time when he worked for a company that went bankrupt. ''That left me without a job and without my last two weeks paycheck. So after that happened, I was determined not to get a job again,'' he says.
>
> Lawrence Industries is a conglomeration of many things, a combination real estate and construction company. They do everything—from owning, selling, buying, repairing, remodeling, and building property. Eddie Lawrence picked this combination because he feels everybody needs land, and everything on this planet needs real estate.
>
> Lawrence is a self-made man at twenty-seven. His father, Kenneth Lawrence, gives a helping hand, although he is not in the business full-time.

But the sophisticated scheme of interlocking firms that dunned customers for multiple fees during the course of a single transaction wasn't Eddie's. It was Fred's.

''I didn't know anything about corporations, and Mr. Tokars told me if you are going to be serious in business, it is to your advantage to have a corporation," Lawrence later explained. "People don't take sole proprietorships seriously, and so it would be to my advantage in the business community dealing with banks and anybody else to have a corporation."

Eddie was more blunt about his partnership with Fred. He was a drug dealer, and Fred wanted to launder money.

"I knew a lot of drug dealers after having been one myself," he said. "And, from that point, we determined that we could set up a business where we could take drug money and buy houses, fix them up and sell them, and we would launder money that way." The business would be its own explanation for large cash deposits in company bank accounts. Fred and Eddie would earn ten-thousand-dollar investment fees from the drug dealers they assisted. Fred would also generate more fees as the lawyer and an accountant attached to each transaction.

The attorney bragged to his young protégé about his finesse with offshore finances. He saw himself as a money broker who "housed" money for his American clientele.

"If he had somebody in the United States who wanted to go to Greece, and if they had a million dollars in cash, they could give him the million dollars cash," Lawrence said. "He would house the cash, and whenever they got to whatever country they were going to, he could fix it to where they could get seven hundred thousand dollars of that country's currency, or whatever was the equivalent to seven hundred thousand dollars of that country's currency. At least, that's what he told me."

Under Fred's tutelage, Eddie eagerly adopted a more rarified lifestyle, exchanged his painter's overalls for tailored suits and the companionship of his high school running buddies for city politicians and cocaine brokers who financed multi-million-dollar enterprises. At night, Eddie would drift among the city's nightclubs on Fred's expense accounts, scouting for drug dealers he would solicit for the attorney's Caribbean money laundry.

One of his first conquests was Michael Morris, a man whom Eddie knew as a drug dealer from Washington, D.C. with drug ventures in several states. Eddie attached himself to Morris, in no small part because he paid his rent in cash and six months in advance. Using Eddie Lawrence Industries as a front, Morris bought two houses and opened a beauty salon in the house Eddie had signed over to Fred as collateral for his defense. He used drug money to finance his real estate purchases and stock and refurbish the salon. Morris also advertised in the *Black Pages*:

Michael Morris has been redeveloping properties over the last three years throughout Atlanta and Decatur. He has taken a personal interest in the black community. Michael feels that these damaged properties offer no value to our community, but more importantly, he cares, and he is committed to reinvesting a portion of his revenues derived from the black consumer back to the local black community.

It was all an elaborate ruse. The revenues Morris reinvested all derived from the sale of crack cocaine. But, like the other drug dealers whom Fred had solicited for his money laundry, Morris was skeptical of giving his dirty cash to the attorney in return for a promise that he could draw on it whenever he pleased.

By then, Eddie was dining out with Fred several nights a week. He trailed the pale, spindly attorney as he strode past lines of people waiting at a nightclub's entrance and sat at the bar with the drug dealer owners, his face a luminous oval in the carbon-colored crowd.

With Fred as his mentor, Eddie was ushered into Diamonds and sat quietly at the bar as Fred greeted Julius Cline, Willie Harris, Andre Willis, and James Mason.

Mason, Fred confided to Eddie, was a patron of his money laundry. He advised Mason on how to wash money through the club. But the attorney kvetched that Mason was spending too much cash too freely, paying forty-five thousand cash for a new, cream-colored Lexus rather than letting Fred launder the money through his Caribbean bank, invest it in real estate, or open another club.

The lure of the nightclubs where Eddie either accompanied Fred or trolled for drug dealers to refer to the attorney mesmerized him. It easily fed his inflated sense of self-importance and bloated his greed. He forgot that the money he spent was borrowed. He didn't care that it derived from drugs. He coveted the influence and attention that James Mason garnered. He wanted his name on a nightclub liquor license. He wanted his customers to greet him at the door.

Morris, too, had been smitten with Diamonds and the idea of investing in a nightclub. Drawing on his drug money, Morris proposed to open a comedy club called Chuckles and a strip club in south Atlanta he christened Peek-a-Boo's. He left the details to Fred and Eddie, who were to lease an abandoned club from friends of Jim Killeen's. Because Morris was a felon, Eddie's name would appear on the liquor license. Morris would also pay Eddie to renovate the club.

But Eddie had other ideas. He would launder Morris's money—but through his own club, not one operated by Morris. With an invincibility borne of arrogance, he hijacked the liquor license and location, then, in a moment of spectacular unoriginality, named the club after himself—"Club Eddie."

One night in the new nightclub's parking lot, Morris waylaid Eddie and beat him for his impudence. Within days, he rammed Eddie's jeep repeatedly as it sat parked on a downtown street near Fred's offices.

"The same thing could happen to you that happened to your jeep," Morris warned him later, "if you don't give me a piece of that nightclub."

Club Eddie was a failure. So, too, was the network of small companies Fred had woven together. With fifteen employees, including office and construction workers, and the amply furnished suite, Eddie had soon spent seventy thousand of Fred's money while generating very little new business and no major drug brokers willing to invest in Fred's money laundry or pay the attorney's exorbitant fees.

Besides, Eddie wasn't a businessman. He didn't even like to work. The quality of his work was inconsistent and often incomplete. He often argued with his customers, incensed that their willingness to hire him entitled them to make demands. Yet Fred defended him, and solicited contracts for the fledgling business from his friends.

One former assistant U.S. attorney who shared an office with Fred hired Eddie, on Fred's recommendation, to renovate his wife's dance studio. But the job dragged on for months, and soon became a sore point with the attorney, Howard Weintraub.

"I expressed to him that I had obligations to other people, and I just could not come every time he called me," Eddie would say later. "He called me at eight in the morning, and I couldn't drive forty-five miles within an hour, just drop what I'm doing just to talk to him about how he didn't like a spot on the wall."

When the exasperated lawyer threatened to sue, Eddie complained to Tokars, who promptly informed his office mate that if Weintraub sued, Eddie would fight it in court and he, Tokars, would represent him.

Despite the pretensions he bought with Fred's money, Eddie remained, in reality, a glorified handyman. And that is how he came to meet Sara Tokars in the spring of 1992.

Fred paid Eddie two thousand dollars to make some extensive repairs in his sons' bathroom. Eddie spent several days at the house, replacing sheetrock and tile, stripping wallpaper, and painting. He met Sara Tokars when she answered the door, and spoke to her from time to time while he worked on one of the few jobs he bothered to finish.

If Sara thought about her chance encounter with Eddie at all, it was probably with a sense of small relief that her penurious husband had finally paid for some much-needed repairs. She had no way of knowing of her husband's odd relationship with the young man—the biweekly dinners, the clubs, the mandate to solicit drug dealers, the subtle advertisements that he was willing to sublimate ethics and honesty for cash.

If asked, Sara would have found it impossible to explain how the husband who forced her to choose between buying groceries and taking her sons to the doctor, who constantly harped on her about any small expenditure, would lavish seventy thousand dollars on a petty criminal and sometime drug dealer. She would have been baffled, had she known, that the shameless social climber she had married would choose to mentor and vehemently defend a man like Eddie Lawrence against far more influential men.

Nor did she know why, out of all the businesses Fred

owned, he chose to place his shares of the holding company he shared with Lawrence into a trust, with Sara as its beneficiary, that Andy Tokars would control. But on June 8, 1992, Fred did just that. And, like the trust Fred had already established, the new trust also gave Andy, not Sara, sole control of the assets and their distribution in the event that Fred should die.

Fred told his brother that he and Sara were running the construction company. Sara was the chief stockholder, he said, and the trust would innoculate the couple against any civil liability associated with the firm.

But, as always, Sara had no financial say, although her name on the trust as beneficiary made it seem so.

Within months it would become more clear. Fred Tokars had something else in mind.

Part III

MURDER

Nine

The Beginning of the End

IT IS EASY TO BELIEVE THAT THOSE WHO PASS THROUGH Texas come to grief. The land, no matter what the season, gives rise to that suspicion. Head west from Fort Worth or north toward Amarillo, and the land has about it a dull, depressing sameness. It is brown, as if the God of green and growing things abandoned it long ago.

The Texas panhandle in particular is a brutal, barren place. The sky in high summer is the dull color of unwashed linen. The overheated earth resembles old enamel. The highway cuts like a scar across the landscape, and there is nowhere to hide.

Perhaps that is why the Chevrolet coupe that Ed Haney was driving on the day Amarillo narcotics officers stopped him on the highway had tinted windows—to insure his anonymity. But those tinted windows, and the conspicuous absence of an auto tag, are what first attracted their attention.

Tinted windows are banned in Texas, a law enacted by the legislature to protect the lives of law enforcement officers, for tinted windows multiply the risk of making routine traffic stops. Officers approaching a car are blind to the occupants, who can see them very well. The tinted windows make police an easy target for men with a reason to kill that they may have unknowingly detained.

Haney was not a killer. He was a courier. He had been hired by a Los Angeles drug dealer and given a new Chev-

149

rolet to drive from Los Angeles to Atlanta. Hidden in the car were more than a hundred kilos of cocaine.

Unfortunately for Haney, the police officers who stopped that morning as he cruised along the Texas plains in the Lumina's air-conditioned comfort weren't merely writing traffic violations. They were trolling for drugs.

It wasn't the first time Haney had traveled cross-country with a load either of illegal drugs or cash. A month earlier, he had driven from Detroit to Los Angeles with nearly half a million dollars hidden in the Lumina's door panels. A twenty-nine-year-old groomsman at a California racetrack, Haney looked a decade younger than his age. He was tall and lanky, with short brown hair and the clean-cut looks of a mother's favorite son. And he was white, which is why he was hired for the job. The drug traffickers that singled Haney out at the racetrack near Los Angeles were African-Americans. They knew that police along the highways were far more likely to stop a black man for some innocuous offense they could turn into a drug search than a clean-cut white boy driving a car his mother might have given him as a graduation present.

But Corporal Brent Clay and the narcotics officers with whom he worked along the Texas flats near Amarillo were far less discriminating than their counterparts in Florida and Georgia, who tended to target cars driven by black men or Hispanics. Parked along side Interstate 40 with binoculars and radar guns, the Amarillo police corporal and his two companions were willing to stop anyone.

Texas—with its long, empty highways that connect both coasts and its proximity to Mexico and the Gulf—has always been a crossroads for the drug trade. Seven years of chasing drug runners had taught Clay something—that race, age, nationality, or political persuasion didn't matter. Everyone was suspect. The chances of being caught were far too slim, the money just too good for people not to chance it. The odds were in their favor. The oldest man he had caught hauling drugs along the irisdescent highway just outside of Amarillo was seventy-two years old.

As it crosses the Texas panhandle, Interstate 40 traces the faded outlines of old Route 66, a highway romanticized and made famous by a far more innocent generation. It is the main road between the East Coast and L.A., which is why Ed Haney was barreling along the interstate that morning. He was en route to Atlanta, his mind on his delivery schedule, a pager in his pocket, and three suitcases full of cocaine in the trunk. The men with whom he was doing business had good taste. It was expensive luggage—simple, elegant, and black.

Clay had been sitting in a police cruiser alongside the highway just over an hour, drinking coffee and peering through binoculars at the traffic. He was looking for a reason to reel in a car. His favorite violation was failure to wear a seat belt. After issuing a misdemeanor warning or, in rare cases, a citation, Clay's question to the driver was always the same, "Mind if we search your car?"

Haney had been feeling good until he saw a police cruiser with the flashing blue lights behind him. He was driving a new car that the men who hired him had registered in his name. He was carrying three thousand dollars in expense money in his wallet. And before leaving California, he had won five hundred dollars at the track—the first place he headed after securing his illicit cargo and pocketing the money he had been given for food and gas.

Haney probably saw the police car on the side of the road as he went by. He may even have nervously glanced at his speedometer, because when he was stopped he wasn't speeding. But here was a police officer, dressed like a mercenary in a black T-shirt, fatigues, and combat boots, walking up to his car on the side of the road. It was almost as if he knew Haney was hiding cocaine in the trunk.

When he stopped him, Clay had no reason to suspect Haney of anything. He made dozens of similar stops each day. But as soon as he saw the driver, Clay knew the boy was doing something wrong. He just looked like he'd been caught, or was about to be.

Clay took his time issuing the citations. The car had tinted windows, and the driver wasn't wearing a seat belt. Then, by way of conversation, he asked Haney why the Chevrolet had only a temporary tag. He spoke deliberately. He seemed inclined to chat. And he wanted to watch Haney sweat.

Haney said his mother had bought the car and given it to

him. It was a recent gift, he said, and the new license plates had not arrived. The car was registered in his name.

By then, Clay's two companions had joined him. Clay watched Haney watching him. Then, in his blunt Texas twang he asked, "Mind if we search the car?"

Haney didn't know what to say. As an unobtrusive camera mounted on the patrol car filmed him, he reluctantly agreed.

Haney didn't know the finer points of search and seizure laws. But if he had, it wouldn't have mattered. The Amarillo officers, with the help of Texas law, had figured out a way to circumvent them. They had brought a drug dog with them.

Haney stepped out of the Chevy. He began pacing nervously as Clay and the two officers who had joined him began searching the car. If he had smoked, he would have been desperate to light up. He was sweating, and on the side of the road in high summer, it was hot.

The officers were taking their time. With Haney's permission, they opened the trunk. Would he mind if they opened the suitcases, one of them asked. Haney began to babble.

The suitcases are locked, he told them. His mother had packed and locked them but had forgotten to give him the combinations. No problem, Clay told him. Give us your mother's telephone number. We'll call her and ask.

By then, the officers had lifted the suitcases out of the trunk. Look, Haney said desperately. I'm in a hurry. I'll just leave them with you and pick them up on my way back through Amarillo.

He was in deep trouble. Rocky the drug dog was already sniffing the bags. He was a German shepherd trained for police work, and Clay swore Rocky could smell the lingering odor of marijuana on money or on the clothing of someone who had smoked a joint the night before. The dog began scratching a suitcase. He had detected the faint, bitter odor of cocaine.

Haney crumpled. "They aren't my suitcases," he said.

He had been hired to deliver the suitcases to Atlanta, Haney admitted. But, he insisted, they weren't packed with narcotics. They were filled with expired credit cards.

"Our dog doesn't sniff out credit cards," Clay said wryly. "The only time he scratches, it's narcotics." And because

Rocky had indicated there were drugs inside the suitcases, Clay told Haney he didn't need a warrant to open them. Under Texas law, the drug dog and Haney's mobility had given him probable cause. Right there, on the side of the interstate in the middle of the Texas prairie, Haney buckled. "I want to help," he said.

That single traffic stop on August 5, 1992 just west of Amarillo would, like the first rattle of small stones on a hillside, trigger a deadly avalanche of events that ended three months later in the brutal death of a woman a thousand miles away—a loving, troubled Atlanta housewife who knew nothing of cocaine or drug dealers and their urgent need to launder their ill-gotten profits, who never knew her fate was sealed on a solitary strip of Texas highway one sweltering summer afternoon.

Ten

Busted

AT 9 A.M. PACIFIC TIME, ED HANEY CALLED A LOS ANGELES pager. He punched in his three-digit identification number and the area code through which he was was traveling. He should have punched in 806—the area code for Amarillo where he had been for the past three hours. Instead, he signaled the pager that he was in Albuquerque, six hours closer to LA. It was supposed to be an all-clear signal and a locator for the drug dealer who had hired him. Now it was a decoy sent by a man in the custody of police.

With Haney's help, the Amarillo police had decided to broaden their horizons. They had decided to go with Haney to Atlanta. The cocaine in Haney's suitcases was worth more than $2 million. Haney could never hope to finance that kind of deal. Brent Clay wanted the men who could.

Arresting one of the drug trade's West Coast financiers and his Atlanta distributor would be a law enforcement coup. But, just as important to the Texas officers, those men had wealth and assets they could legally seize as the ill-gotten gains of the drug trade. Those assets, paid for with the profits of illegal drug sales, were routinely transferred to the law enforcement agencies that seized them.

Like Haney, a gambler who was always short of cash; like the drug traders desperate to finance their rich and reckless lifestyles; the Panhandle Narcotics Task Force was always

154

strapped for funds. In that sense, the drug trade can be a terrible equalizer. Everyone, to some degree, is in it for the money.

But in order to profit from Haney's arrest and capture his employers, Amarillo's narcotics officers needed help. By noon, they had enlisted the U.S. Drug Enforcement Administration and borrowed a cargo plane from the U.S. Air Force to fly Haney's car to Atlanta. Their goal was to make Haney's arrival in that southern city appear as uneventful as his cross-country trip should have been. But the cargo plane broke down in Little Rock, Arkansas. The drug agents, with Haney in tow, limped into Atlanta on August sixth, eight hours later than they planned.

They had left eighty-three kilos of cocaine behind in Texas, although they had brought the suitcases and a kilo of cocaine with them. En route, they discovered more cocaine. Haney, who knew almost nothing about the illegal trade in which he had become entangled, was talkative and trying very hard to be helpful. He was, after all, looking at a very long prison sentence if police weren't impressed with his cooperation. At some point during those long hours in flight and in Little Rock waiting for the plane to be repaired, Haney told his escorts about a trip to Detroit he had made the previous month. His assignment, from the drug dealer who had sent him to Atlanta, was collection of a cash payment. Haney returned to Los Angeles with $485,000 hidden in the Chevy's rear door panels. By that time, his law enforcement companions were bored. They didn't have anything better to do. So they dismantled the doors. They didn't find any money. But they did find twenty-one kilos, almost forty-five pounds, of cocaine.

It was 8:30 p.m. before Haney once more signaled the Los Angeles pager and the unseen monitor of his route. This time he punched in another code, three lucky sevens that had failed him. He hung up, then called a second time with his phone number. When the phone rang a few minutes later, a tape recorder quietly began recording Haney's conversation.

The pager belonged to Shorty Owens, a young former groomsman with whom Haney had worked at the track. Owens had recruited Haney to make the cross-country drive, and, needing money, Haney was glad to oblige. In Encino, Owens had personally packed the bagged kilos of cocaine in the suitcases and hidden twenty-one more bags in the door panels of Haney's car. He was paid fifty dollars for every bag he handled. Now Owens was in Atlanta, registered at an elegant downtown hotel. He had left his pager behind in Los Angeles with his boss, a drug financier and trafficker named Dana Gold. Gold bought cocaine directly from a Colombian cartel in South America. He was a door into the U.S. market.

By the time Haney called him, Gold was agitated and angry. During Haney's cross-country trip, the drug trafficker had grown leery of a deal he could ill afford to cancel.

Gold was then twenty-five. He had been selling cocaine since he was twenty. He had parlayed the profits of those illegal sales into a network of legitimate business ventures, including an Los Angeles gymnasium for professional prize fighters called the V.I.P Boxing Club. Gold had his own stable of boxers and a stable of race horses. He had also adopted the ostentatious lifestyle of the professional athlete he might have been had he not dropped out of the University of New Mexico after just one year and surrendered his basketball scholarship.

He lived in Malibu. He gambled. He played the ponies at Delmar and Hollywood Park. He frequented Caesar's Palace in Las Vegas where he was known as a high roller. Whether he was at the track or a casino, he occupied the most expensive suites.

He wore expensive jewelry, including a four-hundred-thousand-dollar ring; purchased expensive real estate; and married an expensive wife, a Las Vegas night club singer named Sherrelle. But he had few, if any, scruples. He once used the deed to his grandmother's home as collateral for a drug deal while she lay ill in a hospital bed.

Gold's high-profile gymnasium and his role as a manager of prize fighters helped to explain his illegitimate wealth. He kept his cocaine deals a secret. But he insisted, "I didn't pretend to be nothing I wasn't."

And on August 6, 1992, Dana Gold was facing prison. In 1987, he had been arrested and charged with selling five kilos of cocaine, a negligible amount for a man who claimed he rarely made deals for less than a hundred keys. In 1992, he had finally been sentenced to serve five years in prison on that charge, a conviction his attorneys were still appealing. For five years Gold had remained free on bond, financing his businesses and his excesses by continuing to sell cocaine. He had also been losing money.

"People think if you sell cocaine, you automatically are rich," he would say later. "Yes, you do make money selling cocaine, but you can take a lot of large losses. . . . One minute you can have five million dollars and the next minute you can be five million dollars in the hole. That's how it works with narcotics."

And two months earlier, Gold had suddenly found himself $1 million in debt when federal agents arrested his lieutenant, Gino Williams, in Orange County, California with a hundred kilos of cocaine. Gold promptly abandoned Williams, refusing to take his urgent telephone calls from jail.

But because cocaine is, in part, a credit business—suppliers front cocaine to other dealers on credit and are reimbursed once their customers make a sale—Gold had little choice but to pay his Colombian suppliers for the cocaine seized when Williams was arrested.

"I always kept my word good and tried to pay whoever I owed so my word would stay good in the cocaine business," he explained. "If I didn't pay, my word wasn't good, and I would have problems with the people I dealt with."

They would kill him.

Fresh from that $1 million loss, Gold could not afford to lose another shipment, but he was suddenly leery of the Atlanta deal. Haney had taken far too long to drive from Los Angeles to Atlanta. Somewhere on that cross-country trip he had lost more than a day. Gold's instincts told him that something wasn't right. But the specter of another million-dollar loss was more vivid than his ill-defined disquiet. He told Haney to rent a room at a downtown hotel, then page him with the number. Gold said that Shorty Owens, the man who had taken Gino Williams's place and had hired Haney to make the cross-country drive, was already in Atlanta. Owens would call Haney back and arrange to complete the sale.

But Haney, guided by the D.E.A., didn't follow Gold's

instructions. Instead of finding a hotel downtown, Haney took a room at a motel at the outer edges of Atlanta near the county industrial park—a twenty-minute cab ride away. After he registered, Haney paged Gold with the number.

Still unnerved, Gold called Owens and told him Haney was finally in town. Owens had been waiting more than a day for Haney in Atlanta. But it was, after all, his job.

Owens had met Gold at the track and later had taken a job as a janitor at Gold's gym. Over time, as Gold began to trust him, Owens gradually assumed responsibility for the gym's daily operation. Eventually, he began managing the gym. And by the time he flew to Atlanta on August 5, 1992, Shorty Owens was the general managing partner of V.I.P. Boxing. He had also become a willing participant in Gold's cocaine deals after Gold asked him one day, "Are you interested in making some fast money where you can have some of the finer things in life that I have?" And after Gino Williams was arrested, Owens became Gold's new lieutenant.

Owens called Haney. "Why," he demanded to know, "were you so late?"

With an unseen tape recorder rolling, and a lighter prison sentence dependent on his answers, Haney carefully and deliberately lied. He had driven into fierce weather on the plains, he said. It had cost him more than a day.

The excuse was credible. The storms that spread like great bruises across the flat prairie skies in summer can blow a car off course or drown a road in rain.

Owens accepted the explanation. But Haney's next words should have warned him. "By the way," he said casually, "I got a ticket."

At the time, the significance of that simple statement eluded Owens. His mind was occupied with other things. His boss was angry, the hour was late, his Atlanta connection was impatient to consummate the deal. Owens didn't question Haney in detail about the stop. There was no real reason for concern. The cocaine—hidden in the door panels and packed in locked suitcases—wasn't visible, and Haney wasn't black. And Haney didn't tell him that police in Texas don't need search warrants when they make their traffic stops with drug dogs.

Owens told Haney he would meet him at Haney's motel.

The two would return to downtown Atlanta with the cocaine. They would deliver fifty-two kilos to an Atlanta dealer that night.

Less than a half-hour later, Owens arrived. He told Haney he would take the smaller suitcase with him in the cab that was waiting outside. Haney was to follow in his car with the larger suitcases. When he got to the Mariott Marquis with its stone lions out front and its elevators of mirrored glass, Haney was to leave the car with the valet and bring the larger suitcase to Owens's sixth-floor room. Fifty-two kilos of cocaine were to stay in Atlanta for later distribution on the streets. The remainder was to go to Detroit.

It was after ten o'clock when Haney and Owens walked out to the motel parking lot. Haney opened the trunk of the Chevy. As Owens lifted out the smaller suitcase, fifteen federal drug agents and law enforcement officers, guns drawn, scrambled shouting to the car. Owens was thrown to the ground. An agent placed a gun to his head. "You're looking at spending the rest of your life in prison," said a voice behind the gun. "Is it worth it?"

"No," Owens breathed.

"If you come up to the motel room," the voice replied, "we can talk."

Minutes later, in Haney's suburban motel room, Owens agreed to cooperate. He would lead federal agents to Dana Gold and to Gold's Atlanta connection.

Shortly before midnight, he called Gold in Los Angeles. Gold was frantic. In spite of a mercurial temper, Gold had never shouted at Owens before. But that night, he became enraged. Owens and Haney weren't following his orders. Why had Haney rented a motel room so far from the heart of the city? What about the midnight meeting Gold had scheduled to transfer the cocaine?

Owens was contrite. He was also a good actor. Haney, he explained, didn't understand that he was supposed to rent a room downtown. Now they were lost, marooned at a motel in the boondocks. There was no way he could make the midnight meeting. It would have to be rescheduled.

"Is everything okay?" Gold suspiciously demanded.

"Yes," Owens answered, even though it wasn't.

Gold chose to believe him and quickly issued new orders. He would reschedule the midnight meeting with his client, an Atlanta drug dealer whose name, Gold said, was Billy. At 1 a.m., Owens would leave the Mariott Marquis carrying two suitcases. Billy would meet him at the entrance and drive him to another hotel where they would complete the drug transaction.

Owens didn't know it, but the name Billy was merely a convenience. Gold didn't know whether his client or a member of the drug dealer's Atlanta organization would actually handle the transaction. No matter who met Owens, he would introduce himself as Billy. And Owens would give him the suitcases with no further questions asked. Then Gold hung up the phone, still plagued by the uneasy feeling that something wasn't right.

Owens made the trip back to his hotel downtown handcuffed in the back of a federal drug agent's Mercedes. Another D.E.A. agent drove Haney's Chevy downtown and parked it in a lot three blocks from the hotel. Federal agents gave Owens instructions on how to find the lot in the dark amid Atlanta's maze of skyscrapers and one-way streets. Then they began to watch the lot.

Back at the hotel, other agents fitted Owens with a tiny transmitter. At 1 a.m., without the suitcases, Owens began waiting at the hotel's front entrance. At 1:20 a.m., a new charcoal Acura Legend pulled into the hotel drive. The driver, a well-dressed black man, was talking on a cellular phone. He told Owens his name was Billy, and he had Dana Gold on the line.

Drug agents couldn't believe their luck. "Billy" was a suspected cocaine trafficker named Anthony "Al" Brown. For more than a year, federal drug agents had heard rumors that Brown was a major Atlanta dealer. Two men in federal custody had identified Brown as a dealer. But drug agents had never been able to catch him—until now.

When Brown picked up Owens at the hotel's front entrance, he had already circled the block, talking to Gold as he did so.

"Is he short?" Brown demanded as he spotted Owens.

"Yes," Gold replied as Owens approached the car.

But as soon as Brown told Gold that Owens wasn't carrying the suitcases of cocaine, the California drug dealer demanded, "Let me speak to Glenn."

"What the hell is going on?" he shouted. "Where are the suitcases? What the hell are you doing? Is everything okay?"

As the conversation dissolved into a string of epithets and shouted accusations, Owens told Gold, "I'm doing this the way I need to because I think somebody is watching."

At that point, Brown reclaimed the phone. "Let me see what's going on," he told Gold, "and I'll call you back." As Brown pulled away from the Mariott Marquis, Gold hung up, certain now he was facing disaster as another drug deal dissolved.

Federal agents had told Owens to direct his contact to the lot where the Chevy was parked. The suitcases, containing a kilo of cocaine, were in the trunk. But Owens didn't know Atlanta, nor had he parked the car. Confused, he and Brown circled the blocks near the hotel twice before they found the lot. Brown pulled in next to Haney's Chevy Lumina.

"What do you want to do?" Owens asked.

"Why don't you drive around the corner and follow me," Brown said. He paused. "Never mind. We'll just do it right here."

Owens slid out of the Legend and opened the Chevy's trunk. Brown opened the trunk of his own car. In a car less than a hundred feet away, D.E.A. Special Agent Jeff Dalman spoke low into his radio. "Take them down," he said.

As agents' cars roared into the dimly lit downtown lot, Owens began to run. Brown stood his ground, shouting at the officers who cuffed him, "I'm not doing anything wrong."

"Then what are you doing here at one-thirty in the morning?" Dalman asked.

"I gave this dude a ride to his car," Brown responded.

"What's his name?"

"Man, I don't know. I just gave him a ride."

"Why is your trunk open?"

"My C.D.'s broke. I was going to fix it."

"But you were talking on the phone?"

"I was talking on the phone with friends."

"So," Dalman paused. "What about all this money in the trunk?"

The money, Brown said, belonged to him—almost fifty thousand dollars in a blue canvas bag. He was a gambler, he explained, and he'd had a lucky run.

"What type of gambling?" the drug agent persisted. "Who were you gambling with?"

Unable or unwilling to bluff, Brown stonily refused to answer. There was no explanation really for being in a downtown lot long after midnight with more than fifty thousand dollars in cash. The streets at that hour were sweaty but deserted, empty except for criminals and the homeless who had nowhere else to go.

When Brown was arrested, he was carrying $1,700 in cash, a digital pager, and a Georgia driver's license in the name of Alfred Robert Brown, an alias. Inside the Legend, drug agents found weekly reports of Diamonds and Pearls, the Atlanta nightclub frequented by some of the nation's celebrity athletes and by the city's politicians.

There was also a business card for an Atlanta corporation called Peachtree Entertainment, Inc. The company's attorney was Fred Tokars.

Eleven

"Just Do It"

ARROGANCE WAS THE ONLY REAL EXPLANATION FOR AL Brown's careless decision to meet with a cocaine mule he had never met in the heart of downtown Atlanta and place a delivery of narcotics in the trunk of his own sleek luxury car.

There were few other reasons he would fail to secure fifty thousand dollars stashed in a gym bag in his trunk or secure his nightclub's business records and his gun. But by August 1992, Brown had sold drugs in Atlanta for five years with impunity, set up a supply route from Atlanta to Chattanooga and Detroit through which he funneled as much as two hundred pounds of cocaine a week, and laundered his illegal millions through the city's flashiest and most desirable nightclub.

In truth, Al Brown's ill-gotten millions—and his willingness to spend it like a spoiled child—had only made him a sought-after VIP since that night in 1989 when he had easily strutted into Dominique's. A casual hundred-dollar tip and a promise to buy a magnum of champagne won him a celebrity seat when the fashionable dress code that he flaunted should have earned him only an ignominious exit. If those who now greeted Brown each night at Diamonds knew where his money came from, they didn't care, or worse, afforded him even greater admiration and respect.

It had all been much too easy for a man whose currency was poison. So, it is no surprise that Brown told the federal

drug agents who had arrested him that he was the owner of
Diamonds, supremely confident that the club's cachet gave
him an elevated status, immunity, and respect. Instead,
Brown's almost casual admission that night revealed Diamonds and Pearls as an illegitimate enterprise built on drugs
and shored up with deceit. As such, the club and all its assets
were subject to seizure by the federal government. As federal
agents intensified their scrutiny of Brown and his associates,
the club's financial facade of legitimacy began falling away.
And Fred Tokars, the architect of the business venture that
was Diamonds and Pearls, became suspect as a knowing col-
laborator.

Assistant U.S. Attorney Janis Gordon told Fred as much
during a detention hearing where Brown asked for but was
denied release on bail. Immediately after his arrest, Brown
had retained the lawyer to defend him.

By then, Gordon had initiated a full-scale grand jury investigation. Brown had reversed himself and now denied that
he was anything other than a club employee. His business
associates, notably James Mason and his lawyer, insisted he
was merely a doorman with an exalted sense of importance.
Fred even obtained an affidavit from one of the club managers
swearing that Brown had no financial stake in Diamonds and
Pearls. And when Brown first appeared in federal court after
the drug arrest, Fred was by his side.

The attorney's sharp, whiny arrogance as he questioned a
federal drug agent under oath may have been simply part of
his style as a trial lawyer. It may also have disguised the first
raw whirrings of panic.

After the detention hearing, the assistant U.S. attorney approached Fred with a problem. Gordon told him she had
learned Fred was responsible for incorporating the club's
holding company, Diamonds, Inc. The club was now under
investigation as a repository for Brown's drug money, she
told him bluntly. In fact, Fred faced a possible conflict of
interest if he continued to defend the drug dealer.

"If we find any monkey business or hocus-pocus, and the
government decides to seize the nightclub, you may become
a prosecution witness," she said. Under oath, Fred would be
asked to explain how Diamonds and Pearls operated and what

he had been told by its owners about the club's financial underpinnings.

"I don't know if, at this point, there is any funny business relating to the club, but we are looking at it as a possible asset that has been purchased with drug money," she said. "I'm not asking you to recuse yourself at this time. I'm just letting you know I'm aware that you have a possible conflict."

If Fred's apparent conflict proved genuine, she said ominously, "We'll discuss it in the future." It was a polite way of saying the whole thing stank like bad fish in a barrel. But, Gordon added cheerfully, she was always willing to consider a deal if Brown were to tell her where he was buying his cocaine.

For more than a week, Gordon heard nothing from Fred as the federal investigation of Brown and Diamonds and Pearls intensified. Three days after the detention hearing, Mason was subpoenaed and ordered to turn over all of the nightclub's business records to the grand jury. Federal drug agents began questioning him about Diamonds operations, asking pointed questions about how the club was financed and grilling Mason about his own financial status.

The arrest of the kingpin of Diamonds rattled Mason. In an increasingly precarious situation, he did two things. He lied. Then he called Fred Tokars.

But Fred had taken Gordon's warning to heart. By the time Mason was ordered to appear before the grand jury, Fred was scrambling to sidestep Mason and disassociate himself from Brown. He steered Mason to another attorney, Howard Weintraub—the same attorney he had threatened to sue when Weintraub complained about Eddie Lawrence. Within a week, Fred also notified Gordon that Al Brown had fired him as counsel when he suggested—as he usually did—that Brown plead guilty, become a government informant, and testify against everyone he knew who was associated with the drug trade. Fred's recommendation to plead was loaded with self-interest. If Brown were to plead guilty, the grand jury probe into Diamonds would die, the "funny business" associated with the club's creation would simply become irrelevant, and

Fred could easily sidestep the scrutiny of a federal investigation.

Brown's refusal surely left him shaken. For by then, the attorney knew that Brown would probably do time, Mason was a target of the grand jury, Diamonds and Pearls was clearly forfeit, and his own tainted role was surfacing in documents seized by federal agents.

Meanwhile, Detroit police were conducting an investigation of their own that threatened to draw Al Brown and his associates at Diamonds into its tangled loop. Just two weeks earlier, at 3 a.m. on July 25, 1992, Julius Cline—Fred's client, his associate, and one-time business partner—had been gunned down in front of his mother's Detroit home. It was the anniversary of drug dealer Donte Snowdon's death—the murder that had forced Cline to flee to Atlanta in 1986. Cline's killer was proficient. He pumped five bullets into Cline—one in the leg that disabled him, one in the chest, and three in Cline's skull, including a final execution bullet that was fired into Cline's head at close range. The killer left no fingerprints on the .357 Magnum he discarded in a nearby alley. That gun had been purchased in Dalton, Georgia, ninety miles north of Atlanta.

There were other reasons besides Snowdon's death that could have led to Cline's execution two weeks before Al Brown was arrested. A month before he was murdered, Cline had quietly approached Detroit police, hoping to make a deal that would resolve the murder warrant still outstanding against him. When he did so, not only was he buying cocaine from Brown, who was also distributing the illegal drug in Detroit. He was also buying heroin from some of James Mason's Nigerian friends. He owed money to Brown, who was increasingly suspicious of him as a competitor. Mason owed him nearly three hundred thousand dollars, which, as usual, he had no way to pay. And there was the ominous promise Fred had made to Mason regarding Cline, "It will all be taken care of."

But even as Fred was being sucked into the vortices of two independent criminal investigations, he was also facing more civil litigation.

When Zazu's—the Buckhead piano bar that Cline and Ma-

son had opened in 1990—became mired in debt, Mason and
Cline had simply walked away, leaving Fred to tell the club's
former owners that the promissory note Mason and Cline had
signed on behalf of the holding company, Atlanta House
Clubs, was worthless. Neither Atlanta House Clubs, Mason,
nor Cline had cash or assets, except for the club itself, Fred
told the attorneys representing Zazu's former owners.

That misrepresentation might have been sustained had Fred
not made a simple legal error similar to the one that had cost
Cline the Parrot. When Mason eagerly agreed to become
Brown's front man in Diamonds, Fred applied for the liquor
license through Atlanta House Clubs rather than a new corporation that would have insulated Cline and Mason from
their earlier debts.

The legal notice announcing the liquor license application
signaled Zazu's attorney, Patrick McCreary, that Atlanta
House Clubs did have assets, money to purchase and refurbish
Diamonds and Pearls. By the time that Cline was gunned
down in Detroit, McCreary was unwilling to trust Fred's word
that Atlanta House Clubs had no money. He had demanded
to review all of the corporation's business records, corporate
tax returns, liquor and business licenses, bent on rooting out
the deception that had left his clients with the hollow shell of
a defunct nightclub. Mason and Tokars ignored the request.
As Diamonds and Pearls attracted favorable press notices and
record crowds, McCreary grew more skeptical of Fred's assurances that Atlanta House Clubs was both broke and defunct. The day the federal grand jury subpoenaed Mason,
McCreary fired off a letter to Fred saying that since Mason
was balking at providing the documents he'd requested, he
saw no solution but to sue.

McCreary's threat was one more urgent hole in Fred's increasingly leaky legal dike. A civil suit might prove rich fodder for the federal grand jury already probing the corporate
heart of Diamonds and the federal agents who were watching
Mason with growing suspicion. It would reveal that there
were no corporate tax returns because Mason and his business
partners had simply never filed them. It would also amplify
Fred's own role in the financial operation of the trendy, elegant nightclub.

Moreover, such a suit would illuminate an even earlier association with Mason and a drug dealer who had just been executed in Detroit at a time when Fred was seeking to minimize the alliances with criminals he had so diligently forged. If the attorney's actions became suspect, federal investigators could begin analyzing Fred's own finances. In doing so, they might uncover the intricate string of Caribbean corporations and bank accounts Fred had so craftily woven.

As if Brown's arrest and the pending civil suit weren't enough to send a seismic shiver through the financial ground on which Fred stood, he learned in August that his investments in Eddie Lawrence and the interlocking companies he had created for the elevated house painter had been, at best, ill-conceived.

Lawrence ran the four businesses that comprised Eddie Lawrence Industries with an appalling lack of obligation to his clientele. His business practices were similarly cavalier.

"Eddie wanted to go into business today at 9 a.m., and by tomorrow at five he wanted to be a millionaire and never work hard at it," said Fred's accountant, Marian Refert. "The only thing I ever saw Mr. Lawrence work hard at was trying to make time with the ladies."

His management skills were woeful, his staff erratic. He would hire a construction crew only to fire them three weeks later. During his first six months in operation, he hired four office managers and five receptionists, including two exotic dancers he met while foraging for drug dealers in Atlanta's nightclubs.

Part of the reason for the constant turnover in staff was Lawrence's decision to pay them with cashier's checks rather than weekly payroll checks in what one loan processor for Lawrence's subsidiary, Southwest Mortgage, called "a strange arrangement." Eddie always insisted on handling all the company's cash receipts personally.

In fact, Eddie was stealing money. Whenever Southwest Mortgage financed a home improvement or construction loan, a larger finance company that supplied the actual cash would send a check to Eddie. Rather than use the money as it was intended—to hire a crew and buy the supplies needed to perform the job—Eddie would simply pocket it. His customers soon found themselves paying installments on loans for work that was paid for but never completed. Moreover, Lawrence would hire subcontractors or buy building supplies on credit and then neglect to pay the bills.

One loan processor who quit was never paid her final week's salary. When she confronted Eddie, he informed her curtly, "You'll have to take that up with Fred. He's the only one who can pay you. I don't have any money."

By August 1992, Eddie Lawrence Industries was fielding increasingly hostile telephone calls from customers complaining that Lawrence owed them money. Eddie never responded to those calls, telling his staff simply, "I'll handle it," as he breezed through the office. As the phone calls grew more angry, including one from a caller who threatened to bomb the office, Eddie's staff began urging him please to resolve the complaints.

"This is my business, and I'll do what I want to do," Eddie responded, "and I don't have to answer to you."

As the complaints intensified, Eddie simply stayed away. Instead, he poured his energies and Fred's cash into Club Eddie, a gimcrack nightclub that was Eddie's pathetic attempt to make a name for himself and become, like James Mason, a major player on Atlanta's entertainment circuit.

From the beginning of Fred's odd partnership with Lawrence, Fred's accountant had been sending alarming signals that Eddie's accounting practices were suspect. Lawrence repeatedly refused to let her see company checkbooks, bank statements, or company books he had agreed to keep. Instead, he bounced checks, or brought the accountant bills for payment. Yet, she never saw any accounts or checks that reflected company revenues.

"Eddie brought the bills," she said, "but he never brought the money."

Refert complained bitterly to Fred, who was scrupulous about paying his own bills. Yet the attorney demonstrated a remarkable tolerance for Eddie's monetary excesses. He reassured Refert on numerous occasions that he had talked with his business partner and that Eddie was going to show her the books. But Eddie never did. By August 1992, creditors were calling Fred to collect on Eddie's debts, Lawrence Industries was in a shambles, and Eddie owed the penurious attorney seventy thousand dollars.

Sara Tokars unknowingly strayed into the vortex of a rising whirlwind of criminal investigations, civil litigation, and financial ineptitude reeling around her husband.

Three years had passed since she had hired a private detective to follow her husband. Three years had passed since she had surreptitiously copied a sheaf of documents secreted in her husband's safe and entrusted them to her younger sister for safekeeping. Yet, divorce remained Sara's private mantra. Restless, unhappy, and frightened, she had furtive, desperate conversations with her sisters and a precious few close friends. But always, the certainties that locked her into a harsh marriage wheeled like harpies in her thoughts. She had no money. She had no job. She had two small sons. Her husband was a divorce attorney and a judge. He had threatened her. If she tried to divorce him, he would surely win custody, and she would never see her sons again.

Her mistake had been in thinking that Fred would ever let her go, although the logic behind that wistful assumption was plain. The love and admiration that drew Sara to Fred when she was a young divorcee had long been wrung from the marriage. The sense of security she had sought so desperately when she married had metamorphosed into fear. He had little to do with the children and less to do with her, preferring the company of business partners and clients whom Sara regarded as criminals and women she suspected were whores.

Yet he fought her every suggestion that they end the sad charade, as if he took some perverse pride in humiliating Sara by doing as he pleased despite his wedding vows, even as he harped upon her failures as a wife.

Fred's threats certainly sounded credible. By 1992, he was contributing heavily to political races in Atlanta, both in his name and Sara's. He made donations and loans totaling more than seven thousand dollars to the campaigns of U.S. State Supreme Court Justice Leah Sears, Fulton County Sheriff Jackie Barrett, and Fulton County Solicitor General Paul Howard, all of whom waged successful campaigns.

Tokars political contacts would probably not have interfered if his wife had sued for a divorce. But Sara had no way of knowing whether her husband's threats were real or simply a sinister bluff.

Over time, the women who knew Sara most intimately saw their strong, burnished sister and cousin slowly sink under the weight of her husband's petty cruelties, intimidation, and disdain into a mire of insecurity, indecision, and abject helplessness.

Plagued by nagging fears about her husband's clientele, Sara confided to a neighbor and her sister that she had urged her husband to install a home alarm system because she was alone at night so often with her sons. But every request became a confrontation that gradually sapped her will. Sara was ever the supplicant, her husband the final authority. As Fred's nagging questions, implicit challenges, and belittling remarks took their dreary toll on Sara, the most basic chores became insurmountable.

Her marriage "is just awful, terrible," she would confide to her younger sister, Karen, who called her almost daily.

"Oh, Mary," she would tell her cousin whenever she called. "Nothing's changed."

By 1992, fatigued by a string of betrayals but unable to find a way to dissolve her marriage without risking her sons, Sara seemingly resigned herself to a loveless marriage with a manipulative spouse.

"She kept thinking that even though he's not around much, and usually when he is around he's drunk and taking pills, kids do need a father," Karen said. "So she thought that even though he was a terrible father, it was probably better than no father at all because the kids did have an attachment to him."

Sara resolved to live through her boys and try to recreate the lingering warmth of her own childhood for them.

"Sara, how can you go so long without sex?" Karen asked her one day. "Doesn't it bother you?"

"No, I just don't think about it," Sara answered. "I just think about the kids and after a while you kind of forget about it."

But if sex were, indeed, forgotten, Sara's hunger for divorce lingered like scent as she laced her days with children.

Her job as a volunteer in her sons' classes at St. Jude was unsalaried, but it drew her out of the house, reminded her of the woman she once had been, and offered her reflection in more forgiving mirrors than her husband's. Her ebullient nature reasserted itself, and, slowly, a certain independence began to surface like small green shoots on a wind-blistered plain.

Although her husband was a Democrat with political ambitions who had taken the stage with Michael Dukakis during the 1988 Democratic Convention in Atlanta, Sara acquired a "George Bush for President" bumper sticker for display on the rear bumper of her Toyota 4-Runner. She also began seeking, among her friends and former contacts, a job that would generate an income.

Sara had talked with her husband about one idea—establishing hair salons for children in grocery stores that would offer inexpensive haircuts while their mothers shopped. Sara even had a name for the business, Fun Cuts.

She had also scheduled an appointment with Fred to ask for money to buy clothes suitable for an interview and a professional job.

"You have to schedule an appointment?" her friend Tricia Loesel said incredulously.

"We don't talk unless it's an emergency," Sara answered.

But Fred, who had angrily insisted she work after Ricky's birth, now expressed little enthusiasm unless she worked for him. A paying job could mean only one thing—Sara was seeking a way to pay for a divorce.

By then, Fred had also let his wife know that he knew about her credit cards, although she hid the bills in a briefcase in her car, and that she owed about five thousand dollars. He would settle her debts, he said, if she would come to work for him. At his office, she could help him bill his clients and collect on the outstanding accounts. What he didn't say was that if Sara worked for him, not only would he save money he would otherwise have paid a bookkeeper, he could also keep close watch on his increasingly independent wife.

Although she had confided to her younger sister that she didn't want to work for Fred, Sara had reasons other than money to accept. Terrified that Fred might keep his promises to take her sons away if she were to leave him, Sara had already begun a deliberate hunt for information she could use against her husband if she left him—anything she could use to seal her right to custody of the boys. It was that desperate quest and her willingness to contemplate divorce that made Sara, finally, someone to be reckoned with in the drug-dusted world her husband had embraced. A divorce and a bitter custody fight—with the requisite examination of Tokars's assets—would have brought to light his evasions, his relationships with drug dealers, the web of hollow Caribbean corporations and bank accounts under assumed names he had woven with such care. Such revelations would have marked Fred as something more than just a corporate lawyer for the grand jury investigating Diamonds and Pearls. They would have identified him as a willing player in a criminal conspiracy.

Sometime that September, Sara found what she was looking for. Working for her husband collecting payments on open accounts gave Sara unprecedented access to his business finances and, for the first time in their marriage, her first glimpse of Fred's substantial income. Within days, she had collected more than sixty thousand dollars in outstanding bills.

At a political fund-raiser that fall, Fred spotted Sara's cousin, Mary Taylor, who, despite her suspicions was always gracious because, she said, "He seemed to be pleased she was associating with me. Whenever I would compliment her, he would give her money."

"I'm so glad you and Sara are such good friends," the lawyer said effusively as he praised Sara for her skill at collecting his outstanding fees. "No matter what she does, she does it better than anyone else. I really need her in my office."

Taylor was charming, but wary. She didn't want Sara working for Fred any more than Sara did. "I know how you feel," she demurred. "But all of us were raised to be wives and mothers. That's what we live for. You will be glad when you see what kind of young men the boys become."

It was during Sara's temporary stint at her husband's office, that she almost certainly learned about the federal grand jury investigation that was sweeping Fred's business partners and clients into its net. Federal drug agents and I.R.S. investigators were trawling through Diamonds with search warrants seeking business records that would implicate its partners as illicit launderers of drug money. Federal agents were serving subpoenas almost daily. There were panicky calls from Mason, who had been ordered to appear before the grand jury after lying to federal agents. There were hushed or hurried conversations with colleagues as Fred sought to distance himself from clients with whom he had become just a little too familiar.

How much Sara absorbed as she sat quietly at a desk culling through her husband's business accounts and files remains unclear. She was a smart and by then desperate woman with a nearly forgotten business savvy that had helped make the nightclubs she once marketed among the city's best. But somewhere amid the welter of legal files, balance sheets, and ledgers Sara found evidence that she believed would tarnish her husband enough to stop any judge from taking her boys away.

Giddy with relief and a sudden, urgent hope, Sara confided in her neighbor Sara Suttler, "I've got the goods on Fred."

Suttler, an older woman, had walked to the Tokars house to retrieve her young grandson. A playmate of Sara's boys, he spent several afternoons a week happily ensconced at the Tokars house. At Sara's urging, Suttler always came before 5 p.m. Sara wanted no visitors when her husband was at home. But the boys' companionship drew the two women together, and, over time, Sara Suttler became her younger neighbor's confidant. She knew her young friend's marriage had degenerated into a restless misery. She knew Sara Tokars hated her husband but was afraid to leave him.

But on this particular September day, Sara was elated. "I have good news for you," she bubbled. "I can divorce Fred now because I have the goods on him, and he won't get my boys."

"Great!" Suttler answered. "What is it?"

"I've found records of tax evasion," Sara confided. "I've given the documents to a private detective. We're turning them over to the proper authorities. Now I can divorce him and take my boys.''

Early that beleaguered August, Fred met Eddie Lawrence in the dark parking lot by the worn strip mall that housed Club Eddie's. As they talked, the attorney asked with studied casualness, ''Eddie would you kill somebody?''

''It depends on the situation,'' Eddie answered. ''I mean, if my life is threatened, then yes, I would kill somebody. But I'm just not going to walk up and shoot somebody and kill them for no reason.''

''Well, I want to have my partner killed,'' the attorney said. ''It's worth a million dollars. Think about it.''

At the time, Fred didn't identify his partner by name. Eddie was somewhat puzzled. He assumed Fred and Howard Weintraub were partners because they shared an office, and Fred frequently referred to Weintraub as ''my partner.'' But he also knew that Fred and Emily Sherwinter were business associates. He had seen the aggressive ad campaign that had plastered their names on billboards around town. And he knew that Fred was usually less than complimentary of his former law school classmate, except for an occasional crude observation about her physical attributes. Why would he want to kill them? Eddie didn't ask. It didn't occur to him at the time that Fred might have been referring to his wife.

The attorney was more blunt with a Jamaican stripper from Club Nikki who had infatuated Lawrence and worked as a receptionist for Lawrence Industries. Her name was Dion Fearon. Her stage name was Jeda. She had heard Lawrence talk about Fred and contacted the lawyer when she decided to open a business with friends. He had incorporated her new firm in his office and then had kissed her deeply on the lips.

''Maybe we can get together some time,'' he had leered.

By September, Fred was waiving the dancer's legal fees, and Fearon was referring clients to him. She got off the dance floor at 4 a.m., and Fred would call her at 6 a.m. to talk.

''I always knew we would end up somewhere,'' she said.

On September ninth, Fred slipped Fearon eight hundred dollars in an envelope, and arranged a tryst at the Ritz-Carlton near his downtown office.

Fred arrived with beer in his briefcase. He had been drinking. He was light-headed, prone to stumbling, and slurring his words. He was visibly angry with Sara.

She was nosy, he complained—always poking around, going through his things, rifling his personal papers, "getting into my business." He mentioned that Sara had been snooping in his safe.

"She knows too much," he told the stripper. "I'm going to have to have her taken care of."

Eddie would do it, he said. Eddie owed him. And he owned Eddie. "He owes me money," the lawyer told the dancer. "He's going to take care of my problem."

Eddie was also under orders to burglarize the house, Fred confided, so that he could then file an inflated insurance claim.

"There are a lot of ways to make money," he explained to his date. "Insurance is a really good way of doing that."

Before leaving the hotel that night, Fred also talked to Fearon about the murder of Julius Cline. "My friends in New York were involved in Julius Cline's murder," he told her. "Cline was killed because he wouldn't sell his interest in the Parrot."

Meanwhile, Eddie had simply shrugged away his conversation with the lawyer and Fred's query as to whether he might be willing to kill. But within weeks, the attorney broached the subject again while the two were lunching at a downtown restaurant as easily as he discussed sports or the weather. He wanted his partner murdered. If Eddie had a response, he didn't remember it.

But Fred continued to raise the subject whenever they ate lunch or dinner at the fern bars and chain restaurants around Atlanta. Murder for money. A million dollars. Think about it. Eddie indulged his mentor. There was no harm in talking. Conversation wasn't a crime.

Eddie didn't understand that the attorney who lavished money on him and his new businesses was calling in the chits. Fred had made his decision. Eddie would be his hit man. Some financial adjustments were needed before he realized it.

On September ninth, Fred sued Eddie and Lawrence Industries for sixty-five thousand dollars. He explained to Eddie why he did it. He could deduct the money from his tax returns as a bad investment. At the same time, he could insulate the company's assets from irate customers threatening to sue Eddie for fraud and breach of contract. If Fred won a judgment against Lawrence Industries, in which he still held a majority interest, he would be first among the creditors. No one else would collect any compensation from Eddie's thievery. A week later, on September fourteenth, Fred sued Eddie a second time for more than seventy thousand dollars. Eddie never appeared in court or hired an attorney to defend him. When Fred advised him to sign the consent judgment instead of challenging the debt, Eddie willingly did so. He thought he was protecting Lawrence Industries from his other creditors. He didn't need an attorney to represent him. Fred was his attorney.

It was fraud, one that Fred compounded by lending Eddie another five thousand dollars within a week of filing the first suit. But more than that, it was a sinister manipulation that left Eddie deeply and irrevocably in debt. That month, Fred terminated Eddie's line of credit at a local building supply company, removed Eddie as a cosigner on company checks and bank accounts, and replaced him with accountant Marian Refert.

The next time the attorney met his protégé for lunch, Eddie was unwittingly teetering on the edge of a financial chasm. Fred was matter of fact, as if he were finalizing a business deal.

"I want to kill my wife," he said.

Lawrence was stunned. "Why?"

"She's going to divorce me," Fred answered curtly. "She's going to take everything I have, and I've worked too hard. I'm not going to let that happen. She's got to die. That's the only way I see out of it."

Whatever Sara had found had stripped her husband of his arrogant assurance that he could secure custody of their children. "I'll be living in an apartment on Buford Highway," among the city's immigrants and illegal foreign nationals, he spat.

"If you do it," he promised Eddie, "I'll pay you twenty-five thousand dollars." The attorney may have noticed Eddie's incredulous silence as he raised the specter of Eddie's vast debts. Sara's life was also insured for nearly $2 million,

Fred explained. If Eddie were to kill Sara, he was prepared to reinvest $1 million in Eddie Lawrence Industries and sign over his majority interest to Eddie as payment. He had bought the policies years earlier. No one would suspect.

Eddie knew one thing. He wasn't going to do it.

A week later, the two met again for lunch. This time Fred was even more insistent. Sara intended to divorce him. She would expose him, lay waste to his finances, take everything he had worked for, everything he owned.

"Let her have it," Lawrence counseled. "The house, the money in the bank, let her have it. You can always get it back."

"No!" The attorney's rage was plain. "I worked too hard. I went to school at night. She never did anything. All she ever did was spend my money. I'm not going to give it to her. I'll kill her first."

Killing Sara became her husband's furious obsession. In a succession of lunch and dinner meetings, Fred berated and cajoled Eddie with a vituperative litany of Sara's sins. If his financial empire was tumbling, if a grand jury had inadvertently snagged him in its net, he was the victim, and, somehow, Sara was to blame.

"What about the kids?" Lawrence asked during yet another conversation that Fred had turned to Sara's death.

"They'll be all right," Fred answered sharply. "They're young. They'll get over it."

True to form, Lawrence dallied. He procrastinated. He demurred.

"I hope this is what you want, because once it's done, it ain't like you can undo it," Eddie warned his mentor.

"I just want it done. She isn't going to get everything I have. She's pressuring me. I want her dead."

Fred's first plan should have warned Eddie of the contempt in which the attorney really held him. The young black man was so clearly the dupe. Fred would lure Sara to his downtown office, then taunt her into a violent argument. Hearing voices raised in anger, Lawrence would barge in and, while defending Fred, would shoot her.

"I'll tell the police she was going to kill me, that you saved my life by killing her first," Fred promised eagerly. He was, after all, a judge. He had lots of influential friends in high places. He would cover for Lawrence. No charges would ever be filed.

By then, the attorney was carrying a .38-caliber, snub-nose revolver tucked in the back of his pants. "Sara's going to have me killed," he warned. But Lawrence didn't bite. His lawyer might be a judge, but Eddie didn't believe Fred could successfully cover for a young black man who would shoot his wife after entering an office peopled with hundreds of whites. "I just didn't think it would work," he said. "I know in doing murder, if I was going to attempt to do it, I was going to try to do it and get away with it."

Yet Eddie saw nothing cynical or sinister in Fred's suggestion. It didn't occur to him that Fred, a former county prosecutor, might finger him as the killer, and point to his substantial civil judgments against Lawrence as an ample motive for revenge. It didn't dawn on Eddie that he was just a patsy.

By early October, Fred had devised a second plan. He wanted Sara killed at the house, as if she had surprised a burglar. But Lawrence still balked. He might justify his illegal drug deals because almost everyone he knew sold crack to get by. He might excuse his thefts as bad business with difficult, demanding clients, and shrug off his willingness to counterfeit by saying he was simply helping a friend. But he didn't have the stomach to be a killer.

But Fred read Eddie's reluctance as defiance, and it enraged him. He wanted Sara dead, and he expected Eddie to kill her. Otherwise, he explained coldly, he would cut Lawrence off like a recalcitrant child and strip him of his businesses and his income.

"I don't care how you do it," the attorney warned. "Just do it."

Twelve

Barreling Toward Oblivion

BY THE FALL OF 1992, SARA KNEW WITH A GLASSY CERtainty that her husband simply didn't like her, that he found their marriage to be a distasteful and aggravating obligation. She knew she was, at most, a tolerable convenience—available when he needed a charming, attractive companion by his side at political and social events to which he bought access with generous contributions Sara knew nothing about. She was one more cog in his master wheel, fortifying his image as a man who worked hard for and was dedicated to his family—an image that suited his political ambitions.

It was that image that a divorce from Sara would crack. For Fred was truly the couple's darker half. Sara, with her suburban sensibilities, her open nature, and her devotion to her children, masked her husband's more derelict desires. Her genuineness softened the hard edges of Fred's artifice.

Fred's cold hunger for money also made divorce unthinkable for him. When the couple married, Sara had been the more financially successful, drawing an income nearly twice that of her husband. She had left that career to care for the couple's children while Fred built a successful career as an attorney, an accountant, and a professional consultant. If they divorced, Fred knew he would have to pay for that. The life insurance policies worth $1.75 million that provided him with a sinister security in the event of Sara's death also would dissolve. And although Sara may have fled from any thought that her fate was buried in them, Fred was banking not just financial security but riches on his wife's eventual death.

Sara may have recognized that her husband's desire for money, his reputation, and his political future locked her to him. What she never understood was that reason played no role in Fred's determination to dominate her. Divorce was unthinkable because it stripped him of control. The former cheerleader with the doting family was not going to tell him what to do.

Perhaps that was one reason Fred was so angry when Sara told him in November that she had accepted a job with Jim Killeen. He had wanted her to work, but he wanted her to work for him. Instead, Sara had worked for her husband only long enough to find what she thought she needed to force a divorce. In early November, she called Killeen, who had opened his own restaurant after leaving Dominique's.

"Jim, can you use any help during the Christmas season? I'm looking for some extra Christmas money. I'll help you any way I can."

"Sara, you'd be a big help in helping me book Christmas parties. But the restaurant's still struggling, my funds are limited, and I can't pay you a lot of money, certainly not what you're worth."

"Whatever you can pay me will be fine with me," Sara answered.

But days later, Sara called again. Fred had angrily objected to her decision to work for Killeen, telling her, "It doesn't look good."

Killeen, by then, had divorced a second time. Fred, in fact, had been his attorney and won custody of his son for him. But despite Fred's efforts to usurp Sara's longstanding friendship with Killeen by cultivating him as a sometime business associate and client, Sara and her former employer remained close. Undoubtedly, jealousy contributed to Fred's violent objections. But behind his self-righteous rage was a blunter truth: if you're planning a murder, you are more likely to become a suspect if police believe your wife is having an affair. And, in Fred's mind, that was all Sara's decision to work for Killeen could possibly be.

Depressed and uncertain, Sara called Killeen and apologetically declined the job, even though the restaurateur offered to call Fred "to clear the air and make sure that it was not going to be a problem."

"I think I'll just go to Florida," she said.

After all, it was near Thanksgiving. Florida was home—the one haven that Fred could never bully Sara to forsake. She might travel on pennies, paying for gas with the credit card she hid from her husband or with cash she gleaned from a meager weekly allowance, but on that cornerstone of Sara's life, he could never break her. Eventually, he must have hated her for it—the slip of steel at her core that he could never crack or control. She always defied him, her fear fading in a roadside blur whenever she tumbled southward, believing for that moment only that she was running away for good.

"Karen, I'm going home for Thanksgiving," Sara told her younger sister in Buffalo. No one else in the family could make it, and she didn't want her mother and father to spend Thanksgiving alone.

But Sara was chagrined. "It doesn't look too good that I'm going to be able to go home again for Christmas. You know I have to fight Fred tooth and nail every time I go to Florida. Since we're going down at Thanksgiving, there's no way I'm going to be able to go down again at Christmas."

"Oh, Sara. That's terrible," Karen replied. "What are we going to do?"

"I don't know. I'll really work on Fred. Maybe I can get him to agree to a day or two."

Days later, she called again. "Karen, I can go home at Christmas! I can't believe it. I'm so shocked. Fred didn't even put up one fight about it. He said, 'Sure, you can go home at Christmas. And stay in a hotel.' "

It was strange, the two sisters agreed, that Fred would agree to a second vacation in Florida less than a month after the planned Thanksgiving trip "when he usually put up such a stink."

For Fred, it was a cheap and easy promise to make. He had already decided that Sara would be dead by Christmas. He needed only to tighten the financial noose he had looped around Eddie Lawrence, then offer the strangling man a bribe.

Eddie's greed, desperation, and deficit of conscience would insure the outcome the attorney sought.

By then, the federal grand jury investigating Al Brown's drug ring and scrutinizing his associates—among them Sara's husband—unknowingly had sealed Sara's fate. On November ninth, jurors subpoenaed Brown's common-law wife, Vicki Bailey, the mother of his child. At the time, federal prosecutors acknowledged that Bailey probably had no knowledge of any of Brown's criminal activities. They had called her to testify anyway, they said, to obtain information regarding Brown's assets—cars, real estate, guns, jewelry—that might be subject to civil forfeiture. The tactic was a prelude to, among other things, possible charges of tax evasion.

Because Fred had been Brown's attorney and the corporate lawyer for Diamonds and Pearls, federal prosecutors regarded him as, at the very least, a potential witness. By November, the grand jury's investigation had grown so wide that if jurors, or federal prosecutors, had so desired, they could easily have subpoenaed Sara, too.

"As long as Sara lived, she could talk," Assistant U.S. Attorney Buddy Parker would say later. "As long as she could talk, she could describe what she believed."

And in that context, what Sara had to say and what she suspected about her husband would not be dismissed as the fabrications of a vengeful spouse seeking a divorce at any cost, as Ralph Perdomo once had done. This time, her suspicions would be heeded by authorities eager to determine if drug money belonging to Al Brown was being laundered through offshore bank accounts by his lawyer.

Two days after Bailey was subpoenaed, Sara called Karen again. Although she had called to wish her sister a happy birthday, during that conversation Sara confided soberly, "Karen, I have all this new stuff on Fred."

"What is it?" Karen asked.

"I can't tell you now," Sara answered. "I'll tell you at Christmas."

"I didn't press her because she sounded worried," Karen explained later. "She thought the phone was tapped."

Mary Rose Taylor knew nothing of the grand jury's investigation. But instinct and her experience warned her that her cousin's husband was a criminal; the documents in his safe, which Sara had copied three years earlier, were evidence that he was laundering the profits of his white-collar piracies. Her corrosive suspicions made her fear for her cousin. The week before Thanksgiving, as she was preparing to fly to Scotland for the holiday, Mary Taylor called Sara one last time.

"Sara, I just wanted to let you know I'm going to be out of the country for Thanksgiving," Mary apologized. "I wish we could spend it together."

"Oh, Mary, that's okay," Sara answered gaily. "We are all going to go to Bradenton for Thanksgiving."

"Sara," Mary asked cryptically, her worry and affection now evident. "Has anything changed?"

Sara understood the gravity of her cousin's seemingly simple question.

"No," she replied.

"Sara," Mary paused. "Are the documents in a safe place? Are the papers in a safe place?"

"Yes."

"Sara, are you safe?"

Sara laughed. "Oh, Mary," she affectionately chided her cousin. "You worry too much."

Mary Rose Taylor never spoke to her cousin again.

In a dinner meeting that same month, an angry and increasingly impatient Fred Tokars once more confronted Eddie Lawrence. He had issued Sara's death warrant in August, yet she was still alive.

"Why hasn't it been done?" Fred demanded coldly. "I want you to do it. And if you don't, I'll take your business, and I'll leave you with the bills." And in case Eddie didn't believe him, Fred reminded him of the settlements he had signed when Fred had sued him. Those civil judgments, he now informed Eddie, gave him the right to take control of Lawrence Industries and all its subsidiaries. He could, and would, boot Eddie out.

But that didn't have to happen, the attorney soothed the unnerved younger man. If Eddie would just kill Sara, he would pay him twenty-five thousand dollars in cash. Once he collected the insurance from Sara's death, Fred promised he would also invest another $1 million in Eddie's troubled businesses. And he would surrender his majority interest in Lawrence Industries to the younger man.

"What if we're caught?" Eddie asked the lawyer.

"I've got no intention of talking to the police or answering questions about the murder," Fred answered. The lawyer had long bragged that he was tight with the police, a relationship he cultivated during his occasional teaching stints at Georgia's police academies.

"The police are stupid," he insisted, "and the case will blow over. If it doesn't, they won't be able to tie me to the investigation."

"And if they do?" Eddie persisted.

"I'll kill myself," Fred answered.

It seems doubtful that Fred ever intended to pay Eddie the fee he offered, since he promised to pay him only after Sara was dead. In fact, Fred's choice of Lawrence as his hired gun was more than likely a contingency plot to frame Eddie for the murder as a disgruntled business partner who slaughtered Sara for revenge. The scaffolding for such a frame-up was already conveniently in place as long as Lawrence carried out the crime himself. After all, who would believe Eddie if he tried to finger Fred, especially once authorities learned that Fred—the beneficent attorney who had so generously bankrolled the young black man—had finally placed a vice grip on Eddie's financial future? And who would believe that Eddie had killed for no more than an I.O.U. to be collected at some later date? Who would believe that Eddie was a patsy?

And there was the trust for Sara and the boys, which Eddie knew about. Fred's majority shares of the holding company that owned Lawrence Industries were locked in it. Fred had given Eddie the same reason for the trust as he had his brother, Andy—to protect the stock from creditors and him from liability. Because Andy was still the trustee, Sara had no more control over the disposition of that stock than Eddie and little, if any, knowledge of businesses that her husband never discussed. But Fred could, and did, eventually argue that Sara had worked for him. Sara had collected his debts and bills, and Sara had an interest in the companies' financial success and would have strenuously objected to Eddie's cavalier expenditures.

On the surface, at least, Fred had constructed for his business partner an arguable motive for murder.

But Fred misread Eddie. He wasn't a killer. He had no intention of becoming one. He was just a con man looking for an easy dollar, and he saw the opportunity for one more con behind the murder contract Fred had proffered. He would, without Fred's knowledge, recruit a killer from the war zones of Atlanta's public housing projects, a man who lived on a diet of shootings, robberies, and drug deals gone sour; a man willing to kill for a gram of crack, an athletic jacket, or a pair of running shoes. Against the backdrop of the city's violently impoverished public housing projects, the five thousand dollars Eddie offered would seem more than generous and would allow him to skim the remaining balance Fred had promised, which hovered near $1 million. As always, Eddie would corral the cash, without unduly dirtying his hands.

Sometime that November, Eddie Lawrence went looking for a hit man. Never a subtle man, Eddie approached this task with the carelessness that marked all of his endeavors. He started asking around. One of the receptionists in his office, Toozdae Rower, carried a gun, and Eddie had once asked whether she could acquire one for him. This time around, Eddie asked her if she knew anyone willing to pull a trigger for a fee. For five hundred dollars, Toozdae agreed to check around.

She didn't have to go far. Her younger brother, Curtis Rower, was a crack addict who supported his drug habit by running with one of the robbing crews spawned in the city housing projects. He answered to the street name "Cornbread," which is how he was introduced to Eddie, with the assurance that "he'd killed a few people." A broker in stolen guns, he only had a record of smaller crimes, culminating in a car theft for which he was on parole.

Curtis Rower was the most unpredictable of people—a crack addict prone to a desperate paranoia with no moral center and only a marginal I.Q.

He was born in Bankhead Courts, an Atlanta housing project so notorious for crime during his childhood that firefighters, utility crews, and postal workers refused to enter without an armed police escort. Like so many of the impoverished children born in Atlanta, he was the child of drug addicts who was nearly strangled by his own umbilical cord during twenty-two hours of labor.

That violent, oxygen-starved birth left him mildly retarded. It also foreshadowed the lattice of his life. By the time Curtis Rower was one, his parents were blowing marijuana smoke into his face to make the baby high. Discipline skewed early into abuse. His father whipped him for indiscretions that later escalated into crimes, and once left him tied to a tree. His parents often left him with cousins who took the boy with them on the burglary sprees that substituted for a working wage.

By the time he was eleven, Rower was a thief. At first, he stole bicycles. As he grew older, he graduated to cars. By the time he was a teenager, he was addicted to crack and was dealing drugs to support his habit. His main sources of supply were the crackhouses he robbed for drugs and cash.

By the time he turned eighteen, Rower had been arrested twenty times. He was functionally illiterate, his speech a muttered, at times unintelligible, street argot. At the Fulton County Child Treatment Center, where juvenile delinquents were educated, Rower was a troublemaker, easily led and not very bright.

He also was a drifter with no permanent address, staying instead, with his sister, his cousins, or a succession of girlfriends. But like many drug dealers Rower carried a pager, which is how his sister reached him to arrange his first meeting with Eddie.

Eddie picked up Rower in his truck and took him out to talk, in much the same way Fred had always taken him out. Except this time, Eddie was the big man. Eddie was the boss. Eddie was the man with the proposition and the money. That may explain why he boasted to Rower that he was in the Dixie Mafia, and that the southern crime syndicate was recruiting "young brothers with balls."

"How would you be interested in making a quick five thousand dollars?" Eddie asked the younger man.

"Doing what?" Rower was sullen and suspicious.

"Take up a hit."

"What kind of hit?" Rower answered. "What you talking about, a hit?"

"I want this bitch knocked off."

"Damn, cuz," Rower was hesitant. "You're kicking kind of strong, ain't you? Shit, you talking to the wrong one. I don't do no shit like that. You want to buy some guns, I can get you set up where you can buy some guns. But that knock off, I can't help you with that, cuz."

"I'm telling you five thousand, man. Five thousand dollars. Get back with me."

And, Eddie added, "I still want a gun. Call me when you come across one."

Days later, Eddie paged Rower again.

"Can't you come up with no gun?"

"I might know someone," Rower answered. "I can probably get you one for one hundred fifty or something like that."

Eddie was stunned by the price. In Atlanta, stolen guns could be bought on the city's meaner streets and in the projects for as little as thirty-five dollars. "What you got, an Uzi or something?"

"No," Rower said. "But whatever kind of gun I get you, it'll probably be hot cause it will come from a dope truck. You going to have to pay some money for it."

"I'll do that," Eddie agreed.

But Eddie never seemed to have enough cash to pay for the stolen gun he wanted, much less the five thousand dollars he had offered Rower for Sara's murder—a reluctance that left Rower suspicious of Eddie's real intentions. But the two continued to negotiate in front of a growing contingent of Rower's family and friends, who engaged in a running commentary from the sidelines.

Fred would have been horrified if he had known how openly Eddie was soliciting Sara's murder. He had always intended that Sara's murder appear as a random act by an unknown burglar who killed her when she surprised him. Should that ruse fail, Eddie Lawrence would become the perfect dupe. His credibility shot by a history of fraud, his word pitted against that of a former prosecutor who contributed to or ran campaigns for some of the county's more prominent politicians, Eddie's story that he killed Sara at Fred's insistence for the mere promise of money would have simply elicited guffaws.

But Eddie's decision to solicit a hit man without Fred's knowledge, the careless manner in which he did so, and his reliance on the unpredictable, indiscreet conduct of a drug addict salted Fred's carefully constructed scheme with failure.

As Fred squeezed Eddie, the con man pressed Rower to do the deal. Sometime in November, he jammed Rower; Rower's sister, Toozdae; and "Red" Swinger, the father of her three children, into the cab of his pickup and drove them to the Cobb County subdivision where Fred and Sara lived. Swinger, who lived with Toozdae in Carver Homes, a public housing project, had never been to Cobb. "We don't hang out in no white section of town," he said.

But Eddie insisted. "Let me show you the layout," he said. While his passengers drank beer and smoked a little weed, Eddie drove them past the Tokars's home.

"That's where my ex-wife stay at," he told Rower. "You've never seen her."

But his offer was still on the table. He would pay Rower and Swinger to kill the blond white woman who was "standing in the way of a lot of money."

"It has to be done in the house," he said, "and make it look like a burglary. But I can't pay the money up front. I'll pay up after the job is done."

Rower was understandably suspicious of that arrangement. "I want my money," he insisted sullenly. "You own your own business. You can give me half of my money now."

But Eddie didn't have it. Fred hadn't paid him, a matter he didn't mention to Rower. "I'm about to lose my business," he protested. "I need to get her out of the way."

"I don't trust you man," Rower challenged. "You ain't got no money. You keep talking about you want a hit done and all this. Why you can't produce no money? You got the business and all this, but you ain't got no money. There's something wrong. I believe you the police or something."

"Nah," Eddie answered. "I ain't no police. If I had to, I'd do it myself."

"You can't buy no gun. You can't get no gun," Rower continued.

"No," Eddie protested, "I can't do it like that. If you don't trust me, we can do it together."

By then, Swinger had heard all he wanted to hear.

"Red, why you so quiet?" Rower asked as they drove back to Atlanta. "Why you ain't saying nothing? What's up?"

"Man, shit," Swinger said. "I don't do that."

Rower turned to Eddie. "You going to have to do something then, because I ain't going to let you just take me out there."

"Okay," Eddie said. "We'll do it together."

In that pickup pungent with marijuana smoke and beer, the outline of Sara Tokars's murder took shape as Eddie barreled down the interstate away from the white enclaves of suburbia to the city's dingy, rat-infested, bullet-riddled neighborhoods where the foursome were safe from scrutiny.

Back at Carver Homes, as Eddie parked the truck, Swinger pulled Rower aside with a warning.

"Hey, man, you don't even know him. Don't get caught up with him, man. You don't know nothing about him. You don't want to get involved with him. You don't want to get yourself in no trouble like that. You don't know nothing about this man."

"I don't know, man, shit," Rower muttered. "I'm going to do it, you know."

"Man, you don't even know him." Swinger was scared now that he might be implicated in the crime. "I'm going to tell you, you're going to get in trouble, man, messing around like this. You don't know him, man."

And then, there was the money.

"But he say he about to lose his business," Rower patiently explained to Swinger.

"I don't care what he lose. I want him to lose his business," Swinger answered. "I don't know nothing about him. And I don't like him too much."

But Rower was adamant, lured by five thousand dollars— only a fraction of the money that Eddie thought he would collect. "I'm going to do it, man. I'm going to take the hit." He offered Swinger one more chance. "Red, you ain't got to kill nobody, you know, I just want you to go with me. I want you to trash the place and kind of like steal all the jewelry and stuff like that.''

"Man," Swinger replied, "I don't even want to do that."

When they parted company that day, Rower and Lawrence each had a different understanding of whether or how Sara would die. Her murder was incidental to them both. They were more interested in money. Lawrence thought he had hired a hit man without paying him a dime. Rower, swayed by Swinger, had changed his mind about the murder.

"Curtis, I ain't going to kill nobody," Swinger told him after Lawrence had gone. "We ain't got to kill nobody. We just going to try to trick him out of this money."

But whether he intended to kill Sara or simply perpetuate the ruse, Rower still needed a gun.

Swinger, a convicted drug dealer, knew just where to go. Valvickiyor Zinamon, an eighteen-year-old drug dealer known on the streets as Smokey, lived with Swinger's brother. He had acquired a sawed-off shotgun, an evil-looking firearm he insisted he had found lying at a bus stop on Atlanta's West End.

The .410-gauge, single-shot shotgun was chrome and black with the words "Snake Charmer" etched into the trigger plate. It had a pistol grip and an eleven-inch barrel that made it easily concealable under a coat or jacket. It was a killer's weapon, a shotgun masquerading as a pistol, and one of the few firearms in the country that is illegal to own without a federal license backed up by a criminal background check.

This particular shotgun had a hair trigger and a broken stock that had been poorly mended with duct tape. Smokey had broken the butt against the side of another man's head.

"We gonna rob some dope boys," Swinger lied when he first inquired about the shotgun. "It's gonna be a sweet lick"—a robbery worth five thousand dollars.

Zinamon wasn't surprised. In the Atlanta neighborhoods where he lived or plied his trade, armed robbery was a way of life, a lucrative sideline both of drug dealers and their clientele. As long as they targeted drug dealers, the robbing crews operated with virtual impunity. Nobody who made their living breaking the law would call police or testify against their assailants even if they were confronted at gunpoint. Instead, they would simply retaliate in kind.

Zinamon didn't want to sell the gun. But he did agree to lease it to Rower for one hundred dollars cash. Afraid that Atlanta police might roust him, he had given the gun to a friend in Carver Homes for safekeeping. Police rarely patrolled inside the vast public housing development in south Atlanta, where open-air drug markets flourished and rival drug dealers peppered the night with gunfire. No one would search for it there. Eddie drove Rower and Swinger to Carver Homes to get the shotgun. But he waited in the car while Rower made the deal inside.

Rower named the shotgun "Dino" because "it had a hell of a kick." He slept with it. He and his uncle fired it daily into the ground in his aunt's backyard in College Park. By then, nearly a dozen people knew he had agreed to "do a hit" for five thousand dollars. At least four people knew the target was a Cobb County white woman who was simply "getting in the way." At the time, no one seemed to mind or care. But that kind of information in the hands of drug addicts, dealers, and outlaws is a saleable commodity. Silence always has a price, and self-interest is at the heart of every transaction.

At 4 a.m. three days before Thanksgiving, long before night had calcified into an empty dawn, Eddie Lawrence drove through the grim streets of southwest Atlanta to meet Rower and, once again, drive him to the Tokars's home thirty miles north of the city. Fuzzy with sleep and more than likely stoned or falling off a cocaine high, Cornbread thought the hit was going down. They were going to kill Eddie's former wife.

Eddie had something else in mind. A conversation with Fred had left him with the mistaken impression that Sara and the children had already left Atlanta for the holidays. He thought he and Cornbread could case the house before the murder, so Cornbread would not stumble wildly when he returned to kill her.

Eddie chattered as they drove, and through his torpor, Cornbread heard his voluble partner's repeated instructions: "Make it look like a burglary."

It was nearing 6 a.m. when Eddie pulled into the deep quiet of a neighborhood unrattled by gunfire and cruised by the house, cloaked in the deeper shade of a dark stand of trees. There was only one car in the drive. Eddie, who still insisted that Sara was once his wife and that he once had shared the Kings Court home with her, told Cornbread that her husband had already left for work despite the early hour. "I call her, and her husband be gone every morning," he told Rower. "He be gone to work. He leave about six."

He knew that Sara and her two sons were sleeping together in the master bedroom. He knew that the burglar alarm had been deactivated. And he knew that the sliding glass door that opened into the kitchen was either poorly secured or unlocked, the same door that Fred had resolutely refused to repair, despite Sara's repeated pleas.

"The sliding glass door, they don't never keep it locked," Eddie told Rower. "They rich, and they don't suspect things like this to happen."

By then, Rower thought Eddie was going to do the murder. Rower thought Eddie was carrying a knife. He remembered Eddie talking, talking, priming him like a coach chats up a weary athlete. "I'll do this myself if I have to. I'm gonna go up and handle this, and you ransack the house and go downstairs and ransack that down there. And make it look like a burglary."

But instead of jimmying the sliding glass door himself, Eddie stepped aside. It would not be his crime. He would simply be the voice behind it. "You got to open it," he ordered the drug-addled young man who stood beside him.

Rower shied away. He told Eddie the Cobb County police had fingerprinted him following some long-ago arrest. "I ain't fixing to put my hand on it," he said.

Lawrence grabbed the door.

"They can be my fingerprints," he said. "They ain't going to suspect me because I been working for them for six months."

But as the two shadowy figures slipped inside the kitchen, they were met by Jake, the small springer spaniel who belonged to Sara's oldest child. Alarmed, Jake began barking. Eddie reached down to grab the dog, whispering to Cornbread, "That's my little dog. He suppose to know me." Eddie may have thought the dog would remember him from six months earlier when he had traipsed in and out of the kitchen for several weeks as he remodeled the downstairs bathroom. He may have thought the dog was an unexpected but minor irritation, left behind while Sara and the children were away. But then Jake bit him. Jake shrieked, then barked wildly as Eddie dropped him to the floor and booted him across the kitchen.

Cornbread knew then, through the stale, blind fog that slurred his reason, that Eddie was lying to him. "This wasn't never his house. He ain't never lived here."

The barking dog had awakened Sara. As Eddie and Cornbread sweated panic in the unlit kitchen, a light came on upstairs. The two men fled into the moon-dead dark.

As they drove back to Atlanta, Eddie's panic turned to anger. Sara, not his own stupidity, had thwarted him. "They done fucked up. They done fucked up," he muttered angrily.

"Shit," Cornbread thought to himself. "What am I doing here?"

Later that morning, Fred called Eddie and asked the younger man to join him downtown for lunch. As the two walked to a nearby restaurant, Fred asked Eddie pointedly, "Have you been in the house?"

Sara had called her husband at his office before dawn, Fred explained. She had found Jake outside, barking furiously, and the sliding glass door ajar. She had called demanding to know if he had forgotten to secure the door. Fred had let her believe that his own carelessness was the culprit. "She didn't suspect a thing," the attorney said.

Then, because he was used to giving orders or because Eddie couldn't quite seem to formulate and execute his own plan, Fred quickly and methodically gave his protégé instructions as to how and when Sara would be killed.

She was leaving Atlanta for Florida the following day. "When she comes back, I want her killed," he said. "I've made arrangements to go to Alabama to meet a client who's in jail there. That will be my alibi.

"I'm sure," the attorney reassured Eddie, "that you will take care of everything."

The next day, Eddie called Cornbread to reassure the jittery hit man. He spoke as if Sara were still his former wife, although by then Cornbread knew better. "She didn't suspect a thing." He was jubilant. "I talk to her every day because I check on my kids. She didn't suspect a thing. She thought that her husband had left the sliding glass door open, and the dog had got out."

For the next few days, Eddie stayed close to Cornbread, calling him, taking him for rides, worrying him, working him as if he were priming him for a fight, supplying him with weed. "When we get that bitch out of the way, we'll be smooth sailing. We'll get us a bird [a kilo of cocaine]. My folk be down with some people who got some power, and they going to be in."

"All right," Cornbread finally answered. "All right."

On Tuesday, Sara, her two young sons in tow, left her Cobb County home for the last time, her white Toyota 4-Runner outfitted with a V.C.R., a television, games, blankets, pillows, and the dog to distract and amuse her boys during the nine-hour drive along the congested interstate to Sarasota. But this trip was different. This time, Sara's normally penurious husband had given her two hundred dollars in cash from the basement safe. Such an uncharacteristic gesture pleased her. Sara was, at heart, an innocent; she did not wear suspicion well. To her, Fred's offer of money, after so many years of withholding it, reflected the glimmering of an old, expansive generosity that had dissolved soon after Sara married him. In her darkest dreams, she never suspected that her husband's gesture was just a brick in an alibi that would wall him away from any serious suspicion once Sara was dead.

Fred's efforts to construct an alibi never extended to his own discomfort. He made no remarkable attempts at reconciliation. As always, Sara and the children made the day-long drive to Florida alone. As always, Fred, complaining of a bad back and a heavy work load, chose to fly to Florida that night where Sara and the boys met him at the Tampa airport en route to her parents' home in Bradenton.

Sara's voice had a holiday lilt when she called her parents from the Tampa airport that Tuesday night. She had just bought ice cream cones for her boys. The small gesture, the prospect of seeing her family again and the simple, sweet magic of ice cream had conjured up her beloved childhood, and she had regaled her boys with stories about ice cream expeditions she and her sisters had embarked on as children.

On Thanksgiving Day, Sara's sisters noted approvingly that Fred seemed more benevolent than was his wont and less dismissive of his children. The weather was warm, the sun shining, the gathering was light-hearted, and old resentments were buried or at bay. Sara was encouraged that Fred was finally paying more attention to the boys. Maybe it was a turning point. Maybe the bitter wind that had chilled and shriveled their marriage had finally shifted south.

Fred's true reason was far more base. It was Sara's final holiday.

Mindful of the frosty disapproval with which Sara's family regarded his habit of cutting short his Florida visits to fly back to Atlanta, leaving his wife and children to make the long drive home alone, Fred made sure to let them know he had a Sunday appointment with a client that could not be avoided or postponed. In fact, Wilburt Humphries was in an Alabama jail, where Fred had been ignoring him while his ability to pay Fred's exorbitant cash fees remained in doubt. But Humphries provided Fred with the excuse the attorney needed to slip away early and sidestep any pointed questions about why, once again, he was abandoning Sara and the children to brave nine hours of holiday driving alone. That Sunday appointment in Alabama was significant for another, more sinister reason. It gave Fred what he thought was an airtight alibi.

In fact, Fred had another reason to return to Atlanta early Saturday. Around 1 a.m. Saturday morning, Rollins Security, which serviced the Tokars's home alarm system, called the Ambrusko home in Bradenton. Dr. Ambrusko answered the early-morning call in his third-floor bedroom, then called his son-in-law to the telephone. The fire alarm had sounded. Police and firefighters were at the house.

"They're not finding any trouble as far as fire is concerned, but they found an open sliding glass door," the security employee told Fred.

"Okay," the lawyer answered calmly.

"Will you be going back over there?"

"Yes."

"Can I tell them how long you will be, and what you will be driving?"

"No, we won't be going there now," Fred answered curtly. "We're here in Florida."

The security dispatcher was trying to be helpful. Could the company notify anyone locally to come and secure the house?

"I don't think we need to do that right now," Fred said.

The dispatcher was obviously puzzled. "You are clear that the sliding glass door has been open," she asked. "They found the door open. So your house isn't secure."

"Okay," Fred answered.

The dispatcher tried again. "We got a fire alarm. We didn't get an intrusion, but they're showing an open door."

Exasperated, Fred responded, "But we didn't even have the security alarm on." Not only that, but the entire intrusion system had been deactivated the week before.

When the now puzzled dispatcher persisted about the open door, Fred reluctantly told her, "Just have them close it then, I guess. . . . I guess that's really the best advice I can give you."

A half-hour later Rollins called again. The fire alarm had apparently been activated by a malfunctioning hot water heater that had spilled steamy water onto the basement floor. Firefighters had turned off the gas and water, but at least twenty to thirty gallons had spilled out.

"They will try to secure the door as best as possible," she said.

The next morning, Rollins called a third time. The fire alarm had sounded again. Firefighters were en route to the house. When the dispatcher called back a short time later, Sara answered. This time, firefighters had found nothing amiss.

"Has anyone gone out to turn off the burglar alarm?" Sara asked, as if she assumed the system was still armed.

During that brief call, Sara agreed that the security firm could disregard any alarm triggered by a single smoke detector that appeared to be malfunctioning. But before she hung up, she emphasized that only that one sensor should be ignored, as if she didn't know that for more than a week, the entire intrusion system had been shut down, leaving the house unprotected.

Fred would say later that Sara, not he, had decided to shut down the security system until he could return home. It was Sara who had asked him to fly home a day early to oversee the repairs rather than arrange for a neighbor to let a workman into the house. Sara, not he, had insisted that there must be hot water for the children's baths on Sunday night when they returned from Florida.

But, together, the broken water heater and the malfunctioning alarm provided Fred with another excuse to leave Florida early. Police, firefighters, and Rollins security had disrupted his plans. If they had indeed secured the house, Eddie might not be able to get inside.

On Saturday morning, Fred left Tampa shortly after eleven on a return flight to Atlanta. By then, Sara had contacted Sears, which agreed to send a repairman to the house later that day. Free for a day from the oppressive exhaustion that accompanied her husband's constant monitoring of her activities and harmless conversations, a buoyant Sara frolicked with her boys and gaily went shopping for a Christmas tree to install in her parents' condominium. To be sure, Christmas in Florida would never match the Buffalo Christmases of her childhood—the memories of blowing snow, wooden sleds, hot chocolate, and silver skates on a frozen pond as plain as the imprint of Christmas angels and as warm as a child's rising breath. It would not be a Buffalo Christmas, but she would still be home. Of this, her husband had assured her. That afternoon, as she and her children hung the first ornaments, Sara's anticipation was as breathless as that of her boys.

That Saturday, as Sara eagerly plotted the arrival of her most cherished holiday, three hundred and fifty miles away in Atlanta, her husband was finalizing the details of her death.

Soon after he landed in Atlanta on Saturday, Fred placed a call to Eddie Lawrence. He told Eddie that he had returned sooner than expected. The hot water heater in the house had broken. He wanted Eddie to come to the house to repair it, but Eddie said he couldn't make it.

Fred didn't tell him that police had visited the house, or

that the alarm system was apparently malfunctioning and summoning authorities to the house without good reason. He now had one last chance to meet with Eddie so that there would be no misunderstandings, no mistakes, and no more delays.

It was the first of a flurry of telephone calls and digital pages between the two men that weekend. That night, Eddie called Cornbread Rower one more time. They would kill Sara the following day.

On the final morning of her life, Sara woke early and packed the car for the return journey to Atlanta. At 9 a.m., her husband called. The repairman was finally en route. It was a brief, desultory conversation with a hidden motive. Still desperate to control her, Fred was checking up on Sara, eager for her to leave an environment where he could never completely dominate her, anxious now that his deadly plan be set in play. Sara told him she was still packing. She and the boys would be leaving soon.

The repairman soon arrived with a new hot water heater in tow. As he installed it, he and Fred chatted. Ron Chaney was also a musician, and Fred's expensive guitar in the basement had caught his appreciative eye. Before he left, at Fred's invitation, Chaney played a riff. He remembered the lawyer had stacks of cash on his basement desk. He paid for the $550 installation in cash, and gave Chaney a fifty-dollar tip.

As Chaney left the basement, he reminded Fred, "Make sure you shut the sliding glass door and lock it." Fred was standing in the basement doorway as Chaney pulled away.

At 10:45 a.m., Fred called his wife a second time. This time, Sara told him they were going to brunch before they left for home. Fred could hardly argue, but it must have galled him that he couldn't seem to will or bully Sara into foregoing a pleasant Sunday brunch at the club with her parents and her boys simply because he wanted her to. He wanted Sara to be on her way. The longer she delayed, the more difficult it became for him to meet with Eddie, oversee the final details of her death, and still travel to Alabama in time to generate a credible alibi. He chafed at the delay. It would be Sara's last small act of defiance.

A short time later, Fred left for his downtown office to pick

up his Alabama client's file. At the house, he left a note that
was uncharacteristic for a man who rarely communicated with
his wife and rarely let her know where he was or when he
would return.

Sara,

*The hot water heater is fixed, and, as we discussed, I
went to Montgomery to see Humphries. I'll be back
in the morning. I'll call and let you know where I'm
staying.*

                                                   Love,
                                                   Fred

Once at the office, he generated a small trail that would
help establish his alibi that he had been to the office on Sunday, and left the house long before Sara was expected to
arrive. He collected several messages, and his Alabama client
Wilburt Humphries's file, and dropped off some bills to be
paid. Then he placed another call.

Usually, Sara and the boys couldn't bear to leave Florida.
Usually, as they departed, they would all be in tears as Sara
returned with her sons to the dilapidated iron cage that her
marriage had become. But this time, she was happy. In three
weeks, she would be back to celebrate a long Christmas with
her family. The night they arrived, she promised to finish
decorating the tree. She serenaded her father as she and the
boys settled into the car. "I'll be home for Christmas. You
can count on me."

"Sara, why don't you stay overnight?" her father had
asked hopefully. It was already early afternoon, and he worried that she and the children would not be home by nightfall.
Besides, the boys were eager to remain.

"The boys have to be in school, and I don't want them to
get behind," Sara replied.

"Well, they can miss a day," her father said.

That might have been enough. But Fred, Sara insisted, was
anxious. "He really wants me home tonight."

As Sara climbed into the driver's seat, her father asked her, as he always did, "Sara, do you need any money?" But this time, Sara was flush. Fred had given her plenty of cash before she left Atlanta. She had nearly two hundred dollars remaining in her wallet. "Call me when you get home," he said as he kissed her goodbye. "Let me know you're safe." At 12: 30 p.m., she pulled out of the drive, and headed north toward home.

Less than fifteen minutes later, the telephone rang at the Ambrusko house. It was Fred, calling for a third time. "Has Sara left?" he asked.

"Yes, they just left. She's on her way home," Dr. Ambrusko answered.

"Well, I just wondered," Fred said. The hot water heater was repaired, and he was leaving town. He would later deny ever placing that call. But Dr. Ambrusko carefully noted it in his pocket diary, a habit he had acquired as a surgeon and that he did almost without thinking.

Shortly after Dr. Ambrusko spoke with his son-in-law, Eddie Lawrence received a call from Fred. He was relieved. He had gotten no answer when he called Fred at the house. He had paged him several times without result. Fred wanted Eddie to meet him at his downtown office.

The canyons of downtown Atlanta are deserted on Sunday. Office workers and students give way to vagrants, alcoholics, and an occasional bewildered tourist. Even the Dunkin' Donuts a half-block from Peachtree Street, the city's main thoroughfare, is closed. So there were few, if any, witnesses, around to see Eddie Lawrence park his truck at a nearby lot and walk to the small office tower where Fred shared a law office. Eddie strolled by the security guard in the lobby without signing the entry log. He caught an elevator to the ninth floor where he met Fred. He was there only a minute or two. Fred had no desire to discuss his plans with Eddie in his office when he knew that federal investigators were still seeking his offshore accounts.

Fred carefully signed out, another in a string of records and recorded messages Fred left that day to show he had been nowhere near his home for hours before Sara's expected arrival. Once in the basement parking garage, Fred told Eddie he had just called Sara in Florida. "She's on her way back," he said. "She'll be in around eight or nine o'clock. I'm on my way to Alabama."

He told Eddie he had left the sliding glass door open, and the alarm system was deactivated. Fred said he had even persuaded the repairman to play his guitar and unwittingly leave his fingerprints behind.

The lawyer based his final instructions on his wife's routine. Whenever she returned home from her Florida pilgrimages, she left the boys, often asleep, in the car while she unlocked the kitchen door, set down her purse, and turned on the lights. "Kill her when she first walks in the house," the attorney ordered, "when she's in the kitchen. Don't hurt the kids. If you have to hurt the kids, don't do it.

"Just leave the kids alone," he continued cavalierly, "and they'll be all right.

"I'll know you'll take care of everything," Fred reassured the younger man. "Just go ahead and make sure it's done." As the attorney drove Eddie to his truck, he reminded him, "I don't want the boys hurt. I just want Sara killed, and her car taken from the house."

After Fred left him at his truck, Eddie sought out the nearest pay phone and called Curtis Rower. "Cornbread, man, everything is set and ready to go," he said. "She's coming in from Florida, and this will be the only opportunity to get her."

"Well," Rower replied, "you got the money?"

"Yeah, I got a little money to hold you till I get the rest of it."

"Well, okay," Rower agreed. "Come and get me."

That Sunday afternoon was unremarkable for both Sara and her killers. A restless Lawrence went first to his own home, then to a girlfriend's, to his mother's home to pick up his son, then to his son's maternal grandmother's house where he left the boy, then to the home of a second female acquaintance where he waited out the dull, silent hours until 7 p.m. Fred spent the afternoon driving to Montomery, Alabama, more than three hours away—in spite of his bad back that he had reinjured earlier in the week—then made a brief appearance at the Montgomery County Jail.

His client, Wilburt Humphries, was surprised, but pleased,

to see the attorney. He had not been expecting him. Tokars was brusque. He needed Humphries's signature on a legal contract acknowledging that Fred had been retained by Humphries and accepted an initial payment of eight thousand dollars. Humphries, a convicted money launderer, was facing more federal drug charges. He wanted to talk about his case. But Fred was in a hurry. The face-to-face meeting lasted less than ten minutes.

By 6 p.m. Eastern Standard Time, Fred had registered at the Madison Hotel in Montgomery where he indulged in a small dishonesty. He requested a government discount, then flashed an identification that may have identified him as a city traffic court judge. The hotel clerk thought Fred was with the U.S. Justice Department.

A short time later, Fred called his Atlanta answering service from the hotel. He left the hotel's telephone number and his room number, where he said he could be reached in case of an emergency until 11:30 a.m. the following day. He knew that the Tokars's housekeeper, scheduled to arrive at 9 a.m. Monday, would surely find Sara's body first.

Sara spent the afternoon navigating the heavy holiday traffic and listening to the drone of the tiny television and lazy chatter of her two small sons as she barreled innocently toward oblivion.

Between 7 p.m. and 7:45 p.m., Eddie arrived at a College Park house where Cornbread was staying with his cousins. Cornbread had a girl with him, and was cradling Dino, his sawed-off shotgun. He was high on crack. Eddie was driving his orange pickup, an indication either that he hadn't planned to drive with Cornbread to a Cobb County neighborhood where it was liable to attract attention or that he simply wasn't thinking. Eddie would insist later that he never intended to carry Cornbread to the house. After Red Swinger had passed on participating in the contract hit, Cornbread left Eddie with the impression that Cornbread's uncle, Joe, would do it.

The duo dropped Rower's girlfriend at her apartment, then Eddie stopped to buy Cornbread some cigarettes. Sometime after 8 p.m., they cruised by the Tokars's house. Either sloppiness or the reluctance that had tugged at Eddie since Fred first proposed the murder had delayed them. Fred had told him Sara would be home between eight and nine. But the house was dark. No one was home. The killers had time to spare.

Once more, Eddie walked Cornbread through the plan, just as Fred had walked him through it in the parking garage earlier that day. The sliding glass door to the kitchen would be unlocked, the alarm deactivated. "I know how the bitch think," Eddie told Rower. "I stayed with the bitch. She's so dumb she got the alarm turned off."

He continued with his instructions. Kill her as she opened the door from the kitchen to the garage. Don't hurt the kids. Take the car and meet me down the road. He showed him where he would be waiting, at an unfinished subdivision nearly two miles away.

What Eddie wanted to do was leave Rower at the house, then quickly retreat to a safe distance. He had convinced himself that by doing so, he would not actually be responsible for Sara's murder. He would take credit for the deed, but sidestep any personal blame. But Rower was adamant that the pickup remain close to the house where he could see it.

"If it make you feel better, I'll park my truck over here by the house," Eddie finally agreed. "When she come home, take her back down here. I'm going to follow you down there, but you got to kill her. You got to do it."

"All right. All right," Cornbread answered.

Before leaving the truck, Cornbread once more demanded his five-thousand-dollar fee. Eddi· only had eight or nine dollars in his pocket. "I left it at the house," he explained lamely. "You'll get it after the job is done." And if Cornbread hadn't still been riding the euphoria of a cocaine high, he might have abandoned the ugly task right there. Instead, he accepted the feeble excuse with equanimity.

"Okay, it's still the same game." He hopped out of the truck. As Eddie pulled away from the curb he watched Cornbread walk up the drive.

Dressed in black, Rower slipped easily through the sliding glass door and went straight to the alarm system panel. To his horror, the panel lights were blinking. Goosed by fear, he ran from the house and slid breathlessly into the truck.

"That alarm on," he squeaked.

"Uh-uh, it ain't on," Eddie was adamant. "I know it ain't on."

"I don't know how you know all this, but that alarm on," Rower insisted.

Increasingly fearful of attracting the attention of the To-kars's neighbors, Eddie started up the truck. As he drove Rower through the suburban streets, he begged him to go back into the house and wait for Sara.

But Rower was adamant. "No, I ain't going up in that house by myself.

"You're going to have to do something," he challenged Eddie. "You ain't sitting in no truck."

Eddie finally agreed to accompany Rower back to the house to convince him that the alarm system wasn't functioning. The two slipped into the kitchen and climbed the stairs to the master bedroom where the alarm control panel was housed.

It was still blinking. "Leave that alarm alone, man," Rower said, his rising panic accentuated by the cocaine he had ingested. "I'm fixing to get out of here."

"No," Eddie was frustrated. "It ain't on."

"Shoot, that motherfucker's on," Rower was sweating. "I'm gone."

"The alarm's off; the alarm's off," Eddie protested.

"Man, don't you see that thing blinking? Cobb County be out here in a damn minute. I'm telling you, you better come on. Get me out from over here. We can watch and see if the police come."

Cornbread practically ran from the house. Eddie trailed behind, worried that someone would spot the two men or the orange pickup, both so out of place in the sterile serenity of suburbia. They hovered near the sliding glass door. Eddie told Rower he was going to move the truck to a less visible location. Stripped of what little reasoning ability he possessed by a cocktail of panic and crack, Cornbread wanted the truck parked where he could see it from the house. It was nearing 9 p.m.; Sara was expected any minute. Traffic in the neighborhood was heavy with holiday arrivals and departures, and Eddie was terrified someone would spot them. He broke away from Rower. He had to move the truck to a safer location.

Rower stood alone in the yard, watching as Eddie's taillights receded and then vanished into the dark. Eddie never came back to the house.

Instead, as Rower hovered near the sliding glass door to the kitchen, Eddie followed the plan he had been trying to impress upon his addled partner. He pulled the truck into the drive of an unfinished house at a new subdivision two miles away where he had originally told Rower he would wait for him. The truck, which could have passed for a worker's vehicle, was partly obscured by a ten-foot-high brick wall at the subdivision's entrance. Eddie settled in to wait.

Back at the house, Cornbread's cocaine high had plummeted into a cellar of paranoia. Uncertain of his bearings, convinced that Eddie had abandoned him, penniless, and smelling a setup, Rower had only one sure way home—Sara would have to drive him.

For more than an hour, he waited, drifting aimlessly through the house until shortly after 10 p.m., when he saw the lights of Sara's 4-Runner as she turned into the drive. Rower slipped into the kitchen as Sara pulled the car into the garage.

Mike, the youngest, was asleep in the back seat. Sara left him sleeping while she, Ricky, and the spaniel left the car. Perhaps she was still fumbling for the doorknob, her mind already on a hot bath and bed. Perhaps she had just opened the door. But, suddenly, there he was—an agitated black man wearing a dark toboggan and nervously fingering a sawed-off shotgun.

Sara screamed as Jake barked wildly. Rower kicked the dog. "Get in the car," he said.

"Ricky, get in the car," Sara said, her voice shaking from shock.

As her elder son crawled into the front seat, Rower climbed into the backseat next to Sara's sleeping four-year-old. He squatted on the floor. The shotgun barrel brushed her hair as Rower rested it against the seat just inches from Sara's temple.

"All you got to do is drive," he said.

"What do you want?" Sara breathed as she backed the car out of the garage. "Money?"

"You don't have nothing to worry about," Rower said. "Just do like I say and everything will be all right."

As she backed down the drive, Rower, still baffled as to where he was, hesitated. He wasn't quite sure what to do. He was supposed to kill her, but he hadn't been paid to do it. He suspected Eddie had simply abandoned him. Peppering his commands with angry obscenities, Rower ordered Sara to drive him to Bankhead Courts, the housing project where he was raised. Sara, who rarely traveled south of the Perimeter unless she was going to Florida, didn't know how to get there.

"Are you going to kill me?" she asked him.

"Nah, I ain't gonna do nothing to you," he answered as the shotgun nudged her ear.

"What do you want, money?" she asked desperately.

"Yeah, give me your money," Rower answered. Sara reached for her purse as Ricky cowered beside her. "There's a couple of hundred dollars in my pocketbook," she said, pulling out a wad of twenty-dollar bills. "Just don't hurt me and the kids."

"I ain't here to hurt you all," Rower lied. "I just want you to take me back to Atlanta. Just do what I ask, and everything will be all right."

But Sara balked. She feared the city and for her children if she took Rower to what she suspected were the dank and dangerous neighborhoods long abandoned by police.

"I don't know how to do it," she wailed.

"You just drove all the way from Florida. You trying to tell me you don't know how to get to Atlanta?" Rower demanded.

By then, Sara had turned onto Powers Road. As they eased down a hill, Rower spotted Eddie's orange pickup sitting in the driveway of an unfinished house, exactly where he had promised to wait. Rower was jubilant. Eddie could take him home, or he could kill Sara himself.

"Pull in here," he said.

Again, Sara hesitated. She would not drive her children into a lightless cul-de-sac where she stood no chance against the death she knew surely awaited her there. She attempted one more time to persuade the manic black man with the gun in her ear to let her and her children go.

"I'm not pulling in here," she told him firmly. "Can't I just drop you off here?"

"Don't fuck with me," Rower thundered.

"I'm not trying to fuck with you," Sara shouted, her voice rising in panic.

"Just stop right here," Rower bellowed.

Sara pulled to the side of the road near a stop light. "You can take the car," she urged him. "Just don't hurt me or my children." She didn't know that Rower wasn't sure he could drive it.

Just then, Rower spotted Eddie through the left passenger window, walking up beside the car. Sara saw him, too.

"She acted like she know Eddie," Rower would say later. "She looked back and seen Eddie like she was shocked. I don't know if she recognized him, but she was looking like she was in shock."

In that single, fell moment, Sara must have realized that Rower and Lawrence were puppets, and that her husband was plying their strings. She knew Eddie. He had spent weeks remodeling their bathroom. She knew he was in business with Fred. Negotiating for her freedom was fruitless. With an ugly certainty, Sara knew that she was dead. In the final moment of her life, Sara mashed the gas pedal and jerked the steering wheel toward Eddie. The car vaulted to the left, knocking Lawrence to the ground and throwing Ricky low against the front door.

Inside the car, the gun with the nickname and the hair trigger that Rower held cocked with his thumb erupted with a thunderous roar.

The blast caught Sara just below her right ear. As she slumped over the wheel, the car rolled across the road, leaped a curb, plunged through a ditch, and broke through a line of shrubs and small trees. It came to rest in an unlighted field.

As the truck careened into the ditch, Rower tumbled out, still gripping the shotgun with one hand and Sara's purse with the other. He sprinted across the street, passing a limping Lawrence en route to the pickup.

"It's done. Let's go," he said as Eddie climbed into the driver's seat. The two men fled into the night.

Covered in his mother's blood, Ricky reached over Sara's

body and carefully turned the ignition key. The engine stopped. He pulled his little brother from the back seat. They were crying. He held Mike's hand as they ran through a field as dark as a hole in their dreams to the beckoning lights of a nearby house. He wanted someone to call his grandfather. His grandfather was a doctor. He would make his mother better.

Thirteen

"Who Shot My Mother?"

HORROR ABANDONED SARA'S BOYS IN A WORLD WHERE only the shadows were alive. Deafened by the shotgun's ugly roar, they stumbled, sobbing, in the cottony silence across a black field silvered with frost. The warmth dying on Ricky's face was his mother's blood. Caught in his hair were the remnants of her final thought, her last brief breath.

The boys were still wearing shorts, and the icy grass whipped their small, bare legs as they ran—a four-year-old and a six-year-old struggling alone in the briary dark towards a solitary porch light a hundred yards, and a child's lifetime, away.

Teen leaders at the Young Life House, a nondenominational Christian ministry on Powers Road, heard the high, childish voice calling for help, heard small fists pounding on the door over the soothing hum of the television.

"Help! Help! Our mom's been shot!"

David Nelms flung open the door and stared down at the stricken, blood-stained faces of the Tokars boys. Breathless, wracked by fear, Ricky pleaded with the tall stranger in front of him, "Please, my mom's been shot."

"Where has she been shot?" Nelms urgently asked.

The children pointed down Powers Road toward a pair of headlights still visible in the field. Two of the young men dashed from the house toward the abandoned car as a third called county police.

"Who shot your mother?" Nelms asked the children.

"A bad man with a pirate gun, a black man," Ricky answered.

"Why did he shoot her?"

"She wasn't doing what he wanted her to."

"What was he telling her to do?" Nelms asked patiently.

"He was telling her to turn right, and she wouldn't turn right," Ricky explained breathlessly. He remembered their final shouted exchange.

"Don't fuck with me," the man had screamed. "I'm not fucking with you," was his terror-stricken mother's last reply.

She had shoved Ricky to the floor. The car had leapt forward. The world had blown apart.

Nelms quickly retrieved a flashlight and, leaving the boys in the care of the housemate who had called authorities for help, he, too, headed for Sara's car.

It was, of course, too late. The young men found Sara's body slumped over the steering wheel, a broken doll with blood spilling down her face and arms. Blood had spattered every surface inside the car. It had drained under the driver's door, and left a halo around Sara's shattered head. Her right foot was still on the accelerator.

When Dave Anderson, one of the first Young Life leaders to reach the car, yanked the front door of the 4-Runner open, Sara's body tumbled out. He saw the gaping hole in her head as he caught her, knew as Nelms felt for her pulse that they would find none.

"What should I do?" he called to his companions as he struggled with her inert frame. Nelms, who had arrived behind him, helped Anderson lift Sara back into the truck. They shut the car door to await police.

But the musky odor of coagulating blood and the sour scent of death unsettled them. They began casting nervous glances into the pasture where the car was mired and stifled a rising panic that the darker shape of Sara's killer still lurked in the void of that lightless field. They saw nothing.

Using Nelms's flashlight, one of the Young Life leaders flagged down the police car that had been dispatched to the scene. As Nelms made his way back to Powers Road, he saw one of his housemates walking with the Tokars children back toward the car. He gently intercepted them, certain that the boys must not see Sara's lifeless body.

"Are you cold?" he asked them.

"No, we have our sweatshirts on," Ricky replied.

By then, police and rescue vehicles were arriving, bathing Powers Road in the eerie, disconcerting pulse of red and blue emergency lights. After radioing for tracking dogs and reinforcements, Officer Terri Blackmer approached Nelms and the boys.

"Who are these children?" she asked.

"They're the children of the lady in the car," Nelms answered.

Blackmer led the boys to her patrol car where she bundled them in blankets. Ricky's face and matted hair were still streaked with Sara's blood.

"Tell me what happened," Blackmer asked him gently.

The little boy choked back sobs as he told her his name was Rick, that he was six, and he lived with his mother, his brother, and his father in Kings Cove.

"We were coming home from Florida," he said. "When we got home, there was a black man with a pirate gun waiting for us. He had on dark clothes and a green toboggan. He told us to get back in the car. He told my mom to drive. But she disobeyed. My mom started screaming. She pushed me on the floor. The bad man shot my mom."

When an ambulance arrived, Blackmer turned over her two young charges to the care of emergency rescue workers.

The back of that ambulance was where Cobb County Police Detective Pat Banks first met Sara's children. Banks was a ten-year police veteran, a laconic, lanky New Yorker with a thatch of unruly blond hair who favored jeans instead of suits as his plainclothes attire. Divorced, with a small son of his own, he was shaken by the innocent heartbreak he found when he threw open the back doors of the ambulance. As warm air from the ambulance wafted by him, heavy with the sour odor of a child's vomit, he saw two small, young faces the pallid color of the moon. The four-year-old was dazed. Fear, fatigue, loss, and the smell of blood had made him ill.

Emergency medical technicians were still cleaning the child when Banks threw open the doors. Ricky was watching them with an uncanny fortitude.

"I'm a detective," Banks told the boys. "I need your help in finding the person who has hurt your mother."

For the third time, in a delicate voice now heavy with fatigue, Ricky recited the plain, but horrific, story.

"Who's your father?" Banks asked the boy.

"My father is Fred Tokars. He's a lawyer and a judge," Ricky said.

Banks would never forget the ragged sobs that caused Ricky's voice to break unnaturally as he struggled to suppress them. At that time, he still believed his mother was alive, that an ambulance much like the one in which he sat had already taken her to a hospital where his grandfather, a doctor, would find her.

A cold rage gripped Banks as he tenderly bid the boys goodbye. By midnight, the detective was at the Tokars's home. As he stepped through the secluded sliding glass door into the kitchen, the scenario the child had suggested—a burglar surprised by the family's unexpected return—seemed all wrong.

Banks noted with grim surprise the absence of standard security, odd for a house owned by a criminal defense attorney and a judge. The sliding glass door through which he stepped had been left ajar, the metal lock bar that fit into the tracks laid neatly on the carpet just behind the blinds. A second sliding glass door opening into the basement office was unlocked. The frames of sliding glass doors on either side of the fireplace separated from the wall with a single tug. The knob on the door leading to the garage had been reversed so that the door could not be locked from the inside. The detective would soon learn that Tokars had reversed the handle himself, unhappy that he too often found the door locked from the inside when he tried to enter through the garage. In spite of the holiday weekend, the security alarm had not been set.

The telephone was off the hook in the master bedroom. Sara's jewelry boxes had been rifled. Children's toys were scattered throughout a house in obvious disrepair. But a night burglary at the end of a long holiday weekend made no sense to Banks. A burglar would surely realize that people would be returning to their homes on Sunday night as they prepared to return to work and school. The end of a long holiday weekend was not the most ideal time to burgle a residence.

Nor did it make sense that a burglar would target a home a mile inside a subdivision without a getaway car. And as he walked through the Tokars's home, Banks noted that the televisions, videocassette recorders, answering machines, and other easily pawnable electronics all remained in place. Nothing appeared to have been taken. Nothing had been dropped or left stacked by the door. There was little to suggest that Sara's murder was the end result of a burglary gone bad.

Meanwhile, Sara's father had been calling the house for hours. A meticulous man, he had carefully gauged Sara's driving time from Bradenton to Atlanta, allowing at least one stop for gas. All his daughters always called him as soon as they arrived safely at their destinations. Sara was no exception. By 9:30 p.m. Sunday, Sara had not called, so Dr. Ambrusko called her. No one answered. He wasn't really worried. Holiday traffic was probably heavy. His daughter had more than likely been unavoidably delayed. He waited a half-hour then called a second time. Again, there was no answer.

It was nearing 10:30 p.m. when Dr. Ambrusko called his daughter again. This time, the line was busy. Relieved, he told his wife, "She's probably trying to call us now," and hung up the phone. But Sara didn't call. He tried again. Sara's line was still busy. He was puzzled. He was also growing worried.

It is certain that Curtis Rower was in the Tokars's house when Dr. Ambrusko placed the first calls to his missing daughter. Authorities have speculated that Rower—wired on crack, his nerves jangled by a drug-induced paranoia and his growing certainty that Eddie Lawrence had abandoned him—may have taken the telephone off the hook because its insistent ringing proved demanding and unbearable.

By the time Dr. Ambrusko placed a fifth call to his daughter's house, it was after 11 p.m. and Sara was dead in a field. The line was still busy. An operator obligingly checked the line before notifying Sara's parents that it was clear. It was

simply off the hook. Now alarmed, Dr. Ambrusko called
Cobb County police and asked them to. check the house. It
was unlike Sara not to call. She was also nearly three hours
overdue. He had no idea that, by then, police detectives were
already scouring the Tokars's house for clues.

About midnight, five Manatee County sheriff's deputies arrived at the Ambruskos' door. "We'd like to talk to you,"
one said. "May we come in?"

"Sure, come on in," said the bewildered man.

Then, one deputy gently asked the elderly couple to sit
down. "Your daughter has been murdered," he said. Her sons
were still alive. They had no more details than that.

Shocked, but determined to know what happened and to
see if, by some chance, his daughter were still alive, Dr. Ambrusko called Cobb County police a second time.

"I couldn't get the whole picture from anyone," said the
retired surgeon. "I was interested in whether she was dead
or there was a possibility we could revive her."

All police could tell him was that Sara's death was instant.
Her children were all right and in their uncle's care.

Cobb police had notified Fred while his children were still
shivering in an ambulance, unaware that their mother was
dead. They had left an urgent contact message with his answering service, which had called him in Montgomery at the
emergency number he had carefully left earlier that afternoon.
The answering service connected the attorney with police dis-
patchers who patched him through to officers at the scene. If
Fred dissolved in hysteria on the telephone that night, no one
remembers. He asked police to allow his younger brother,
Andy, to take the children until he could return from Alabama.

Certainly, once he had spoken to police, Fred did slide into
hysteria. After a distraught call from Fred, Andy, in turn, had
called his eldest brother, Jerome. Jerome, a physician, had
left immediately for Montgomery with his wife to retrieve
Fred and drive him back to Georgia before dawn. Alone in
his hotel room—his descent into the sordid depths of Atlanta's underworld complete—Fred Tokars began to drink.

*   *   *

As Ricky and Mike were crawling out of their mother's car, Rower and Eddie Lawrence were scrambling for the anonymity of the interstate. Eddie, limping from an earlier, accidental gunshot wound in his foot, had trailed behind Cornbread as he sprinted for the pickup, still holding the shotgun and Sara's pocketbook.

Rower said little as the duo raced for the highway. Dazed, he finally muttered, "It blew my high." The agonizing cocaine paranoia that had blossomed as he waited for Sara to return, the angry confusion that ended only as he knocked the shotgun hammer loose, the adrenaline that fed him as he ran, had made him crash. But, at least with Sara's purse crushed tightly to his chest, he was nearly three hundred dollars richer.

"I ain't got no blow," he whined. "I need to get me some powder."

As Eddie obligingly steered the truck southward toward John Hope Homes, yet another public housing development where drug dealers sold crack from their apartments with impunity, Cornbread began explaining to Eddie why he hadn't killed Sara at the house. His story was slightly different than his fears. He didn't tell Eddie he was sure he had been betrayed and left as fodder for the Cobb police. Instead, he offered another, slightly giddy version.

"Man, I didn't want to kill her at the house and take the chance of trying to drive the jeep because I might not know how to drive it. I didn't want to get stuck at the house with somebody dead. Shit, man, you were two mile away. I had no way to contact you. It was a lot easier for me to kidnap her and make her drive."

Eddie accepted the explanation. Sara was dead. Fred would be appeased. Eddie's businesses, and the company titles he had assumed, were secure. So far, he had avoided paying Rower. He might not ever pay him. After all, Eddie wasn't the one who had pulled the trigger. He could afford to take Rower to John Hope Homes and let the agitated gunman bury the details of the crime under an avalanche of crack.

At John Hope Homes, Rower dumped Sara's pocketbook in one of the fifty-five-gallon drums that residents used for refuse at the rotting, yellow stucco apartments. Either Rower didn't find what he wanted, or he didn't find enough. When he returned to the truck, he told Eddie to drive to another drug dealer's den at yet another cluster of deteriorating public apartments where he bought more cocaine and marijuana with what was left of Sara's money. By the time Eddie dropped Cornbread off at his cousins' College Park house, Rower was beaming on a cocaine high. Eddie told him it would be several days before he could pay him for the hit, but Rower didn't seem to mind. For the moment, he was too giddy to care.

Rower's hand shook as he unsteadily inserted the key into the lock. He fumbled with the knob as his girlfriend sought to open it from within. He cursed her as she pulled the door open. She was purposely keeping him waiting on the porch. He strode inside, holding the shotgun, and wearing a navy nylon warmup suit. He was carrying the clothes he had worn when he left under one arm. His face was smeared with blood.

"I did it. I did it. I did it," he hailed his cousin, Lamar.

"All right, man! All right!"

As the cousins erupted in laughter, Lamar called to Rower's girlfriend, a fourteen-year-old runaway who was staying at the house. "Lashara, you and Aishah get some bleach and a towel." Rower's white leather athletic shoes were spattered with blood. As Lashara poured bleach on a washcloth, Lamar wiped the drying blood away. The girls quickly dumped Rower's clothes into the washer.

"What's wrong wit' you?" Rower's uncle, Joe Tanner, called from the living room as Rower, pumped and glassy, strode toward a back bedroom, the shotgun wrapped in his coat.

"Nothing wrong wit' me. It's done."

"What's done?"

"You don't need to know everything," Rower flipped back a reply. "Watch the news."

At 11 p.m., Atlanta's television stations were broadcasting the first live reports of Sara Tokars's murder.

Rower quickly stripped and stepped into the shower. He didn't lather up. He simply stood there. But as the water washed the last of Sara's blood away, Rower began to shiver.

Lashara toweled him dry. As he crawled into bed, he asked her to hold him, and she joined him, curling against him like a cat. She held him as he trembled, but he was too jittery to sleep. Within thirty minutes, he was up again.

Nervous now about his successful incursion into Atlanta's suburbs and his easy escape, his expertise as a hit man validated by the late-night news, Rower needed more drugs to jack him up. He and his cousin cruised over to Carver Homes where they acquired more dope with the last of the money he had stolen from Sara. When they finally returned to College Park, they were still silly, still loopy with glee over a white woman's death and the promise of five thousand dollars still to come. By dawn, at least six people knew who had killed Sara, not counting the dope boys to whom Rower and Lamar may have dropped grinning hints as they purchased their eightballs, weed, and bags of crack. Rower was about to tell two more.

Early Monday morning, he appeared at his sister's doorstep in Carver Homes. Red Swinger heard him banging on the door, and tumbled naked down the narrow stairs to let him in. Rower followed him into the back bedroom and flipped on the television.

"Hey, man, there's shit all over the news," he boasted.

"What you talking about?" Swinger asked him, puzzled.

"You know," Rower said as images of Sara and the bloody white Toyota flashed across the screen.

"No. No, you didn't man," Swinger gulped in horror. "I know you didn't do that."

But Rower was babbling, too high or scared or pleased with himself to listen. "The patio door was open, just like Eddie said. I was in the house. They pulled up. I made them get back in the truck. One of her damn kids wasn't acting right. I started to shoot him. But I knew not to do that. Eddie told me not to, not to bother the kids. Just her. We was riding down the street. I tell the bitch to turn. She won't turn. Eddie was waiting. I did it, man. I did it."

Panic clawed at Swinger. He had ridden with Rower to Cobb County to case the Tokars's house, helped him locate the shotgun Rower had obviously used. Swinger's girlfriend, Rower's sister, had introduced Rower to Eddie and put the ball in play. This death was not just another drug slaying that police were likely to ignore. When Rower finally left the apartment, Red Swinger was pacing, swallowing his fright, considering his options.

Back in College Park, Rower was still flying, still eagerly absorbing news reports of Sara Tokars's death, unable to contain his glee.

"What was wrong wit' you earlier?" Lashara asked him.

"Baby," he boasted, "I killed a white 'ho."

"Well, ain't she pretty," he teased Lashara later as a smiling photo of Sara and her children appeared on the television screen.

"Yes, she's pretty," the fourteen-year-old answered. "It's a shame someone killed her."

Rower answered insolently. "Yep, it's a shame what a nigger will do for money."

"Yep," she echoed. "You know it's just a shame."

At 7 a.m. Monday, the telephone rang at Karen Wilcox's home in Buffalo, N.Y. Her husband, Neal, answered. Karen's mother was calling. "Please, please," she said, "get Karen."

When her younger daughter answered, Phyllis Ambrusko could not tell her, at first, that Sara had been shot. Instead, she began reciting the events, as she knew them, that had ended in her daughter's terrible death. Sara was driving home. There was a man in the house. He made her and the children get back in the car. "Karen," she said, "he shot her."

"He shot her?" Karen breathed. "Is she dead?"

"Yes." Her mother was crying.

"Are the kids okay?"

"Yes." Karen dissolved in tears.

Awash in grief, Karen couldn't digest the awful reality. "Every time the phone would ring, I kept thinking somebody was calling to say it was just a mistake."

On a lonely flight to Atlanta later that day, her thoughts sharpened by a razor's edge of grief, Karen fixated on a single looming suspicion. "Fred did this. He hired somebody to kill her."

Karen—the shy sister, the one who married her high school sweetheart—not only knew about Sara's unhappy marriage, she knew there was no way to save it. She knew that Sara wanted out. And, in his efforts to avoid divorce, Fred had threatened and cajoled her sister, using Sara's boys as bait. Karen's hard suspicion took root. Fred knew Sara would fight him for custody. His only way out was to kill her.

Mary Rose Taylor had flown in from Scotland with her husband late Sunday. By 6 a.m. Monday she was awake and had instinctively flipped on the early morning television news. Splashed across the screen were the images of her cousin's blood-soaked car, the solemn faces of Cobb County detectives, the dispassionate reporters who had followed the story throughout the night. Sara wasn't safe. She had been murdered as her children watched. Badly shaken, Taylor first called Captain Julian Deal, the Cobb County detective who had described Sara's murder to a growing band of reporters. She knew Deal from her own days as a journalist, knew he would tell her what reporters couldn't, knew she could confide in him. As she learned the slender details of Sara's slaying that Ricky had recounted to police, conviction rose from the crucible of grief in Taylor's chest. Sara was the victim of a contract killer. Whether directly or indirectly, Taylor knew that Fred had played a role in his wife's ugly death. She was equally certain that the key to the riddle of Sara's murder lay buried in the documents Sara had once lifted from her husband's safe. Taylor knew only that Sara had assured her the documents were safe. She had no idea where Sara had secreted them. She knew only that she must find them before they fell into a conspirator's hands. Deliberately now, Taylor placed a second call to Sara's youngest sister.

The shock of Sara's death had driven Krissy to her knees. Still clutching the phone, she had convulsed in wretched sobs, screaming for her sister as the grieving voice of her mother echoed softly in her ear. Finally, exhausted, she had collapsed into a fitful sleep. The telephone's insistent ring awakened her. Dazed with fatigue and grief, Krissy picked up the receiver. Her cousin's voice was low and urgent. Had Sara ever given to her for safekeeping the documents she had copied from Fred's safe?

"What documents?" Krissy asked blearily. She couldn't remember. Lost in an avalanche of grief was that summer day in 1989 when Sara had called her sister from Fred's basement office as she thumbed through the sheaf of documents she had found. Forgotten or dismissed as too dramatic was Sara's admonition to take copies of the documents to police should anything ever happen.

"Could they be with Sara's will?" Taylor pressed her cousin.

"I'm not even sure I have the will," Krissy answered.

"Krissy, we must find it," Taylor insisted. "I'll help you."

Taylor found what she was seeking in some boxes in Krissy's basement that had seemed too unimportant to unpack. There they were, alongside Sara's handwritten will. By noon, Taylor and Krissy had given them to the detectives investigating Sara's death.

Supported by her cousin, Krissy told them what Sara had schooled in her. Fred represented drug dealers. He always transacted his affairs in cash. He would not let Sara have a checking account. He forbade her to have credit cards in her name because he didn't want his purchases, or his money, traced. He was hiding money from the I.R.S.

A wizened dawn crept across the city as Fred drove through the outskirts of Atlanta to the house he intentionally had left so vulnerable to intruders. Confronted with the enormity of Sara's murder, he had grown hysterical with every drink and each passing mile that brought him closer to home and the corpse that had once been his wife. He was stricken with fear for his own personal safety, terrified that his own indiscretions would be uncovered, his arrogance swamped in a deluge of remorse. When he called Sara's father, he was nearly incoherent, moaning like a manic animal as he begged, "Will you help me?"

"We're all coming to help," Dr. Ambrusko promised. "The whole family is flying in." They would all be staying at an Atlanta hotel in nearby rooms where they could mourn even as they undertook the business of burying his daughter and finding a safe harbor for her children.

One of Fred's first calls was to Howard Weintraub, the criminal defense attorney with whom he shared an office. At 8 a.m., Weintraub and Fred's brother, Andy, escorted Fred to a Cobb County police precinct near his home. Fred was unshaven and disheveled, his breath rank with the odor of stale beer. His emotions tilted wildly as he stumbled over urgent questions that induced spasms of nausea and tears he seemed helpless to control.

"Where is she right now? I just need to see her," he sobbed brokenly.

"She was shot. The wound's in the head, and I don't think you want to see her," Detective Brad McEntyre explained gently.

"Oh, no," Fred convulsed in sobs. "I'm sorry."

"Are you all right?" McEntyre asked.

"I feel terrible," Fred answered.

He seemed genuinely shaken by Sara's death. But as a former prosecutor who surely knew that the first twenty-four hours after a murder are critical in solving it, he sidestepped even harmless questions as he spiraled toward hysteria.

"My little boys were there," he cried. "Oh, no. What did you tell them about my Sara? They're such cute little boys. Oh, no."

He asked for a trash can because he felt ill. He asked for a rag to wipe his face. He asked for water. He told police that he was cold. Yet, he could not rein in the terrible sobs that wracked him as the detectives struggled for any clue that might lead them to Sara's killer.

"I can't remember," he told McEntyre. "I just can't think about it right now. I just can't do it. I'll do it later on."

When the detectives finally asked the distraught lawyer to accompany them as they walked through his home to determine if anything traceable had been taken by Sara's assailant, Fred at first resisted the suggestion. The investigators were puzzled by his disinclination, particularly when he knew that stolen items pawned or sold could help them track a killer. They also found it odd that Fred had acquired the services of a criminal defense lawyer before he ever talked to them about his wife.

What they did not know, or suspect, was that when Fred spoke with them that day, he knew that something had gone awry, that his clear instructions to kill Sara at the house had been forgotten or ignored. He did not know whether the house had been burgled. But if Eddie had, indeed, ransacked the house, Fred wasn't going to volunteer a clue that might lead police to his partner in the sordid crime. Instead, he would have to coin his answers in the lawyer's realm of imprecise replies. Eventually, Fred acquiesced. He would accompany police on a walk through his home.

Howard Weintraub drove Fred to the house. But when Detective Pat Banks met them there he smelled fresh beer on Fred's stale breath. He hastily pulled Weintraub aside.

"Do you know this guy just showed up with beer on his breath? Where did he get beer at eight in the morning?"

"I gave him a couple of beers to calm him down," Weintraub replied.

The detectives and the attorneys entered the house through the sliding glass door to the kitchen where Rower had slipped inside. They moved from room to room, tracking what they thought were the footsteps of Sara's killer. Banks pointed to the metal bar on the carpet near the sliding glass door.

"I believe I locked that door and put the bar in place," Fred said. "But I'm not sure."

Upstairs in the master bedroom, Banks queried the attorney about Sara's jewelry boxes, open and askew.

"No, that's not right," Fred acknowledged. "They shouldn't be there. But maybe Sara put them there," he offered. "Sara could have put them there."

When he left the house on Sunday, he said, the princess telephone in the master bedroom was still in its cradle. He had not taken it off the hook.

As they descended the basement stairs, Banks noted with interest that Fred did not go immediately to his safe, which was standing ajar. Instead, the attorney directed detectives to his electric guitar, which was propped against a music stand.

"Well, that guitar isn't where it used to be," he said. "It's been moved."

He didn't mention that he had encouraged the repairman to play the guitar after the hot water heater was once more functional. He didn't mention he had done so to generate an unidentifiable, and misleading, set of fingerprints as a false trail.

"Nothing else was taken?" Banks asked pointedly. "Just the guitar has been moved?"

"Yeah," Fred insisted. "That guitar is not where it should have been."

"What about the open safe?" Banks asked.

"I don't think it was open." Fred was maddeningly vague. "But, then again, my wife has the combination, and so maybe she's been in there.

"I think I had fifteen hundred dollars in the safe," he offered. "But I can't remember."

"Look, it's really important," Banks said, his frustration evident. "We need to see if anything is missing."

"That file folder," Fred said, pointing to a manila folder atop the safe. "That file folder should be in my file cabinet under S. It's got the combination in it. But unless you knew where to look for this file folder in the file drawers, even if you looked under S, the tab on the top where you label it has been trimmed. There would be no way to open the file cabinet, and quickly pull the file with the safe's combination inside."

And so it went as detectives waded through Fred's distracted and noncommittal answers. He didn't know if anything was missing. He had nothing to contribute to the investigation of Sara's murder. He was sorry he couldn't be of more help.

That morning, while Fred was still drifting through the house with detectives, Leah Sears dropped by. It was a generous gesture of support by an influential and highly respected state supreme court justice. As she hugged him, hovering television cameras caught the brief exchange of sympathy on tape. It would become one of the defining television moments in the coverage of Sara's murder—and one that would trouble Sears as she pursued her reelection campaign.

As the news of Sara's death spread, media trucks began lining Kings Court, the street facing the Tokars's home. As reporters, police, neighbors, and sympathetic well-wishers made their brief pilgrimages to the house, Fred called in reinforcements to secure the door. The man he called was Billy Carter, the former G.B.I. agent with a temper and a criminal assault conviction. He was also Fred's private investigator, and a one-time front for a drug dealer who had invested in the Parrot. Carter told those who inquired at the door that he was "a family friend." He was also an odd choice, considering that Fred's name was still floating at the nether edges of a federal investigation that had targeted his client, Al Brown, Brown's drug trafficking network, and the operation of Diamonds and Pearls.

In the hours immediately following Sara's murder, John Ambrusko couldn't quiet the questions. They reverberated in his mind as he methodically tracked his daughter's last steps, her final desperate actions. As he walked through the Tokars's house, paused on the stairs where Sara had first confronted her killer, drove to the Powers Road intersection where she had steadfastly refused to turn, noted the incomplete and vacant subdivision devoid of inhabitants or lights, questions scrolled through his head that only his son-in-law could answer.

"This is not a robbery," he told himself. "This was an execution."

"Who knew?" he demanded when he finally faced his son-in-law in Atlanta in those days after he first confronted the abyss of Sara's loss. "Who knew what time she would be home? You knew. You called me. You knew when she left. What you've got to figure out is who else knew?"

Fred's pale face still quivered with hysteria. But the elderly doctor was intent; his analyst's mind had distilled from the chaos of violence the key questions that, if answered, could unearth a killer.

"Who knew?" he persisted. "Who knew that side door was open? You knew. Who else knew? Who knew Sara had told the security firm to disconnect the alarm? You knew. Who else knew it?

"That's how we have to start thinking about this," he pressed. "It wasn't a robbery. Nothing was taken, as far as we know. If you're going to kidnap somebody, Christ, you don't shoot them. The way it was carried out, it looked like an assassination."

He tried to rattle Fred from his unresponsive torpor with his questions, hopeful that his son-in-law could enlighten him and lead them to Sara's killer, that the answers might give him some relief from his intolerable grief. But Fred remained distracted and uncommunicative, a weak man sodden with self-pity who sidestepped police and all but ignored his two small boys and the shadows stamped on their souls by the shotgun's single atomic blast.

Like some distant bell, Joni Ambrusko heard Sara's urgent voice in the hours that followed hard on her sister's death. Younger than Sara, Joni was her closest sister in age and the one who looked most like her—slender with platinum hair that fell below her shoulders; wide, dark eyes and girlish bangs that still kissed her forehead nearly twenty years after she had followed in Sara's celebrated wake through high school.

Joni then worked for the mayor of Jacksonville, Florida, handling public relations and special events. For seven years under three different mayors, Joni had worked to secure an N.F.L. football team for the city. She also was a newlywed, married four months to a Navy pilot who had flown F-18 fighter jets during the Gulf War. When Dick Crain and his comrades, flush with victory, had come home from that distant desert half a world away, Sara and her boys had joined Joni on the tarmac, waving an American flag and cheering like a schoolgirl as Dick Crain swept her sister in his arms. Sara had also helped her sister plan her wedding when Joni's job proved too demanding, ordering flowers, calling the priest, securing the church.

"Sara," Joni had once asked her older sister, "you've spent your whole life taking care of all of us. What about you? You're so unhappy. We have to find a way to help you."

"Don't worry about me, Joni," Sara replied. "I'll find a way."

Now, Joni heard the echo of her sister's voice ringing through her grief. "Please go to my kids. Get my boys. Take care of them."

At that moment, Joni had no clear sense of the enormity of that disembodied plea or what it would ultimately cost her to keep the promise that she whispered like a rosary. She knew only that she would carry out Sara's final wish.

When she reached Atlanta, Joni and her husband first drove to Andy's house to see the boys. Fred was sitting with them on the couch watching television when she swept in, a highly energetic woman who would channel her desperate grief into finding her sister's killer and caring for her children. Mike was asleep in his father's lap.

When he saw his sister-in-law, Fred began to wail. "Joni, what am I going to do?" he sobbed. "I've worked so hard. I'm going to leave Atlanta. I'm going to have to close my practice. What's going to happen to me?"

Joni was terrified for the children. Their inconsolable father was frightening them. He was also demanding everyone's attention.

Bowed with grief, numb with fatigue, Sara's sisters and their husbands arrived in Atlanta throughout the day—Karen and Neal from New York, Mary from New Jersey, Therese and Gretchen from California. "It was difficult for us to really understand just what had happened," Karen said.

Sara's extended family rented a suite of hotel rooms and moved with the children there. Joni and her husband took the room that adjoined Fred's, where the Ambruskos assumed he would stay with his sons.

"He was so hysterical," Joni said. "I kept asking him not to act like that around the boys because they were so sad."

Once Rick and Mike arrived at the hotel, the sisters assumed an almost manic gaiety to distract their tiny nephews from memories colored by blood and the dark. The boys knew their mother was hurt. In their childish faith, they still did not know she was dead. The heartsick task of telling them that what had happened to their mother was irrevocable was left to Sara's older sister, Gretchen, a hospice nurse.

Sara's boys were asleep when Gretchen reached Atlanta late Monday night. At 2 a.m. Tuesday, she heard a desperate knock at her door. It was Joni.

"Gretchen, you've got to come. I can't control Fred. I just can't control him.

"I've had trouble controlling him all day," she said as the two sisters hurried to the room their brother-in-law was sharing with his sons. Fueled by liquor, driven by hysteria rooted in remorse and fear, Fred had skidded into a crying jag. He was nauseous and staggered sloppily around the room, self-absorbed as always and completely oblivious to his sleeping sons. Joni was petrified that he would awaken them, terrify them with his antics, blurt out their mother's death as he caromed about the room.

"I'm so scared," he moaned as he collapsed against Gretchen and heaved into the waste can she held for him. "Oh my God, my heart's pounding a mile a minute. My stomach is a wreck." He began babbling wildly. "I can never go back in that house. They're in there. They're going to get me. I just know it. I've got to get bodyguards. I'm going to quit. I'm just going to quit."

"I know, Fred, I know," Gretchen soothed as she offered her brother-in-law a Valium to calm him. But as she listened to Fred wallow in what seemed less like grief than a rising panic, her heart narrowed imperceptibly. Absent from his raving monologue was any mention of Sara, her final, terrible moments, or the stunned anguish of his sons.

"I'm a hospice nurse. I meet grieving families every day," Gretchen told Detective Pat Banks five days later. "I'm telling you I've never seen anyone react like he did." As she comforted her brother-in-law until well past dawn, Gretchen scrutinized Fred's face, studied his eyes, seeking some original well of grief from which his drunken histrionics sprang. But, while Fred's lower lip quivered and collapsed as he howled or swept his knuckles across his eyes, Gretchen never saw any tears.

"Call my mother," he begged before he finally succumbed to the Valium and exhaustion. "I want my mother."

Only once did Gretchen see tears welling in Fred's eyes—when she told his sons that their mother was dead. The little boys were crying as Gretchen told them that Sara was in heaven with God, the Virgin Mary, and the angels; that she, herself, was now an angel and that she would be listening when they prayed.

When Norma Tokars flew in from Florida later that day, Gretchen took the older woman aside to speak with her frankly about her middle son.

"We can't control him like this," Gretchen explained. "You need to take him to your house and give him something to knock him out because he's going to just freak these little kids out acting like this." Sara had been her children's anchor in a flotsam world with an absent and indifferent father. They needed now to know that they were not lost or alone or running from a bad man with a pirate gun.

Fred's mother remained at the hotel that night, as his two brothers and his sister joined the awkward assemblage of Sara's family and in-laws. Weepy, still sour with alcohol, Fred clung to Norma Tokars like an insecure, overindulged child. Curled in a fetal position on the hotel bed, oblivious to his own children, he called plaintively, "Mommy, lay down with me," until Norma finally acquiesced, and he slipped into a troubled stupor.

As soon as Fred awakened early Wednesday, he began pressing his mother to make a beer run, insisting that a swallow or two would "calm him down."

"Norma, please don't give him any," Gretchen begged when she learned of Fred's agitated demand.

"Well, I think he's a bit of an alcoholic," Norma explained.

"There is no such thing as 'a bit of an alcoholic,' " Gretchen replied. "He is one. Sara knew it. That's when he was worst, when he was drinking."

But Norma trundled out to fetch beer for her boy, just as Howard Weintraub had stopped to buy his colleague beer on Monday morning on the way from the police precinct to the Tokars's house. In fact, by Wednesday, Fred had been drinking steadily for nearly sixty hours.

"To me," Gretchen said, "it was more anxiety than sorrow."

"It was shocking how little he was with the family or his children," Joni noted. "He was gone during the day. Sometimes he said he was at meetings, or at the office. Sometimes he didn't say." None of those meetings were with police. Fred, through his attorney, had postponed all discussions with detectives, including any with his children, until after Sara's funeral.

Throughout that first week, Fred exhibited a rising paranoia that baffled the Ambruskos. He refused to have significant conversations on the telephone, telling his in-laws they might be tapped. "Look, Krissy, I bet you there are people over there watching us all the time," he told his sister-in-law one day as he stared out at an adjacent motel.

Two days after Sara's murder, he authorized his lawyers to hire private investigators, including a retired F.B.I. agent, who doubled as bodyguards and set up a command post in the motel. And for nine days, a security detail accompanied him and his sons whenever they went out in public.

On one outing to a Cobb County video game palace teeming with families and children, he at first refused to go inside, saying he had left his gun behind. Only after he borrowed the pistol that Krissy's fiancé kept in his truck did he feel safe enough to enter.

Yet, said investigator Tim Huhn, Fred never told his bodyguards who they were supposed to be protecting him from. And the lawyer never told them that he had actually been threatened.

Meanwhile, Mary Rose Taylor had taken Sara's sisters and her parents quietly aside.

"This is the beginning of a long ordeal," she told them gravely after they had gathered in a hotel room. "I believe Fred was either directly or indirectly involved in Sara's murder."

Dr. Ambrusko roundly rejected the suggestion that the younger man of whom he had become quite fond would kill his daughter. Even Sara's sisters, who knew how unhappy Sara had become, believed Taylor's suspicions were unfounded. But Krissy was convinced her cousin was right.

The Ambruskos laid their Sara to rest on Thursday, December third, at a Sandy Springs cemetery north of Atlanta. More than three hundred people attended the funeral mass at St. Jude of the Apostle, where the children knew Sara as "the lady with the red boots"; where she daily had walked each of her sons to his classroom door, vowing to do so until she was asked to stop; where she left behind an unfinished Christmas toy drive she had organized for needy children. Her brothers-in-law bore her coffin, her sisters trailing like the Mercies as her husband, his face contorted, swiped at his eyes and continued clinging to his mother. Notably absent from the mass and the procession that accompanied Sara's coffin to the tomb was Jim Killeen, one of her dearest friends and the man most knowledgeable about the depth of her husband's involvement with the drug dealers who had turned the city's most popular nightclubs into money laundries.

By then, police detectives were growing impatient. Tips that had flowed into the police department in the hours after Sara's murder had proved fruitless. Investigators feared that Sara's children might soon simply shut down, eradicating the terrible details of their mother's death from all conscious thought. They were eager to learn if any of Fred's criminal clientele or the disgruntled spouses of divorcées he had represented might be seeking retribution. The images of the Hollywood thriller, *Cape Fear*, where a prosecutor's family is methodically stalked by a killer he sent to prison, flickered at the edges of their credulity—every cop's worst nightmare. They needed to know who had slaughtered such a lovely woman within inches of her children and just how ephemeral was the security ring around their own families and loved ones.

On Friday morning, the day after Sara was buried, Tom Charron, Cobb County's district attorney, announced, "We have allowed the husband, the children, and the family time to grieve until after the services." Detectives, he said, would interview Fred today.

Instead, Fred again demurred, asking for a few more days to soothe his shattered family. In a prepared statement Fred issued to the media through his public relations firm, the attorney offered the following explanation.

"We have been devastated by the loss and need to share our grief privately as a family for a short period of time. I have cooperated as best I can in the investigation and will continue to do so. I met with police investigators for two hours on Monday and gave a preliminary statement. I will meet with police again as soon as possible." He didn't mention that he had given police nothing they could use.

Assigned the odd responsibility of handling public relations in a murder case, Fred's spokeswoman, Brenda Fontaine, offered an equally odd explanation after distributing her client's news release: "Our own speculation is that Fred represented some really strange people, and that Sara was more worried about them than Fred was."

That Friday, someone else did go to the police. Defense attorney Guy Davis, Jr., an old friend of the private detective Sara had hired to follow her husband in 1989, contacted Cobb police on behalf of Ralph Perdomo. Feeling guilty, spooked by Sara's eerie prescience in asking him to go to the police "if anything ever happens to me," concerned both about his safety and his liability, Perdomo had hired his old friend Davis, another former cop and private eye, to act as his intermediary. Now a player in a sensational homicide, Perdomo had sent the thin investigative file on Fred's adulteries to police. He had also passed along the information that Sara had urged him to go to the police, and her distraught allegations about her husband, his drug-dealer clientele, hidden cash, foreign bank accounts, and tax evasion. The information dovetailed with the folder Krissy Ambrusko had given to police the previous Monday. Taken together, the files gave detectives their first glimmerings of a motive, one that pointed as stoutly as a compass at Fredric Tokars.

Police detectives, frustrated by Fred's intransigence, mentioned Perdomo's file to his attorneys, perhaps to goose him into some response. They abruptly stopped saying that Fred was "not a suspect" and, lacking any semblance of cooperation from him, leaked word of the file's existence to journalists baying at the precinct door. Perhaps that is why, that night, Fred embarked on a rambling confession of his indiscretions during his six-year marriage to Sara as he sat at the dinner table with her elderly father, her mother, and her sisters.

The dated, brief documentation of an old affair accompanied by the echo of Sara's voice pleading, "If anything happens to me, take this file to the police," must have shaken the attorney badly. For Fred had never given Sara proper credit as an observant, intelligent woman who possessed stamina and courage. It had never dawned on him, as he plotted her murder, that his wife might have collected or hidden evidence of his crimes and indiscretions. She had seemed so weak and acquiescent it never occurred to him that the possibility he would separate her from her sons—and that threat alone—had driven her to build and leave behind what would become the core of the murder case against him. He would make her pay for it eventually, dead though she was, for pursuing him from the dust to which she had been so brutally consigned. But for now, Fred was simply attempting to control the damage that was leaching away his sympathies and his alibis.

"You know," he began his monologue that night, "Sara once hired this investigator. I'm not perfect, and I've had a few flings. But they never meant anything, and I didn't ever want to leave Sara.

"Sara used to laugh about it," he stumbled on, oblivious to the indignity of his admission and the shock or icy anger now evident on his in-laws' faces. "As we would go up to bed at night, she'd say, 'Now, how much do I have to service you?' " He laughed nervously.

Sara's sisters knew better. Sara never talked like that. She would never laugh, had never laughed, about her husband's suspected extramarital affairs.

"It was so long ago," Fred added lamely, "but I want you to know because it will probably come out in the media that there was this little infidelity."

At that moment, choking on silence as thick as sawdust in her throat, Sara's mother left the table. She could no longer bear to listen. Fred ignored her abrupt departure.

"Did you know about it?" Fred asked Karen at the end of his sordid and ill-timed admission.

"I kind of suspected it," Karen cautiously admitted, unwilling to betray a sister who had always confided in her and who had often vented her hurt and ire about Fred's illicit life. "You suspect that, really, of all men."

"Did you know the investigator?" he asked.

"I just don't know anything about that," Karen answered uneasily.

Fred's admissions, made only a day after the family buried Sara, merely accelerated his polarization from the Ambruskos. His refusal to cooperate with police seeking Sara's killer only widened the divide.

As Fred's younger brother, Andy, left the hotel late that night, he draped a protective arm around Fred. Fred, who had been drinking heavily, staggered. "Now, don't talk to the press," Andy admonished him. "And don't talk to the police."

Karen overheard the brief instructions that her former boyfriend was quietly imparting to his brother. "Oh, my God," she breathed, "you've got to talk to the police."

"I don't want to talk to the police right now," Fred acknowledged in a conversation with his mother and Gretchen in his hotel room a day later. "I'm trying to stall talking to them, hoping that they will find the person who killed Sara, because I'm afraid if I talk to them now, they are going to look into my business dealings. I have gotten some money from some criminals and some drug dealers that I was supposed to put in an escrow account and declare on my income tax. If they look into that, I'm afraid that I could go to jail for tax evasion."

"But Fred," Norma protested, "this is a question of priorities."

"If there is something that you know that can help this investigation, this tax evasion question is irrelevant," Gretchen pleaded. "You've got to go to the police."

Instead, Fred sowed bold seeds of distrust and doubt about the Cobb police, even as he suggested that his former nightclub partners, both jailed and dead, might somehow have effected Sara's death.

He warned Krissy that police would ask her if she and Fred had engaged in an affair because they had cosigned a lease on the Fulton County apartment where Krissy had once lived. Fred had acquired the lease to sidestep county residency requirements for county political offices and judgeships.

He told Joni's husband, Dick Crain, "Cobb County police are a bunch of uneducated idiots who can't do their job."

"Christ," Dr. Ambrusko exploded when Fred made similar excuses to him, citing attorney-client confidentiality as one reason he was still sidestepping a conversation with police. "You should be down there pounding on the table. You should be making every effort to find Sara's killer now, not try to postpone this thing."

"But postpone is exactly what he was doing," Dr. Ambrusko would remember later. "I felt Fred should have been much more aggressive in trying to solve who was behind this.

The police were doing everything they could. He was not aggressive enough in trying to help them. Yet, whenever I discussed it with him, he assured me he was not involved.''

The news media, Sara's family, and the legacy of a hollow affair that Sara had left with Ralph Perdomo finally forced Fred from his curious silence about his life and Sara's death. By Saturday, Atlanta's news media were reporting the existence of Perdomo's files, and Sara's cryptic plea to go to the police "if anything happens to me." It was, one journalist suggested, "the first big break" in the case.

Driven by private promises to their dead sister to find and prosecute her killer, stunned that Sara may have had a premonition of her danger, and furious that their brother-in-law continued to stonewall Cobb investigators, Sara's sisters trooped to the Cobb County Police Department in Marietta on Saturday afternoon to share their anguished suspicions with police. By Sunday, Fred was reading published accounts revealing he had rented an apartment on Roswell Road in Sandy Springs, in a neighborhood that, throughout the eighties, boasted a reputation as a magnet for boisterous party animals who changed partners more often than they changed their socks. The implication was clearly that Fred was having an affair and, if so, he had an articulate motive for murder.

On Sunday afternoon, Fred, accompanied by two criminal defense attorneys, met with Cobb detectives. His colleague, Howard Weintraub, who had accompanied Fred on his first visit to police the morning after Sara's body was found, wasn't one of them. Perhaps Fred, always penurious, was simply shopping for an attorney who wouldn't bill him, but rather accompany him as a favor to a friend. Jerry Froelich clearly fit that mold, unwilling at first to characterize himself as Fred's counsel. Rather, Froelich, a former federal prosecutor whose New Jersey accent defied more than a decade in the South, described himself simply as Fred's friend.

But Fred may also have had something else in mind. Both Froelich and Frank Petrella specialized in federal criminal law, while Sara's murder was still strictly a state investigation. The federal grand jury was still investigating the drug-trafficking and money-laundering enterprise that had, as its hub, the nightclub Diamonds and Pearls. Al Brown had been indicted and was awaiting trial in jail. James Mason had been subpoenaed to testify before the grand jury. Federal agents were culling through boxes of records, some of them incorporation papers bearing Fred's name. If authorities had not yet identified Fred as a suspect in Brown's criminal enterprise, they had clearly labeled him as a witness.

Fred knew that to sidestep prosecution or avoid a lengthy prison sentence, one of his former business partners—especially Mason, who bore no loyalty to anyone—might offer to testify against a lawyer with prominent political ties whose wife had just been murdered. Weintraub was already representing Mason, which also explained why Fred may have turned to Froelich and Petrella. But if Fred fingered Mason and Brown first as possible suspects in Sara's murder, any testimony they might offer later would be tainted with intimations either of retaliation or a coverup.

Fred's first remarks left little doubt in the minds of the investigators that the attorney had any intention of cooperating.

"Are you under the influence of any alcohol?" Detective Ron Hunton asked pointedly, remembering Fred's beery breath as he had staggered through his home just hours after Sara's murder.

"I am under medication," Tokars answered. He was, he said, taking the prescription painkiller Antivan, a second codeine based muscle relaxant, mixing them with Valium, although he told the detectives, "I haven't taken a lot of that today."

"Do you understand and know what you are saying?" Hunton pressed him.

"I, yeah, I'd better. Yeah, I mean, I——." Fred paused.

"Yes?" Hunton repeated.

"Yeah," the attorney grunted.

"You do? Okay."

"Well, yeah, as best I can," Fred explained. "Well, my memory, right now is, like, boggled. My mind is boggled, and it's just that, I'll do the best I can."

Intentional or not, Fred's statement was slick with legal implications. If, during the course of the interview, Fred said something that might incriminate him at some later date, his attorneys could argue that the drugs had incapacitated and confused him, leaving him mentally incapable either of distinguishing the truth or defending his own best interests. He had made the statements while on medication simply as a courtesy to police to facilitate the investigation of Sara's death.

The detectives questioning Fred quickly became exasperated with his astonishing lack of memory. The attorney wouldn't give them even the most basic information about himself, his wife, or their marriage. He couldn't remember the address of his downtown office building without checking his business card. He was unclear about his work history and vague about whether he was partners or simply sharing office space with attorneys Howard Weintraub and Emily Sherwinter. He couldn't remember his secretary's name, the exact color or model year of his car, when he leased it, or whether the Toyota 4-Runner was in his or Sara's name. An insurance broker, he couldn't remember which company had insured his car and Sara's vehicle, and under whose name the policies had been obtained.

"I mean, I'm sorry, it's just like, my mind isn't connecting the way it should," he offered as an explanation.

When Hunton began questioning Fred about Sara's final trip to Florida, Fred pleaded ignorance. He couldn't remember what day Sara and the boys left Atlanta for Florida, when he left, where he was or what he did before he followed his family to Florida, or the day of the week on which Thanksgiving fell.

"Thursday," Hunton reminded him firmly. "It was Thursday."

"My mind is just a little boggled," the attorney said apologetically. "Everything is blending together right now."

As he explained how Sara had driven to Florida with the boys while he flew into the Tampa airport, Fred may have realized just how selfish he sounded in the sterile interview room, on tape, and face to face with two less than sympathetic listeners, for he began offering explanations that sought to justify his self-centered behavior.

"That was the way we always went. I've got a bad back and the driving bothered it. It would require me to stop and rest more frequently than the kids. We had tons of stuff that we would bring down. It would be hard to take on the plane. It was hard to have everyone in the car. Plus, it's expensive, you know, with four people flying."

Gradually, Fred's discomfort at the critical stares and unsympathetic silence of the police detectives became Sara's fault.

He had been in an auto accident in early November that had aggravated an old back injury, but, he whined, "My wife really wanted me to be down there with the kids. And I really was injured from this accident. My neck was really killing me, and I was taking this medication."

The truth was that Sara would have been happier if her husband had simply stayed at home.

Fred's lack of memory persisted as Banks and Hunton questioned him about the Thanksgiving holiday. He didn't remember the details of the security company's calls to Bradenton, why they called, or even the family's personal security code. He did, however, remember that Sara was the one who told the security firm to deactivate the alarm after the hot water heater broke and began spraying water on the floor.

Fred insisted it was Sara's fault that he left Florida early. "I didn't really think it was that big a deal to have hot water," he shrugged. "But my mother-in-law, Phyllis, said, 'You have to go home,' or she implied that I had to go home. And I said, 'All right, I'll go home.' "

Again, Fred's memory failed him. He couldn't remember when he returned to Atlanta, whether he went out or stayed at home that Saturday night, whether he stopped by his office, when the repairman arrived Sunday to fix the water heater, how he repaired it or whether he installed a new unit.

"I don't really remember. My mind is just a little fuzzy," he repeated.

Nor could he remember where he had left the telephone in the master bedroom, whether he had taken the receiver from its cradle, whether his cufflink box and Sara's jewelry boxes had been left lying open on the dresser, whether the two .38s, the Beretta or the shotgun he kept in the house were missing, how much money, if any, he had stored in the safe, whether he had secured the safe and whether any of the money, bank books, or other documents he also kept in the safe were missing.

"You don't know how much money you had in your safe?" Hunton asked incredulously.

"I don't really know," Fred said. "I'm not sure."

He sighed, hesitating. "See, my mind is just so blurred . . . I thought I had about $7,500, maybe a little more, maybe a little less. I can't remember." What he did remember, he insisted, was giving Sara money—more than $2,500—and that she had spent a lot of it in Florida.

Banks continued to press him. The detective wanted to know why the house was so ill-secured, why the sliding glass doors opening into the kitchen and the basement were unlocked, why the metal security bar by the kitchen door was still resting on the carpet and the alarm system deactivated even after the hot water heater was repaired. It was a carelessness bordering on recklessness that, at the very least, demonstrated a decided lack of concern for the safety of Fred's wife and children.

"Before you left the house on Sunday, Mr. Tokars, what did you do?" Hunton was blunt. "Did you lock the doors? Turn the alarm system on? Tell me what you did."

Instead, Fred launched into a rambling monologue about the alarm system that sounded almost bitter, as if he had resented it from the day Sara insisted on its installation. His children had torn away screens and broken doors where the sensors were installed, and, on occasion, actually damaged the sensors. The system was difficult to activate and frustrating to use. It took too much time to secure all the doors and windows in order to activate the system. Neighbors and the cleaning lady often let themselves in by jiggling the broken lock on the kitchen door, sounding the alarm when Sara was out of town. Sometimes, the alarm sounded accidentally for no apparent reason. The family often didn't activate the alarm at night because, "My wife was spending a lot of time in the evening out of the house. I would be with the kids, and she would go to see her sister."

Besides, it was Sara who had told the security firm to de-

activate the system the weekend she was killed, Fred emphasized. "When I left for Montgomery, you couldn't even turn
the system on because she had deactivated it the day before.
Or at least that's what Sara told me," the attorney said. "I
don't know whether she did or she didn't.

"I feel as though I locked the house," the attorney continued defensively. "I did not try to turn on the alarm system,
and you're asking me about something that is like a blur in
my mind. I don't even remember leaving. This is like a nightmare to me, and I feel like I'm dreaming right now, talking
about something that I don't even really remember happening.

"I apologize." He sighed heavily. "I just don't know."

Fred didn't remember much about his trip to Montgomery
either. He didn't remember what time he left, the name of his
hotel, whether he registered there or went first to the county
jail to visit his client.

Hunton wanted to know why he chose to drive rather than
fly, given a back injury that had kept him from driving to
Florida with his family, and why he didn't just return to Atlanta that evening so that he would have been at home before
Sara and the boys arrived.

"I was just zonked," the attorney answered. "This was a
vacation. I drank a little over the vacation. I had been taking
medication." He said he had intended to drive back early
Monday morning, although to be in Atlanta by 7:30 a.m. as
he planned, he would have had to have left Montgomery a
time zone later by 3 a.m.

"Was anyone with you at the hotel?" Hunton asked.

"No."

"Did you meet anyone along the way? Did you pick up
anybody, male or female?" the detective persisted.

Maybe it was the potent cocktail of prescription drugs
chased with alcohol that Fred had ingested. Maybe he had
grown careless, or arrogant, or exhausted. Maybe he just
wasn't listening. Or maybe he was telling the truth. But his
airy answer stiffened the detectives' growing suspicions that
Fred was, somehow, at the murky bottom of Sara's end.

"I don't remember if I did," Fred said in response to Hunton's question as if he had been asked what he had eaten the
night before for dinner. "I don't think I did."

"You say you don't remember if you picked someone up or if you were with someone?" Hunton probed.

"Oh, no," Fred corrected himself. "I definitely didn't pick anybody up."

Hunton moved on. But he reposed the question one more time before the interview had ended.

"Mr. Tokars, let me make sure that I've got this clear. You're quite sure that when you checked into this hotel, or motel, or whatever it is in Montgomery, that you did not check in with anyone else and no one else was with you, and you've made no reference to anyone else being with you," Hunton pronounced each word deliberately. "Is that true?"

"Yes."

Frustrated in their attempts to learn anything from Fred that would help them to trace the killer who had entered the Tokars's home and kidnapped Sara and the boys, the detectives shifted the conversation to possible suspects who might try to strike back at the attorney and former prosecutor by murdering his wife.

"Have you had any problems with hang-up phone calls?" Hunton asked, aware by now from Sara's sisters that she had fielded a number of hang-up calls she assumed were from Fred's mistresses and whores.

"I don't know," Fred was guarded. "I mean, I don't think I have. Occasionally, Sara would get one that would hang up, and she would joke, like, 'Oh, your girlfriend called,' but I don't remember how recent, you know what I'm saying?"

They knew from Sara's sisters enough to know that if Sara made such a statement, it surely wasn't a joke.

"I mean, it was like a joke," Fred continued lamely, "and it did happen to me sometimes, and I'd say, 'Oh, they asked for someone else, Sara. It was your boyfriend.' "

So commonplace were his affairs that Fred just didn't get it, still did not understand that refusing to leave Sara for another woman did not absolve him of his infidelities.

"Had Sara expressed any concern to you about any strange people or anything strange going on before she was killed?" Hunton asked.

"What was that?" Fred was vague. "Could you say that again?"

Hunton repeated the question.

"She always talked about my clients," Fred offered.

"But there was nothing specific that she complained about, that she worried about?" Hunton pressed.

Fred was unsure how much Sara had told her sisters or what they may have confided to police. "She might have mentioned something about a client or person. But again, my mind is like, so dazed right now. I don't really know. If she had, it didn't seem to me to be anything to worry about."

"Have you ever received any kind of threats from your clients?"

"I don't want to say threats," Fred hesitated. "I guess I'm sort of ashamed of it, but they were all scumbags, and they had done bad things, and yeah, they would say things to me. I discounted a lot, maybe, of what I shouldn't have discounted. But I never felt in my heart that there was anyone who would hurt me or my family. Maybe I should have been more aware or more concerned."

Asking about clients who might have been unhappy with Fred's representation or defendants he had imprisoned as a prosecutor were obvious questions. But Fred couldn't afford to have detectives uncover any defendants with a connection to his one-time client, Eddie Lawrence. Counterfeit charges against Lawrence had never materialized, so he should attract no suspicion in a murder. Nonetheless, Fred began laying a series of false trails for the Cobb detectives, casting doubt and suspicion on his more violent customers, especially the ones who had never paid his exorbitant cash-only fees in full. Most of them were already in prison.

His Montgomery client, Wilburt Humphries, "was trying to trick me into coming to Montgomery to represent him, and then I wouldn't get paid the fee," Fred offered. The two had already quarreled over Fred's twenty-five-thousand-dollar fee, and Fred had abandoned him in court after Humphries had ponied up only half. Humphries, his family, and his friends were angry. Humphries, Fred said, "was pissed. It wasn't a pleasant conversation."

"Did he or his people make any specific threats?" Banks asked.

"None of them said, 'I'm gonna kill you if you don't

come,' or 'I'm gonna hurt you,' " Fred answered. "They just got mad. You know, you're welcome to look at them, call them, talk to them." He even offered the detectives his file on Humphries, despite his earlier protestations to Sara's family that he couldn't discuss his clients without violating their confidentiality. It was, of course, what Fred did best—giving up a client to law enforcement, often as part of a plea bargain on behalf of other clients, once he no longer had any use for them.

Jerry Froelich actually raised the issue, interrupting Fred as detectives pushed for the details of Fred's conversations with the client he had just maligned.

"There's one problem," he reminded Fred. "You've got attorney-client privilege."

In addition to Humphries, still in jail in Alabama, Fred offered up Reynaldo Victorine, the leader of a drug gang with roots in the Virgin Islands.

"Two or three of the key witnesses who saw this guy murder somebody have disappeared," Fred said. "He supposedly had this guy killed for looking at his girlfriend wrong."

And Fred insisted he had argued with Victorine over a ten-thousand-dollar fee he had refused to refund after the government's key informant disappeared and prosecutors were forced to drop the charges.

"It's happened to me many times, but he was a little more vicious," Fred said. "I guess my level of anxiety grew about four or five weeks ago. I don't know for sure if he wanted to see me during Thanksgiving, but I made it appear as though I was going to be out of town."

Then, there was a Cherokee County drug dealer whose family had also hired Fred. When he failed to make bond, the dealer had asked Fred to go back to court. The attorney demanded additional money.

"About a month ago, he just started to really use the real nasty cuss words, threatening type words," Fred told the two detectives. "And it got to the point where I wouldn't go out to the jail to see him anymore."

"Is there anyone else, Mr. Tokars?" Hunton asked.

"I don't know whether this is important," Fred paused coyly, "but James Mason is a guy I represented for about four years''—the one man most likely to hand Fred to federal prosecutors as the operator of a money laundry.

"He's had one close business partner get murdered," Fred was rolling now. "And he ended up getting all the property from that. And then Al Brown, his new business partner, was arrested and jailed and looked like he'd be in jail for a long time. And Al Brown's brother came to town to sort of manage his brother's affairs, and then he was murdered.''

He never would have considered Mason a suspect in Sara's murder, the attorney said, except that his security guard, Billy Carter, had just informed him that Mason's employees were spreading word that Fred owed Mason twenty-five thousand dollars.

It was an artful lie, although it had been poorly executed. It capitalized on the fact that federal prosecutors had already warned Fred he was a witness, that the sloppy legal work Fred had done on Mason's behalf had eventually cost Mason and Cline the Parrot club and might have generated a grudge, and that Al Brown had fired him when he tried unsuccessfully to persuade Brown to enter a guilty plea. Mostly, it stamped with a permanent question mark any incriminating testimony that Mason or Brown might later care to offer about Fred.

"Did you own any interest in the Parrot?" Hunton asked.

"I don't think the Parrot's even there anymore," Fred sidestepped the question. "Mr. Mason hasn't had any interest in it in a while."

Hunton repeated the question.

"No," the attorney sighed. "Not legally, no." He didn't mention he had been a corporate officer until the Parrot's holding corporation, and its officers, were sued.

"When was the last time you saw James Mason?"

"I don't know. I can't remember."

The detectives didn't ask Fred to elaborate. They weren't aware of the federal money-laundering investigation, didn't know how close a grand jury was to sweeping Fred into a drug conspiracy, had no clue that less than two weeks before Sara's death the grand jury had subpoenaed Al Brown's wife to testify about his assets, and weren't convinced that, if Fred was failing to report his taxes, he would kill his wife to conceal it. They were looking for more obvious motives for murder, reasons such as adultery, excessive insurance policies, or divorce that drove the other homicides they usually confronted in Cobb County.

"What kind of insurance policies did you have on Sara?" Hunton asked.

"I think there are three or four of them on her, and three or four of them on me," Fred volunteered. He was, among other things, an insurance broker. The policies—one for $250,000, one for $1 million and one for five hundred thousand—were investments, he explained. His life, as well as Sara's, was insured, he insisted. "I've got the same ones that she does."

At that point, the detectives became convinced they had ferreted out the $1.75 million motive for Sara's murder.

But Fred assured them he had money in accounts and safe deposit boxes all over the city—revenue generated not only by his lucrative law and accounting practice, but by a series of private ventures. Buried amid the tally of bank accounts and corporations was the attorney's passing mention of "four or five little related ventures" that included a construction company, a mortgage company, and a real estate firm. They were the same businesses he had set up, and then stripped, from Eddie Lawrence.

Again, Fred's commercial enterprises held only passing interest for the detectives.

"Mr. Tokars, tell me about your relationship with your wife," Hunton said.

"What do you want to know?" Fred was guarded.

"Were you happy?"

"We had our ups and downs."

"Most recently, has there been any talk of divorce on your part or her part?"

The question, borne of the emotional and bitter interviews with Sara's sisters, cut to the heart of Sara's death. By then, Banks and Hunton both were certain they knew the answer. They were curious to know how Fred would answer it, whether and how often he would lie. But Fred had been waiting for this question. By then, the attorney had seen published accounts that the private investigator Sara had hired had gone to police. Detectives must surely know he had indulged in an affair. They would also know that the three-year-old information, and the motive it implied, was stale.

"You know, occasionally, I'd have a fling here or there with someone," the attorney acknowledged. "There was one girlfriend that Sara thought I was ready to leave town with, and she hired an attorney or investigator. That was on the news last night. At any rate, we went to counseling.

"Sara always thought that I drank a little too much," he continued thoughtfully. "She was concerned I was representing bad people and running around and drinking."

"So, as far as you know, Mr. Tokars," Hunton pressed, "Sara had never seen an attorney concerning a divorce?"

"I think three or four years ago," Fred answered slowly. "But I don't think she had recently. I didn't feel as though things were bad right now. I felt as though things were good.

"You know, I loved Sara very much," he continued. "She was, like, the perfect wife for me. And yeah, like I said, we had our ups and downs. But I've never touched her in my entire life. I've never hit her. I don't think I've ever hit anybody in my entire life."

He had said too much. No one had asked him if he had ever struck Sara or the children. He didn't know it was the one last secret she had withheld from all her sisters. Fred rattled on, oblivious.

"And, you know, we might have an argument here and there, but I felt like we had a good marriage, or at least as good as the ones I've seen as a lawyer doing divorce work. I would be shocked if I thought that she was considering a divorce right now from me. I would really be shocked, and I would be hurt." He was waxing indignant, and Banks and Hunton were convinced they had caught him in yet another lie.

"Did she sleep with you?" Hunton asked.

"Yes." A lie.

"Did she have sex with you?"

"Yes." The detectives were certain they had their man.

"Do you use any other addresses outside Cobb County?"

But Fred was ready for that question, too. For years, he explained, he had shared a lease with Sara's youngest sister as a way of maintaining a Fulton County address so he would be eligible for political appointments in Atlanta.

"I'm sure you saw the paper this morning," he said. "My wife actually helped me look for the apartment. It's a dive. There's no furniture in it. The heat's not turned on. It was never designed as a place where I was gonna live or have a girlfriend or anything."

It was really just a ruse, an empty address through which he registered to vote in Fulton County that would, at least on paper, make him eligible for a post as a county magistrate judge. But the dishonesty inherent in his explanation didn't seem to faze him.

"What are your plans for the future?" Hunton asked Fred pointedly. "Are you planning on staying in Atlanta? Are you thinking about moving somewhere? Or have you given it any thought?"

"I don't know." Fred gulped. "I'm gonna come up with a reward. It's gonna be hard. Obviously, I'm not going to be making money as a lawyer any time soon." The last thing Fred wanted to do was offer a reward for information that might ferret out Sara's killer and lead directly back to him. But Sara's family and her neighbors had already decided to open a reward fund. To keep from casting suspicion on himself, Fred had no choice, not only to go along but to take the lead, as if losing Sara and hunting down her killer really mattered to him.

"I don't plan on leaving," the attorney continued. "My mother's here. She really needs me. My two brothers are here. Plus, I'm more concerned about my kids and getting them back into the routine they were in."

"What kind of relationship do you have with your kids?" Hunton asked carefully. Sara's sisters had told him tearfully that Fred paid only rare attention to his boys.

"I think it's good," Fred answered. "I love my kids very much, and I was always there for them." His voice assumed a defensive edge.

"Did the kids ever refuse to stay with you?" Hunton asked.

There was a long pause. "Whenever Sara would leave, about a third of the time, they'd say, 'No, Mommy, don't go.

Don't go.' But as soon as she left, everything was fine." The defensive tone waxed sharper.

"The kids did that with baby sitters, and they did it this morning when I was ready to leave. They didn't want me to leave. They loved their mother so much, and she was a very wonderful person, and I know you look at me like, what a rat for having cheated on her, but my kids meant a lot to me. And I spent as much time as I could with them, and I had very little social life as a result." Fred now sounded aggrieved.

"I would work hard, and then I would be with my kids. I wasn't hanging around with millions of girls at millions of fancy hotel clubs or country clubs. I wasn't playing golf or tennis. I was there with them as much as I could be."

"Did you ever have Sara investigated?" Banks lobbed the question at the now sullen attorney. Fred shook his head. "Are you sure?"

The attorney waited so long, the detectives weren't sure he intended to answer. "I think I'm sure," he hedged. "I don't believe I ever did." It was clearly an unexpected question, and Fred didn't know what other cards the detectives might be holding as he fashioned his next answer.

"If you have something to refresh my memory," he said carefully, "but I don't think that I ever did. Let me think for a second here. I don't think that I ever did."

It was a curiously guarded answer that suggested the attorney had something to hide. But the detectives did not pursue it.

"Mr. Tokars, do you have any idea who may have wanted to kill Sara?" Hunton asked.

Again, Fred hesitated, as if he were trying to decide what hidden information might have prompted such a question. "I just can't even imagine it," he said.

"What do you think happened?" Hunton rephrased the question. But he was truly looking for clues to the still unfathomable answers. "What do you think? Why did this happen?"

"I don't know," Fred replied. "I wish I knew. I've thought about this, and I've slept, like, two hours a night, and the rest of the night I'd roll in my bed thinking about it, and I think they were probably after me, but I just don't know."

He didn't say who "they" were. Banks and Hunton didn't ask. But Banks did gently admonish the former assistant district attorney who had prosecuted cases in one of the nation's most violent districts, "You need to start thinking about people that you prosecuted, people with a major sentence who would roll out after about seven years, people who got life sentences."

"I will." Tokars heaved a final sigh. "It's a nightmare."

It was an abysmal performance. By the time Tokars left, his two criminal defense attorneys in tow, Hunton and Banks were convinced that the trail left by Sara's killer ended in her husband's lucrative pockets. Fred had lied to them, dissembled, balked at providing them with even the most harmless information, thrown about red herrings like bait.

He didn't sleep with Sara, but had willingly lied about it. He had threatened her if she divorced him. He had slept around. And, dead, Sara—a suburban homemaker—was worth $1.75 million. Fred, himself, had characterized the policies insuring Sara's life as "an investment" in their future. As far as the two detectives were concerned they now had motive to spare.

They had little interest in the murderous drug dealers, all in prison, whom Fred had fingered as possible suspects. But they had missed the significance of Fred's intimations about James Mason and Al Brown and gave only passing consideration to the documents Sara had taken from her husband's safe that had so alarmed her cousin, Mary Rose Taylor.

Banks and Hunton didn't yet know how Fred had come to kill his wife, but they were now certain that he had. Drunk, drugged, or simply a bad actor, the attorney had not fooled them. Driven by two of the Seven Sins, Fred had ordered the execution of his wife for money and for lust.

But in the hours immediately following his interview, narcissistic to his core, Fred believed he had outwitted Banks and Hunton. He had sidestepped their questions. He had given only noncommittal answers. He had said nothing that could be refuted later. He appeared addled by prescription drugs. He had masked the demarcation between truth and fiction with carefully executed turns of phrase. He had volunteered information on the policies insuring Sara's life, the sexual liaisons that Ralph Perdomo had revealed, his rental of an apartment in Fulton County a month before Sara died. He deemed his explanations to be reasonable, unwilling to believe that the legal tactics he employed had simply made him look uncooperative, evasive, and guilty.

So confident was Fred that he could skate unscathed through a battery of suspicious questions that he called *The Atlanta Journal-Constitution* after he left the Cobb County Police Department and gave reporters what became a front-page interview.

It was a seemingly open, even avuncular, conversation with a man who had just been questioned by police for three hours. But whether he was apologizing, bragging or confessing, Fred openly acknowledged what he had already told police and Sara's family—that he had indulged in an extramarital affair four years before Sara's murder and that she had hired a private investigator to follow him. But, he insisted, his marriage had been repaired, and he would do "whatever it takes" to help police find Sara's killer.

Was Sara afraid of anyone?

"I have never hit Sara, my children, or anyone in my life," the attorney responded hotly—answering, just as he had during his interview with Cobb detectives, a question that had not been asked.

But now, in the wake of Sara's death, Fred said he feared for his own safety and that of his two children so much that he had hired twenty-four-hour security to protect them. He didn't mention that one of his bodyguards was Billy Carter, the "family friend" who had shooed reporters from the door the day after Sara died.

He began sobbing as he recounted a tender story about his sons—the same one that he had already told police.

"We went to a movie the other night, and Michael looked at me and said, 'Dad, Mom would have liked this.' I think he knows she's gone, but he doesn't really understand it yet.

"I've been thinking over and over and over and over why and who would have done this," Fred continued mournfully. "It's the hardest thing in the world to understand. I just don't know."

He declined to say more, offering the sympathetic explanation, "I have been asked by police and my attorney not to talk publicly until after the case has been solved. I would like to speak with you further, but I think I should follow their advice. I am hoping they will solve this case and solve it soon."

Police, at least, had never asked Fred not to speak about the case. In fact, police detectives had assured Sara's family that continued publicity might actually flush Sara's killer from hiding.

In one final, emotional footnote, Fred added, "If this thing destroys my law practice, then so be it. I've told police, 'Everything I have is open to you, everything.' I'm willing to do whatever it takes to catch this guy."

Fourteen

Hung Out to Dry

WHEN RICK WHEELER, ONE OF EDDIE LAWRENCE'S SOMEtime business partners, saw the accounts of Sara's death on television and heard that police were looking for a slender, African-American man, he knew that Eddie had to be involved. He knew Eddie worked for Sara's husband. He had been to the Tokars's house with Eddie just a month before the murder. He was friends with Cornbread Rower's sister, Toozdae. And he knew that Eddie had been looking for a hit man.

On Monday, November thirtieth, as police were still scouring the Tokars's house for clues, Wheeler called on Eddie. He wanted to talk about the murder. In a sly street argot, he taunted Eddie with Sara's death, noted with ill-contained glee that police were seeking the slender, black man who had killed her, a man who just might be Eddie Lawrence. He badgered Eddie to confess, and mocked his silence when Eddie's answer was a simple, sullen "no."

Fred Tokars was going to set him up, Wheeler warned. Eddie would find no solace there. And it was only a matter of time before Toozdae Rower, Rower's crack-addicted sister, turned state's evidence against her brother and her boss because Eddie hadn't paid her either.

What Eddie ought to do, Wheeler argued, was blackmail Fred, the puppeteer behind the scrim who had pulled their strings and had the most to lose. But Eddie maintained his

252

obstinate silence. If Wheeler were seeking more lurid details to inflate the information he could sell or barter to police, he failed. But, in the end, what he did know was enough to corroborate the stories of the frightened or disgruntled circle of acquaintances who soon turned on Lawrence and Rower like a pack of wayward dogs. Sara's murder was unlike the crackhouse slayings and drug robberies to which they were accustomed that were, by and large, crimes ignored by police and the media. Sara was the innocent wife of a prominent man who was kidnapped from a safe, suburban enclave and then slaughtered in front of her two young sons. For months, her face would haunt the airwaves, and her killer would be zealously pursued.

But even as Eddie stoutly protested his innocence, Wheeler's taunts dogged him. His swagger sagged. His cocky, braggart's manner dwindled, leaving him anxious and deflated. He held to one hope, that Fred would still come through for him. Yet, since Sara's murder, Eddie had heard nothing. Now, he needed reassurance. He also needed to be paid.

One day after Wheeler's visit, Eddie paged Fred. Fred's voice was curiously removed when he returned the call.

"Who's this?" he asked as if Eddie's telephone number had suddenly eluded him.

"It's Eddie," Lawrence replied, startled that, after months of calls and companionable dinners, he would need to remind his mentor who he was.

"How are you doing?"

"I'm doing all right."

"Did you hear about Sara's murder?" The attorney's voice was flat.

"I heard about it." Eddie paused, waiting for Fred to commend him, and to tell him how and when he would deliver the money.

Instead, the attorney offered, "It's a terrible tragedy, isn't it?"

"Yeah." A thin thread of worry creased Eddie's voice.

"Well, I'm going to Florida," the attorney said. "I'll see you in about three months." He hung up the phone. Their conversation had lasted seventy seconds.

He had said nothing about money, nothing about the insurance, offered no thanks or praise. Instead, he had jilted Eddie and was preparing to abandon him. It was the last time the two men ever spoke.

For three more days, Eddie waited. By Friday, with no more word from Fred, Eddie once more sought out Rower. He had promised him five thousand dollars. He would deliver it within ten days.

"Just relax. Everything is cool," Eddie told the young killer. "Fred is a man of his word. He does what he says. If the man told me he was going to give me money, he will.

"Don't run your mouth either," he warned Rower. "And keep your sister from running her mouth."

Gone was the charade that Sara was Eddie's wife, that Eddie was the one who wanted Sara dead because she "was standing in the way of a lot of money." Now, he was shifting gears, the blame, and the responsibility to his attorney as the one who had really solicited Sara's murder.

The subtleties were lost on Rower, who only wanted money. But he seemed content with Eddie's explanation, as long as Eddie padded it with enough cash to purchase beer and drugs. Three days later, Rower wasn't as forgiving. He was out of money, Sara's face was a haunting constant on television, police were hunting him, and he still had nothing to show for it. Eddie gave him what he had in his pockets. It was barely a hundred dollars.

Eddie's stalling also unnerved Toozdae Rower's boyfriend, Red Swinger, who had never thought of Eddie as reliable.

"Curtis," he warned Rower, "them people ain't giving you your money. They might come back and try to hurt you, and they might try to come back and hurt me or Toozdae, too."

When he couldn't shake Rower from his lethargy, Swinger, in desperation, shared his fears with his mother, including the detailed account of Sara's slaying that Cornbread had related when, coasting on cocaine, he had pounded on his sister's door within hours of the murder. In case anything happened to him, Swinger wanted someone else to know just who might be at fault. His mother told her boyfriend, who was a sheriff's deputy. That deputy, and others who had heard, eventually went to Cobb police, for, by then, police and Sara's family were raising money for any information that would lead to Sara's killer.

Tom Lord, a neighbor and banker whose children attended school with Rick and Mike and whose wife had taught with Sara, had volunteered to set up the reward fund.

Joni broke the news to Fred. "Isn't that great?" she marveled as she gave Fred the neighbor's name and number. "He wants you to call him, or he will come down to the hotel."

"No." Fred curtly cut her off. "No, we're not going to do that. We're not going to meet with him. He's just feeling guilty. He probably had an affair with her."

It was a bold slander of both his dead wife and someone generous enough to offer help. Outraged and hurt, Joni remained undeterred. She conferred with her sister and, together, they approached Fred a second time.

"Let's at least hear what he has to say," Joni pleaded. "He says he wants to help."

Once more, Fred refused.

But Joni and her sisters agreed to establish the reward fund anyway with the help of Sara's friends and the generous banker who had contacted them. Determined to find her sister's killer, Joni wrote press releases and fliers which she and her sisters distributed.

"Why are you and your sisters doing all this media?" Fred exploded at Joni one day.

"Because we are trying to find out who murdered Sara," she responded hotly. "We're trying to get word out about the reward."

"Joni, I thought you were smart," Fred shot back. "You shouldn't be doing that."

"But the police said it would be a good idea," she argued. "There have been no breaks on the case."

"Those cops are idiots," he sneered.

Finally, Fred informed Sara's sisters that he was establishing his own twenty-five-thousand-dollar reward, which his legal team announced in a press release a week after the family buried Sara. He may have done it for appearance's sake. He may have done it simply to reestablish his control. He may have decided it was an easy gamble, a generous gesture by a grieving husband that would never come to fruition. For Fred still assumed that Eddie had slain Sara and confided in no one. But now that at least a dozen people knew of the circumstances surrounding Sara's death, dangling those rewards was akin to chumming for sharks.

Soon after, an anonymous woman, her face hooded, appeared at the Cobb County Police Department's front desk. She refused to go any farther than the lobby. She didn't want to appear as if she were passing information to police. When a detective captain supervising the investigation into Sara's murder came to the window, she quietly told him that a man named Curtis Rower was involved in Sara's death, that Rower had a sister who was a secretary at Eddie Lawrence's office, and that Lawrence had at least one business partner, a man named Rick Wheeler.

That week, Toozdae Rower began to pressure Eddie for the five hundred dollars he had agreed to pay her for arranging an introduction to her brother. On Friday, December eleventh, she left a message for Eddie. "If we don't get our money, I'm going to turn state's evidence." Besides, the reward money was fifty times what Eddie owed her for her services. The impact of such an action on her brother didn't faze her. One day later, on Saturday, December twelfth, Eddie called them back.

By then, Cobb County detectives had put out the word that they were looking for Eddie.

When Eddie met them at the police department, Detectives Banks and Hunton told him right away that theirs was a homicide investigation surrounding the murder of Sara Tokars. They wanted to know whether Eddie and Fred were business partners; they wanted to know why. They wanted to know who held the majority interest, why the companies Eddie ran for Fred were struggling, and why Eddie had bounced two company checks, then repeatedly refused to pay them.

They also wanted to know when Eddie had last talked to Fred and the details of that final seventy-second call.

"I hadn't talked to him since the incident," Eddie explained as he edged around Sara's murder. "I feel like if I'm a friend, I should call."

It was obvious the two detectives had reviewed Fred's tele-

phone records because they asked Eddie if he had talked to
Fred the day before his wife was killed as well as on the day
she died.

"Yes," Eddie acknowledged carefully. Fred had asked him
if he could repair the hot water heater. Eddie said he had no
one available to do it. He remembered even less about their
Sunday conversation.

"Did he ever talk to you about his relationship with his
wife? How about girlfriends?" Banks asked.

"No," Eddie replied. "We never really got personal."

The two detectives began probing for an alibi. Where was
Eddie the night Sara was murdered? Was anyone with him
after 8:30 p.m.? Could anyone vouch for his assurance that
he was home in bed alone?

"Mr. Lawrence," Banks asked candidly, "do you have
ideas as to who killed Sara Tokars?"

"No, I don't."

"Did you kill Sara Tokars?"

"No."

"Why would someone want to kill Sara Tokars?"

"I don't know."

"You know anybody that wants to kill Fred Tokars?"

"No, I don't." Eddie's answers had shrunk to monosyl-
lables.

"Did Fred Tokars speak to you about finding someone to
hit his wife?" Someone, somewhere, had handed them the
blueprints of Sara's murder.

"Never."

"He's never mentioned that to you?" Hunton was insistent. "You would remember that wouldn't you?"

"Yeah."

"He's never mentioned the desire to have his wife out of
the way?"

"Never."

They had sweated Eddie for forty minutes. By the end of
the interview he was virtually noncommunicative. He had answered their questions with half-truths, with small, slick lies,
and, in a voice as implacable as a mask, with several stunning
denials. The detectives had little choice but to release him.

"I wasn't going to confess to murder," Eddie would say later. "I just told them I didn't do it."

When he walked away from the police station that day, Eddie may have thought he had finessed the two detectives. He may have believed, in his cocky, errant way, that they had nothing they could pin on him and that Fred would enlist his powerful friends to defend him if police harassed him further.

The media quickly disabused him of that notion. By Monday night, Eddie's photo was all over the news. Reporters knew police had questioned, but not charged, him in connection with Sara's murder. Before the news had ended, Eddie fled Atlanta.

The realization that police were willing to go public rattled Eddie to his self-centered core. If he had ignored the signals during his Saturday interview with police that they knew more than they were saying—the pointed questions about Fred's illicit girlfriends, Eddie's troubled business ventures, and Sara's murder, the curious inquiries about his telephone calls to Fred within a day of Sara's death—by Monday he knew his interview was merely prelude to a full investigation.

Eddie didn't know that anonymous tipsters, not Fred, had first informed police that the two men were partners in a troubled web of small business firms. In his December sixth statement to Detectives Banks and Hunton, Fred had made a single generic reference to the mortgage and real estate firms and the construction company he owned with Eddie. While he had given detectives the names of seven business partners in at least three different ventures and cast suspicion on a number of his clients, Fred had inexplicably omitted the name of Eddie Lawrence. After questioning Eddie, the detectives were certain they knew why.

Eddie left Atlanta that night, fleeing to a motel in Covington in the city's far-flung suburbs where he registered under an assumed name that he soon forgot. On Tuesday, he learned that Cobb detectives were looking for him again. They had told his family they had a few more questions. Eddie wanted nothing to do with them. But by Wednesday, Eddie had changed his mind. Running from police only made him look guilty. And it never crossed his mind that white detectives working in Cobb County north of Atlanta could ever tap into any underground network of urban informants capable of coughing up the name of Curtis Rower. On Wednesday, December sixteenth, he called police and agreed to meet with them a second time. In an interview later that day, Banks and Hunton asked Eddie again if he had murdered Sara. Once again, Eddie told them no.

"They didn't have a warrant for my arrest," he would say later, "so I wasn't going to confess."

But by that time, what police did have was information that Eddie Lawrence's name was scrawled across Sara Tokars's murder. Tipsters were calling police with information about Eddie and Curtis Rower. Detectives had tracked down Rick Wheeler and persuaded him to take a polygraph exam after he told them Eddie had asked him to kill Sara and that the two had scouted out the Tokars's home. They had also begun hauling in Eddie's office girls—among them former stripper Dion Fearon and Rower's sister, Toozdae—to ask them what they knew about Eddie and Sara's husband, Fred. Fearon, who had shared a room at the Ritz-Carlton with Fred on more than one occasion, had paged the attorney in a panic when she learned police wanted to question her. Fred was her lawyer, and she was afraid to talk to the detectives without one. Fred had told her, "I can't help you."

Eddie may have thought that at the end of that second interview he would once more skate unscathed through the police department's doors, that the bad check charges he had accumulated were not enough to warrant incarceration, or that he could explain them simply as stemming from his financially troubled business, a matter more civil than criminal. He was wrong. The detectives jailed him. He was transferred to the Fulton County Jail where he faced six felony check fraud charges. A seventh was pending in Wheeler County. They didn't want Eddie unexpectedly leaving town again until they could prove what they already knew—that Eddie was near the sinister center of the plot to murder Sara.

The publicity surrounding the slaying had aggravated Cornbread Rower's capricious, drug-fueled paranoia. Slumped low in the seat of his car, he would troll the southern edges of the city for hours. At his uncle's house, he began hiding in a rear bedroom and sleeping under the bed. A week after the murder, Red Swinger found Rower sitting at his uncle's kitchen table, staring morosely at what remained of the .410-gauge shotgun that had killed Sara Tokars.

"Dino's sick," he said plaintively. "Do you want to go with me to help me get my money?"

But by then, it was too late. Eddie Lawrence, the man that Rower and Swinger knew as "Dexter," was in the Fulton County Jail.

Five days before Christmas, Detectives Banks and Hunton once more were seated in an interrogation room with Sara's husband and the two criminal defense attorneys who flanked him. This time their questions were aggressive and accusatory.

Hunton threw a mugshot of Lawrence on the table.

"You know that man?" he demanded.

"It's Eddie Lawrence," Fred said innocently.

"We talked on December sixth of this year for some three hours, and this man was never mentioned," Hunton said with cold deliberation. "Never mentioned."

"I'm not sure that I know what you're talking about."

"You never told me anything about Eddie Lawrence," the detective responded heatedly.

"Well," Fred replied, "you never asked me anything about him."

Three days after Sara's funeral, Banks and Hunton had asked Fred for any information about anyone who might have a grudge against Fred that would give him a reason to slay Sara, and the attorney had failed to mention a business partner he had sued for seventy thousand dollars. When they had asked him about his business associations, he had sidestepped naming Eddie Lawrence. Now, they wanted to know why.

"Everything I've ever done with Eddie Lawrence is a matter of public record," Fred explained. "I have nothing to hide."

With that, the attorney launched into a long-winded and, at times, defensive explanation as to how and why he became partners with Eddie. He talked of referral clients, real estate in lieu of fees, corporate entities, business opportunities in Atlanta's majority African-American community, personal

promissory notes, arcane tax writeoffs, and business investment losses. Throughout, he described Eddie as "valuable,"
an "expert witness" in real estate who "knew numbers."

"He can't be too good with numbers," Hunton responded
wryly. "He's been hanging bad paper all over north Georgia."

"It's come to my attention," Fred acknowledged ruefully.
"It bothers me. But I tell you this—a lot of my clients who
make a lot of money also bounce checks. My wife was probably, unfortunately, one of the people I used to criticize for
bouncing checks."

It was the first and only time he mentioned Sara.

"What was his reaction when you sued him?" Hunton
asked. Fred had not mentioned the civil suits he had brought
against Eddie just two months before Sara's death.

"That was a consensual suit," Fred answered. "I assume
you have the suit because they're made a matter of public
record." But mention of the suits that he had used to hogtie
Lawrence financially made him stammer. He also began backing away from Eddie, prefacing his explanation with, "Towards the end of my relationship with him. . . ."

Eddie was in obvious financial trouble, Fred explained. Clients were threatening to sue. Eddie "messed up a little job."
He "wasn't exactly" managing his money well.

"I wanted to be first in line," Fred explained. "I wanted
to have first dibs on everything."

As his explanation veered into the minutia of tax losses
and accounting practices, Fred must have realized that the
scheme he was outlining bordered dangerously on criminal
fraud.

"Whether it's right or wrong," he added sheepishly, he
had sued Eddie for the money he had invested in their partnership, claiming it was not an investment but a personal loan.
He had also represented Eddie and advised him after the suit
was filed.

As Banks and Hunton pressed him for more details about
his relationship with Eddie Lawrence, Fred acknowledged
telling Eddie he would sink no more money into Eddie's businesses. He also admitted that he had stripped Eddie of his
credit.

"What did Eddie Lawrence think about the fact that the business might go under, that he had been cut off?" Banks asked. Such an action could well be a motive for murder.

Fred launched into another babbling monologue about his high hopes for the enterprise without ever answering the detective's question.

"Has Eddie Lawrence ever been out to your home?" Banks asked the attorney pointedly.

"Oh, yeah. Numerous times. He did work on my home. He put in a bathroom."

Hunton leapt on the statement. They had caught Fred in a lie.

"Do you remember that last time we talked, we asked you who did the work on the bathroom and you just couldn't remember?" Hunton challenged him.

"On what bathroom?" Fred's response was suddenly guarded. "I don't remember you asking me that question."

The words seemed to stumble from his mouth.

"I mean, the bottom line is this ... I don't believe ... I don't remember being asked specifically about that type of question. It wouldn't have been nothing that I would have hidden. My wife knew Eddie Lawrence. My kids watched him do the work out there. It would have been ludicrous for me to try to have hidden the fact that I knew him or that he did work on my bathroom."

That, in fact, was exactly what Fred had done.

"That's just my honest explanation," the attorney continued. "I don't remember being asked that question. There's a lot of things I don't remember that have occurred in the last three or four weeks because it's been very hard on me.

"But I most certainly never would have withheld that piece of information."

Still missing from his conversation with police was any real mention of Sara. He showed no apparent curiosity as to why the detectives had zeroed in on Lawrence. He never asked whether they truly thought Eddie might have killed his wife. There was no shock, no horror, no remorse or revulsion, no personal recriminations—all normal reactions for a man who had just been informed that his wife's killer may well have been his business partner. Instead, the attorney's verbal tap dance was wholly self-absorbed.

Hunton chose that moment to rattle him further.

"Talk to me about the phone conversation you had with Eddie Lawrence Saturday and Sunday. Those two days, the last one was the day your wife was killed."

The almost amiable nature of the question belied its significance. Banks and Hunton had taken the considerable trouble of checking the telephone records of both men on the days leading up to Sara's murder. Two conversations the day before and the day of Sara's death with a business partner he had failed to mention placed Fred squarely on their list of murder suspects.

Fred responded with the stock answer defense attorneys always provide to clients under oath. Don't lie. Just forget.

"I don't remember the exact details about what happened on those two days," Fred answered slowly. "I don't remember specifically what happened or what didn't happen. I don't remember exactly who I talked to. You're asking me to remember things I just don't recall right now."

But, he added, "I have met with Eddie Lawrence and talked with Eddie Lawrence since the inception of our relationship. There's nothing that I had to hide about that."

Was the attorney's memory lapse that of an honest man understandably distraught by the brutal trauma of his wife's shocking death? Or was he scurrying to escape his own culpability in the inept way of criminals certain that they would never be caught? Banks and Hunton were certain it was the latter.

"Wait a minute," Hunton said. "Are you telling me you don't remember talking to him Saturday and Sunday?"

"I don't remember if I did or if I didn't. But if I did, it wouldn't surprise me."

He paused, certain now that police had pulled, not just Eddie's phone records, but his. They knew he had talked to Eddie the day that Sara died. His memory cleared. He had talked to Eddie. He couldn't be sure, but he had probably called him about the broken hot water heater. But his memory remained steadfastly blank when it came to the specifics of their conversations.

The Cobb detectives were now actively trying to catch Fred in a lie. They asked him questions about Dion Fearon, the stripper, although they didn't mention that Fearon had told them about her affair with the attorney and Fred's assurance that he would kill his wife. They asked him why he had earlier told them he hadn't talked to nightclub proprietor James Mason for months when he had, in fact, talked with Mason the day Sara was buried.

"I don't believe I said that." Fred was wary. "James Mason was an ongoing, regular client of mine. Months?"

"That's what you said."

"No, I can't believe I said that."

The detectives moved on, seeking other lies. Tom Lord, one of the Tokars's neighbors, had offered to establish a reward for information leading to the killers.

"And according to Mr. Lord, you told him not to do that; the police had this great lead, and we were close to making an arrest," Hunton said. "Did you tell him that?"

"I never told him that. Keep in mind that was a very emotional time for me. I was probably drinking too much. I was medicated. Tom Lord pestered or called our room at least six or seven times in a two- or three-day period."

Fred floundered, then settled on an explanation. "I wanted to have the reward fund set up through my family. I felt it would look better." And, he added lamely, "I was taking the advice of my attorney."

Pat Banks was getting impatient with Fred's inconclusive answers, his nearly perfect lack of recall, his unwillingness to volunteer any information unless prodded into doing so, his apparent ease with degrees of truth. Banks was tired of the game, as if Sara's death was a grand charade where the right answers were forthcoming only if one phrased the questions precisely.

"Mr. Tokars, do it the easy way," he demanded. "Is there anything that you remember about how your house was the Sunday that you left?"

Again, Fred was coy. "Can you ask me specific questions about what you mean?" He would volunteer nothing.

Hunton, too, was frustrated with what the detectives now saw as an intentional absence of cooperation that bordered on obstruction. Their questions grew noticeably more harsh.

"Mr. Tokars, do you remember telling someone that the reason that you were delaying talking to the police was because you had to figure out how to answer the questions?" Hunton demanded.

"Hold it. Hold it." Fred's attorneys had been remarkably quiet throughout the increasingly hostile interview. Now Jerry Froelich interrupted vociferously. "Don't even answer that. I want to make it clear," he spoke deliberately to both detectives, "the delay was me, and it's always been me. Any delay in meeting with you was because of my advice and because I couldn't be there. I didn't think he was physically or mentally capable of meeting, and I thought there were more important things right then—taking care of his family."

Banks and Hunton retreated. But before the two-hour interview ended, they returned once more to Eddie Lawrence.

"Did you know that Eddie Lawrence was connected in any way with a counterfeiting ring?"

"I felt comfortable that he wasn't involved," Fred answered.

"Would he get angry enough to lash out at you and try to send you a message?"

"I don't know." Fred half-heartedly dismissed the suggestion. "I have no evidence of him ever having a violent past. He was never violent around me. I don't have any evidence of him being violent to anybody."

"How about this." Banks was still seeking any motive that bore Eddie's silhouette. "Is he aware of how much you might keep in your safe? Would he be in a position to speculate that there might be large amounts of money in your home?"

"I think most of my clients would be in that position," Fred answered.

"Was there any bad blood or animosity between you and Eddie over what's been going on recently with the business?"

"I don't want to say bad blood," Fred said. "I would be frustrated sometimes at some of the things, yeah." But he insisted, after he informed Eddie he didn't want to funnel any more money into their joint venture, "He didn't argue with it."

But Banks kept pushing for answers, searching for more

links between Fred and Eddie that might cause police to widen their nets to include the elusive attorney. Again, he asked Fred about a conversation he had with Eddie the day Sara was killed and whether he had mentioned to his partner that he was leaving town.

The attorney remembered nothing of that conversation or whether it had even happened. And, although he acknowledged meeting Eddie quite often for dinner in the weeks leading up to Sara's death, he remembered nothing about them or when they had last shared a meal.

"Has Eddie ever made any threats towards you?" Banks pressed.

"No."

The detectives, by now, were even more convinced that Fred was protecting Eddie.

"Mr. Tokars," Hunton finally asked, "you've had a number of days to reflect on this. Is there anything else that you can tell us that might help us find who killed Sara Tokars?"

"It's sort of an open-ended question," Fred answered. "I mean, I've agonized and I've thought about it, and you can be assured, if I think of anything that we will definitely provide it to you. Any leads my lawyers have gotten I've asked them to turn them over to you."

It was a sterile, noncommittal answer from a lawyer, not a bereft and anguished husband.

By then, Fred and his lawyer had sent private investigator Tim Huhn to the Fulton County Jail to speak to Eddie Lawrence. Huhn's instructions were to find out what Eddie would say about his relationship with Fred and whether he was talking about Sara's murder.

When deputies brought Eddie from his cell, Huhn introduced himself, and told Eddie that Fred had hired him to hunt for Sara's killer. By then, Eddie was watching television news accounts with growing trepidation. He had seen Froelich on the news, chastising police for casting doubt on Sara's husband as he ardently defended his innocence. Eddie didn't know whether Huhn was an emissary from Fred sent to test his loyalty, or whether he was really an agent acting on behalf of Cobb police. He did know that he wasn't about to confess a murder to a stranger, no matter whom he claimed to represent.

"I've been expecting you," Eddie said.

Cobb County detectives had already informed him he was "definitely involved" in Sara's murder, and they had warned him that Fred had hired Huhn and Carter to kill him so that he wouldn't talk. But the police had promised to guarantee his safety if he cooperated with the investigation and had offered him a new identity, promised to move him out of state, and even suggested he might claim the reward, now nearly fifty thousand dollars, for helping solve Sara's murder.

"Do you have any knowledge of who was responsible for Sara Tokars's death?" Huhn asked.

"No."

"Was Fred involved in any way?"

"No."

If Huhn's questions were, in fact, some sort of loyalty test, Eddie figured he had passed it. If the private investigator was working hand in glove with police, Eddie had given him nothing to strengthen the case against him.

As Huhn was leaving, Eddie told him, "I'd like to get out of jail, get this matter resolved, and salvage my business with Fred." It was a message he hoped that Fred would understand.

But if Eddie wasn't talking, a circle of acquaintances that included Rick Wheeler and Rower's family were. After Eddie had rebuffed suggestions that he blackmail Fred in exchange for his silence about Sara's murder, Wheeler, enticed by the reward, surrendered Eddie's name and the bare outlines of the murder-for-hire plot to the Cobb police. Eddie, he said, had offered him five thousand dollars to "do a job" and had driven him by the Tokars's home before he had rejected the deal. He knew about Toozdae Rower and her family that thrived on crime. He and Toozdae had already discussed giving police her brother's name in order to claim the reward, in part for the crack it could buy.

Meanwhile, Red Swinger's mother's boyfriend had also called police and related a fifth-hand but startlingly accurate

account of Sara's murder—drawn from Rower's own account
to Swinger just hours after the slaying.

Three days before Christmas, Cobb investigators arrested
Swinger, a convicted drug dealer, for violating his probation.
They told Swinger they "already knew everything" about
Sara's murder, including his own casual involvement.

Transferred from an Atlanta jail to one in Cobb County,
where law enforcement authorities punished drug crimes more
harshly than in the city, Swinger had good reason to be worried. He became even more alarmed when detectives informed
him that they knew he knew about Sara's murder before it
happened and had done nothing to prevent it. Such knowledge
could brand him as an accessory to the crime.

"They told me the whole thing," Swinger said. "They told
me what had happened. They told me my involvement. They
told me just like it was, and I'm trying to figure out how they
know all this."

Eager to avoid criminal charges that would link him to
Sara's death, Swinger gave the detectives a formal statement
implicating Rower, his sister, Eddie Lawrence, and
"Smokey" Zinamon, the man who had sold Rower the .410-
gauge sawed-off shotgun that had ended Sara's life.

Before dawn on December twenty-third, Swinger accompanied the detectives to Toozdae's Carver Homes apartment
where she was detained for questioning. Once Toozdae corroborated Swinger's story, identified her brother as Sara's
killer, and gave the detectives her aunt's address where her
brother usually slept, she was released. While detectives were
waking a county magistrate with an urgent, predawn request
to search the College Park home that harbored Sara's killer,
Toozdae called her brother, warning the family to flee.

"Get the hell out of the house. The police are coming.
They know everything. And they know where you're at." Just
how they knew had conveniently slipped her mind.

Instead, Rower hid under the bed where police found him
less than two hours later, wallowing in the dregs of a drug
and alcohol stupor.

Banks and Hunton bundled Rower, cuffed and hungry, into
the backseat of their unmarked police car. En route to the
police department, they stopped at a fast food restaurant to

buy Rower juice and a sausage biscuit. Back at police headquarters in Marietta, they sat him down in an interview room,
uncuffed him, and gave him time to smoke a cigarette and
eat.

About 8:30 a.m., nearly two hours after he had been
dragged out from under his bed, the detectives told him they
wanted to talk to him about the murder of Sara Tokars.

"We've already talked to Red Swinger. We've already
talked to your sister, Toozdae. They told us about your involvement," the detectives informed the rank young man
with the sleep-glazed eyes.

"I don't know nothing about it," Rower replied. Nevertheless, he agreed to talk with them. But first, he insisted on
calling his grandmother. He was certain the police were lying
about taking statements from his sister and her boyfriend. His
grandmother would know whether Toozdae really had talked
to the police. His grandmother counseled him to tell police
the truth.

What followed that conversation was an informal, unre-
corded, hour-long interview during which the detectives
pushed Rower to confess. They knew he had killed Sara.
Swinger and Toozdae, his own sister, had given him up. They
played the more damaging portions of their taped interviews
with Toozdae and Swinger to prove it. By 9:30 a.m., Rower
had waived his right to an attorney and agreed to tell them
what happened.

He told them that he had met Eddie through his sister when
Eddie was in search of a gun "because somebody done tried
to rob him and he done got shot." He told them Eddie had
offered to pay him five thousand dollars "because I want this
bitch knocked off." He knew the small, intimate details of
Sara's life that police had withheld from the media—that Sara
slept with her children, that the sliding glass door leading into
the kitchen was either broken or unlocked, that the alarm
panel was in the master bedroom and that it had been deactivated before he had slipped inside.

He gave them detailed directions to the Tokars's home and
volunteered that he and Eddie had made an earlier attempt to
kill Sara shortly before Thanksgiving but had been thwarted
by the family dog. He admitted kidnapping Sara and her sons

at gunpoint after waiting for them for several hours in the house. He told the detectives, in a voice devoid of emotion or remorse, that he had hustled Sara and her boys into her four-wheel drive, slid into the backseat behind Sara, and leveled the shotgun at her neck as he ordered her to drive.

In his slurred, halting street patois, Rower insisted that he had not intended to kill Sara, even though Eddie had hired him to do so. Afraid that Eddie had abandoned him in a suburban subdivision far from the streets and public housing developments where he could go to ground, he had decided to kidnap her instead.

But even if Rower had changed his mind, the murder plot was resurrected once the gunman spotted Eddie parked in the driveway of an unfinished subdivision and ordered Sara to turn into an unlighted cul-de-sac where the houses were still under construction. Sara disobeyed him, pulling instead to the side of the road. As Rower blandly recounted Sara's final desperate moments, he implicated Eddie Lawrence as more than just a choreographer of death. Eddie, he told police, was standing just outside the car door as the fatal shot was fired.

"I told her to stop because I had seen Eddie. I had my door open. It was cracked. Then Eddie came to the side of the truck. She acted like she know Eddie 'cause when she seen his face, she was looking at him like she recognized him. Eddie tried to grab the gun, and I snap back from him, and it went off. I thought she had ducked. Eddie fell. She pushed the gas. When she pushed the gas, it kind of hit the curb. When she pulled off, it knocked him down."

As the two men scrambled into Eddie's pickup, Rower said Eddie grabbed the murder weapon and tossed it behind the seat. "He said he was going to dismantle it and throw it in the Chattahoochee."

Police would soon learn that Rower had lied to them at least twice as he confessed. There was no struggle over the sawed-off shotgun with the unreliable hammer. A forensic examination of the blood spattered inside the car proved that Rower's passenger door was closed when he fired the .410 shotgun point-blank at Sara's head. Six-year-old Ricky Tokars, sitting helpless in the front passenger seat just inches from his mother, never saw a second man open the rear door or wrestle for control of the gun before a blinding explosion took his mother's life. Nor did Rower surrender the vicious weapon he had affectionately named "Dino" to Lawrence that night. Loathe to dispose of the shotgun, he had kept it for at least a week after the murder, as residents of the Connell Street household where he returned after the murder later informed police.

But Rower's insistence that Eddie had left his pickup as Sara's car was idling at the roadside and that Sara had recognized him as he approached the driver's window explained why Rower shot Sara on a major thoroughfare instead of executing her in the house, where there was less chance of discovery. It also explained why the car veered across the road, jumped a curb, cleared a ditch, broke through an eight-foot hedgerow, and barreled hundreds of yards into a field—the last desperate act of a woman driven to save her children as she saw in Eddie's face the shadow of her husband.

Eddie wasn't the only person Rower implicated during his hour-long confession. He also implicated Sara's husband, although it appeared that he only learned of Fred's involvement after the murder, when he still hadn't been paid.

Edgy about the manhunt for Sara's killer, eager for cash to fuel his drug habit, Rower had called Eddie demanding five thousand dollars and his sister's five-hundred-dollar fee for introducing the killers.

Eddie swung by the house later that day to pick up Rower. "My people, they going to come through with the money," Eddie sought to reassure him.

"Your people? Who your people?" Rower demanded. "Is Fred? You just go on and tell me. Stop doing me, man. Don't try to dick me. Just tell me the truth.

"That's when he said, 'Fred,' " Rower told police. "He said, 'Fred gone out of town, and when he come in town, give it a little time to get off the news. When he come in town we get our money. I'm going to tell you the truth. I owe Fred a lot of money. This man ain't nobody to be fucked up with.'

"I know that Fred put the hit on," Rower told police. "Eddie told me that it was his lawyer's wife."

Later that morning, Banks and Hunton swung by the Fulton

County Jail where Eddie was awaiting trial on check fraud charges, cuffed him and drove him, once again, to Marietta for questioning. As they escorted him to an interview room, they passed the open door of a second room where Rower could be seen smoking a cigarette and sipping a soft drink. Eddie's knees buckled. The detectives knew they had their second man.

By the time Eddie sat down, he was shaking. "I want to do what I can, but I have to call my lawyer," he said. "Can I call him?"

When Atlanta attorney Bruce Harvey met with Eddie at the Cobb County Detention Center later that day, Eddie told him everything. "I told him that I was involved and what I had done," Eddie said. "And he told me, 'Don't tell anybody else. Don't say anything. Just shut your mouth, and let's see what happens.' " Police would not interview Eddie for another seven months.

The telephone rang at Dr. John Ambrusko's Bradenton home about 6 p.m. on December twenty-third. The elderly doctor answered the telephone in the dining room. Cobb County Detective Captain Julian Deal was on the line.

"We've arrested two men for Sara's murder," he informed Sara's father in the sterile police manner that is second nature to homicide detectives. "Eddie Lawrence and Curtis Rower."

The names meant nothing to Dr. Ambrusko.

"Is Mr. Tokars there?" the captain inquired.

"Yes. He's standing right here," Dr. Ambrusko replied.

"I would like to speak to him."

Dr. Ambrusko handed the receiver to his son-in-law.

The dining room assumed the dim, cottony calm of the sea before a squall. Fred listened for several minutes.

"Okay," he said. "Okay."

Then, he handed the telephone back to his father-in-law. "He wants to speak to you again," he said curtly.

Deal's voice was low and urgent. "I just told Fred what I told you about the fact that we had arrested two men and charged them with Sara's murder," he said. "What was his reaction?"

"Well, he didn't seem to have any reaction at all," Ambrusko said.

"Well, you know, one of these men is an associate of Fred's," Deal explained. "They are business partners."

Dr. Ambrusko slowly hung up the phone, a grieving and now deeply puzzled man.

"He said this one man they arrested was a business partner of yours," he told his son-in-law accusingly. "Can you tell us something about it? Who he is or anything about him?"

"It's Eddie Lawrence that he is referring to," Fred said slowly. "And he's a good guy."

"Yes, but how can he be involved in this?" Ambrusko demanded.

"I don't believe he is. Why, even my mother knows him."

"What kind of recommendation is that about what kind of person he is?" Ambrusko roared.

By then, Sara's sisters were shouting shrilly at Fred. They had known for years of Sara's fears regarding Fred's business associates and clients. The stunning horror that their sister had been right to be wary and that her husband had exposed her so nonchalantly to such danger infuriated them.

"Why would he want to kill Sara?" Krissy demanded. "Could he be mad at you?"

"He's a good guy. They've got the wrong guy," Fred insisted.

"Did you get in a fight?" Sara's older sister, Mary Bennett, cried.

"What's your definition of a fight?" her brother-in-law answered tartly. "We didn't have a physical altercation, if that's what you mean."

Joni, in particular, was outraged. She had remained in Atlanta after Sara's funeral to promote the reward fund and had seen news accounts of Eddie's arrest when Cobb police first questioned him concerning Sara's murder.

By then, Fred, doggedly insistent that he was leaving Atlanta for good, had flown to Sarasota with his sons. Unsure what to do with the children, he had willingly left them with Sara's parents. When Joni returned to Florida a few days later, she had confronted her brother-in-law with Eddie's arrest.

"Who is Eddie Lawrence?" she had demanded to know.

"They are talking to him about Sara's murder. He may know something, and you need to go to the police."

Instead, Fred had, once again, dismissed the Cobb police as "idiots," as he airily insisted, "Eddie Lawrence is a good guy."

"No matter what I said, he kept giving me excuses why he didn't want to talk about Eddie," Joni said. Now she screamed in her anger and her grief, "Who is this guy? What kind of business associate is this?"

"I just don't believe it," Fred insisted obstinately. He refused to discuss it further. "I can't talk about it. I'm just too upset."

"What's the problem, Fred?" Krissy demanded. "Do you want to talk to your lawyer first before you talk to us?"

Fred insisted later he was simply "in a state of shock." Sara's family, he said, were "vicious" and "just brutal" in their accusations. Sara's eighty-year-old father, he said, even threatened to have him "taken care of" by a former Buffalo patient reputed to be a Mafia henchman, an allegation that Joni later angrily dismissed as false.

By then television camera crews had amassed at the end of the Ambrusko driveway, seeking reaction to the arrests. In Atlanta, Cobb District Attorney Tom Charron had bluntly identified Fred as a suspect, telling reporters, "We've made that very clear to him."

Fred's attorney, Jerry Froelich, had countered by revealing that Fred had taken a private polygraph examination four days before Rower's arrest. The exam, administered by a former F.B.I. agent, had convinced Fred's defense team that the attorney had no hand in but was terrified by Sara's death.

But police still speculated publicly that Fred knew the motive for Sara's death, although he might not have known beforehand that she was going to be killed. They made false promises that more arrests were imminent, statements intended to spur and enlist the media in a campaign that would make Fred's facade blister and crack under the intense and critical public glare.

Fred, who had been drinking, desperately wanted to return to his motel near Lido Beach, but he didn't want to pass through the media gauntlet or entertain their aggressive and suspicious questions. He finally called a cab, gathered up his sons, and hustled them away from his in-laws' house.

His children "wanted to know why everyone was screaming at me, and they wanted to know what was going on, and they were crying," Fred recalled.

"And I just said, 'I'm going to get the heck out of here.' "

Neal Wilcox, the husband of Sara's younger sister, Karen, followed him. The family's faith in Fred's judgment had been wholly shattered, leaving only shards of sharp suspicion.

"We were a little concerned where he was going," Wilcox said, "and that he was going to be okay."

Later that night, after their children were asleep, Wilcox talked with Fred. But the attorney's words that night were devoid of remorse, shock, or rage—all natural responses to being told that a business partner had been charged with executing his wife in front of their two children. Instead, Fred's words fluttered at the wild edges of panic, as he confided to his former high school chum, "I'm worried about police making a deal.

"The police are after me, not after these guys," he chattered. "They are using these guys to get to me. I'm worried that the police are making a deal for their testimony against me."

That evening, after leaving the Ambrusko home, he had also placed a call to Captain Deal during which he extended a belated but still qualified offer of help. "I've already given you a lot of information about Eddie," he said, as if he had volunteered the details of his troubled partnership with Lawrence to police without being prodded to do so. "If there's anything I can do, I'll talk to my attorney, and, if we decide we can give you the information, we will. I'll give you everything I can on it."

Deal was not impressed. "That had generally been Mr. Tokars's response to everything—that he would do whatever was requested or asked. But then, somehow or other, nothing ever happened." In fact, despite his phoned assurances, Fred never gave Cobb detectives struggling to solve Sara's murder any more information about Eddie.

To distract and amuse the children, and celebrate the birthday of one of the small cousins, Sara's sisters had planned an excursion to Busch Gardens on Christmas Eve day, a family tradition. They had assumed Fred would accompany Rick and Mike, fragile and bewildered in the aftermath of their mother's death. But the unspoken schism between Fred and Sara's family was widening. All they seemed to think about was Sara and the boys. Fred thought they should have been thinking about him.

"I felt really terrible," he said. "They were screaming and yelling at me, and I was emotionally and psychologically drained. And the atmosphere was just too tense. I just couldn't face the Ambruskos. And I didn't really want the media following me and Rick and Mike around wherever I went."

That morning, he curtly informed his sons that they weren't going anywhere with Sara's family. They were going to spend a quiet day at the beach.

The children didn't understand. They wanted to go, needed the comfort of their cousins and a raft of aunts who reminded them of their mother and could distract them from their haunted dreams. Exasperated, Fred acquiesced, sending word with the children that he was staying at the motel because he had work to do.

But the old resentments he had long harbored against Sara—his ill-concealed fury that his wife had always defied control whenever her family was concerned and that she drew from them what little strength she had to challenge him—Fred now extended to her family. His sons were abandoning him for their aunts, who glared at him with cold, accusatory eyes.

"It felt like I was losing the last thing I had," Fred wretchedly explained. "I couldn't explain to them what was going on. I had lost Sara. I had lost my law practice. I had been driven cut of Atlanta by the media, and all of a sudden, Rick and Mike were saying, 'I want to be with them.' And so I felt I was by myself."

That morning, a story in *The Atlanta Constitution* had stated unequivocally that Sara was killed because she had found documents in Fred's basement safe indicating that money was being laundered through businessses owned by the attorney and his associates. Law enforcement authorities suggested those businesses might include the Atlanta nightclubs and club managers Fred had represented, several of whom had been under investigation for months.

The bold, authoritative statements stripped across the top of the newspaper's front page baffled and terrified him. He had underestimated Sara. Now, the attorney gagged on a legacy he thought he had buried with her. He had choreographed her murder meticulously. Eddie Lawrence should have been the solo killer, easily framed as a hostile, embittered business partner if guilt alone were not enough to insure his silence. Yet, police had arrested another man along with Lawrence whom Tokars didn't know. And, if the media were credible, federal authorities now had documents Sara had taken from Fred's safe containing evidence that he had laundered drug money in the Caribbean for his clients. That federal investigation, launched in August, and subtle hints by federal prosecutors that Fred might be tainted, had been the flash point that ignited Sara's murder.

But, in devising his wife's death, Fred had never considered that Sara had defied him, entering his basement sanctum where he secured the few documents linking him to his illegal offshore enterprises. A scrupulous and tautly suspicious man, he had never missed any of the documents that Sara copied. And he had failed to catch her. In doing so, he had lost control. Although he had killed her, Sara had won.

Alone again in a motel room, just as he had been on the night Sara died, Fred began to drink, indiscriminately washing down sedatives and painkillers with alcohol chasers. He chained the motel door, then shoved an easy chair against it.

At noon, Sara's father called the motel room to invite Fred to lunch. The elderly surgeon had always been fond of Fred and was reluctant to abandon him despite a gnawing uncertainty about his daughter's death. But he also had unanswered questions about his daughter's murder that he doggedly pursued. At noon, he called the motel room to invite Fred to lunch. No one answered. A half-hour later, Dr. Ambrusko called a second time. Fred still didn't answer the phone. At 1:30 p.m., he called again. When no one answered, he called the motel clerk, worried now—with Sara dead and Fred's business partner in jail—that something fearful might have happened, or that Fred had succumbed to heart failure from the stress.

The motel clerk was unconcerned. "It's a beautiful day. He's probably out by the pool."

But twenty-five days earlier, an unanswered telephone had signaled his daughter's death. After a fourth unanswered call at 2 p.m., Dr. Ambrusko and two of his daughters drove to the motel, found Fred's car parked in the motel lot, and hurriedly searched the nearby beach. Fred was nowhere to be found.

Worried, Dr. Ambrusko asked the motel clerk to lead them to his son-in-law's room. It was locked, and no one answered the door. When the clerk declined to break down the door, Dr. Ambrusko called the Sarasota police.

When police broke through the door, they found Fred semiconscious on the bed in a "catatonic state," suffering from an overdose of alcohol and pills.

Before he had passed out, surrounded by empty beer and prescription pill bottles, he had penned a letter to his children, his mother, his younger brother, and other "friends and family" in a scrawling, erratic hand.

Dear Rick, Mike, Norma, Andy, and friends and family:

I am sorry for the pain and sorrow my lifestyle has inflicted upon you. I never wanted to hurt Sara or anybody to die or get hurt.

I am a weak person and cannot stand the pain and sorrow any longer. I only want to end it.

Last night, I was asked: How could you work with anyone who could do this? And I had no answer. Please make sure my little Mike and Rick are taken care of. I love them so much. So did little Sara.

Andy and Mother Norma are the only 2 people who have stood by my side to the very end. Without them, I would have died a long time ago.

I took the lie detector test only because I knew that I was innocent. Ever since I took it, I wanted to die.

Sara Tokars and her two sons, Rick *(left)* and Mike. This photo was taken shortly before her murder and was distributed by her sisters at her funeral and presented to juries in three separate trials. It became Sara's defining portrait.

Courtesy of Janice Sanborn

THE MANY FACES

Prior to and during his 1994 federal trial, Tokars dressed meticulously in business suits.
Billy Downs/Reprinted with permission of The Atlanta Constitution *and* The Atlanta Journal

After his federal conviction, Tokars's appearance became gaunt and haunted.
Dwight Ross Jr./Reprinted with permission of The Atlanta Constitution *and* The Atlanta Journal

OF FRED TOKARS

During his 1997 death penalty trial, Tokars dressed in sweaters and wept copiously as his brother read aloud Tokars's 1992 suicide note.

Andy Sharp/Reprinted with permission of
The Atlanta Constitution *and* The Atlanta Journal

Defense lawyers introduced this photo at Tokars's murder trial in an effort to rehabilitate his image.

Crack addict Curtis Rower, sentenced to life without parole as the hit man who killed Sara.

Joe McTyre/Reprinted with permission of The Atlanta Constitution *and* The Atlanta Journal

Edwin Marger, once a lawyer for Haiti's "Papa Doc" Duvalier, represented Rower after he confessed.

Eddie Lawrence was a drug dealer, a con artist, and a thief who became Tokars's business partner.

Lawrence *(center)* is sentenced for his role in Sara's murder. He's surrounded by his lawyers, Bruce Harvey *(far right)* and Mark Spix *(center right)*, and Cobb County D.A. Tom Charron.

Dianne Laakso/Reprinted with permission of
The Atlanta Constitution *and* The Atlanta Journal

Jerry Froelich, Tokars's defense lawyer, cultivated a combative courtroom demeanor.

Jimmy Berry, Tokars's defense lawyer, was a formidable veteran of more than two dozen death penalty trials.

Legal legend Bobby Lee Cook *(center)* and Wyoming lawyer Ed Moriarity *(right)*, two of Tokars's defense team, celebrate Cook's 70th birthday during Tokars's murder trial.

Assistant U.S. Attorneys Buddy Parker *(left)* and Katherine Monahan secured Tokars's federal conviction.

During his 20 years as Cobb County D.A., Tom Charron sent a dozen men to Georgia's Death Row.

Cobb County first Assistant Attorney Jack Mallard earned the nickname "Blood" for his aggressive prosecutions.

Sara and Ricky in her parents' pool. This photo was shown to the jury at her husband's death penalty trial during testimony about the impact of her death on the family.

There is just too much pain for me. Even though I passed.

Yesterday, little Ricky asked me who was the best person in [his] mom's family—I hesitated, and he said Joni. I want Joni to take care of Rick and Mike. I want Andy to take care of my money for the education of all Tokars and Ambrusko children.

Please make sure that all children have a chance to go to college.

I want Andy to replace me as trustee for my mother because he is so strong and honest. He will be very good at that.

I ask that all my and Sara's money go to a college fund for the Tokars, Ambrusko, Wilcox kids. I also want to keep our house in Canada as it's my real beginning. Mike, Rick, Sara, and the Wilcoxes loved it. Please try to keep it for them as there's nothing like it left.

Please call Bob Brenner and tell him that I love him and have always admired him. Whale and Neal and Oakie were also the best friends in the world. I'm sorry for not spending enough time with them. I just worked so hard.

Sara really loved Christmas, so do what you need to do to make everybody happy. She really was very special to me. You won't ever know.

I know your loss was bad, but mine was really worse. Every day I felt like I was going to die without her. She was always great with everybody.

The real pain comes from trying to help catch the murderer and defend myself. There are people all over Atlanta who know and love me. They know I would never hurt anybody. I really had it made, and I can't explain to you how hard it was to lose everything in one day.

Mike and Rick have been sheltered from the press so far. Let them see everything and draw their own conclusions. They will see I could never hurt Sara or anyone else. The press killed me.

Please explain to my friends my weakness and let them know what happened. I can't live with all this pressure. I'm sorry for all the pain and suffering that I have caused everyone. But I loved Sara, never hurt her, and I have now died for her.

I love you Sara, Rick, Mike. Give my judge's badge to little Ricky. Give my D.A.'s badge to little Michael. Make sure they know how hard I worked for them both.

The press have made me feel like a suspect. I shouldn't be. The torture has weakened me to the point where I can't take it any more. I want to die. I'm very sad. Please help my children, Norma, Andy, and my family.

The letter was by turns maudlin, generous, and self-aggrandizing. It was loud with remorse and sloppy with self-pity. It also looked as if Fred had edited it before he finally passed out. But Fred's suicide attempt was less a manifestation of despair than it was an act of utter cowardice in which he indulged in one final grandstand play for attention, oblivious of the impact on his already traumatized children. He, not Sara, was the victim, according to his note. "The media," he had written accusingly, "killed me."

It worked, but not as well as Fred might have hoped. The attorney's suicide attempt abruptly tore the spotlight away from his murdered wife, a victim reduced to a blond, suburban stereotype forgotten by all but her family in the hunt for sufficient evidence to arrest her killer husband.

On Christmas Day, Fred regained consciousness at Sarasota Memorial Hospital where his mother and his siblings had gathered. He told them about the Ambrusko family's shouted accusations and the television cameras that dogged him with their boom microphones and intrusive, telescopic lenses. Moreover, Dr. Ambrusko, he said accusingly, had threatened to enlist the help of a Buffalo mafioso to kill him.

Within hours, the husband of Fred's sister filed a formal complaint with the Sarasota Police Department alleging that Sara's eighty-year-old father—the man whose actions had successfully stymied Fred's suicide attempt—had committed a felony by making terroristic threats.

On holiday in Fort Lauderdale, Fred's attorney, Jerry Froelich, told the media that Fred had sunk into a dark depression.

"He thought this thing was over," Froelich said. "Then the police started releasing other things that he might be involved in, which he absolutely denies."

It was left to the Ambruskos to explain to Sara's sons what had happened to their father and why he, too, was missing from the sad celebration around the tree on Christmas Day.

Two days after Christmas, doctors decided that Fred was no longer a threat to himself and cleared him to leave the hospital. Instead, Fred remained hospitalized for two more days, while a growing pool of media, joined by Cobb County homicide detectives investigating Sara's murder, maintained a vigil at the perimeter of the hospital grounds, hoping to catch a glimpse of the man police had told them was now a suspect in his wife's murder.

The attorney left Sarasota that Tuesday without telling the Ambruskos or saying goodbye to his sons. "I was a physical and emotional wreck," he said later. "I had just tried to kill myself, and I needed to go back to Atlanta. I needed to close down my law practice; I needed to close down my house; and I really didn't want to take Rick and Mike and expose them to the media. I was really concerned they had really been traumatized, and I wanted to get them into school. The Ambruskos offered to allow them to stay there and enroll in school, and I was just trying to take care of them, and I needed help."

Fred was greeted by television camera crews as soon as he disembarked at the Atlanta airport. They surrounded him, ravenous for a sound bite, hungry for a confession, starved for a grief-driven grimace or a single, poignant tear. They had become the brutal engines of a police agency that, for the moment, had little but suspicion and tenuous statements from a killer to guide their public pursuit of Sara's husband.

"It's our job," one television reporter said defensively. "He may be mad because the journalism is aggressive. But it's the police calling him a suspect. Whether he likes it or not, we come along with that—all of our trucks and our cameras. It's a package deal."

That intrusive, thoughtless scrutiny and his own desire to reassert control led Fred to call a New Year's Eve news conference in the high glass lobby of his attorney's midtown office building. He was accompanied by two burly security guards, as if he feared he was as vulnerable as Sara and threatened by unseen adversaries with a similar fate. His voice quavered as he made his brief statement, a sniveling performance that convinced no one who watched it that he was truly weeping.

"On November twenty-ninth of this year, a tragic event took place which has altered my life and the lives of my two sons, Rick and Mike," he began. "I never could have believed that I would have to stand here and defend myself against the innuendo and unsubstantiated allegations that have been in the media during the last month.

"The murder of Sara is the most devastating event that has happened to me. Not only was my wife taken from me, but she was taken from my two sons, Rick and Mike.

"I emphatically deny an involvement in Sara's murder, and even the suggestion that I may have been involved hurts me deeply."

He launched into a pitiable apologia for his suicide attempt.

"On Christmas Eve, I was in Sarasota with Sara's family and my two sons, Rick and Mike, where my family and I have spent Christmas vacation for years. For the first time in seven years, Sara wasn't there with us. Just last year, we stayed at the same hotel where we were staying this year.

"After drinking too much and after taking some back pain medication, I began to think of Sara and my two sons, Rick and Mike, and became extremely depressed.

"I started to think of the lifestyle I was losing, not only my wife, but my whole lifestyle. Unfortunately, I did something to put my life in danger. I made a bad mistake. I want to live, for my children and for my family.

"My personal and business life has been closely scrutinized by the police and the media on a daily basis. This scrutiny and its impact on my family and children has been devastating. My children and I need to go on with our normal lives. That has been impossible so far.

"Everywhere I go, I'm followed by cameras, by media people. My children can't live a normal lifestyle under these circumstances. I'm begging you just to please leave us alone. Don't camp out in front of our house; don't camp out in front of anyone's house where my children are at. Let them develop a normal lifestyle. I'm eventually going to get over this, get through this, but it's going to be a lot harder on my children. So I'm begging you just to leave us alone. Allow the police to complete their investigation.''

In his self-absorbed stupor, Fred had tacitly confirmed the worst suspicions of police, the press, and Sara's family. He had told them publicly that Sara's death was an aside, that what drove his depression were thoughts, not of Sara, but of "the lifestyle I was losing," a compromised lifestyle of drug dealers; noisy, dim-lit nightclubs scented with dirty money and cocaine; of strippers and prostitutes and political fund-raisers; and a petty flim-flam man he had turned into a killer. Clearly convinced he was the victim, and that the media hounds had made him so, he unwittingly told them what they needed to know, that Sara's death mattered far less to him than its unforeseen and unexpected consequences.

In Florida, Fred's words clawed at Sara's family like some angry animal.

"What I remember about that news conference is he was overwhelmed because he was losing his way of life," Dr. Ambrusko said. "He didn't say anything about anything else I remember. But he mentioned he was losing the life that he had, and that's what seemed to be emphasized, that he was broken up because he was losing his way of life."

On New Year's Day 1993, Sara's terrified children returned to Atlanta with their aunts. Sitting in a darkened room at the Cobb County Police Department, Ricky watched through a one-way window as five black men shuffled into a tiny room and lined up facing him. One of them had murdered his mother. He was so small that Joni had to lift him to a tabletop so he could see. He was so shaken and so scared he barely looked at them at all. He couldn't identify Curtis Rower, slumping nonchalantly. They all terrified him. Any one of them could have pulled the trigger.

That night, the little boys returned to Florida with their aunts. On the drive back to Bradenton, Ricky, saying nothing, sat curled in Joni's lap. About thirty minutes from his grandparents' home, he whispered in Joni's ear.

"Joni, I'm scared to go home. I'm afraid Nana and Papa will be murdered when we go in."

The hollow echo in his tiny voice was the prelude to hysteria. As Joni tried to reassure the child, as fragile as a wounded bird, he only grew more desperate.

"I know Nana and Papa will be murdered, shot in the head. And if we go in, we'll be murdered, too."

He was panic-stricken, his eyes wide with grisly memories. Desperately, his aunts sought a pay phone and called their parents to assuage the haunted child. The elder Ambruskos reassured the boy. They were well and eager to have him home. He relaxed, and his aunts pulled back onto the interstate. Ten minutes later, he whispered again in Joni's ear.

"I'm so scared, Joni. I'm so scared to go into the house. I'm afraid Nana and Papa will be dead, and there will be blood all over."

Joni reminded him that they had just talked to his grandparents by phone. They were alive and well. But Ricky was inconsolable. Again, his aunts pulled off the highway, found a pay phone and called home. Again, Ricky listened eagerly for his grandparents' voices, afraid now to hang up lest they be killed as soon as he said goodbye. This time, they agreed to turn on every light in the house and stand in the drive where he could see them. Only then would Ricky say goodbye, climb back inside the car, and resume the ride home, still fearful of what he might find when he arrived.

Fifteen

To Ransom the Children

MEANWHILE, FRED TOKARS WAS DISMANTLING HIS SONS' slender lives. After his suicide attempt, he left for Atlanta without a word to his children, who had not seen him since Christmas Eve morning when they set off for Busch Gardens with their cousins. Their mother was dead. Their dreams were haunted by an unknown killer and a black night dissolving in the ruby halo of their mother's blood. Now their father had simply walked away from them without either explanation or farewell, leaving their care and nurture to his dead wife's elderly parents and her sisters.

Distracted by Sara's terrible death, Fred said he surrendered to his bewildered grief. "I needed help with them because I was used to working full time, more than full time in work, and I wasn't used to raising children," he would offer. "And I really didn't want to take Mike and Rick back to Atlanta to expose them to the media. I was really concerned. They had been really traumatized. I was just trying to take care of them."

But even though he voiced those sentiments to anyone willing to listen, for nearly a month, as Fred eradicated the remains of the only life his children had ever known, all he offered his bereaved and stricken sons was silence.

He placed the east Cobb house, with its eerie memories of a drug-driven intruder hovering in the shadows by the kitchen

285

door, on the market. For, in truth, the Tokars children were afraid to return to a home where they believed they would never be safe again. But in preparing the house for sale, Fred did what he had never done for Sara. He cleaned it, painted it, and installed a new garbage disposal. He also rented a giant dumpster where he junked much of the contents of the house, among them Sara's effects, the boys' toys, and the beds in which they had slept.

"It was as if he were erasing Sara," her youngest sister said. Neighbors who observed the obscenely wholesale disposal quietly called the Ambruskos to warn them. On Super Bowl Sunday, Sara's sister, Joni, dropped by to salvage what she could of Sara's belongings. Fred bluntly rebuffed her, insisting that he had placed Sara's belongings in storage. Retrieving them that day was impossible, he said. He had invited company in to watch the game.

"I just think it would be better to leave Atlanta," he told his sister-in-law by way of explanation. He seemed oblivious to the possible consequences for his sons who, having lost their mother, would now also lose their small friends on the suburban street where they had spent their lives and at the close-knit Catholic day school they attended.

Insisting that the intrusive lenses of the media and the errant suspicions of police had devastated his Atlanta law practice, Fred dissolved his law firm, relinquished the lease on his downtown office, and cashed in his retirement savings accounts. They could have been the acts of a genuinely beleaguered man. They were also the actions of guilty one.

As Eddie Lawrence and Curtis Rower were hauled into Cobb County Superior Court and the broad outlines of Sara's death gave way to sharp detail, Fred hired a second defense attorney, a gentleman lawyer named Bobby Lee Cook, with an international reputation as a lethal inquisitor and an ardent defender of the damned. At the time, Fred insisted that his investigators would cooperate with police and provide them with all their findings. "When the facts are all out," Fred insisted belligerently, "a lot of people will owe me an apology."

Yet he fought vigorously to prevent Cobb police from reviewing the results of his parallel investigation, sending his attorneys to court to quash subpoenas secured by the Cobb County district attorney in spite of repeated promises to cooperate.

In January, Fred's attorneys fired the first volleys in a defensive campaign to clear him. Offended by what he insisted was a legal "rush to judgment" on the part of Cobb police, Fred's lawyer, Jerry Froelich, issued a defiant challenge: "I bet you right now that they will cut the deal of the century with Eddie Lawrence if they can get my client. It's my greatest fear, that they will give away their case against Eddie Lawrence to get him."

In fact, Froelich was a true believer, a man who unabashedly and uncritically absorbed Fred's growing animosity toward his wife's family.

During those early months, as the rising winds of suspicion swirled around Fred, his sons remained an afterthought. Without legal guardianship and with no instructions from Fred, the Ambruskos were unable to enroll them in school or have a child psychiatrist treat them for what would later be diagnosed as post-traumatic stress disorder. In fact, Fred said he would only consider allowing his sons to talk with a psychologist if he received written assurances that whatever they might say would never be used against him in court. Sara's elderly parents and sisters struggled to keep the boys occupied and steer their minds away from their memories. After closing the house and his practice, Fred returned to West Palm Beach with his mother, without a word to his in-laws or his sons. Not until the third week in January did he return, unannounced, to Bradenton as the boys were sitting down to dinner.

Joni Ambrusko collared him for a family conference. The children were in limbo, she told him. Without Fred's permission, they couldn't go to school. He had sent them no money for food, clothing, doctor bills, prescription medications when needed, or tuition for a Catholic school where the Ambruskos hoped to enroll them. Fred insisted that he had sent nothing for his sons' upkeep on the advice of his attorneys.

That day, Fred agreed to allow the boys to remain in Bradenton indefinitely with their maternal grandparents. If Joni, still a newlywed, could find a school for them in Jacksonville where she lived with her husband, a Navy fighter pilot, Tokars said he might move his shattered children there.

But instead of talking about his sons' future, Fred wanted to talk about Sara's insurance and $1.75 million in death benefits to which he thought he was entitled.

"What about the insurance, Joni?" he asked. "We need to settle the insurance." Sara's family had already notified the two insurance companies holding the policies of the ongoing investigation into their sister's death and asked that the companies delay paying the benefits until after the investigation was complete or Fred, her beneficiary, was no longer a suspect.

Joni told him there was time enough to settle the insurance once Sara's murderer was behind bars. But the explanation did little to assuage Fred. He wanted the money, and he was willing to use his children to get it.

So, although Joni and her father reached what they thought were agreements in principle with Fred that day, he left without giving them written permission to enroll his sons in school. And during the intervening weeks, he equivocated as to whether he would let them remain in Bradenton, permit them to move to Jacksonville with Joni and her husband, or move them to his mother's home in West Palm Beach.

"You have to sign this so we can get these kids into school," John Ambrusko would tell Fred every time she saw him.

"I don't want to sign it," Fred would respond. "I'll sign it went I get back."

"Can I fax you the forms?" Joni would plead.

"I don't have a fax in West Palm Beach," he answered.

Sometimes, the Ambrusko family couldn't even find him. But as long as Fred's in-laws cared for his children absent legal guardianship, their lives hinged on his decisions or his increasingly recalcitrant inability to make them.

"Each time there was a different roadblock," Joni recalled. "And Fred would say, 'We've got to get this life insurance settled.' "

Sara's father suspected that a desire to control lurked behind his son-in-law's chronic ambivalence.

In the weeks following Sara's murder, the relationship between Fred and John Ambrusko gradually stiffened into an

abrupt civility. Almost daily, new revelations surfaced in the
Atlanta media implicating Fred in unsavory, and often criminal, activities. But when Sara's hurt and outraged family demanded explanations, Fred replied that he had entered
counseling after Sara's murder—a respite he had denied his
sons. He had been advised not to discuss Sara's death, he
said. "I have to start looking forward, not back," he said.

Dr. Ambrusko was undeterred. "You've got to defend
yourself," he urged his son-in-law. "They're all pointing at
you."

"They're all going to apologize for that," Fred answered
brusquely.

"If anybody pointed a finger at me with these innuendos,
I'd lead the charge down there," Sara's bewildered father
persisted. "I'd be down there pounding on the desk and saying, 'I want this cleared up.' Why the hell aren't you doing
that?

"You've got to get in there and start fighting, because this
looks bad, Fred. It looks bad for the children."

Instead, Fred would rail against the family, reserving a special ire for Joni, the sister who most closely resembled his
wife. Why was the family continuing to give interviews to
the media, he demanded, when "we need to let it die down."

"Are you crazy?" Joni fired back. "We've got to find the
murderer. The kids are witnesses. Somebody doesn't blow a
woman's brains out because she's a kindergarten teacher."

"It happens all the time," her brother-in-law answered.

"His response was always the same," Joni sighed long
after. "The cops were idiots, and I was stupid to be doing
it."

"Did you have anything to do with Sara's death?" Dr.
Ambrusko once demanded of Fred in a voice riven with frustration and grief.

"I was not involved," Fred answered smartly. "And some
day, you're going to find a lot of newspapers apologizing to
me for what they've written."

"I hope you're right," the elderly doctor said. "I do."

But by then, he was sadly certain he knew otherwise. He
had the answers to the questions he had first posed on the

day he traced his daughter's terrifying final minutes, answers that would illuminate a killer.

Fred was the only one who knew what time Sara would return home from Florida. He had called as she was pulling down the driveway with her sons on that final, fatal journey home. Fred knew that the security alarm had been deactivated and that the lock on the sliding glass door to the kitchen was broken. Fred, not Sara, had been the last to leave the vulnerable house with two sliding glass doors unlocked and open, the metal bars that normally secured them lying worthless on the carpet. Fred knew.

By then, Dr. Ambrusko was determined to keep the children, which his son-in-law, for the time being, seemed content to allow. His decisions were guided by a single principle, "What would Sara want us to do?"

Too often Sara had mentioned that the children hated to be alone with their father. Too many times, she had ruefully lamented her sons' near desperate determination to follow her everywhere and their tears if told they had to remain behind.

Sara, he knew, would want her family, not Fred, to care for and raise her sons. But more than his dead daughter's wishes governed Dr. Ambrusko's hardening determination to secure custody of Sara's boys. Even after Sara's murder, Fred had seen fit to ignore his children, the only living witnesses to the crime. He had attempted suicide on Christmas Eve. He had an obvious drinking problem. His business partner was in jail for arranging Sara's death. And police had publicly labeled him as "uncooperative" and openly identified him as a suspect. Fred saw his sons every other Saturday, as if he had simply divorced Sara rather than arranged her execution.

Given Fred's recalcitrant behavior and the still murky circumstances of Sara's death, Dr. Ambrusko felt he had no prudent choice but to restrict his son-in-law's access to the children. For two months following the arrests of Lawrence and Rower, Dr. Ambrusko refused to let Fred take his children alone on outings, despite his son-in-law's enraged objections. In February, he finally relented after Fred threatened to secure a court order to take the boys. But, still fearing his son-in-law might flee, the elderly surgeon secured a promise from Fred to check in every two hours whenever he was on an outing with his sons.

"He always wants to take them by himself," Dr. Ambrusko said. "He wants to be with them alone. . . . We don't know how to handle it."

Meanwhile, every decision governing the boys required authorization from Fred that the attorney resolutely, at times belligerently, withheld. He continually threatened to move them, saying Sara's family was "hostile" and was turning the children against him. He refused to enroll his children in school, telling Joni every time she raised the issue, "We need to settle the insurance first."

As his consternation blossomed, Dr. Ambrusko realized, "This guy's got us all tied up in a knot the way he did to Sara." With a sudden, ugly clarity, he knew the son-in-law he had long defended was concerned only with himself. Fred had used their children as a weapon against Sara. Afraid of losing them, she had bowed to his demands. Now, her family was in a similar trap.

"Sara, please help us," her older sister Gretchen would breathe into her pillow every night.

The family's growing anguish over Sara's sons was compounded by events unfolding in Cobb County. During a February second bond hearing for Curtis Rower, Sara's confessed killer, Cobb County District Attorney Tom Charron demanded to know if Rower had, in fact, told his sister's boyfriend that "Fred" was supposed to pay for Sara's five-thousand-dollar contract murder. Rower abruptly refused to answer, returned to his jail cell, and forfeited his request for bond.

Six days later, on February eight, Charron hauled Rower's sister, Toozdae, back from New Jersey where she had fled after her brother's arrest and jailed her on a material witness warrant so she would be available to testify before a county grand jury. Fred knew Toozdae. She was on his payroll, having worked at Lawrence Industries most of 1992. Charron announced that she would remain in jail until a county grand jury met to hear evidence concerning Sara's murder.

Within hours, Fred filed a legal declaration of residence in

Florida's Palm Beach County courthouse, using as his address that of his mother's West Palm Beach condominium. By then, Cobb police had learned that Fred had applied to renew his passport, cashed in some retirement savings accounts, and was making plans to leave the country. Fred's attorney, Jerry Froelich, said that Fred was planning to take his widowed mother to London in March. He wasn't planning to flee. But police couldn't help but question the timing of the trip. A week earlier, Fred's other defense lawyer, Bobby Lee Cook, had insisted publicly that Fred was moving to Florida to be closer to his sons. At the time, the attorney had privately offered to place $1.75 million—the insurance benefits from policies that Fred had purchased on Sara's life—into a trust for the Tokars boys if Sara's family agreed not to sue Fred over Sara's death.

Alarmed at the implication, the Ambruskos hired an Atlanta law firm to negotiate formally the custody of the Tokars children and pursue the boys' claims to some portion of the insurance money, even though their father was the sole beneficiary. In the weeks following his wife's murder, Fred had contributed nothing to the upkeep of his children. But he viewed the Ambruskos' decision to seek legal counsel as a blatant grab for cash, a prelude to laying claim to some or all of the $1.75 million from insurance policies he had purchased on Sara's life that benefited him.

On February twenty-second, Tokars returned to the Palm Beach courthouse where he filed a declaration of legal guardianship. In it, he designated his brothers, Andy and Jerome, as guardians both of his sons and their property should he become incapacitated or die.

That same day, a Cobb County grand jury was hearing evidence associated with Sara's murder. On February twenty-third, the grand jury publicly indicted Lawrence and Rower for Sara's robbery, kidnapping, and murder, and the kidnapping of the Tokars boys. Sealed by the grand jury for release at a later date was a document naming Fred Tokars as an unindicted coconspirator in his wife's violent death. District Attorney Tom Charron signaled that, despite the two indictments, the murder investigation was "ongoing." But he acknowledged that he anticipated no new indictments in the foreseeable future.

That news must have come as a tremendous relief to Fred, who had no way of knowing he was an unindicted coconspirator. He could only surmise that Eddie had kept his mouth shut about Fred's role in Sara's death. He had been right after all. Cobb County police were stupid. He was too clever for them. They might suspect him, but they would never find enough evidence to arrest him. He had, in fact, committed an almost perfect crime. He could afford to be magnanimous. On February twenty-fifth, the Tokars boys finally returned to school at a Catholic parish near the Ambrusko's Bradenton home. Ensconsced in his mother's condominium, plagued by pain from an old back injury, Fred collapsed in bed. His mother, Norma, became his nursemaid, and Fred's world reverted to one where he, not Sara or the children, was the absolute and narcissistic center.

In March, Fred underwent a laminectomy to relieve his now chronic back pain and sciatica. The operation, according to his mother, left him a temporary invalid. But, as the weeks passed, he regained his mobility with the help of a cane, and he would accompany his mother to the club to watch her hit golf balls. His small sons remained incidentals in his life, as, in fact, they had always been. He missed Mike's fifth birthday, the child's first without a mother who had once spontaneously swept him into her arms to dance.

Gradually, Fred and his mother began traveling every other weekend across the state to Bradenton to visit Ricky and Mike. But Fred's old anger at his wife's family simmered unabated, stoked by media reports that linked him to drug dealers who were his occasional business partners as well as his clients; reported that he was under investigation for laundering drug money; and elaborated on his highly questionable business partnership with Eddie Lawrence.

"You get your family together and sign that insurance settlement," he would rage at Sara's father whenever they would talk. By then, the pretext that the money was for the boys was gone. Fred was demanding seven hundred thousand dollars, a dollar amount on which he was unwavering and for which he seemed increasingly desperate. In return, he would grant Sara's parents custody of his sons.

In early April, news of a second, unrelated federal investigation that threatened to taint Fred surfaced. The F.B.I. was investigating allegations that Atlanta's traffic court solicitor, an investigator, and several unnamed judges, including Fred, were taking bribes to dismiss drunk driving charges of habitual offenders. The F.B.I. in Atlanta had long suspected there was a well of corruption in the close-knit traffic court community of bailiffs, lawyers, and politically connected judges—who drank heavily, indulged in casual affairs, and lunched together daily at an Atlanta sports bar where their names were engraved on plaques along the walls.

In February 1993, a federal drug felon named Charlie Harris told police he had paid Fred secretly to dismiss cases. Fred had done it, he insisted, not in a courtroom, but by altering each case's computer status at night.

"He pulled all the tickets up and dismissed all of them," Harris told police. "Between two or three days later, he come out to my house, and I give him two thousand dollars."

Harris, of course, was not the most reliable of informants. He had an unsavory reputation for being willing to sell anyone, innocent or guilty, for a quick buck or an easy deal. But Harris's confidential accusations were, in part, confirmed April sixth, when the unclothed body of Atlanta Traffic Court Solicitor Ken London was found below a treacherous hiking trail in the north Georgia mountains. London, one of Tokars's colleagues, had been missing a week when he was found, dead of hypothermia and cocaine asphyxiation. He had left behind a suicide note and a briefcase full of traffic tickets that dozens of defendants, charged with drunken driving, had apparently paid him to dismiss.

And suddenly Fred was implicated in a growing bribery scandal that threatened his judicial reputation.

Throughout the spring, Fred remained in Florida with his mother, while his children lived with the Ambruskos. But that changed soon after an investigation published in the June issue of the city magazine *Atlanta* concluded that Fred was a controlling and abusive husband and an inattentive father whose motive for murder might well have been divorce. A

divorce and bitter custody fight—with the requisite examination of Fred's assets—would surely have brought to light
the fact that Fred was not only representing drug dealers, but
he was in business with men who were their front men. Moreover, the magazine reported, three weeks before Sara's death,
the federal grand jury investigating Diamonds and Pearls had
subpoenaed drug dealer Al Brown's common-law wife, seeking information on financial assets that might be subject to
civil forfeiture. While seeking evidence of tax evasion by
players that already included Fred, it could have easily subpoenaed Sara, too.

Sara's family had talked extensively with the writer who
had pieced the story together like a damning puzzle, unaware
of just how much of the truth behind Sara's murder they had
bared.

Fred's attorney received an advance copy of the story, and,
within twenty-four hours, Fred angrily penned the first draft
of two retaliatory lawsuits that harshly demanded sole custody
of his sons and all his wife's life insurance money.

Fred did not actually file those suits until June 11, 1993—
the same day that Cobb County police detectives flew to Florida to talk with Ricky Tokars a third time about the night his
mother was murdered. Less than an hour before the Palm
Beach County Clerk of Court office closed for the weekend,
Fred sued his in-laws, John and Phyllis Ambrusko, for formal
custody of his children, even though he had never legally
relinquished it and, as their natural parent, remained their legal guardian. He demanded the emergency intervention of a
judge to remove his sons from the Ambrusko home.

In the civil suit, Fred said that the Ambruskos were "acting
as parents" and had physical custody of the Tokars boys not
because he had abandoned them to their care but because they
harbored "a false belief" that Fred had been involved in his
wife's death.

It also accused the eighty-year-old surgeon and his wife of
allowing the use of "foul and abusive language" in the children's presence and demanded that they be stopped from
making "disparaging remarks" about their son-in-law in
front of the children.

The accusation that the Tokars boys were being taught foul

language referred to a lewd fraternity drinking song that the
children had learned from their youngest aunt. In fact, they
had learned a similar off-color song from their father, which
they had once, wracked by giggles, sung to Krissy.

"Oh, that's nothing," Krissy replied. "I know one that's
much worse. But you'll have to wait until you're in college."

"Oh, please, Aunt Krissy," they begged. "Please sing it
for us." So she did, never dreaming that the boys would
memorize the ribald verses so quickly or with such glee.
When their father overheard them singing the song during one
of his occasional visits, he had them call his answering service, identify themselves, and leave a timed and dated recording of the song which he later turned over to his lawyers.

For the next four years—long after the children themselves
forgot the risque lyrics—Tokars's defense attorneys repeatedly cited "The Melba Song," as it came to be known, as
the single most significant reason that Sara's family should
not have custody of the Tokars children. They simply
couldn't find anything else.

But if Fred was retaliating against imagined slights and the
family's growing criticism, he was also fighting Dr. Ambrusko, the family patriarch, for control. The Ambruskos had
refused to return his children to him, Fred complained in his
lawsuit, although he hadn't asked. The family treated him like
"an intruder" in his sons' lives and only permitted him to
visit every other weekend. Now, he wanted them back.

But more than the children, Fred Tokars wanted money.
That day, Fred also sued the Ambruskos, Sara's six sisters,
and the two insurance companies that had issued $1.75 mil-
lion in policies on Sara's life.

Shortly after Lawrence and Rower were jailed, Fred had
appeared eager to place all of the insurance money in trust
for Rick and Mike in return for the Ambruskos' promise not
to sue him for Sara's wrongful death. The offer effectively
eliminated a motive for Sara's murder at a time when police
had publicly named Fred as a suspect and were pressuring
Lawrence to identify his former business partner as the one
who orchestrated Sara's death.

But five months later, Fred remained free, even though
Lawrence and Rower, by then, had been indicted for the mur-

der and the Cobb County district attorney was vowing to seek the death penalty against them. Moreover, Lawrence had given an interview to a reporter with *The Atlanta Journal-Constitution* in which he signaled Fred that he stoically intended to stay silent about his mentor's role in Sara's murder.

"The worst thing they can do is kill me," Lawrence said in a telephone interview that was published May eighth. "They're trying to use me to get to Fred. I've had plenty of time to create a lie about him, but I'm not going to. I don't think he'll ever be arrested. Tell them Eddie Lawrence said there will be no plea bargain. I'm innocent. I will be found innocent."

Much later, Lawrence would say that he had wanted Fred to know that he would die before he testified against him. "I wanted to let him know that I was not going to change my story," he said. But Eddie also still held out hope that Fred would keep his promise to transfer nearly $1 million into Lawrence Industries accounts and surrender his majority share of the partnership either to Eddie or his heirs.

If anything, Eddie's public statement enhanced Fred's contempt for Cobb police and strengthened his conviction that they would never prove he had ordered Sara's murder. But a month later, when his real motives for killing Sara began circulating on Atlanta newsstands, Fred abruptly abandoned all pretense of surrendering to his sons any of the proceeds from the policies he had bought on Sara's life. The premiums had been paid. Sara was dead. Fred was the sole beneficiary. Now he wanted his money. Then he would leave the country.

In a second lawsuit Fred aggressively claimed all of it, just as police had always suspected he would. He accused the two firms that had issued the policies of breaching their contracts and blamed the Ambruskos for the insurance firms' refusal to honor them. Claims that the Ambruskos had made on behalf of Fred's sons were intended to cause "embarrassment, humiliation, and economic injury" to their son-in-law and to deprive Fred of his children. The interference of the Ambrusko family was unfair.

When Fred arrived in Bradenton on Sunday to retrieve his children, he told the Ambruskos they were going to Disney World and would be back in Bradenton by Tuesday. Tuesday

morning he called to say they were having such fun they had
decided to stay another day. He promised to return to Bradenton with the boys on Wednesday, June sixteenth. At no
time during either of those two conversations did Fred mention to the Ambruskos that he was suing them for custody
and for interfering with his claim to $1.75 million in benefits
that had accrued on Sara's life. And he never told the couple
or any of their daughters that he and the boys weren't coming
back. He simply packed them in the car and left. By the following week, they were in Canada, where his mother owned
a beach house on the Great Lakes.

But if his bitter animosity toward Sara's family drove
Fred's actions during those first two weeks in June, so surely
did a flaring and irrepressible panic. Between the pages of
Atlanta lay his blueprint for Sara's murder. For the first time,
someone had publicly documented his deteriorating and domineering marriage and linked Sara's desire to divorce her husband to the federal investigation of Fred's drug-dealer
clientele. Canada may have been the Tokars's family vacation
home, but it was also a country that shunned capital punishment and refused to extradite Americans accused of crimes
to which the death penalty was attached.

On Monday, the day after Fred and the children left Bradenton, the Ambruskos' Atlanta law firm, the venerable King
& Spalding, received an urgent, vociferous letter from Fred's
attorney, Jerry Froelich. It formally withdrew all settlement
offers, presumably regarding custody and the life insurance
benefits.

"It is the position of my client that he has given the Ambrusko family more than sufficient time to make decisions as
to potential conflicts between them," Froelich wrote. "Hopefully, the Ambrusko family will realize that their actions and
words, especially those within the last two weeks, are not in
the interest of Fred's children." He never mentioned the lawsuit.

Neither the Ambruskos nor family attorney Dwight Davis
knew what Froelich was talking about. The interviews with
Atlanta had been given months earlier, and, on their attorney's advice, the family had long since stopped speaking to
the media. That Monday, the Ambruskos still didn't know

Fred had sued them or spirited the children out of the country. They would not see or speak to Rick or Mike again for nearly three months.

Thus began an increasingly vitriolic exchange of letters between Froelich and King & Spalding attorneys, who later described them as "hostage negotiations to ransom the Tokars children from their father." In them, Fred bartered his sons for $750,000, nearly half of the unpaid insurance benefits. He was more than willing to surrender his children's care to the Ambruskos in exchange for cash. He was not willing to surrender his control.

On June fifteenth, Froelich sent a letter to Frank Jones, an attorney at King & Spalding, proposing to settle a lawsuit the Ambruskos still knew nothing about.

"First, my client will have sole and exclusive custody of his sons, Rick and Mike. This is non-negotiable," Froelich wrote. Fred, the absentee father, would now allow his wife's family to see the children just once every three weeks, during the summer, and at Christmas. However, that arrangement was contingent on whether the family would agree "not to make any detrimental remarks or accusations to the children about Fred."

Froelich said that if the Ambruskos rescinded claims they had filed on behalf of the boys for Sara's insurance benefits, Fred would establish a five-hundred-thousand-dollar trust fund for each son that would remain inviolate until they turned twenty-three. Fred would receive the remaining $750,000 in cash.

The letter grew more threatening.

> My client has been attempting to settle the above issues for quite some time, but it has appeared that the Ambrusko family has been delaying making a decision in this matter. If the Ambrusko family is truly interested in the welfare of Mike and Rick, they will agree to the above terms. Litigation in these matters will only lead to a complete rupture of any possible relationship between Fred's sons and the Ambrusko family. . . .
> We are prepared to fully litigate all issues of custody of Rick and Mike and the proceeds of the insurance

policy, but we believe it is in the best interest of the children to settle these matters.

We believe Fred has cause of action against members of the Ambrusko family but have not filed those claims in hopes that there can be a settlement in this matter.

The family was given three days to sign.

On June eighteenth, Jones wrote back in the second of more than a dozen letters the two attorneys would exchange while the Tokars boys summered in Canada, forbidden to see or speak to members of their mother's family.

The sole concern of the members of the Ambrusko family is the well-being of Rick and Mike. . . . They want to allow Mr. Tokars to have unlimited access to the boys and yet at the same time permit the boys to remain in the stable environment that has existed in recent months, during which they have resided with their maternal grandparents, Dr. and Mrs. John Ambrusko of Bradenton, and their aunt, Joni Ambrusko Crain.

Although the family resented the subterfuge that Fred had employed to whisk the boys to Canada without even allowing them to say goodbye, they remained willing and eager to negotiate. They asked that the boys be allowed to live with their maternal grandparents during the school year for at least four years. They also asked that the children's trusts be increased to $625,000 each. Income from the trust funds could then be used for the boys' upkeep and education by whomever the children were staying with at the time. Fred could have the remaining five hundred thousand dollars. In return, the Ambruskos would not make any detrimental remarks about Fred either to the children or to the media and would release all claims to Sara's insurance on behalf of both their family and her children.

On June twenty-second, Froelich rejected the counteroffer.

My client, Fredric Tokars, has restrained himself and me from commenting or responding to the many state-

*ments the Ambrusko family have made to the media,
many of which are incorrect. Fred has done this in order to preserve the relationship between his sons, Rick
and Mike, and the Ambrusko family. However, as I
stated to you at our meeting, it has reached a point
where Fred is concerned about his sons if the present
conditions continue.*

   *After much thought over the weekend, Fred decided
that he would attempt to settle his differences with the
Ambrusko family in order to preserve the relationship
between Dr. and Mrs. Ambrusko and his sons.*

   *Before considering this offer, Fred wants me to ask
you to assure the Ambrusko family that he had absolutely no involvement with Sara's death and hopes that
the individuals responsible for it are punished. Further,
he loved Sara very much, greatly misses her and her
loss has been and continues to be a great sorrow in his
life.*

That said, Froelich again threatened Sara's family, suggesting—as Fred had once suggested to his wife—that if they
did not acquiesce to his demands, he would secure custody
of the children and they would never see the boys again.

   *Fred is fully prepared to litigate any and all issues and
believes he would be successful. However, he does realize that success would most likely end all relationships between his sons and the Ambrusko family. He
does not wish to do this, but he cannot allow anyone
to drive a wedge between him and his sons and he will
not lose the people he holds most dear, Rick and Mike.*

The settlement Froelich held out was stringent and so re-
strictive that the Ambruskos were reduced to the role of babysitters with no real authority. Fred would retain legal and
physical custody of the children although they would be allowed to stay with the Ambruskos during the school week
for two years. He alone would decide where the children
would attend school, although the Ambruskos had already
enrolled them in a Catholic day school in their Bradenton

parish, and what "if any" medical and psychological attention they would receive. And, if Fred didn't pay, the children would do without, unless their grandparents sacrificed their savings.

The Ambruskos were also asked to agree in writing that Fred had not abandoned Mike and Rick to his in-laws for six months following Sara's death. More than that, Fred demanded that the family "admit that Fredric Tokars is a fit parent capable of raising his sons."

But through the agreement, on which he hinged his children's visits, Fred also sought to muzzle Sara's family, and the proposed agreement barred Sara's parents, sisters, in-laws, and cousin Mary Rose Taylor, from speaking to the media, to psychologists and doctors, and anyone seeking to write a book or produce a movie about Sara's murder.

If they wanted to see the children again, Froelich demanded that the Ambrusko family

> stop talking with any and all members of the media about anything directly or indirectly related to the murder of Sara Tokars or of the history or background of Sara Tokars or of the history or background of any member of the Ambrusko family or any relative including but not limited to the following subjects: about the murder of Sara Tokars; about Rick and Mike Tokars; about where Rick and Mike Tokars are living; about where Rick and Mike Tokars are going to school; about Fred Tokars or any member of his family, and about their or Mr. Tokars's relationship with Rick and Mike.

His sons, the only eyewitnesses to the crime, could speak to police investigating Sara's murder only if "the investigatory process is approved in advance by Mr. Tokars, is reasonable under the circumstances, and is done in a manner that takes into consideration the best interests of Rick and Mike." Nor could the children travel without their father's permission.

Again, Fred insisted on securing $750,000 of Sara's insurance money as well as interest accrued since her death. He also insisted that he be allowed to claim the boys as dependents on his taxes.

There was more. Restrictions that sought to portray the Ambruskos as if they were poor candidates for custody by suggesting that they used profanity and abusive language in front of the boys, fed them ill-balanced meals that centered on cake and candy, and spoiled them with too many toys. Embedded in each allegation was a kernel of truth. Besides learning the ribald fraternity song from Krissy, both boys had put on weight since their mother's death. And Sara's extended family had bought them toys to distract them from the horror of their mother's death and make them feel that Bradenton was their home, not just a pit stop on the way to somewhere else.

But then, Fred had always seemed obsessed with the children's toys. He complained incessantly when Sara bought them, declined to buy them presents, and, after Sara died, he dumped dozens of their playthings into a dumpster and had them hauled away.

The proffered settlement captured Fred at his most vindictive. In it he barred his children from spending time alone with their youngest aunt—the most outspoken of the sisters and the one closest to Sara—or visiting her Woodstock home. He demanded that Sara's few belongings and photos that her sisters had taken from the Tokars's house be returned along with any copies the family had made. In particular, he wanted one photo that included the entire family. Although Fred had adorned his office walls with photographs of himself greeting an assortment of public officials, he had no photos of Sara and the children displayed either in his office on Peachtree Street or in his basement office at home. His attorneys, seeking to show that Fred was, in fact, a family man, found few photos of him with his sons. It was, they decided later, the Ambruskos' fault. They assumed such photos actually existed, although Fred had spent little time with his children. Sara's sisters, they hinted, must have stolen and destroyed them.

Again, the Ambruskos were given just three days to decide. And again, their attorneys submitted a counteroffer that gave the Ambruskos joint custody of the Tokars children and

$2,500 a month to pay for the boys' school, medical, and living expenses, and psychiatric care. The family also asked for one hundred thousand dollars to reimburse Dr. John's retirement savings for expenses he had incurred caring for the children and defending himself in court against his son-in-law. The Ambruskos also modified some of the agreement's more restrictive clauses, permitting the children to talk to police as long as the investigation into Sara's murder was conducted "in a reasonable manner." They also agreed not to challenge Fred as an unfit parent unless he was indicted or arrested.

In return, the Ambruskos agreed to ask the insurance companies to release $650,000 to Fred as long as it was distributed over four years. Mindful of Fred's attempts to portray them as unfit and still worried about his often excessive behavior, the Ambruskos included their own list of restrictions. The third counteroffer forbade adults caring for the boys from indulging in alcohol or drugs, driving while under the influence, or exposing the children to violent movies, unhealthy environments, and unwholesome people. They agreed to most of Fred's other terms except for the one attacking Krissy.

The offer provoked a belligerent and hostile response.

On June thirtieth, Froelich fired off a letter that said, in part:

> My client has attempted to settle this matter because he believes that litigation of this matter will forever destroy any relationship Rick and Mike have with the Ambrusko family. We believe my client's proposal is more than fair, and your most recent proposal to be so far from what is acceptable it is not worth responding to.
>
> My client has been attempting to settle these issues with the Ambrusko family since March 1993. It appears the Ambrusko family merely wants to stall.

Alarmed that so much money on both sides was being spent on attorneys who couldn't agree on behalf of clients who weren't speaking, Joni decided to circumvent the lawyers. In early July, she flew to Canada where she called Fred, seeking an agreement that would satisfy her brother-in-law but allow her to bring the children back to Bradenton. Even though Lawrence and Rower were in jail, the investigation of Sara's murder was ongoing and Joni feared that, if one of her sister's killers were still free, the Tokars children—the only eyewitnesses to the crime—could be in danger.

"We were worried about the boys," Joni recalled. "I thought maybe I could talk to Fred on my own and leave all the lawyers out of it."

Fred refused to see her.

"Fred, can't we just settle this?" Joni begged him by telephone. "It is costing so much in legal fees. Let us bring the boys back, where we know they're safe until the investigation is over, and we know there aren't killers still out there. Fred please, you have to understand our concern for their safety. There might be someone waiting to murder you or murder the boys. Bring the boys home until police can assure us they are safe."

But Fred seemed content to let the lawyers continue their tedious negotiations. What he cared about most, he told her, was settling the matter of Sara's life insurance.

"Go to the insurance companies and tell them to give me $750,000 and put the rest in a trust fund for the boys," he said. Only then could she see the children again.

Froelich insisted that Fred wanted the matter settled amicably because he loved the children "too much to put them through all this." At the same time, Fred told the Ambruskos, "I love them enough that I will never agree to any kind of language that would relinquish them to you totally."

In the meantime, Fred had ended all contact between Sara's family and his children. On July fourth, Sara's sister Karen Wilcox and her family were vacationing in Canada when her children spotted their cousins with Fred and his mother at a fireworks display. The cousins ran into each other's arms. Fred and his mother quickly separated them, hustled Rick and Mike into their car, and drove them away in tears before the fireworks began.

So, for the sake of the boys, the Ambruskos acquiesced to Fred's harsh demands. In a letter dated July eighth, they agreed to forgo joint custody as long as Fred gave them the right to make emergency medical decisions for the children, consult with their teachers, review their school and medical records, and sign school consent forms whenever the children were with them. They accepted most of the points on which Froelich insisted when he had met with family attorneys the previous day.

"That's what Sara would have wanted us to do," Joni said.

The family's lawyers asked that the Ambruskos be reimbursed $75,000 in expenses and legal fees incurred because Fred had chosen to sue and $2,500 for the boys' upkeep. The family agreed to make a formal statement saying that Fred had not abandoned his children in the months following Sara's death in deference to Fred's concerns about his public image, but insisted that if he were arrested or indicted for any felony, they would assume joint custody of the boys. The family still wanted $1 million set aside in trusts for the boys. But they agreed to increase Fred's share of the insurance to $675,000.

The next day, Tokars issued a new set of demands. He was now unwilling to allow the boys to stay in Bradenton with the Ambruskos during the school year. The $750,000 was not negotiable.

Yet, he denied ransoming the children for the money. "When Sara died, I told everybody right from the beginning that I wanted all the money to go into a trust for the benefit of Rick and Mike," he said later, as if his lawyer's correspondence were small, aberrant works of fiction. "That was the first thing that I said to anybody when they started to talk about insurance. I had plenty of money. I had about a half a million just sitting in the bank . . . Money was no problem for me. I was always able to make money.

"They wanted money so that Joni could quit her job and could get a new house. There were negotiations that related to the insurance policies, but I, myself, said I would give up all the money and put it into a trust. It wasn't until six months after I had spent every nickel I had on lawyers fighting the Ambruskos, fighting the media, that I ever said I wanted any of the money out of that insurance policy. And, legally, I was entitled to all of it.''

On July twenty-ninth, Tokars's attorney sent the Ambrusko lawyers another abrasive letter.

> *Your clients' latest offer of settlement . . . clearly demonstrates to me that they are not interested in the best interests of Rick and Mike but have their own agenda with no concern for the welfare of the boys. . . . This settlement offer is our final offer. It is non-negotiable. Do not send any further proposals to me because we will not accept them.*

In return for $750,000 in insurance, Tokars would allow his sons to "visit" the Ambruskos on days when school was in session and on the nights preceding school days. But he alone would choose what school the boys would attend, what physicians and counselors they would see. They were forbidden to make overnight trips out of state without his permission, a clause which smacked of an attempt to avoid future line-ups or interviews by Cobb police still investigating Sara's death. He had reduced the children's trusts to $450,000 each and attached a list of tax provisions, all designed to capitalize on tax deductions while sidestepping any liabilities. Joint custody of the children would fall to the Ambruskos only if Fred were indicted for his wife's murder. If he were indicted on any other felony charges stemming from the ongoing federal money-laundering investigation, he would retain full custody of his sons.

On August second, the Ambruskos countersued Fred on behalf of Rick and Mike. In a letter to Froelich notifying him of the lawsuit, the family's attorney, Frank Jones, expressed a remarkably gentle and diplomatic frustration.

> *We believe the negotiations were unsuccessful because of a series of arbitrary deadlines and unreasonable positions taken by your client. . . . Let me express my personal appreciation for the many hours that you have devoted to the task of attempting to work out a settlement . . . I know that you have acted in complete good faith, and I realize that you are bound by the instructions of your client.*

But the letter, a professional courtesy intended to be conciliatory, only provoked another outraged response from Froelich.

Your belief that settlement discussions were unsuccessful because of "arbitrary deadlines" and "unreasonable positions" taken by my client is disingenuous. This matter was not settled because my client was not willing to give in to your clients' unreasonable demands to give up custody of his sons, Rick and Mike. The Ambruskos, though they have no legal rights to custody of Mr. Tokars's sons, wanted language that gave them some form of legal custody. It is clear that the Ambruskos believed that they "inherited" Fred's children upon Sara's death ... Your raising of the issue of language is disingenuous in that your clients' last proposal did not contain language that you previously "agreed to" but to be blunt, was so contrary to what we had discussed and what would be acceptable that it was an insult to me and my client. There were no arbitrary deadlines. My client had been attempting to settle the issues we discussed since April. After four months of negotiations it became clear that the Ambruskos had no intention of settling this matter.

Finally, let me make it clear that there was no settlement in this matter for three reasons: first, though my client met all of the Ambrusko family's economic demands, the Ambruskos wanted my client to give the Ambrusko family custody of his children. This he would not do. Second, members of the Ambrusko family wanted to be able to fulfill their own egotistical needs and goals by being involved with the media. Finally, and most importantly, the Ambrusko family was not interested in the "best interests" of Mike and Rick. If the Ambruskos had the best interests of Mike and Rick as their primary concern, they would have settled this matter a long time ago and not made the many public statements, many of which were untrue, they made to the media. The Ambrusko family was only interested in fulfilling their own selfish interests. It is clear to me that

*the "best interests" of Rick and Mike never entered
into the Ambrusko family's considerations in this matter.*

*I believed that you wanted to settle this matter, but
it became clear to me that we would never be able to
reach an agreement because of the agenda of the Ambrusko family. This letter also is to notify you that I will
not accept service on behalf of Mr. Tokars. You will
have to serve him.*

On August sixteenth, one of three civil attorneys in Florida
whose help Fred enlisted in prying loose Sara's life insurance
benefits wrote his own letter to the Ambrusko family lawyers
in Atlanta, accusing Sara's parents and sisters of "blatant efforts to drive a litigation wedge between Fred and his children," as if the Palm Beach lawsuit he had filed three months
earlier didn't exist. The letter went on to say:

*Mr. Tokars does not want the funds available to be
distributed to his children dissipated by fee and cost
obligations incurred by members of the Ambrusko family. . . . If your clients are still acting under the influence
of their misguided and baseless suspicions that Fred
was involved in Sara's homicide, then I expect they will
continue to endanger the welfare of Rick and Mike by
continuing to try to use them to seek revenge against
Fred.*

Angered by a second attorney's willingness to overstep the
bounds of professional courtesy to cast aspersions on the Ambrusko family, Frank Jones strongly defended the beleaguered
family and chastised his Palm Beach counterpart.

*In view of the comments in your letter about the Am-
bruskos, let me say just a few words in response so as
to "set the record straight."*
*Your allegation that the Ambruskos do not want what
is best for Rick and Mike is cruel as well as inaccurate.
This family recently lost a beloved daughter and sister.
Since that tragedy, the family members have completely*

*reorganized their lives so as to help Rick and Mike cope
with the tragic loss of their mother. For over six months
they nurtured and cared for the boys. The Ambruskos
did this willingly and are thankful that Mr. Tokars
agreed that they should take care of the boys during
this traumatic time.*

*It is hypocritical and misleading for you to suggest
that the Ambruskos initiated this dispute over the insurance proceeds. The litigation regarding the insurance proceeds was begun by Mr. Tokars in Florida. He
filed a lawsuit at a time when the parties were engaged
in settlement negotiations, apparently for the purpose
of gaining "leverage" in those negotiations. This was
hardly a good faith act on his part.*

But by August 1993, suspicions that Fred was involved in
his wife's murder were anything but baseless, despite the
protestations of his growing battery of lawyers. For by then,
federal investigators could prove that Fred willingly had laundered illegal profits for Detroit drug dealers who numbered
among them Anthony "Al" Brown, Jessie Ferguson, and Julius Cline.

Sixteen

"Counsel is Not a Potted Plant"

THE DAY AFTER POLICE CHARGED EDDIE LAWRENCE WITH Sara Tokars's murder, his brash attorney, Bruce Harvey, paid a visit to Cobb County District Attorney Tom Charron to announce, "It looks like I'm in a pretty good position here."

For nearly two decades, Harvey had been one of Atlanta's more provocative lawyers. His appearance, temperament, and his blunt, casually profane conversational style identified him as an independent thinker, a man perpetually at the edges of outrage.

He was, and remains, an anomaly. In court, where the majority of his clients appeared in orange jailhouse garb, Harvey pleaded their cases in the dark, hand-tailored suits and monogrammed oxford shirts of a corporate lawyer. What distinguished him from that polished legal circle was a single, elegant braid of graying black hair that hung nearly to his waist. That rope of hair, which his wife of more than twenty years braided for him every morning, attracted notice, both good and ill, and set him apart as surely as a dark star. His hair had always been Harvey's public statement of individuality, just as the small tattoo bearing his wife's initials, P. H., on the half-moon of flesh between his left thumb and forefinger attested to his union with a woman he adored.

Harvey was a member of a diminishing league of lawyers driven by ideals, outrage, and a basic sense of fairness. His courtroom demeanor was that of a caged and restless panther. His job was not to toady to the criminal justice system but to challenge it, to demand that it shed its rusty, antiquated biases so that justice remained blind and her scales balanced. He loathed the misuse and abuse of authority. Trickery, deceit, brutality, or a simple lack of candor evoked a visceral reaction in Harvey, who more than once has stomped angrily from a courtroom, overturned chairs, or lunged at a prosecutor he suspected of introducing lies as evidence in court. Yet he is an artful storyteller, whose accounts of his own past have occasionally assumed the color of a minor, harmless legend.

The earrings that have adorned his lobes since long before it became fashionable, two stunning dragon tattoos that undulate across his shoulder blades, and a small five-pointed star tattooed on a ring finger all have contributed to his legend. So does the coal-colored Porche with the vanity license plate that boasts, "Acquit," a Harley hog he once accepted as a retainer from a Hell's Angel defendant, and his habit of parking the motorcycle in the foyer of his downtown law office next to the coffee table displaying back issues of "High Times." He was for much of his career a chain-smoker who shunned meat, not for health reasons but because he couldn't stomach the thought of a slaughterhouse.

He has represented some of Atlanta's most notorious criminals. He has built his practice on defending drug dealers, so much so that he has earned the enmity of federal and state drug agents. As a result, his name occasionally surfaces in police investigative files weighted down with unfounded suspicion and innuendo by investigators who never understood that while Harvey may bend the rules, he doesn't break the law.

One-third of Harvey's clients never actually pay him for his services. And more than once he has waived his legal fees to defend a broke and desperate client. He is one of the Atlanta legal profession's better trial lawyers and one of its most elegant writers, a man who reads law for recreation and argues it with often profound clarity.

Harvey's name circulates freely in the city's jails, which is why Eddie Lawrence's brother called him after police had questioned Eddie about Sara Tokars's murder then surrendered him to Fulton County authorities who jailed him on outstanding bad check warrants.

Before he ever met with Cobb County D.A. Tom Charron, an irate Harvey had barreled into a Fulton prosecutor's office to argue, "Let's drop these chickenshit bad check charges.

"What is this guy doing in jail on a bad check charge?" he demanded, knowing that defendants like Eddie usually were allowed to post bond within hours of their arrests.

"Don't you know who this is?" the prosecutor replied.

That's when Harvey learned he was plunging headlong into Atlanta's most sensational case since the 1981 child murders. Ten days later, he marched into Charron's office, certain that Eddie's testimony was so critical to prosecutors that they would eventually negotiate a deal.

Although Cobb County police had the gunman and Eddie, his accomplice, in custody, the man they were certain had masterminded the murder still eluded them. Eddie could give them what they wanted. Eddie could give them Fred.

Moreover, "We didn't believe they could prove Eddie was guilty," Harvey said. The murder case against him was built on the self-serving confession of Rower, a borderline mentally retarded crack addict who couldn't always discern the line between reality and what he had seen on television.

"Eddie was a small-time hustler and manipulator who wanted to view himself as a player," Harvey said. "He wanted to move up. He wanted more respect. He was enamored with and involved with Fred Tokars, whom he viewed as the same kind of player on a larger scale in the world he wanted to get into. He fell under the spell of Fred Tokars. He was easily manipulated by Fred, who is a classic manipulator. That was always our theory," Harvey said. "That also is truly my impression of reality."

But if Harvey were to urge Eddie to testify against Tokars in return for a lighter prison sentence that would allow him to sidestep the electric chair, Eddie's testimony could put Tokars on Death Row in his place. "We had a considerable moral dilemma with any kind of plea," Harvey said.

On principle, he opposed the death penalty and the license it gave the state to kill. Murder, illegal under other circumstances, became justifiable when committed by the state. It was biased. It was cruel. There was no margin for error. And too many times the state had imposed it only to learn later it was wrong. More than once, Harvey had nearly spent himself into bankruptcy representing condemned men.

He decided to delay a deal and fight. On January sixth, at an arraignment hearing for Lawrence and Rower, Harvey waded into the fray. A visiting judge threw out the arrest warrants that police originally had obtained, saying they were so vague they failed to provide critical details that would have given police probable cause to arrest Rower and Lawrence, who were already in custody when the warrants were obtained.

Prosecutors countered that police had that critical information but had withheld it from the warrants to keep it from falling into the avid grasp of a news media circling like raucous crows. Dissatisfied with the visiting judge's ruling, they promptly turned to a Cobb County magistrate and asked him to reissue the arrest warrants. Normally those warrants would be issued in the privacy of a judge's chamber after a police investigator briefed him under oath. This time, then Cobb County Magistrate James Bodiford convened a public hearing which, in an unusual move, he permitted television cameras, reporters, Lawrence and Rower, and their attorneys to attend. Local radio broadcast the hearing live from the courtroom. But Bodiford barred Harvey and Rower's defense attorney, Edwin Marger, from questioning police Detective Ron Hunton or objecting as he summarized under oath the damaging statements from witnesses and informants that had led investigators to arrest Rower and Lawrence.

Incensed, Harvey stamped out of the hearing. "That's fucking ridiculous," he fumed. It was a foretaste of the public circus that Sara's murder had become.

The next day, Harvey filed an outraged formal objection to the proceeding, declared that Lawrence was being held illegally, and chastised Bodiford for the public arrest warrant hearing.

No authority exists for holding a *public* arrest warrant hearing. An arrest warrant hearing by its very nature is a private hearing between an informed police officer and a neutral and detached magistrate often in the magistrate's chambers. . . . The policy behind having a neutral and detached magistrate not having an open arrest warrant hearing is to guard against the very kind of public pressures which were exhibited at the "Bodiford hearing" where heinous and infamous cases inflame the public and prevent even the staunchest magistrate from being completely neutral and detached.

In Bodiford's "public and notorious hearing" Harvey argued, he "was reduced to being just another spectator along with the news media.

"Counsel," he admonished, "is not a potted plant." It was vintage Bruce Harvey. It was also the first volley sounded in a motions war that Harvey and cocounsel Mark Spix waged for more than seven months against the state on behalf of Eddie Lawrence.

Harvey had known Spix for a decade. Introduced by a mutual friend, they had first met at a bar, where Harvey was railing against a particularly egregious ruling in a death penalty case. Spix, a former Ohio prosecutor who had resettled in Atlanta at the urging of a law school classmate, listened patiently to Harvey's vituperative analysis of the ruling, his caustic asides about prosecutors, and his snide suggestion that Spix, himself, might well think like "a Nazi." Then he agreed with him.

"Put up or shut up," Harvey ventured. "Help me out."

The duo won the appeal. So, Harvey enlisted Spix's help a second time. Spix, who had once believed in capital punishment as an appropriate response to outrageous crimes committed by "people not worthy of their next breath," accepted.

By then, Spix had come to believe that the death penalty was little more than a crapshoot where the deciding factors were money and race. Capital punishment offended his sensibilities. Some of the worst offenders bought their lives because they could afford the best attorneys or because the high publicity spawned by their sensational crimes attracted good lawyers who were willing to work for free.

It was an affront to Spix's deep-seated sense of fair play.

In court, where the duo often appeared in tandem, Spix was Harvey's foil—a gentleman lawyer and businessman whose easy manner, tailored suits, polished appearance, trademark suspenders, and meticulous corporate image charmed rather than challenged the judges, the straight man to Harvey's merry prankster.

Despite his own outbursts of temper that, on occasion, pushed him perilously close to contempt, when paired with Harvey, Spix always appeared so magnanimous. "Sure, you want the moon and the stars," judges and prosecutors might tell Harvey. "But let me hear from Mark. Maybe he'll accept one of the continents."

It was, of course, a myth that, when they stopped to think about it, mightily amused them both. For while Harvey looked like an outlaw and a rebel, Spix was the true adventurer, the scuba diver who vowed to plumb the depths of every ocean in the world; the daredevil who, while chumming for sharks, suited up and jumped over the side to watch them; the registered Republican who drove a Lexus to work but kept a Harley, a candy-apple-red convertible, and a pickup at home in the garage; the sunny, ebullient wise guy who admired Humphrey Bogart's debonair but dark romanticism.

Yet he was a man of creature comforts who joked that "roughing it" was a hotel without room service in a city without a nightclub.

Life interested him. Where Harvey was guarded, often editing his own conversations even while they were in progress, Spix was genuinely gregarious, a man who slipped easily into conversation and listened unreservedly, a man with a knack for disarming people because he imposed no personal judgments.

He was the great balancer, the team player, and, like Harvey, an intelligent and thoughtful wordsmith in a profession prone to tedium. Empathetic and loyal to a fault, he cultivated enduring professional friendships that even as fractious a case as Sara Tokars's murder were unable to rend asunder.

Among the 121 motions with which Spix and Harvey inundated the court were requests for orders barring Sara's sisters from court proceedings that they attended with the dedication and devotion of parishioners; a motion to compensate jurors for lost wages and provide day care for jurors with small children; a motion declaring the state's penalty statute unconstitutional, and a motion to prevent display of Georgia's state flag.

The Georgia General Assembly was then embroiled in a debate to retire the state flag which was emblazoned with the Cross of St. Andrew—the Confederate battle flag.

The flag, adopted in 1956 by a legislature bent on thwarting integration, was designed by a Savannah newspaper editor and designated the "white man's flag," Harvey wrote.

The 1956 adoption of this flag was done in direct defiance of the United States Supreme Court's rulings on segregation. Indeed on the date of its current adoption, then Governor Marvin Griffin, addressing a joint session of the Georgia House and Senate, remarked, "We must not desert future generations of Georgians. We must never surrender." . . . The mere appearance of this flag in the courtroom, because of the message it sends, is inappropriate and raises the appearance of state-sanctioned hatred and partiality.

Lawrence, Harvey contended, "is entitled to removal of such a badge of slavery."

Spix soon weighed in with an omnibus motion that Harvey dubbed "A Motion for More Justice and Less Surprise for Open File Discovery" asking Cobb County Superior Court Judge George Kreeger, who had been assigned to try Rower and Lawrence, to order Cobb County prosecutors to release thousands of pages of witness statements and interviews they had collected during the murder investigation. It was, Spix said, a simple matter of leveling the playing field.

Indeed, the sole justification for withholding such items as police reports or other type items is the State's desire to enjoy a tactical advantage. After expending a great deal of time, employing expensive expert assistance, and indulging in all other prerequisites of the sovereign to prepare its case, the State wants more. It wants the accused to be unprepared in confronting his accusers, to be confused and weak. It wants victory more than justice. . . . To quote the Supreme Court of the United States, which recently has shown a great deal more enthusiasm for the quest for truth than for what some regard as technicalities, "The adversary system of trial is hardly an end in itself; it is not yet a poker game in which players enjoy an absolute right always to conceal their cards until played."

Over prosecutors' outraged objections, Kreeger granted the sweeping motion.

And so it went. As winter spilled into spring and gave way to the high heat of a Georgia summer, Harvey and Spix issued dozens of subpoenas seeking any information on the case that might strengthen Lawrence's bargaining position. They subpoenaed every newspaper and television station in the state that had published or broadcast stories on the murder for notes, published articles, outtakes, videos, and ratings. They subpoenaed both state and federal investigative files and testimony given before the federal grand jury investigating Fred Tokars's links to the Detroit drug dealers and nightclub owners who had once been his clients. In doing so, they so angered Assistant U.S. Attorney Buddy Parker that he vowed to go to jail for contempt before he would hand over grand jury testimony or the files detailing the federal investigation.

It was a massive scavenger hunt unwittingly aided by the media, which continued to publish and broadcast leaked information that Lawrence's lawyers then righteously demanded.

"The news media had information. The feds had information. The state was resisting giving us what we had a right to get," Harvey said. "We never really knew what they had on Fred. In one sense, it was a major bluff. We figured if they really had something, they would have indicted him."

Their tactics, their passion, and their sense of novelty as they occasionally tweaked the criminal justice system amused and intrigued Kreeger. When a friend casually commented, "I can't believe some of the stuff you're giving them," Kreeger responded. "They're interesting.

"Sometimes," he mused, "judges like to have fun, too."

"We were court jesters," Spix said.

They were also racing against inevitability.

By then, the two lawyers knew that the federal investigation swirling around Fred Tokars was also threatening to engulf Lawrence. The Secret Service's eighteen-month-old investigation of Alex Yancey's counterfeit operation was still open, fed by revelations linking Lawrence, Yancey's one-time partner, to Tokars, and the two of them to Atlanta nightclubs suspected of being drug money laundries.

"We had a one-half-inch-thick file on the counterfeiting investigation," Spix said. "Eddie didn't even know he had flunked the polygraph. Fred had never told him. We knew eventually they would indict him."

What they didn't know was the scope of the federal government's investigation into Fred Tokars's business affairs and his increasingly questionable relationships with his criminal clientele. Nor did they fully understand where Eddie fit into the intricate puzzle that now included Sara's murder.

"Fred was clearly distancing himself from Eddie," Spix said. "These two black guys [Lawrence and Rower] were being hung out to dry. We needed credible information that Fred was part of the conspiracy, that Fred may have had an interest in deleting Sara Tokars. If Fred successfully distanced himself, he would really become our enemy."

That was why the two lawyers had subpoenaed sealed grand jury testimony. But something in their response to the federal government's move to block them attracted the attention of U.S. District Court Judge Ernest Tidwell. On June eighteenth, Tidwell issued an order requiring the federal government to show, within five days, why such evidence should not be made available and ordered federal prosecutors to trundle thirty thousand pages of documents detailing the investigation to his chambers for review.

In Cobb County, Kreeger decided to postpone a ruling on state prosecutors' similar efforts to hold Harvey and Spix at bay until Tidwell completed his review and decided whether he would authorize release of at least some of the subpoenaed files.

"He was actually listening to them," said Assistant U.S. Attorney Buddy Parker, who was supervising the federal investigation. "We were filing briefs on the matter and fighting like hell because they wanted to know what the federal grand jury had. We had a lot. Obviously, we weren't wanting to disclose anything."

"We knew then we had gotten past frivolous," Spix said.

Meanwhile, Rower's attorney, Edwin Marger, was broadcasting his own client's confession as he pointed a condemning finger at both Tokars and Lawrence as the masterminds who bore ultimate responsibility for Sara's murder.

"Here was Ed Marger," Harvey said, "jumping on the table and saying, 'I'm guilty, and he's guilty, too.'"

But as long as Tokars remained free, Eddie's testimony remained valuable to Cobb County prosecutors, who needed it to secure Fred's arrest and conviction for Sara's murder. Eddie was the link in the chain that bound Fred Tokars to the final, terrible drive that his wife and sons endured before she was slaughtered in front of them. Yet, if Eddie went to trial before prosecutors offered an acceptable deal that would not only keep him off Death Row but guarantee his release from prison before he was an old and broken man, he would become Tokars's ally. He would deny his involvement and, by necessity, Tokars's involvement as he scrambled not to implicate himself.

"We clearly were building a defense that if the shoe dropped before they came to the table with something we could live with we were going to try the case," Spix said.

Even so, Spix and Harvey knew that if state or federal investigators doggedly pursuing Tokars secured the evidence they needed to indict him, it could very well be used against Eddie.

For the time being, Eddie was a rook in a legal chess match bent on capturing Tokars. Harvey meant to make a deal before he lost his limited advantage. In his conversations with Cobb County District Attorney Tom Charron, Harvey emphasized that Charron's constituency was so outraged by the evil details of Sara's fearsome death, arranged by a husband who was a wealthy, politically ambitious former prosecutor and sometime judge, that county voters "would have traded Curtis Rower, a borderline mentally retarded man, for Fred Tokars any day.

"The moral outrage," Harvey said, "was against the middle-class white guy for even considering what was done, not with a borderline crackhead who was going to get the death sentence. I played that card very hard."

But Harvey and Spix also believed Lawrence's story, one

that dovetailed with what they knew of both men. They knew Fred was an ambitious legal hustler. They also knew him as a defense lawyer addicted to exorbitant fees he collected for equally exorbitant promises to overturn criminal cases where there was little or no error, cases an ethical attorney would reject on principle. They despised him as they learned that he had doled money out to his wife as if he were a miser while peeling hundred-dollar bills off hefty rolls of cash he carried to pay for expensive meals, hotels, and hookers. They scoffed at media descriptions of Tokars as "prominent," "politically-connected," and "a rising star."

"I was unaware," Spix said, "of Fred's meteoric rise."

But Eddie's lawyers knew that the myth of power and prestige in which Fred cloaked himself appealed to Eddie. "We believe what Eddie said ultimately had the ring of truth to it," Harvey said. What convinced him of Fred's ultimate guilt, he said, was Eddie's account of why Fred wanted Sara killed in November. Sara had been urging her husband to repair the garage door at their home, which operated wildly and often rolled down as Sara pulled her car into the garage. At one point, Eddie had taken one of his erstwhile business associates to the Tokars's house to see if the door could be repaired.

"I'll never forget it as long as I live," Harvey said. "Fred was insisting, 'You have to do it. You have to do it. She's still ragging me about the garage door.' "

For Spix, the turning point came when Eddie told his lawyers that Fred had brushed aside questions about his sons as he gave instructions about how to make his wife's murder resemble a burglary. "He said, 'The kids will get over it,' " Spix recalled. "Now there's the malignant heart."

Still, Charron seemed content to wait, applying pressure of his own that he hoped would force Lawrence to succumb. That pressure could be had by enlisting the hungry and un-witting news media, still baying after the Tokars story like a pack of jackals.

Although defense lawyers had successfully sealed many of the witness statements prosecutors had, albeit reluctantly, turned over to them, prosecutors' notices that they intended to present such evidence, together with provocative summa-

ries, were being published in court records where they were
seized upon by the media, to the detriment of Lawrence and
Tokars.

On June twenty-eighth, prosecutors filed a Notice of Intent
to Use Evidence of Similar Transactions stating that other
witnesses had contacted police with damaging information
about Lawrence. While those witness statements to authorities
had been sealed by Judge Kreeger in a futile effort to quench
the astounding publicity surrounding the murder, summaries
of those statements became part of the public record which,
for the first time, named Tokars as an unindicted coconspirator.

One of those witnesses was Donald "Duck" Coggins,
whom Lawrence had allegedly solicited "to get this guy for
me" as he sought "some guys to beat up a guy."

A second witness, Calvin Johnson, had told authorities that
Lawrence and Tokars had solicited him twice "to do a hit."
Sealed along with the statements was a polygraph examination showing that Johnson's statements concerning Lawrence
and Tokars were a crass deception and notes that police were
never able to confirm his story.

But over the next three nights, WXIA-TV, Atlanta's NBC
affiliate and the station that most aggressively had pursued
the Tokars story, broadcast a three-part interview with Johnson that reporter Dean Phillips had taped the previous January, before Johnson ever contacted police. Johnson claimed
he had met Eddie in a nightclub in December 1991, that Eddie
had given him $2,500 as a "retainer" on a contract murder.
A short time later, Eddie canceled the "hit" but renewed it
in June 1992. When Johnson insisted on meeting Eddie's
partner, Eddie allegedly arranged a meeting with Tokars in
the parking lot of Lenox Square, an upscale mall in Buckhead.

There, Tokars allegedly informed Johnson, "My wife and
the other two need to be taken care of" and to make it look
like a burglary. Johnson said he would do it for one hundred
thousand dollars. A week later, Lawrence again canceled the
deal.

In a scathing but darkly humorous motion he subtitled
"When Alice in Wonderland Met Donald Duck (Coggins),"
Spix demanded an immediate court hearing to bar prosecutors

from filing their notices "in such an oblique fashion as to render them more prejudicial than the actual facts of the transactions.

"Johnson FAILED a state-administered polygraph!" Spix wrote. "The state should be sanctioned for even offering such rubbish for public consumption."

Moreover, Spix continued,

WXIA Channel 11 (11-Alive) News has broadcast Calvin Johnson's lies for consecutive days in a circuslike atmosphere proclaiming he, and Channel 11's newscaster, are "informed sources." Now a significant segment of the television viewing public has been led to believe that the worst or most specific of the alleged similar acts is true, whereas the state's own evidence suggests OTHERWISE.

"The court," he said, "cannot admit such evidence."

At the hearing, convened a day later, prosecutor Jack Mallard, in his droll South Georgia patois, responded to the indignant allegations of the defense lawyers. "If there was a polygraph involved, it's certainly not admissible in court," he growled.

"These type of incidents didn't directly involve Sara Tokars. But defendant Lawrence had a certain bent of mind or intent to get back at someone who gave him problems. I would submit that Sara Tokars was one of those people who gave him problems."

As for Johnson, Mallard purred, "it's a question for the jury as to whether Johnson is telling the truth or not."

"If the state really believed it, Mr. Tokars would not wear the moniker of unindicted coconspirator," Spix responded hotly. "The entire notice is nothing more than character assassination of Mr. Lawrence."

Unable to locate Johnson to testify at the impromptu hearing, Spix and Harvey had subpoenaed Dean Phillips and convinced Kreeger that their right to question him superceded Georgia's media shield law because they were simply inquiring about a public broadcast and because Phillips, having sent Johnson to the police, was a potential witness in the case. As such, they had a right to probe for bias.

The lanky reporter with his mop of brown hair, craggy face, and a jacket that looked as if it had been slept in had broken a number of stories on Tokars, including the attorney's ties to the Parrot Club and drug dealers Al Brown and Julius Cline. He was the first to report the details of the documents taken from Fred's safe that Sara's sister, Krissy, had given to police the day after Sara's murder. He had not only interviewed Johnson. He had broadcast interviews with Sara's private investigator, Ralph Perdomo, and Tokars's former law partner, Emily Sherwinter. Shrouded in shadow, Perdomo insisted on camera that Sara knew she was going to die, and Sherwinter said she feared for her own family after her office was burglarized and electronic records concerning the Parrot nightclub were stripped from her office computer.

Phillips was competitive, a hound who smoked as aggressively as he pursued the news. Harvey, a passionate smoker himself, used to join the rumpled reporter on the sidewalk outside the courthouse during breaks where the two would cadge cigarettes from each other and, between drags, loudly dispute the merits of the case.

Phillips clearly thought he and Harvey had an understanding, borne of nicotine, sidewalk ribaldry, and a modicum of bluff. What he didn't know was that, just that morning, Harvey and Spix had acquired by way of subpoena nearly two hundred pages of documents from Perdomo outlining his bald efforts to sell his rights to a Hollywood production company eager to film the story of Sara Tokars's murder. On one of those contracts, Harvey had found Dean Phillips's name.

For months, Harvey and Spix had been trolling with subpoenas, seeking the details of a movie deal on Sara's murder. ABC had announced less than two months after her death that it planned to underwrite and broadcast it. Now, Harvey folded the facsimile of the contract and placed it in his breast pocket.

Harvey had heard that Phillips had a habit of slipping into his shoes without donning socks. He thought it was amusing. So he waged a bet with Spix. If Phillips showed up without socks, he would grill him on the witness stand. If he wore socks to court, Spix could question him. When Phillips appeared in court, he was wearing a suit. But he wasn't wearing socks. He was cavalier about his subpoena. As they smoked,

Harvey thought the reporter "had an attitude." It annoyed him.

"Every fucking body in this case was out to get something, which really bothered us," he would say later. "That bait was out there the entire case. Everybody was dangling it. We wouldn't do it."

As he strolled to the witness stand and slouched easily in the chair, the cocksure newscaster exuded a debonair lack of concern. He had been singled out for his exclusive newscasts with state witnesses in front of other news organizations covering the hearing, none of which had been able to match his three-part interview with Calvin Johnson. Life was good.

Harvey fired the first warning shot. He would not ask Phillips about his sources. He was more interested in movie deals.

At first, Phillips answered Harvey's questions casually, referring to him by his first name as if they were still standing on the sidewalk blowing smoke.

Harvey cut him down. "You can call me Mr. Harvey," he spat.

After quickly establishing Phillips's credentials, Harvey began aggressively questioning the reporter about whether the NBC affiliate had exclusive rights to the information he gathered.

"I know where you're going with it," Phillips responded. "But yes, they do."

"Does Channel 11 have exclusive rights to your services or can you use what you gather for your own individual financial gain? Have you sought permission about participating in a possible motion picture to be made about the murder of Sara Tokars?"

The other reporters in the courtroom were suddenly alert. Rumors of a movie deal had been circulating for months. But it had never actually intruded on the investigation of the murder case.

"I approached my managers in the early spring," Phillips said shortly. "They said go ahead."

"Yet you've been involved in the coverage of events surrounding this particular case?" Harvey demanded.

"Correct."

It was an ethical bombshell.

Pulling the contract from his pocket, Harvey began asking about witnesses whom Phillips had interviewed whose names appeared, along with Phillips's, on the contract signature line—Emily Sherwinter, Ralph Perdomo, and Steven Labovitz, whom Sara had consulted about a divorce, and the only one who hadn't actually signed the document.

Calling her "the former law partner of a named suspect," Harvey asked, "Ms. Sherwinter acknowledged she had been approached for a movie and book rights?"

"Sure. She said it on television."

Perdomo, Phillips reluctantly acknowledged, had never provided him with copies of the documents the private eye said he had given to police, documents Phillips erroneously believed had come from Fred Tokars's safe.

By now, Phillips knew what Harvey was doing, although the reporters watching his testimony were still uncertain, unaware of the contents of the document in Harvey's hand. Harvey was tainting the witnesses by implying that the monetary promise implicit in the movie deal he wielded shaded their testimony and drove their willingness to appear on television to talk about the Tokars murder. By entering into partnership with witnesses for his own pecuniary gain, Phillips found himself in the uncomfortable position of having to defend his own news reports as unbiased and objective. He began downplaying his exclusives.

In response to Harvey's aggressive questions, Phillips insisted that he had talked to Perdomo "just as had every other reporter in this city. . . . He had already been on television on another station."

His interview with Labovitz "was only a very small portion of a news story. That was a hundred and fifty stories ago."

"At no time did he invoke attorney-client privilege?" Harvey asked.

"I don't advise him," Phillips responded sullenly. "He's a lawyer."

"Did there come a time when you entered into a business relationship with Emily Sherwinter, Ralph Perdomo, and Steve Labovitz?" Harvey asked pointedly.

"The answer, I guess, is yes," Phillips said. "It's very unclear."

"Have you made any contacts with media groups about the possibility of a movie or a book?"

"I did not contact anyone. They contacted me."

Then, in a series of sharp, accusatory questions, Harvey elicited from the now surly Phillips his reluctant acknowledgment that he had formed an unofficial partnership with Sherwinter, Perdomo, and Labovitz as early as January 1993 to sell their rights concerning their roles in the Tokars case to a Hollywood production company. If a movie were made, the quartet stood to gain as much as three hundred thousand dollars from the sales. Phillips, Harvey intimated, had used his authority as a reporter to enhance the marketing potential of his unofficial partners and emphasize their significance to the story—a significance that Harvey knew, at least on the part of Perdomo and Sherwinter, was vastly overblown. Phillips's series of exclusives on the Tokars murder suddenly appeared as biased, governed by greed rather than the truth.

"We agreed it had to be done accurately first and foremost," Phillips insisted. "Number two, we were in it together."

Harvey now insisted on intimate details about the nature of Phillips's business relationship with the trio of state's witnesses. He extracted from Phillips an admission that he had freely provided transcripts of his broadcasts to at least one production company. Harvey began reading from other proposal letters he had acquired that morning from Perdomo. He didn't know what he had. He was winging it. Phillips himself objected a time or two while his attorneys sat by and said nothing.

Said Harvey, "I ran for the border."

Every production company memorandum, every negotiated option fee, every contract offer—most of which had nothing to do with Phillips—became fodder for Harvey's insinuations that the prosecutors, the witnesses, and even the media were so biased against Lawrence, so motivated by money, that a fair trial was impossible.

The letters Harvey now held bolstered that contention. "The viability of the story depends on whether Fred Tokars

is charged either with his wife's murder or related crimes,"
the lawyer read as Phillips shifted uncomfortably.

Was Phillips aware of offers from Patchett-Kaufman? Multimedia Motion Pictures? Hearst Entertainment Media? A letter from Amy Fisher's biographer saying, "Only a woman could do this story."

"I spent so little time on this as opposed to the massive amount of time I have spent investigating this news story," Phillips answered sheepishly as Harvey continued with his roll call of Hollywood film companies. "I have no recall of these things, no. Of course, it's in the grapevine."

What about negotiations with Creative Artists? Cates-Doty Productions? "In the perfect world yet to come (in storytelling, film-making terms)," Harvey read Phillips from another letter, "we would see Fred Tokars arrested, charged, tried and convicted (largely based on your work, information, and testimony)."

In truth, Phillips knew little of the contract negotiations or just how busy Perdomo had been marketing a story that made the detective who had walked away from Sara Tokars because she couldn't pay him out to be a hero. The one deal he signed with Treasure Island Productions was never consummated, partly because Labovitz never signed, and partly because, by then, another movie producer had secured a network deal.

"They never signed the contract," Phillips protested from the witness stand. "We never got a return copy."

"Are you still involved in the consortium?" Harvey pointedly asked.

"It doesn't sound like it exists," Phillips countered.

"How many times did you interview or cover Emily Sherwinter or Ralph Perdomo?" Harvey demanded indignantly. "How many times did you make a decision to place Ms. Sherwinter or file footage of Mr. Perdomo on the air? The information that you gathered, and put on TV, do you have a separate file for what is news and what is available for your life story? What's the difference between Dean Phillips, news reporter, and Dean Phillips, Treasure Island signee?"

"In my investigation of Sara Tokars, I make a salary."

"Not if you can get a three-hundred-thousand-dollar deal," Harvey riposted.

But the defense attorney wasn't through. He demanded to know if Phillips had paid Calvin Johnson any money to appear on camera. When Phillips's lawyers finally objected, Harvey fairly shouted in open court, "I want to know if Dean Phillips is paying a potential state's witness."

"The question is outrageous," Phillips responded hotly. "Absolutely not!"

Harvey spun on his heel. "How many times have people asked you about helping get reward money?" he countered. "Who has asked you about reward money? Did Mr. Johnson make any request to you with regard to the reward with this case?"

"No," Phillips hesitated, "but I asked a very logical question that a reporter should do. I asked if he was interested in the reward money."

"Did you ask if he had taken a polygraph?"

"No."

"Did you ask Mr. Johnson in terms of what he aired if any information he had provided had been corroborated?"

"No."

"Did you make any attempt to verify his information?"

"Obviously."

"Do you have anything that would verify that information?" Harvey asked.

But when Phillips's lawyers objected that the question sought to rend the veil of confidentiality that, in Georgia, shields a reporter's private notes and interviews from public scrutiny, Harvey responded, "Mr. Johnson has this to do with the movie deal. If the money gets better and Mr. Tokars is indicted, and you're putting people on the air who've failed a polygraph, it sure is relevant to a movie deal."

A short time later, Phillips stepped down from the witness stand a discredited man. News reports that night on local television and in the morning paper castigated him for continuing to report the Tokars story after inking a secret movie deal with prosecution witnesses and for publishing Johnson's sensational accusations against Lawrence and Tokars without once mentioning that he had failed a polygraph exam.

Phillips would become the first, but not the only, Hollywood casualty associated with the Tokars murder. Before the case was complete, there would be others, key witnesses who would be likewise tainted and branded by the implication that their testimony had a price tag. The day after the hearing, WXIA pulled Phillips off the air, as his supervisors insisted they knew nothing of the unconsummated movie contract.

Phillips always insisted that he had informed his bosses about the proposed movie deal, and that the news director had asked only, "Who's going to play me in the movie?"

A week later, Phillips was fired.

Harvey and Spix emerged from the hearing jubilant. The tainted prosecution witnesses only strengthened their hand as they negotiated for Eddie's life. It was a turning point. Now they were certain they could broker a deal that would keep their client from living out the remainder of his life in prison.

In yet another motion, which they subtitled "A Further Flight into Fantasia," they couched cogent legal arguments in occasionally arch commentary.

The state, they argued, was attempting to use the statements of alleged coconspirators against Lawrence without ever alleging a conspiracy existed. Prosecutors, Harvey wrote, were guilty of "semantic sleight of hand" in a "Houdini-like attempt" to escape the rules of evidence.

> *This tactic is reminiscent of the classic "Georgia search warrant" where law enforcement officers go to both the front and back doors of a home; the officers in front knock on the door and announce themselves, followed swiftly by the officers at the back door shouting, "Come in!"*

Harvey went on to quote Samuel Taylor Coleridge, Clarence Darrow, and U.S. Supreme Court Justice Learned Hand, before closing with a passage from Shakespeare's *MacBeth* that damned the statements of coconspirators as the province of liars and fools.

SON: And must they all be hanged that swear and lie?
LADY MACDUFF: Everyone.
SON: Who must hang them?
LADY MACDUFF: Why, the honest men.

Son: Then the liars and swearers are fools, for there are
    liars and swearers enow to beat the honest men and
    hang up them.

                                        —*Act IV, Scene ii, line 51*

Harvey's Shakespearean reference prompted prosecutor
Jack Mallard to respond in kind in a motion filed July twenty-
third.

Comes now the state of Georgia, and in reply to Learned
Counsel's breathing of fire but blowing of smoke, let me say:

ORATORY IS GOOD, BUT . . .
THOU SHALT NOT HAVE FLIGHTS OF FANTASY AND
INDULGE THYSELF IN HYPERBOLE WITH GRANDIOSE
QUOTES FROM MACBETH.
THOU SHALT SPEAK ONLY OF THE LAW IN THIS
FORUM; NAY, NOT MACBETH NOR LITERATURE, BUT
LET US HAVE EXPRESSIONS OF THE LAW . . .
THOUGH ANCIENT . . . WHICH RULE THE LAND.
ENOUGH! ENOUGH! *MACBETH,* NO MORE!
                                        —*Mallard, on Criminal Law*

But by then, such sly ripostes eddying the often achingly
dull legal waters were no more than an amusing aside. Eddie
Lawrence had cut a deal with the state and handed over Fred
Tokars to the prosecution.

The day after Harvey had eviscerated Dean Phillips, Charron called Eddie's lawyers with an invitation to talk. They
had been fighting for seven months. A federal judge had taken
seriously their subpoena of federal grand jury records and was
reviewing thirty thousand pages of documents generated during the federal investigations of Tokars, Lawrence, and Tokars's drug-dealer clientele. Judge Kreeger had decided to
postpone his own ruling on their subpoenas of state grand
jury records until after the federal judge had issued his ruling.
They would never be in a better position to deal.

Harvey and Spix informed Charron there would be no deal
unless federal prosecutors were also willing to sit at the table.
They knew, by then, that Fred had set up a half-dozen cor-

porations for Eddie in quick succession and that the duo "were playing fast and loose with a lot of cash" that virtually guaranteed a federal investigation. They knew that Eddie's counterfeiting partner, Alex Yancey, was still on the run. But if he were caught, his testimony could convict Eddie for his role in the scheme.

"Obviously, Harvey and Spix knew what we were up to," Parker said. "And what we were up to was letting Cobb County nail Eddie on the murder." Using that murder conviction and Eddie's counterfeiting activities as previous bad acts, Parker then intended to try Lawrence along with Tokars as part of a racketeering conspiracy in which they laundered dirty money through seemingly legitimate businesses for Atlanta drug dealers. "He would be looking at life without parole. And that, of course, is what drove them to demand that Charron get us on board with a joint deal."

Even if Eddie were to go to trial in Cobb County and win an acquittal, "I'd still take the evidence that had been developed, still indict him, and still keep going at him," Parker said. "In defending himself on the murder case, Eddie ultimately may have had to incriminate himself in other areas."

Parker was meeting with the federal grand jury investigating Tokars, Lawrence, and the drug dealers with whom they had allied themselves when there was a knock at the door. A marshal handed him a message. "Tom Charron is on the phone in the grand jury clerk's office. He wants to talk to you immediately." Parker excused himself from the grand jury deliberations to take Charron's call.

"Buddy," Charron said when the federal prosecutor answered the phone, "we've got a possibility of cutting a deal with Eddie Lawrence. We want to sit down with you right away."

Within twenty-four hours, Charron, Jack Mallard, Harvey, Spix, and two federal agents had gathered in Parker's office in the federal building overlooking the gray concrete expanses of downtown Atlanta.

"What do you want us to do, Tom?" he asked.

At the time, Georgia's death penalty statute did not include the possibility of life without parole. A jury could sentence a defendant in a capital murder trial either to death or to a parolable life sentence. Murderers were eligible for parole after only seven years. Charron estimated that if Eddie accepted a life sentence in return for his testimony against Fred Tokars, more than likely he would win parole after twelve years, provided Sara's family didn't oppose his release.

"Look we clearly have him. He's dead on counterfeiting," Parker said. But the federal prosecutor knew the grand jury was still six months away from handing down the sweeping racketeering indictments then engrossing him. And during June, Parker had become absorbed with Sara Tokars's murder, convinced that there was a timely connection between the money-laundering investigation his office had spawned and her ugly death, that her murder, in fact, might have been ordered to protect the criminal enterprise in which her husband was entangled. Yet, he still did not have enough evidence to support what he was certain was the truth.

If Eddie would plead guilty to federal counterfeiting and racketeering charges that included Sara's murder and become a star witness for the government, not just against Tokars but also against several significant Atlanta drug dealers, Parker agreed to ask that the life sentence Lawrence would normally face be limited to a dozen years—the rough equivalent of the actual time Eddie would remain in state prison for murder. Parker also agreed to place Lawrence in the federal witness protection program, not so much because the prosecutor feared Tokars might retaliate but because "Eddie was going to come forth with more drug trafficking information" about the dealers he had solicited for Tokars's money laundries. Lawrence's sentence would be delayed until after he testified and would ultimately depend on the judge's discretion as well as Parker's recommendations.

Once Charron and Parker had agreed to a plea bargain, Harvey and Spix left to convince Eddie, who had watched his lawyers "kicking butt and cleaning up" as they won motion after motion in state court, that pleading guilty under the circumstances was the smartest thing to do.

Eddie might be impressed enough to think his attorneys could really beat the charges against him, but, in reality, "We were facing a massive assault by two sovereigns and these small victories we were winning had nothing to do with winning the case,'' Spix said.

To convince Eddie that he needed to consider seriously the deal state and federal prosecutors had brought to the bargaining table, Spix and Harvey gave Eddie copies of damaging statements that key witnesses, including Curtis Rower, Rower's sister, Toozdae, and her boyfriend, ''Red'' Swinger had given to police—statements that placed Eddie squarely at the center of the plot to murder Sara Tokars and that would, without question, be used against him in court.

''You can't win forty-eight motions and tell a guy like Eddie that you're losing,'' Spix said. ''He thinks you're kicking ass. We had to say, 'No, Eddie, there's this thing called evidence.' ''

Nowhere among those documents were transcripts of statements that Fred himself had given to police. In fact, Eddie never saw more than a fraction of the state investigative files that his lawyers compiled, contrary to the bitter allegations that Fred's own defense lawyers would later thrust at them, insinuating that Harvey and Spix had given Eddie the tools to fabricate his testimony against Fred so that he could tell police what he knew they wanted to hear. Even the files that the lawyers did leave for Eddie at the Cobb County Jail rarely made it to his cell. Rather, deputies stockpiled the files Spix and Harvey left for him at the booking desk, doling them out to him twenty pages at a time because they said so much paper in a single cell would constitute a fire hazard.

On July twenty-fourth, Eddie, his lawyers, and state and federal prosecutors secretly signed off on the deal. On July twenty-eighth, Eddie was taken quietly into federal custody and, on the pretense of needing medical treatment, was whisked away to a secret location to be debriefed.

There was a reason behind the intrigue: security. When Spix and Harvey were first informed they were needed at Eddie's formal debriefing, they were told the location was so confidential that even they could not be trusted to know it. Plainclothes investigators in unmarked cars would meet them at a prearranged location and drive them there by a circuitous route. But the secrecy of those precautions had less to do with Eddie's safety than it did with preventing the news media

from scenting the fundamental shift in the legal winds that
signaled a break in the now eight-month-old murder. For if
the media knew Eddie had cut a deal with federal and state
prosecutors, it was inevitable that Fred would find out as reporters called both him and his attorneys seeking comment.

Still north of the border with his boys, Fred certainly could
flee, or, at the very least, successfully fight extradition, based
on the death penalty he would otherwise face. But authorities
were far more fearful that the Atlanta lawyer, whom they
were now convinced had with a bloodless efficiency arranged
his wife's brutal murder in front of her sons, would now use
his own children as hostages. Since his Christmas Eve suicide
attempt, law enforcement authorities also viewed Fred as an
unstable and ultimately unpredictable man who might well
try to kill himself a second time and snuff out his sons' lives
along with his own.

Spix accepted the fundamental logic and simply ignored
the implied slur that he or Harvey would intentionally tip the
media. But Harvey wouldn't tolerate the unfounded suspicion.
He was profoundly wary of accompanying federal agents to
an unknown location where he would remain incommunicado
for an undetermined period of time. The action smacked of a
secret police state, and he defiantly rejected it.

A gauzy summer dawn had already faded to a morning
limp with the dirty glower of a rising heat, when Cobb
County detectives Hunton and Banks met Spix near Marietta,
ushered him into the back of their dark, unmarked Crown
Victoria, and, somewhat apologetically asked him to lie down
on the seat. There was an afghan in the back so that Spix
could cover his head as they drove, another directive by federal authorities who had arranged the debriefing. He tolerantly
ducked his head below the window but declined to don the
blanket. Banks and Hunton didn't press him. They cork-
screwed through the county for nearly an hour before turning
off on a rural two-lane road in the county's northern arc. The
din of Atlanta's incessant traffic faded.

They stopped in front of a worn, semirustic lodge nestled
in a tired fringe of trees. As they stepped from the car's re-
frigerated cool, they were enveloped by the nylon swelter of
a Georgia summer. But the placid setting was fractured by

the maddening clatter of a circling helicopter, another one of the federal government's security measures to insure the safety of Eddie Lawrence, who was now formally in their custody. Sheriff's deputies were posted outside the lodge. It looked like an armed camp.

Until the team of investigators arrived, the lodge had sat, locked and unused, in the summer heat. There was no power. As Spix crossed the threshold, he was assailed by a wall of stale, baked air. Eddie was already there. He was wearing civilian clothes, but the foxy odor of confinement clung to him. He stank.

The lawyer spotted the name "Barrett Lodge" engraved on the stone mantel by the fireplace. Situated on a small lake near Kennesaw, the lodge was often used as a gathering spot for county politicians.

"Are you guys so smart you planted a fake cornerstone to fool me?" he said with a wry grin. "Or did I just find out where we are?" The agents looked sheepishly at each other. So much for scripted secrecy.

In keeping with federal protocols, no one recorded the interview. Instead, the eight men who surrounded Eddie at the lodge that day—Spix, Banks and Hunton, F.B.I. agent Mike Twibell, I.R.S. agents Les Furr and Jerry Culver, Secret Service agent Mike Davis and D.E.A. agent Jeff Dalman—made their own notes as they fired their grapeshot questions at Eddie. As they sought to close the holes in the fabric of four independent investigations, including Sara Tokars's murder, they found that Eddie wasn't the common thread. Fred was. The debriefing was supposed to last about two hours. Instead, it staggered on for nearly twelve, steeped in the sour odors of male sweat, stale fast food, and too many cigarettes.

For a dozen hours, Eddie talked, unraveling Fred's tangled web of business associates and criminal clientele. What emerged amid the warp and woof of that extended dialogue was the classic pattern of a money launderer.

Eddie tied the lawyer first to Yancey—the master forger of counterfeit bills. Before he had swapped Yancey for Eddie as a client, Tokars had asked Yancey to bring him some of those bills for distribution in the Bahamas.

Knowing Eddie was a criminal, Fred had set him up in

business, creating a series of small companies through which drug dealers would purchase and renovate real estate with their dirty cash.

Fred also acted as a money broker, Lawrence said, housing money for drug dealers, dispersing the cash he housed to those who entered the country needing money and agreed to reimburse him using wire transfers. It was a clean explanation of a financial legerdemain that Eddie knew little of, but that a legal accountant and former prosecutor who lectured on laundering money would understand far too well. Fred had even showed Eddie a booklet he had published on the subject, one that federal prosecutors had acquired long before Eddie had agreed to cooperate.

"The only thing Fred talked about was money," Eddie said, "and how he was going to make it."

Eddie said Tokars had told him he had laundered hundreds of thousands of dollars in drug money that way.

Fred had sent Eddie to carouse in Atlanta's nightclubs with directives to enlist drug dealers for his money laundries. One of them, Michael Morris, told Eddie he laundered drug money through the beauty salon he had paid Eddie thousands in cash to renovate. He had also attracted the attention of the D.E.A. Fred had laundered more than $150,000 for him.

Eddie also knew about Julius Cline, Al Brown, Willie Harris, and James Mason—unpublished information his lawyers didn't know about their illicit ties to two nightclubs, the Parrot and Diamonds and Pearls, that matched details federal agents had uncovered independently since Al Brown's arrest the previous year.

Eddie said Fred had told him that Mason and his associates were spending their illegal cash so ostentatiously they were bound to attract the attention of law enforcement authorities.

And finally, Eddie revealed the stark details of Sara's murder, a plot that Fred had scripted after first approaching Eddie about killing a "partner" because they were dissolving their partnership and "he would lose everything."

Federal agents seemed unfazed by Eddie's matter-of-fact narrative. But the statement chilled Spix, who knew that Tokars then shared a law practice with Emily Sherwinter that had in fact dissolved that same summer. Nor did Eddie know then that Fred had once approached Sherwinter to suggest that he purchase a $1.5 million policy on her life, an offer which she rejected soundly because she didn't trust him.

By August 1992, Fred's overture to kill a partner had evolved into a plot to kill his wife before she could divorce him. Eddie insisted that Fred wanted Sara killed because a lawyer had called to warn him she was going to file for divorce, an allegation no one ever substantiated.

Not until Eddie explained how Fred had first suggested that he kill Sara in Fred's office did it dawn on the diminutive con man that the lawyer was using him and might have killed him, too. At the time, Fred swore he could convince his powerful friends in Atlanta's legal community that Sara was going to kill him, and Eddie had saved his life.

Spix was certain there would have been two shots fired and two bodies on the floor of Fred's office if Eddie had followed Fred's instruction. One of those bodies would have been Eddie's.

Eddie said he arranged to have Sara killed because Lawrence Industries was in financial trouble and he was desperate for money. The $1 million Fred promised to plow back into their partnership and twenty-five thousand in cash he agreed to pay Eddie within a week of Sara's murder offered Eddie "a way out."

"Now, I wonder if he ever intended to pay me," Eddie said as he looked around the room.

Eddie's version of Sara's murder differed in one significant respect from Curtis Rower's confession. While Rower had told police that he and Eddie had done everything in tandem, in Eddie's account he distanced himself from Sara, the kidnapping, and the final shattering shotgun blast that killed her. Rower had told police that Eddie had entered the Tokars's house with him to reassure him that the security system was deactivated. He insisted that after he kidnapped Sara and the boys, he didn't intend to kill her. It was Eddie who was the catalyst for Sara's death, Rower maintained. When Sara had defied Rower and pulled the car to the side of Powers Road, Eddie had appeared at the driver's window. Sara had recognized him, screaming as she slammed the accelerator. Eddie had wrenched open the back door and struggled with Rower for the shotgun, the crack addict still maintained. In the melee, it had discharged.

Police were certain Rower was lying about the struggle over the shotgun. Sara's older son, Ricky, never mentioned a struggle or a second assailant. Now, Eddie insisted that he had never left his pickup, but sat parked in the driveway of an unfinished home on Powers Road, waiting for Rower to return with word that Sara was dead. Eddie acknowledged that as he sat in his truck that fatal night, he recognized Sara's 4-Runner as it passed him. In Eddie's account, the 4-Runner swerved off Powers Road and into a field without ever idling by the side of the road. Minutes later, he said, Rower had sprinted to the pickup. They drove south for fifteen minutes before Rower told him that he had killed Sara in the truck in front of her children, not in the house as they had planned.

Eddie's version, which became the state's official version of Sara's murder, was at odds with testimony by Ricky Tokars and a passerby that the 4-Runner had idled for several minutes on Powers Road while Sara argued desperately with Rower. And, except for the final struggle over the shotgun, only Rower's version explained why Sara screamed and shoved Ricky to the floor, how the 4-Runner came to veer off the road, through an eight-foot hedgerow and seventy-five yards into an overgrown field, and why Rower pulled the trigger when he did by the side of a well-traveled road. But it made the state's deal with Eddie more palatable if Eddie wasn't just outside the car when Sara died.

As Eddie wrapped up his account of the murder Fred had arranged, he included an odd fillip at Howard Weintraub, a lawyer who shared office space and sometimes clients with Fred, whom Eddie blamed, in part, for his financial vagaries. He had fought bitterly with Weintraub over his failure to complete a renovation of a dance studio belonging to Weintraub's wife. Now, he casually embroiled Weintraub in the murder plot to kill Sara. He insisted that Fred had promised to deliver the first twenty-five-thousand-dollar payment to Eddie for the murder, using Weintraub as the go-between. It made no sense to anyone aware of the emnity between Eddie and the lawyer he had stiffed for construction work he never completed. But it entangled the unsuspecting lawyer in the investigation of

Sara Tokars's murder—Eddie's small, but vindictive payback that no one really believed but were forced nonetheless to consider.

What convinced investigators listening to Eddie's twelve-hour confession that day that, by and large, he was telling them the truth were the small details that Eddie had no other way of knowing—details that law enforcement authorities could, and did, verify or that Sara's family had confirmed during secret grand jury hearings while Eddie was incommunicado in the county jail.

When talking with drug dealers, Fred would always mention that he was a judge to impress them into thinking he could manipulate the justice system in their favor.

He had insured his wife several years before her death to avoid undue suspicion. He had also contacted someone else about having Sara killed.

Fred would ask his mother to work at Lawrence Industries for a day or two so that, if it were ever necessary, she could testify as to what a good person Eddie was.

If Eddie were ever to be arrested for Sara's murder, Fred said he would kill himself.

The day Sara was murdered, before Fred left for Alabama, he had asked a repairman to play his guitar so there would be an unidentified set of fingerprints inside the Tokars's home.

Sara had bought a Christmas tree shortly before leaving Florida to return home. Fred had told Eddie about the purchase even as he told him what time Sara would arrive.

Fred planned to avoid police after his wife's death by checking himself into a hospital with complaints about his back.

And, finally, there were the eerily accurate details of Fred's schemes to launder money, the lawyer's Caribbean bank, the references to tax laws and ways of shielding illegal drug profits from detection, and the criminal enterprises operated by Julius Cline, James Mason, and Al Brown.

It was those details that made Eddie so credible, Buddy Parker would say later.

"We pressed Eddie," he said. "We told him, 'We know you committed crimes, but you're trying to distinguish yourself as being different from Curtis Rower and Fred Tokars. And yet, you're in the middle, literally, of a knowing and willful murder. Why are you different?'

"He said he had never been involved in any violence and really wouldn't have done it except that Fred had gotten him to where he was. Fred had threatened him. And, of course, the threat was essentially the same threat that Fred felt from Sara, and that was that she was going to take everything from him.

"Before Eddie Lawrence met Fred Tokars, he was this painting contractor. He was a two-bit drug dealer. He was a two-bit crook. And in less than nine months, he's being taken by a white judge to fund-raising parties for a black justice of the Georgia State Supreme Court and at City Council President Marvin Arrington's house. He's being touted in corporate records as a company president. Fred has given him eighty thousand dollars to establish himself. He's in the *Black Pages*.

"Fred invented him. And that's why Eddie Lawrence was credible. That's why Fred ultimately threatened to take it all from him. He made him. He could also destroy him."

Seventeen

The Gathering Storm

IT WAS TOO EXPLOSIVE A SECRET TO BE KEPT FOR LONG. Within nine days, reporters at *The Atlanta Journal-Constitution* knew, although only unofficially, that Eddie Lawrence had inked a deal. What they and their television counterparts did with that information became a significant and occasionally alarming sidelight as authorities began closing in on Fred Tokars.

On Friday, August sixth, Harvey and Spix were lunching at a Marietta pub when Don Plummer, a reporter for *The Atlanta Journal-Constitution*, stopped by their table. "I know that Eddie has made a deal," he told the lawyers in a slow, disarming bass. "He's going to plead in exchange for life on the murder and ten years on the federal charges. I have this information from a strong enough source that I can print it. I want your response."

Harvey's face went momentarily blank. He looked at Spix, then back at Plummer. Eddie hadn't even testified before the federal grand jury. If the story leaked now, the deal might well be canceled.

"We need to talk," Harvey replied, as he nodded in Spix's direction. While Plummer waited, the two lawyers adjourned hastily to the front of the restaurant where they could converse privately and regroup.

"If we lie, it's an empty song," Harvey told Spix.

"We can beg him not to run it," Spix answered. He knew Plummer as a fair-minded reporter. He believed Plummer was among the more humanitarian journalists he had met. The lawyer knew he would listen carefully. Give him a sincere and compelling argument to contemplate and he just might change his mind.

The two lawyers motioned to Plummer and walked with him to the sidewalk in front of the restaurant, out of earshot of the other diners. "It's true," Spix told the reporter bluntly. "But you can't run it."

"I can run anything I want to," Plummer answered matter-of-factly.

"Hear us out," the lawyer replied.

Then Eddie's attorneys laid out the consequences they feared if Fred learned Eddie had cut a deal and become the government's star witness against him. They were certain Fred was unstable enough to be dangerous, a bully and a coward who might take his own life and his sons' lives, as well, in one last defiant act to win control.

As the lawyers watched the women in summer dresses strolling through the square, Plummer pondered what they had told him. "I believe you," he said. But the decision to hold the story wasn't his alone. His editors would also have to be convinced that the lives of the Tokars boys were truly at risk if Eddie's deal became public before Fred was in custody. They, not Plummer, would have to make the final call.

The following Monday, Harvey and Spix met in downtown Atlanta with Plummer, federal beat reporter Bill Rankin, who had also gotten wind of Eddie's deal, and two editors to renew their plea for discretion. The publicity surrounding the Tokars case since Sara's murder, the awful circumstances of her death, and her husband's position as a public official who had been hustling to inject himself into Atlanta city politics made new information about Tokars even more compelling, the competitive pressures far more fierce.

Cobb County District Attorney Tom Charron, Assistant District Attorney Jack Mallard, U.S. Attorney Joe Whitley, and Assistant U.S. Attorney Buddy Parker had all been invited to attend the rare meeting and make their case as to why the story should be held. Only Spix and Harvey came, although the U.S. Attorney made his own private appeal a short time later.

"We thought they were genuinely concerned," Harvey said later of prosecutors who had privately impressed on the lawyers that Fred was a threat to his children. "But we were the only ones at the table."

"If the children's lives are really at stake, where are the others we invited?" one editor demanded. "Why aren't they here?"

The irony wasn't lost on Spix. "Here we are, two defense lawyers who don't have any children of our own making the argument that the Tokars children's lives are in danger."

Nevertheless, the journalists eventually agreed to hold the story until Fred was arrested. In return, Spix and Harvey had to tell them everything they knew. Newspaper executives remained suspicious of the arrangement to which they reluctantly agreed. But no one wanted to risk the boys' lives if Fred was truly the unstable killer he appeared to be.

Yet, Eddie's defense lawyers left the newspaper that day feeling like goats—shills who would say what they must to secure for Eddie his "get out of jail" card and protect a plea agreement that, long before it was made, was derisively dubbed "the deal of the century" by Fred's lawyer, Jerry Froelich.

In fact, the duo had a far better understanding of Fred than almost anyone at that time who was connected with the case. They knew that Fred had manipulated and then discarded Sara, because he had done the same to Eddie. In the corrupt regime that Fred inhabited, everyone was expendable or could be purchased for a price. Harvey was certain that Fred would poison himself and his children or ram his car headlong into some bridge abutment if he thought that, in dying, he could amass the kind of public sympathy that his dead wife had garnered and distract the public from the damning litany of facts that identified him as the culprit in her murder.

Two days later, Eddie testified before a federal grand jury in Atlanta. Assistant U.S. Attorney Katherine Monahan, who was assisting with the case, listened as, for hours, Eddie answered Parker's questions about counterfeiting, drug deals, money laundering, and murder.

"I think he leveled with us," Monahan said later. "I don't think he had anything left to hide. I think he felt like this was his last shot at any kind of rehabilitation, that if he were ever going to get out from under this and get out of prison, that he had to come clean. He had to tell us the truth, and he couldn't leave anything out."

That afternoon, federal marshals brought Eddie to a Cobb County motel near the interstate for one more secret interview with Cobb police.

Harvey and Spix were waiting for Eddie in the motel parking lot where they were soon joined by the Cobb County district attorney, a second prosecutor, and three police detectives. They entered the motel room—seven white men, at least three of them armed, and a solitary black man hooded and in chains in a county where the Confederate battle flag still flew in front of public buildings. Harvey detested the implications. That wasn't the only thing that bothered him about the motel setting.

"I was afraid people would recognize me," Harvey said. "I was afraid they would call my wife and say, 'I saw your husband walking out of a motel room with another guy.' It was goofy."

It was also the last time Eddie's lawyers were allowed to see him until nearly six months later.

After Eddie's Barrett Lodge debriefing, Buddy Parker had accelerated dramatically the pace of the federal grand jury investigation. He sought sweeping racketeering indictments against Fred as the lawyer and money-launderer in a racketeering enterprise that washed its drug money through Atlanta's nightclubs and protected its criminal enterprises with intimidation and violence. To shield those criminal activities from discovery, Fred had murdered Sara.

As Parker delved into the background of each nightclub that had some link to Fred, he slid into Atlanta's sordid underbelly—a grim, reflected world lit only by neon, headlights, and half-smoked cigarettes. Drugs were the corrosive at the city's core, a nether region where deviance was succored, crime glorified, violence reptilian, and perversion just another gentle amusement. The information he amassed as he tracked Tokars through the maze of clubs and corporations the lawyer had spawned left Parker, at day's end, feeling slimy and in need of a shower.

At the heart of his case were the documents that Sara had secretly copied and given to her sister for safekeeping and the old appointment calendars police had taken from the Tokars's house during the days immediately following Sara's murder. Among the attorney's calendars and corporate records, Parker had found repeated references to the drug dealers federal authorities had targeted as well as notations of more than $1 million in wire transfers and deposits to banks in the Bahamas, in Switzerland, and Germany.

"These are the symptoms of an attorney involved up to his eyeballs with his clients and helping launder their money," he said.

By then, Parker had acquired information that Fred—confident that the authorities, in spite of their suspicions, had unearthed no evidence of his crimes—intended to leave Canada in late August, return to his mother's Florida home, enroll his sons in school, and continue his battle for his wife's life insurance money.

Parker also knew that the newspaper was aware of Lawrence's deal. The vagaries of the media were such that the prosecutors knew their days were borrowed. Television reporters had also heard that Eddie had appeared before a federal grand jury. They, too, suspected a deal. There was no time to spare if federal authorities hoped to arrest Fred before he had a chance to flee.

But the U.S. Justice Department is a bureaucracy, and the Georgia prosecutors could not proceed without the approval of their supervisors in Washington, D.C. So, while federal prosecutors Katherine Monahan and Larry Anderson shipped drafts and revisions of what eventually became a twenty-three-page indictment of nine people to Washington for approval, Parker shepherded a succession of witnesses before the grand jury.

By Monday, August twenty-second, the details of Fred's arrest had been set and carefully coordinated with Tom Charron in Cobb County. Charron, who had personally sent more criminals to Death Row than any other prosecutor in the state of Georgia, wanted Tokars to face the death penalty for Sara's

murder. According to the plan, Charron would convene a
Cobb County grand jury on Thursday, August twenty-fifth, to
indict Tokars for the murder-for-hire of his wife. That afternoon, the federal grand jury would vote on the racketeering
conspiracy that swept in Tokars, Lawrence, and seven other
drug dealers and money-launderers. Early Friday morning, as
soon as the Tokars children left for school, the F.B.I. would
arrest Tokars in West Palm Beach. Charron would hold the
first news conference at 9:30 a.m. and Eddie Lawrence would
publicly plead guilty for his role in Sara's murder. Friday
afternoon, U.S. Attorney Joe Whitley would hold his own
news conference after which Lawrence would plead guilty to
the federal charges lodged against him.

By Monday, August twenty-second, Fred's impending arrest was an open secret among reporters who for nine months
had covered the evolving story of Sara Tokars's murder. But,
with one glaring exception, every news outlet sat on the story
and stayed away from Fred, fearing that harm would come to
Sara's children if they publicized Eddie's deal or if the Atlanta lawyer, in his growing paranoia, decided he was being
watched.

The exception was WXIA-TV—the Atlanta television station whose reporter had inked an aborted movie deal with
prosecution witnesses. On Monday, August twenty-second,
the station sent a cameraman to stake out the Tokars's West
Palm Beach condominium where Fred and his children were
staying. At the time, WXIA had no real information about
Fred's arrest, only strong rumors and hunches that made their
reporters giddy with suspicion that something was about to
happen. Cameraman ''Big Al'' Ashe flew into Palm Beach
that day to stake out Fred's residence so that, when authorities
arrested Fred, he could capture it on video and scoop the other
networks in the process.

''Our sources had indicated there was concern for the children's safety,'' said WXIA reporter Paul Crawley, who had
worked with Dean Phillips on the story. Their instructions
from the station's news director were ''check it out,'' ''don't
get in the way,'' and ''don't jeopardize anyone's life.''

They didn't think that staking out the condominium with a
camera in the middle of August on an isolated, residential

beachfront road would violate any of those directives.

Ashe rented a van, found the address in the telephone book—the only Tokarses in West Palm Beach—cruised by the condominium, then returned to peruse the resident list by the gate. As he turned the van around to leave the complex, Fred drove up to the gate with his two boys.

"He looked straight at me," Ashe said. "We were maybe fifteen feet apart. I'm a big, black guy. I didn't have a delivery van." And it was, after all, Palm Beach. "Given the fact that he is so paranoid, I guess he got suspicious."

Fred pulled through the gate, circled the building, drove through a rear exit, and looped back around to the boulevard. Meanwhile, Ashe had pulled into the lot and was hunched over reading a map and trying unsuccessfully "not to be seen." Thinking he had narrowly avoided discovery, Ashe pulled out of the parking lot and turned left onto South Ocean Boulevard where he discovered that, without intending to, he was now following Fred.

"At that point, I was trying to pretend I was part of the landscape," Ashe said. There was nowhere to turn off the boulevard and Ashe decided that to make a sudden U-turn would have attracted even more attention. But he soon began to worry that he had flushed Tokars out of hiding and that now the elusive lawyer would hole up with his children at a place without a listed address. Ashe told himself, "If he's taking off now, at least I'm going to know where he is."

Suddenly, Tokars made a hard left into a municipal parking lot where a number of police patrol cars were parked. Ashe turned in right behind him.

"So, this guy wants to turn me in to the cops," Ashe thought. He decided to leave, pulling away as Fred made a wide arc through the lot. "When I went back by the condo later," Ashe recalled, "his car wasn't there."

Chastened, Ashe decided to change cars. He traded the van for a baby-blue Lincoln Continental before he picked up his partner, reporter Paul Crawley, at the airport the following day. Ashe then cruised by the condominium again.

"Kind of obvious, aren't we?" Crawley remarked as the Lincoln cruised down Ocean Boulevard.

"Not in Palm Beach, man," Ashe replied.

As Al slowed and pointed out the Tokars's condominium, Crawley noted a dark, four-door sedan occupied by a clean-cut young white man facing the condo. Although it was dark, the car's headlights remained off.

"Don't look now, but there's this car parked in front of the chain-link gate facing Tokars's condo," Crawley said. It was an F.B.I. stakeout.

"Let's try something," Crawley said as the baby-blue Lincoln cruised past the condominiums. He directed Ashe to bring the car around, and they drove by the Tokars's condo a second time, then slowly pulled into the driveway. They cruised around the back of the complex, just as Fred had done when he had attempted to elude Ashe. As they came around the side of the complex they turned their headlights directly on the watcher in the dark sedan. The lights hit him in the face.

"Okay," Crawley noted. "This guy is definitely staking him out.

"I'm gathering he saw us," he continued wryly. "We better change cars again."

What the news crew did not know was that Fred had also spotted the F.B.I. stakeout and had confronted the agent, demanding an explanation for his presence near the condominium. He asked him who he was and what he was doing. He told him he suspected he was either with the F.B.I. or a private investigator employed by his wife's family to spy on him and his children. He wanted to know if a large black man matching Big Al's description was working with him. Fred told the agent he had spotted Ashe looking at the occupant register by the gate.

The confrontation alarmed the Palm Beach F.B.I. agents who had been assigned to arrest Fred once the Atlanta grand jury indicted him. They knew few details of the investigation. But they did know Fred was wanted for the murder of his wife. They knew he had tried to kill himself. And they feared what a man like him might do to his children if provoked.

As a result, the agents had decided that they would arrest Fred, if at all possible, while his sons were in school. F.B.I. supervisors in Florida placed an urgent call to Parker in Atlanta pleading with the prosecutor to allow them to arrest

Tokars immediately. Instead, Parker received permission from Justice Department lawyers in Washington, D.C. to present the final indictment to the grand jury on Wednesday August twenty-fifth, a day earlier than Parker had intended.

That Wednesday morning, Crawley and Ashe returned to Ocean Boulevard condominiums about 6 a.m. Someone was still watching Tokars, this time a gray-haired man in a metallic-blue sports car that was parked in the same spot as the dark sedan had been. Ashe parked in a condo lot directly behind the car so they could observe what they now were certain was an F.B.I. stakeout as well as any activity at Fred's condo.

At 7:10 a.m. a school bus pulled to the gate and Fred appeared with his two sons. As the children left for school, a man wearing blue jeans and pinstripe shirt with the air of an Ivy Leaguer, a pager on his belt and a cellular phone in hand, called to Tokars and engaged him in a brief conversation.

"He smelled of the F.B.I.," Crawley said. "The guy was either asking about the building or asking directions. We knew he was a cop."

Inside the Lincoln, Ashe raised his camera and began to film. But as the school bus pulled away from the curb, Fred spotted the baby-blue Lincoln with the television news crew inside. He started across the street in their direction, then veered over to the metallic-blue sports car and addressed the man sitting inside.

He demanded to know who the man was and whether he was an F.B.I. agent.

The man at the wheel was in fact an F.B.I. agent, although he refused to identify himself when Fred confronted him. Receiving a less than satisfactory response, Fred walked purposefully to the rear of the car and pointedly eyed the license plate.

Minutes later, Fred left the the complex. The baby-blue Lincoln lumbered out of the neighboring parking lot to follow. Several miles down the road Fred pulled into a public parking lot and the television news crew passed him. Somehow, they thought Fred hadn't spotted them. They decided to stop for breakfast. But if Fred had, by some chance, failed to spot the baby-blue Lincoln in his rearview mirror, the F.B.I.

certainly hadn't missed the news crew's bold maneuver.
Shortly after Crawley and Ashe sat down to breakfast, a gray-
haired man strolled into the restaurant. It was the man they
had seen in the sports car. Big Al darted out of the restaurant,
leaving Crawley ducking behind his newspaper. The agent
walked slowly by Crawley, eyeing him deliberately as he did
so. Then he left the restaurant. The news crew's waitress
rolled her eyes and shrugged. "We figured he made us,"
Crawley said. As he left the restaurant, he spotted the F.B.I.
agent waiting in the parking lot in a dark sedan with tinted
windows. Crawley and Ashe decided to trade in the rental
Lincoln for another van.

After renting a minivan with tinted windows, Crawley and
Ashe decided to rent a condo in the resort from which they
had been conducting their stakeout. That way they could park
there legally and be close to their quarters at night. As Big
Al was registering, he mentioned to the desk clerk that he
was impressed with the visible security.

"Oh, no. He's not ours. He's the F.B.I.," the clerk answered. Spotting the parked sedan and its occupant, the resort
security officer had gone over to the car the previous night
and asked, "Who are you? What are you doing here?" The
agent had flashed his badge at the security guard.

"That," the desk clerk finished triumphantly, "is how we
knew who they were."

Crawley and Ashe camped in the van all day, running the
motor and the van's air conditioner to stay cool in the sweltering heat.

"We figured we would watch them watching him," Crawley said. "We would watch them watching him and hope he
didn't realize we were watching him being watched." They
thought they were being unobtrusive. But the security guard
who had spotted the F.B.I. had also made note of the news
crew and the camera gear stashed in the van. He thought they
were federal agents, too.

That afternoon, a school bus delivered the Tokars boys
about 3:25 p.m. It was drizzling rain, and, as Ashe shot footage of the children, Fred looked directly at the van. A short
while later, the F.B.I. sedan pulled away from the curb,
merged onto Ocean Boulevard, and disappeared. WXIA's

sources had informed the news crew that the F.B.I. would not arrest Tokars in the children's presence. Crawley and Ashe decided the F.B.I. was leaving for the night. There would be no arrest until after the children left for school the following day. They disembarked from the van and adjourned to their rented room to prepare dinner and watch the Atlanta Braves game on TV.

But the F.B.I. hadn't really pulled up stakes. It was a ruse to dupe the television news crew into leaving so they could more easily lure Fred from the condo and arrest him. Parker had called from Atlanta shortly after the children arrived home. The grand jury had handed down a sealed indictment naming Fred Tokars as a money-launderer and a killer.

When Parker called the F.B.I.'s Palm Beach agents with news of the indictment, he assumed they would arrest Fred the following morning. He underestimated their collective case of nerves, fed by the television news crew galumphing around the condominium, Fred's own heightened suspicions that he was being watched and followed, and his willingness to confront two different agents who were not subtle enough to avoid his scrutiny. When he appeared on his balcony with a video camera and began filming both the F.B.I. and television news stakeouts across from his condominium, the agents became convinced that he would do something even more rash. As the afternoon waned, their fears for the Tokars children escalated. They worried that Fred would harm his children once dark fell.

After the television crew departed for dinner, the F.B.I. quickly decided to bend Fred's overweening vigilance to their tactical advantage and lure him away from the children. Knowing the attorney was watching the parking lot from his condominium, an agent dressed in casual attire strolled over to Fred's parked car. He began peering insolently into the car, trying the door handles as if he intended to vandalize or steal it. Fred appeared on the balcony with his camcorder. Oblivious, the agent continued to prowl around the car. Then Fred did exactly what the F.B.I. had hoped. He called the Palm Beach police. A mile up the boulevard, Cobb County detectives Banks and Hunton were waiting at a motel for word that Fred had been taken into custody. Aware of the ruse, they flagged down a Palm Beach patrol car that was en route to the condominium.

"You're going to get a call to 3030 South Ocean Boulevard, apartment seventeen, if you haven't gotten it already. Play along with this. This is a federal arrest. The person you are being called about is a federal agent."

When the patrol car arrived at the condo, the police officer promptly confronted the agent prowling around Fred's car, cuffed him, and placed him in the patrol car. Fred appeared again on his balcony. The police officer called to him, asking that he come downstairs to identify the prowler and make sure his car had not been damaged. When Fred, wearing oversized shorts, a Braves T-shirt, and rubber flip-flops, shuffled downstairs, federal agents took him into custody in the lobby, cuffed him, and hustled him away.

As they drove Fred to the Palm Beach County jail, Atlanta D.E.A. Agent Jeff Dalman noted that Fred appeared remarkably calm, as if he had been expecting the arrest.

"You don't seem surprised," Dalman said.

"Well," Fred answered frankly, "I think it will all blow over."

Within minutes of Fred's arrest, the telephone rang at the Ambrusko home in Bradenton. Fred was in custody. The children were still at his mother's condo. Federal agents had already talked with Florida's child welfare agency, which had agreed that the children could be placed in the care of a relative instead of in a foster home. They would need to leave immediately. But, for some reason, the boys were now terrified of their mother's sisters and had shied away even from speaking to them by telephone. Someone whom the boys still trusted had to come.

Joni Ambrusko was at the movies with her nieces and nephews when her family paged her with the news. She quickly shepherded her small charges out of the theater, and drove to her parents' home where she and her brother-in-law, Neal Wilcox—the boys' favorite uncle—decided to leave immediately for West Palm Beach, a three-hour drive away. They had not seen or talked with Rick or Mike since their father had taken them from their grandparents' home fourteen weeks earlier. There was no time to waste.

Meanwhile, Pat Banks had arrived at the condominium. He found the boys crying on the balcony.

"Hey, guys," he called. "It's Pat. You remember me."

"Have you arrested my dad?" Ricky asked plaintively.

Banks and the federal agents who accompanied him gently sidestepped the child's anguished question.

"We just want to talk to him," F.B.I. Agent Reid Robertson said.

Banks tried valiantly to calm the children. He told them jokes. He told them that, sometimes, grownups do stupid things. He told them they weren't to blame for anything that had happened. Then he told them to pack their bags because "some special babysitters" were coming to get them.

Mike, now five, chattered happily with Banks for the first hour. But as dark fell, the child dragged a blanket from his bedroom, curled up on the couch, looked up at the police detective with a beatific smile, then fell asleep.

Ricky, the older child, remained distraught. "Am I going to go to school tomorrow?" he asked the detective worriedly. "I have to go to school. I have to return a library book."

Finally, he, too, curled up beside Banks. "You aren't going away, are you?" he asked in a small voice.

"I'm going to stay right here," Banks reassured the agitated child. Soon, Ricky too had drifted into a dreamless sleep.

By then, the Atlanta news media had learned of the arrest and were arriving en masse. The WXIA news team had run from the resort across the street just as federal agents pulled away from the curb with Fred in handcuffs inside.

About 8:30 p.m. a dark sedan squealed to a stop in front of the jockeying cameras and a federal agent stepped out. As reporters began clamoring for information, I.R.S. Agent Les Furr held up a greasy sack. "They're just Happy Meals from McDonald's," he said, brushing aside the microphones that were thrust at him.

They were for the Tokars boys. The children woofed them down.

Meanwhile, Fred was calling his lawyers. Jerry Froelich was apoplectic with rage. Froelich was a former federal prosecutor. Though, as a criminal defense attorney, he often played the role of a junkyard dog in court, outside of the courtroom he was a gregarious man with a bluff charm that won him courtesies from the prosecutors who were his adversaries. In federal court, he was the ultimate insider.

Throughout the summer, Froelich had assured federal prosecutors that if Fred were ever indicted, they had only to notify him, and the Atlanta lawyer who was his client would surrender voluntarily. There was no need to cuff Fred and jail him in front of his children. He scoffed at any notion that Fred was guilty of murder, but insisted vociferously that if the federal government succeeded in indicting Fred he would neither harm the children nor run.

Now, Froelich learned from Fred and from the media that he had been neatly sidestepped. He had not been given the courtesy of a telephone call or the opportunity to hand over his client to authorities without any media hoopla. It was, he was certain, the Ambrusko sisters' fault. They had colluded with federal authorities and Cobb County police to wrest custody of Sara's boys from Fred. He was offended, highly insulted and defiant. The government had conspired with Sara's family. Fred was being framed for Sara's murder so her sisters could take the children.

Convinced that custody and insurance, not money-laundering and murder, had dictated Fred's arrest, Froelich placed an angry call to a Palm Beach attorney whom Fred had enlisted ten weeks after Sara's death to secure his custody rights and the ascendancy of his family, not Sara's, as his children's guardians.

Palm Beach lawyer Peggy Rowe-Linn then placed a call to the Tokars's condo. Banks answered the phone. Rowe-Linn informed Banks curtly that she intended to take custody of Mike and Rick on behalf of the Tokars family. Fred, she said, wanted the children to stay with his brother, Andy.

"I'm not a local police officer," Banks said. "State social services has told us we can give the children to a family member. I'll do what I think is in the best interest of the boys."

"When I bring over the custody papers, you'll have to give the boys to me," Rowe-Linn responded sharply.

Joni Ambrusko beat her there. About 9:30 p.m., Joni and

her brother-in-law arrived from Bradenton. Their car had broken down, but their Atlanta lawyer, who had hopped a plane to Florida as soon as he received the news, luckily spotted them and hustled them into his sedan.

Joni expected the boys would be as happy and relieved to see her as she was to see them. Instead, they were terrified. Much later the children told her that their father had spent the summer convincing them that it was Joni who had arranged to have their mother murdered. Perversity, jealousy, or an evil cruelty had prompted Fred to school his children to believe that their aunt was a killer. Moreover, he warned the boys that their Aunt Gretchen, a nurse, had tried to poison him. Surely they remembered that she had given him some pills to calm him down. But it wasn't medication. It was poison. That is why he had been hospitalized at Christmas. Gretchen had tried to kill him, too. He had further terrorized his sons by telling them that their maternal grandmother, Sara's gentle mother, was a witch. Joni could only fold them in her arms and tell them in her small, sweet voice that it simply wasn't true.

Fred's arrest propelled the Ambruskos into action. The following day, Sara's parents, accompanied by their daughters, appeared at an emergency hearing at the Manatee County Courthouse in Bradenton, where they sought and won temporary custody of the Tokars boys. In a handwritten notation, the judge limited Tokars's contact with his sons to telephone calls. He also forbade Fred from discussing with his children anything about his imprisonment or the criminal charges against him, including their mother's murder. That same day, Eddie Lawrence entered formal guilty pleas in federal court in Atlanta and in Cobb County for his role in Sara's murder.

In federal court, Parker laid open the sweeping indictment naming Fred as the lawyer for a criminal drug ring that used his practice to conceal cash generated from illegal narcotics sales. No less than eight Atlanta area nightclubs and at least twenty-one corporations were created as legitimate fronts that were used to launder or conceal the origins of the illegal profits.

Indicted along with Fred were drug dealers Al Brown and Jessie Ferguson; Eddie Lawrence, James Mason, and Fred's investigator Billy Carter—the men who operated the businesses and nightclubs that were used to conceal the drug profits; and Aaron Hudson, an accountant for Mason and Brown whom authorities suspected of fabricating tax returns for the ring. Julius Cline, who had been shot down in Detroit four months before Sara's murder, and a fourth drug dealer, Andre Willis, were named as unindicted coconspirators. Eddie's old pal, Alex Yancey, still a fugitive on federal counterfeiting charges, was also named in the indictment which charged Tokars with obstructing the U.S. Secret Service in its investigation of Yancey and the agency's attempts to take him into custody.

Ring members, including four of Atlanta's most significant cocaine dealers, shielded their illegal activities from discovery with violence, Parker said. Among the victims of the ring's brutality was Fred's wife, Sara Tokars.

"In divorcing Fred Tokars," Parker said, "Sara Tokars could, in fact, destroy his life as he knew it because she believed him to be involved in money-laundering activities. Sara Tokars could, in fact, have been a valuable witness to the government in acknowledging Mr. Tokars's candid admissions to her as to his role and involvement in money-laundering. She posed a threat to him and his life and all that he had built in this community."

Part IV

===

ON TRIAL

Eighteen

Sins of the Wolf

FROM THE DAY OF HIS ARREST TO THE DAY SIX MONTHS later when he went to trial, Fred assumed the colors of a hapless victim.

Sara's family might have lost a sister and a daughter, but he had lost a wife, the mother of his two young sons. He had watched his law practice dissolve under the heavy weight of public suspicion. His life had been traded like some cheap bauble by a resentful business partner who had murdered Sara, was careless enough to get caught, and then lied to police to save himself.

As far as Fred was concerned, everyone else was to blame for the dire circumstances in which he now found himself. He was an oppressed and blameless victim of Sara's family, who had never liked him; the media howling for a prominent suspect in their drive to sell the news; arrogant and ignorant police; a Hollywood production machine that was enlisting witnesses against him because it made a better story; and his own partner, a young, black man he had mentored and entrusted with business investments worth seventy thousand dollars. He was the good guy who had been conned and framed. He was blameless. He, not Sara, was the ultimate victim.

In truth, Fred preferred that role. His nature demanded that he hold the absolute center of attention. Narcissistic to his

361

core, Fred had, in a perverse way, drawn the focus away from both Sara and his children, the true victims of a brutal, heartless crime. By the time Fred was arrested, Sara had largely been shunted aside and then forgotten, dismissed by nearly everyone except her family as an attractive, but naive suburban housewife and largely forgotten in the coy games of cat and mouse Fred had played with the media and police for nine breathless months. In his mind, Fred became the victim of a murder he, himself, had instigated. It would become the heart of his defense.

To that end, he enlisted his attorney, Jerry Froelich, and cultivated his sympathies even as he played to the defense attorney's own biases and beliefs.

Froelich was forty-nine when Fred recruited him to represent him the day after Sara was killed. It may have seemed like an odd choice, for, although Froelich was well known as a criminal defense attorney, he generally appeared in federal not in state court where a murder would be prosecuted. He was a former federal prosecutor who, in private practice, had acquired an expertise in the arcane rules and regulations governing federal banking. He had parlayed that knowledge into a fortune, suing banks on behalf of customers who had been charged excessive interest.

But he had also defended men with known ties to the Mafia against federal charges that they engaged in racketeering, money laundering, and extortion, which explains why Fred may have turned to him, fearful that Sara's death would be folded into the federal drug and money-laundering investigation that Fred surely knew had mushroomed into allegations of racketeering.

How Froelich came to represent the mob's lieutenants in New Jersey and Miami said as much about the feisty, blunt Atlanta lawyer's character as his eventual decision to back away from them and decline all further offers to represent their minions in court.

Froelich was born in Newark, New Jersey. Like Fred, he was a doctor's son. He was also the oldest of eight children. He and his siblings attended a Catholic day school in Newark where, as a compact but spirited teenager with a reckless urge to win, Froelich played football. A son of a Notre Dame alumnus, Froelich, a ferocious Fighting Irish fan, had always intended to matriculate there. But when Notre Dame deferred his acceptance, Froelich, then a senior, found himself suddenly bereft of options. A friend of his had won a wrestling scholarship to Spring Hill College in Mobile, Alabama and had dared Froelich to apply. With the bluff moxie that he later exhibited in court, Froelich did, calling the college admissions office to insist not only that he had mailed an application to Spring Hill, but that, since he had not received an acceptance notice, the application had been lost. The ruse grew more elaborate as Froelich persuaded admission counselors in his bold New Jersey brogue that Spring Hill was his first and only choice and that the turn of events had not only devastated him, but had stripped him of any chance to begin his freshman year that fall.

Chagrined and apologetic, admissions counselors shoehorned him into the freshman class, and Froelich left New Jersey for Mobile. He had never been south of Pennsylvania.

Froelich never intended to stay more than a semester in a state so foreign to his northern sensibilities. But an auto accident that shattered his legs and hospitalized him for fifty days in New Orleans endeared him to the South and solidified grateful friendships with college classmates that he still maintained more than three decades later. Classmates hitchhiked from Mobile to New Orleans to visit him. Family members of friends he knew only casually dropped by. It touched him, engendering a fierce loyalty that had always been, and remains, part of Froelich's better nature. So, he stayed. And, although he returned to New Jersey after graduation where he coached football at his old high school while going to night law school, the South eventually drew him back.

It was while he was in private practice in New Jersey that Froelich ran into the brother of one of his high school football teammates near the steps of the federal courthouse. He was in trouble, he told Froelich. An association with known mobsters had led to a federal indictment. "I can help you," Froelich said.

By then, Froelich had cultivated a combative courtroom demeanor. In trial, he was a junkyard dog—aggressive, demanding, explosive, temperamental. Trials were wars to him; fair play what he could successfully get away with and still avoid an order of contempt. Yet there was about him an impish charm with which he offset even the most outrageous behavior.

Given the offenses, he won an extraordinarily easy sentence for his former teammate's brother. And soon one of his former teammate's buddies, another associate of the mob, had called needing help in a criminal matter. Such representation quickly swelled into a lucrative practice. But eventually, Froelich realized that he was being drawn into a relationship that occupied far too much of his time and blurred the firm line between a lawyer and his client. He was being invited to weddings, pressed to attend family dinners of men he knew were criminals. Representing such men didn't bother him, for he believed in everyone's right to a fair and impartial defense. But he never associated with his clients, never socialized with them or joined them in business ventures.

One night in Miami, he took his parents to a restaurant where the waiters soon began dropping by his table with gifts of fine wine, appetizers, and other expensive delicacies, compliments of a man in the corner for whom Froelich had done legal work and who owned an interest in the restaurant. He was also a Mafia don. Eventually, he and his party joined Froelich and his parents, who chatted happily with their new dinner companions, blissfully unaware they were dining with some of Florida's more notorious mobsters. It was an outrageously expensive dinner. But Froelich politely declined to accept the mobster's largesse, gulped, and paid the bill. As he drove his parents home that night, his mother mentioned that their charming companions had invited them to a daughter's wedding. As Froelich explained to his mother who their dinner guests were and that they were not going to any wedding, he silently vowed that he would decline to represent such clients any more. The danger of compromise was just too great.

From its very inception, Froelich was offended by the Tokars case. The lawyer was more familiar with the comparative sanctity of investigations conducted by federal law enforcement agencies, foremost among them the F.B.I., where secrecy was institutionalized and agents far less likely than local police to chat, even unofficially, with reporters. He was used to the comfortable, often cozy camaraderie at the federal courthouse that existed among prosecutors, judges, and defense lawyers, many of whom, like Froelich, were also former prosecutors. He expected certain courtesies, even from his adversaries, a certain civility that suggested prosecutors would keep him informed of the progress of any investigation involving men or women he represented.

Cobb police played by a different set of rules. The Tokars investigation—which relied to no small degree on news reports to flush out witnesses and informants, pressure suspects, and, in general, keep the case alive—came as a rude shock.

Time and again, Froelich reacted ferociously to the wholesale access the Atlanta media appeared to have acquired to interviews and information the lawyer had assumed were confidential. The intimate details of Fred's affairs and the phenomenal $1.75 million in insurance with which he had secured Sara's life that the media divulged enraged him, in part because he could do nothing to stop it. Such leaks were unprofessional and unethical, he howled. Police had a "hidden agenda." They had targeted Fred from the beginning and, absent proof and aided by Sara's family, had conducted a "media lynching." They had cut "the deal of the century" with Lawrence. He seemed oblivious to the damaging nature of the facts, including Fred's own decision to discuss publicly a previous affair. Instead, he scoffed angrily at reports revealing multiple motives that had led Fred to murder his wife, dismissing them as "negative spin."

"They're not interested in the truth. They're interested in Fred Tokars," he complained bitterly. "They have made up their minds and aren't going to listen to anything."

Lawrence's testimony was suspect, Froelich said in one pretrial hearing, because he "is a young black man who is looking at the chair. He is in the most conservative white county we have in this state. And he is accused of murdering a white woman in front of her two children in the most highly publicized case that this state and this city has seen. Do you think truth enters into it when the government comes to him and says, 'Tell us what we need, and you won't get the death penalty'? He'll tell you anything you want to hear. I don't think there is a more powerful reason to lie."

Hollywood production companies that continued to circle the murder like gulls in a trawler's wake also clearly disgusted Froelich. Sara's murder marked one of the first cases in which movie production companies attempted to negotiate deals with witnesses before the investigation was complete, the last arrests were made, and the case had gone to trial.

"I think the obvious story line that is going to be the most successful is if my client is involved," he worriedly explained. "The story line fades if my client is not involved." A random murder of a white woman by two black men wouldn't sell. A city judge and former prosecutor who hired two such men to kill his wife to protect a drug ring from discovery was another matter entirely.

Froelich feared that people who stepped forward to testify against Fred would slant their stories to enhance their chance for fame and fortune. Even Fred had been solicited, he offered.

Froelich had rejected those early overtures, saying curtly, "My client is not interested."

"How much will it cost to get you interested?" one producer responded.

But what most troubled Froelich about the case and Fred's arrest was his deepening belief that it was built on unwarranted assertions of corruption stemming from Fred's criminal defense and civil practice. It amounted to an attack on lawyers like himself. He, too, had defended drug dealers and mobsters. He, too, had incorporated businesses for a fee. Sara's family might believe there was some sinister motive behind Fred's willingness to defend criminals and his refusal to discuss his practice with Sara. But Froelich insisted that Fred was prohibited from sharing information about his clients with his wife by the Legal Canon of Ethics. Fred, according to his lawyer, was simply doing a job.

"People who do criminal defense work like me, unfortunately, represent people with problems," he explained. "There is nothing wrong with that."

The difference was that Froelich, unlike Fred, knew where to draw the line between representing a defendant and going into business with him, between representing legitimate business interests and helping criminals hide their money. But he saw in Fred something of himself that led him to draw public comparisons between himself and the younger lawyer he was now defending. Fred was a criminal defense attorney like him. He was doing what all lawyers do for a fee. There was nothing wrong with it. Fred had convinced him he had nothing to hide and no reason to kill.

Fred surely played to those surface similarities. But then, he had always done that with people he wanted to impress, divining with an uncanny accuracy what would be most appealing and then reflecting that persona, an elusive mosaic in which the pieces were constantly shifted and rearranged.

Both he and Froelich were from large families. Both had younger brothers who looked up to them. Both were the sons of doctors who worked long hours and mothers who assisted in those practices. Both were descended from sturdy immigrant stock and raised in industrial northeastern cities. Both were competitive athletes in high school. Both had gone south to college, attended night law school while working other jobs, then worked as assistant district attorneys before opening their own criminal defense practices in Atlanta. And although Fred was far more guarded about his religious affiliation than Froelich, he had married a Catholic wife and sent his children to Catholic school.

Unlike Fred, Froelich had never married. But he had close friends who had weathered devastating divorces so he was willing to believe Fred as he complained about his wife's family and their insistence that Sara wanted to divorce her husband.

"What you should consider is that when people believe they're going to go through a divorce, they're going to think the worst," Froelich said. "They are going to say the worst. They are going to blow things out of proportion."

Perhaps the backgrounds and experiences Froelich shared with Fred explains why his defense grew so aggressively personal. A man capable of lasting loyalties, in defending Fred, Froelich became an angry, true believer in his innocence. But in Froelich's increasingly vituperative attacks on Sara's family, particularly her six sisters, were the echoes of Fred's own misogyny.

Fred, he would argue, bought a home for his wife in a nice

neighborhood, gave her "plenty of money whenever she wanted," paid off her credit cards, paid for a maid, sent their children to private school, bought them gifts, and gave Sara a new Toyota 4-Runner. Sara, he insisted, was content.

Sara had married Fred because she was attracted to his prominence in the legal community, Froelich would argue expansively, even though Fred was one of fifty assistant district attorneys in Atlanta when she married him. Or, at least, "she thought he was well known.

"She was an attractive woman to have on his arm when they went out," he explained. "But people who knew her said two things about her, that she was dumb as a rock and obsessed with her kids."

Froelich hotly derided suggestions that the Cobb County house was ill repaired and poorly furnished; that Sara, not Fred, paid off her own debts and secretly acquired credit cards she was forbidden as a desperate way to extend her weekly allowance; that Fred did not give Christmas or birthday presents to his family; that Sara taught voluntarily at her sons' school to earn their tuition; and that her new car was leased. "Sara loved Fred, truly loved Fred," Froelich asserted. "She didn't care about his affair. She knew he had had one, but she had forgiven him. They had gotten counseling. It was no big deal."

But she was an accomodating woman. So, Froelich speculated, when her sisters would call to pour out stories of troubled relationships or marriages, "She didn't want to tell her sisters she was happy and make them feel bad. She didn't want to tell Krissy, who hated Fred."

He scoffed at formal statements by Sara's sisters and friends that she couldn't divorce him because he had threatened to secure sole custody of the children. "Don't you think if she wanted to leave, if he hated her spending his money, he would have told her to take the kids?" he demanded. "She would have gotten into her Toyota and gone to Florida with the boys to live with her parents."

He disavowed any suggestion that Fred was abusive, that he dominated Sara, that he was emotionally cruel or ever physically assaulted her. He didn't believe it; he didn't, in fact, believe that Fred fit any pattern of domestic abuse. Such arguments were only tools women used to excuse their own weaknesses, he said.

Instead, Fred was a victim of "these women" as he often referred to Sara's sisters and her cousin, Mary Rose Taylor. They were dysfunctional, chronically unable to sustain a close and loving relationship with any man other than their father. It wasn't normal for sisters to be so close, he said, to share the personal intimacies of marriage. Froelich said his large, closely knit Catholic family had never discussed such intimacies. "No man," he said, "stood a chance."

Froelich reserved his particular bile for Taylor, whom he held singularly responsible for Fred's arrest. "If my wife had gone into my office, taken and copied documents without talking to me, I'd divorce her that day," he said. "Mary Taylor pushed Sara to see a divorce lawyer, frightened her, made her cry," with her notions that Fred was laundering money and engaged in criminal activities. After Sara's murder, it was Mary Rose Taylor who warned Sara's family that Fred was probably involved, contacted child custody lawyers and then set in motion negotiations for a movie deal, Froelich said bitingly, as if Taylor were somehow responsible for the federal grand jury's decision to investigate and then indict Fred. "Sara never believed she was in danger from Fred Tokars. It was Mary Rose Taylor who scared the bejesus out of her."

Mary Rose Taylor had been right.

By then, Froelich was simply parroting Fred's own bitter inferences and suspicions. But so certain was he, that he boasted easily, "I know Sara better than anyone, better than her sisters, better, even, than Fred."

In hearing after hearing, as Fred watched with an occasional ill-contained smirk, Froelich vilified Sara's family. He demanded to know if Dr. Ambrusko, the family's then eighty-year-old patriarch, had engaged in an adulterous affair with his secretary. He accused Krissy Ambrusko of hating Fred, scurrilously claiming the lawyer had told Sara that her youngest sister had obtained an abortion and contracted a sexually transmitted disease. Sara's sisters, he barked, were framing Fred so they could steal his children because they weren't able to have children of their own. They, not Fred, were greedy for the $1.75 million that had insured their sister's life. Yet, he presented little evidence to substantiate the ugly allegations that he bellowed in open court.

"This case is going to be a war," he proclaimed. "We'll be the last ones standing when it's over."

Such abuse of a victim's family in defense of a suspected killer is rare. When Sara's family privately anguished, "Why are they attacking us so much?" their lawyers could only comfort them, promising that their stalwart testimony would help the sister they had lost by unveiling how utterly without scruples or remorse her husband truly was.

Buddy Parker choked on the hypocrisy of it all. For sixteen months, he had methodically tracked the trail of companies Tokars had incorporated, the Caribbean bank accounts he had established under false identities, calendar notations the lawyer had made, and the drug dealers with whom he socialized. What emerged from those documents and the files Sara had copied and then entrusted to her sister was a portrait of a money launderer, not a victim.

Men like Tokars angered Parker. They misused their skills to legitimize criminal empires built on drugs. They sucked their substantial livings from the poor, the weak, the reckless, and the innocent. Such men, suited in legitimacy, had contributed to the death of a childhood friend who died in the early morning hours of 1977 after overdosing on heroin at a New Year's Eve party. His friend's death at twenty-five didn't convert Parker into an avenging judicial angel. But when he joined the U.S. Justice Department's criminal tax division one year later, he embarked on a prosecutorial career that by 1979 allowed him to pursue the drug barons who imported billions in illegal narcotics and disguised their illegitimate profits behind the facade of legitimate businesses. For Parker, his young friend's death stood as a bleak reminder of the human cost attached to such astounding but illegal fortunes.

As the supervisor of Atlanta's Southeastern Drug Enforcement Task Force, Parker had indicted the dons of the Colombian Medellin Cartel. He had brought a Panamanian bank that laundered cartel money to its knees. He had arranged the first extradition of a Colombian from his native country to face federal drug conspiracy charges on U.S. soil. When trying several cases, Parker had worn a bulletproof vest, and fellow prosecutors had begun posting hand-lettered signs on their office doors announcing, "I am not Buddy Parker" half in jest and just in case.

The detective work involved in unraveling the facets of such elaborate and deadly criminal enterprises absorbed Parker, a trial lawyer with master's degrees in business administration and taxation law.

For months, he had sought with a dogged ferocity to elucidate Fred's authentic motive for murdering Sara Tokars. Eddie Lawrence had said that Fred wanted Sara dead before she could divorce him. Parker was certain that divorce alone wasn't a sufficient answer. Sara had been dallying with divorce since 1989. It was not until August 1992 that Fred had told Eddie, "I'm not going to let her destroy me. She's going to take everything I have."

What really threatened Fred, Parker wondered, when in August 1992 he first approached Eddie about the murder? By then, Fred knew how to launder money. Hiding money from Sara and a divorce lawyer posed little problem for him.

What did he mean when he insisted, "She's going to take everything I have"?

Parker kept returning to the grand jury investigation of Anthony "Al" Brown. Fred's decision to kill Sara had been made in tandem with the escalation of that investigation. As the grand jury witness list had swelled, sucking in men like James Mason who worked intimately with Fred, his position had grown more precarious. Sara had unknowingly stepped into those murky waters.

Sara had worked at her husband's law office collecting overdue accounts. She certainly believed he was hiding money from her and the children and may have decided he was hiding money from the federal government as well. She had confided to her neighbor, Sara Suttler, "I've got the goods on Fred. I've found evidence of tax evasion." Whatever Sara Tokars thought she found was enough to guarantee her death.

"I firmly believe Sara threatened Fred," Parker said. "She thought he would capitulate," surrender the children without a fight, and agree to a swift divorce.

Parker didn't believe Sara truly understood the explosive

nature of the information she had acquired. She just wanted to leave Fred and take her children with her. "Sara had no inkling of the full extent of the law, or the investigation, or the depths to which her husband had sunk," he said.

Whatever she knew, incomplete though it might be, was significant enough that a federal grand jury would cease looking at her husband as simply a witness and begin looking at him as a target.

Even being named as an unindicted coconspirator could cost Fred his legal and accounting careers, his ambitions for a judgeship, and his growing circle of influential political acquaintances. The corporate, civic image he had cultivated so carefully would be indelibly and irreparably stained.

He would be revealed as a deceiver.

Parker stumbled onto the parallel he sought as he was browsing through a bookstore the month before the federal trial was slated to begin. He lifted a copy of Dante's *Inferno* off the shelf. Dante's poetic narrative of a traveler's journey through "a darkling wood" and his spiraling descent through deepening circles of evil was the parable Parker sought that would explain Sara's murder.

"It crystallized so many things," Parker said. "When Sara married Fred, she saw him as a white knight on a white horse. She wasn't totally off base. He had not yet sunk to the depths of hell. He had not yet taken that final journey."

Parker found Fred in Hell's eighth circle, a hypocrite in golden robes guilty of the sins of a predator, the sins of the wolf. It became the crux of his prosecution, the sins of wolves who masqueraded among the innocent as sheep.

On March 1, 1994, fifteen months after a single blast from a sawed-off shotgun ended Sara Tokars's life, her husband arrived in Birmingham, Alabama, in chains. He was dressed in a navy prison jumpsuit, white socks, and navy prison slippers. His hair was neatly trimmed high above his ears. He had cut the wild riot of brown curls at the nape of his neck. Once in Birmingham, he exchanged his uniform for the pressed gray suit and button-down shirt of a corporate lawyer. To the occasional annoyance of his legal team, which, by 1994, had swelled to four criminal lawyers, he would take diligent notes and play an aggressive role in his own defense.

If convicted, Fred faced a federal sentence of life without parole. A number of his codefendants—determined not to be tried with a man who had generated such sensational publicity—had already pleaded guilty and agreed to testify against him. But even though Fred remained under indictment for Sara's murder in Cobb County, he no longer faced a federal murder-for-hire charge. Parker had been forced by the U.S. Justice Department in Washington, D.C. to drop it, although associated charges of kidnapping, robbery, and making interstate telephone calls to arrange a murder remained intact.

The reason: Cobb County District Attorney Tom Charron had powerful friends, among them U.S. Attorney General Janet Reno. Once Fred's defense lawyers revealed that a clause in Georgia's state constitution might prohibit Charron from trying Fred for murder if federal prosecutors did so first, the Cobb County district attorney successfully lobbied Washington to excise Sara's murder from the federal indictment. Pressured by his superiors, Parker had reluctantly agreed.

"We were so convinced that we had the better case," Katherine Monahan said later, "that we had a better chance of convicting him, that we had the wider base in truth because we had had what we believe was the real motive—the coverup for the money laundering."

U.S. District Judge Orinda Evans moved the federal trial from Atlanta to Birmingham after Fred's lawyers railed against the Atlanta media's interminable fascination with the case and shouted for a change of venue. Froelich had argued for either Miami or New York, cities where criminals and legitimate businessmen forged their bitter alliances to launder billions, cities that would dwarf Fred's sins. But Evans, after agreeing to transfer the trial to a city less saturated with the details of the crime, selected the steel mill town three hours due west of Atlanta that three decades earlier had steeped in its own poison of violence.

Parker was an Alabama boy. Born in the tiny town of Ozark, Parker had grown up in southeast Alabama, and his sonorous bass still echoed the broad dialect of his roots. He had eschewed the college credentials of the southern Ivy League to attend the University of Alabama with his friends.

He had gone to college, to fraternity parties, and to law school with men and women who would later run the state. In those legendary days when Coach Paul "Bear" Bryant was synonymous with Alabama, he had once sold his law books to pay a football bet—a predicament more than one Alabamian would appreciate if not thoroughly admire. His mother and sister were practicing lawyers. He recognized these jurors with the comfortable familiarity that a southern heritage begets.

Froelich, a graduate of Spring Hill College on the "Red Neck Riviera" in Mobile, boasted his own sincere Alabama ties. But the lawyer's excitable New Jersey brogue marked him as a foreigner in a courthouse where federal marshals insisted jurors still believed that those who went to trial there must have done something to deserve it.

When Froelich arrived in Birmingham, he was a tired man. He and cocounsel Bobby Lee Cook had recently completed an eight-week corruption trial involving several Atlanta City Council members that had threatened to taint the city council president, to whom Fred had contributed. The judge had held court for ten hours a day, six days a week.

Froelich and Cook had vigorously protested Evans's decision to begin Fred's trial March first. They were exhausted; they had to review forty thousand pages of material the federal government had gathered during its investigation. The month of February had been taken up with federal hearings in Atlanta and preliminary hearings on the murder counts in Cobb. So frustrated were Fred's attorneys that they had hauled the boxes of documents to a court hearing where they attempted to resign *en masse*, claiming that, with so little time, they could not adequately represent him.

But Evans was adamant. She pointed out sharply that Froelich had hired on as Fred's criminal counsel within days of the murder and that Cook had joined the team within weeks. Both had been publicly, and in Froelich's case aggressively, associated with the case for more than a year. They had vociferously broadcast their intention of conducting their own independent investigation nine months before Fred's arrest. They had a motion pending for a speedy trial in Cobb. Evans told them bluntly that they couldn't have it both ways, demanding a speedy trial where it was expedient while attempting to delay a similar trial in another jurisdiction. She wasn't going to play their game.

So, Froelich was seething by the time he got to town, a frustration that erupted during a fractious pretrial hearing after Froelich subpoenaed every single one of Sara's family to prevent them from sitting in the courtroom where the jury could watch them and see something of Sara's reflection in their haunted eyes, and where, as witnesses, they could hear testimony other than their own.

The prosecution had also subpoenaed three of Sara's sisters, her father, and two of her sisters' husbands to testify. But Froelich was determined to keep them all away from the jury even after the prosecution had questioned them.

In a pretrial hearing, Evans tossed out the subpoenas Froelich had issued for Sara's elderly mother and her older sister, Mary Bennett, telling the lawyer in her blunt manner that he had failed to make a good-faith show of cause. Infuriated, Froelich demanded an apology from the judge for questioning his motives and veracity. She pointedly ignored him.

In the fifteen months since Sara's murder, her sisters had maintained a steadfast vigil at every state and federal hearing involving her accused killers—Rower, Lawrence, and her husband. The raw agony of their grief, an unfounded but profound guilt that they couldn't somehow save her, and their stoic loyalty washed across their open faces as they sat, holding hands, small charms, and talismans—all that was left of their sister—crushed in their palms, their heads bowed in one more prayer for Sara before each hearing formally convened.

They were like avenging angels. They had sacrificed jobs, placed careers and marriages at risk to make their pilgrimages from California, upstate New York, New Jersey, and Florida in memory of their sister. They had sat stiffly and silently as Froelich flung tawdry accusations at them in public hearings. Warned against any emotional displays in court, they would flee to the ladies' room to throw up or cry bitterly at such appalling savagery.

They had lost Sara and now they were forced to witness in stunned disbelief the public rape of their integrity and their character in court. They were trusting women who believed, naively, that truth would prevail. They were outraged and deeply hurt that they were considered fair game in the name of a fair trial.

Sara's outspoken baby sister, Krissy, bore the brunt of the attacks. Time after time, in pretrial hearings, Froelich sought to savage her, claiming he had an "absolute right" to do so, to show a jury Krissy had cooperated with law enforcement and then tailored her testimony to destroy Fred. Froelich contended that Krissy was not driven by a desire to see her sister's killer caught and punished but by a hatred of her brother-in-law that stemmed from personal revelations she had shared with him and that he, in turn, had passed on to her sister. Krissy had always acknowledged that she never particularly liked Fred and that they had fought over his treatment of Sara. But Froelich insisted that, despite that animosity, Krissy had confided intimate details of her sex life to a brother-in-law she despised while withholding them from a sister whom she trusted and adored. Because Fred had betrayed such confidences, Krissy now was more than willing to lie about him to a judge and jury, Froelich said.

"This is not to show she's a bad person," he insisted.

"I don't believe that," Evans snapped.

Froelich's temper flared. "Your honor, I take offense at that. I expect an apology."

"I do not see what difference it makes what the reason for the bad relationship is," Evans continued. "Miss Ambrusko may have pretty good reason to believe that Mr. Tokars killed her sister.

"Assuming it's true," she said deliberately, "it's just unnecessary. You already have plenty of ammunition."

"You do not have not the right to judge the amount of ammunition or the type of ammunition I have," Froelich snapped. "You are saying to me, 'Put your hands behind your back and let me handcuff them.' Your honor, I would like an apology."

Froelich would carry that freewheeling, caustic anger with him throughout the federal trial. It infected his defense, his cross-examinations, his news conferences, and his judgment. He would stand before the jury indignant and as outraged as a blinded bantam rooster at a cockfight, sputtering with an unreasoning rage that even baffled his associates and friends. He began muttering audibly after bruising legal rounds, "I can't get a fair trial here," or, "Man, where are we?" in furious exasperation.

"We're not going to have a trial," he barked during one hearing just before the trial got underway. "Throw the rules of evidence out the window. It's insanity."

Outside of court, he was even more succinct. "These women," he spat whenever he was asked about the case. "These women."

But Sara's sisters bore it, because they had to, for Sara, seeking atonement for a wrong they never committed, doing penance for a sin that wasn't theirs. They had made a promise to their sister at her crypt, that they would care for her sons as if the children were their own and that they would find her killer and bring him to justice. They would keep vigil at every hearing and every trial because they knew that Sara would have done it for any one of them. Because they hadn't saved her, they would be guided by their promise to do "what Sara would want."

Monday, March 7, 1993 was one of those unbearably bright, topsy days of false spring in Alabama. But it was in a sterile, windowless courtroom muffled by dark draperies where, largely devoid of drama, the brutal story of how Sara Tokars came to die unfolded.

It was a utilitarian courtroom that lacked the polished grandeur of Birmingham's old federal courthouse—the polished stone, Corinthian columns, vaulted ceilings, grandly arched windows, finely grained wood, and elaborate moldings that exalted the law. In this courtroom, the most gruesome acts of violence assumed the bland colors of banality. Outrage, grief, retribution, a simple plea for justice all seemed curiously out of place.

Shoehorned awkwardly in the courtroom's eight pews were Sara's parents, her sisters, and their lawyers; Fred's mother and his older brother; journalists and sketch artists; Cobb County District Attorney Tom Charron and his lieutenant, Jack Mallard; court personnel; and casual observers—some law students, some simply curious, some associated with lawyers for both the prosecution and defense. It was an understandably self-conscious assemblage.

Dressed in charcoal-gray pinstripes, accented with the suspenders of a country lawyer, Parker approached the lecturn. He could be imperious in a courtroom, a minister of justice who argued his cases with a missionary zeal. That day, he was an instructor for a jury that was largely working-class and far removed from the convoluted financial chicanery that gave drug dealers the means to spend their illegal profits and still avoid detection.

There were eight men and four women in the jury box. Among them, three had been divorced, three were single, and half were married. Some lived in Birmingham, Alabama's largest city. Others spent their lives in the small, rural towns embedded in the Appalachian foothills of north Alabama. Most worked for an hourly wage. Two were or had been coal miners. They were joined by a bill collector, a mechanic, a janitor, a cook, a delivery man, a truck driver, a warehouse supervisor, an electrician, a quality assurance inspector, and a telecommunications company manager who called herself a workaholic. One had a brother who had been convicted of manslaughter. They had all answered questions about the nature of their divorces, whether they had ever been drawn into a custody battle, or suspected their spouse was having an affair, whether they hated homosexuals, or were biased against blacks.

Parker confronted them all. "Greed. Torture. Drug trafficking. Money laundering. Racketeering. Fear. These are the subjects and topics you will listen to and hear about during your service as jurors in this case."

Tokars and his codefendant, James Mason, and the other men indicted with them who had already pleaded guilty to their crimes, appeared as pillars of Atlanta, as respected members of the circles in which they moved. Instead, Parker said, they had taken their lessons, and identities, from a children's fable. They were wolves in sheep's clothing, men who devoured flesh and killed, drug dealers who imported tons of cocaine worth millions. Fred Tokars helped them conceal the ill-gotten source of their fortunes. He gave them what they hungered for but lacked—legitimacy.

The Alabama-born prosecutor then sought to ally himself with the jury, people whom Alabamians would describe, if asked, as "solid" and "good folk."

"I come from L.A., Lower Alabama," he said. Until he arrived in Washington, D.C. in 1977, "enterprise," he said, wasn't a criminal conspiracy, it was an Alabama town.

But the drug dealers that Fred solicited were all strangers, Yankees, carpetbaggers from Detroit. They sold cocaine. They knit their illegal trade with cruelty, assault, and torture. When they had to, they killed to cover their crimes. They made all their purchases in cash because "cash leaves no footprints." No checks, no trail of bank withdrawals or deposits.

"We're talking millions," he told the jury he complimented as "hardworking individuals" who "labor throughout the week" for money "derived from honest conduct." His outrage was plain.

Fred Tokars, "a prosecutor who tried drug cases," became a man who represented drug dealers and "took a lot of cash.

"There's nothing wrong with attorneys representing drug dealers for their past criminal activities," Parker said. "What's wrong is when attorneys help drug dealers continue their conduct, continue their illegal ways. What's wrong," he lifted a copy of a news article Tokars had penned in 1990, "is best stated by Mr. Tokars himself." He read the headline: " 'How lawyers help drug dealers launder money.' "

It was a service the lawyer provided, Parker said, sheep's clothing for predators who indulged in threats, assaults, torture, murder. Against that backdrop, Sara Tokars was "a ticking time bomb. She was a witness who could be a witness against him." Tokars had enlisted Eddie Lawrence to kill her "because she was going to divorce him and take everything he had; not his money, but his position, his power, and his prestige."

Froelich leaped to his feet. "Your honor, he's getting out of control," he shouted.

"The implication is terrible," Froelich argued after Parker completed his opening statement and sat down. "So you represent drug dealers. It doesn't mean you've broken the law. You have drug dealers who are clients and some of them pay

in cash. That happens to be a fact of life.'' But the jury might
not know that. In his own opening statement, Froelich would
have to blunt Parker's earlier insinuations.

He asked Fred to stand. In a charcoal suit, a white button-
down shirt, and a maroon tie, Fred looked bland, a bookish
accountant in steel-rimmed glasses anchoring a placid face
utterly incongruous with the leather-jacketed, gun-wielding
drug dealer whose poster-sized photo Parker had posted earlier on an easel in front of the jury.

"Fred Tokars does criminal defense work," Froelich said.
As a criminal defense lawyer, he explained, "You meet people who have problems. You meet people who deal drugs.
You meet people who are paid in cash. There's nothing illegal
about that.''

Then, as Fred sat down, Froelich launched into a rambling,
litany of the wrongs he insisted in offended tones had led to
Fred's arrest. Fred was an innocent, even naive, dupe; a victim of the government, police, the media, and in-laws who
never liked him and wanted to steal his children. "There was
tremendous publicity in Atlanta that is going to become very,
very important in this case. Every aspect of Fred Tokars's life
was put on television every day. Everything was leaked to
the media, everything. It became a sensation in Atlanta.

"Unfortunately, the Ambrusko family decided the day Sara
was murdered that Fred did it, and they decided those children
weren't Fred's, they were Sara's.''

Sara, he suggested, was a spoiled divorcée from a wealthy
family who had worked in a singles nightclub that was "the
hot spot of Atlanta'' before she married Fred after "a whirlwind romance.'' Fred was a responsible lawyer who had
given her everything she ever wanted. Again, Froelich singled
out Krissy Ambrusko for particular abuse, describing her as
a woman who had never worked for a living, who had relied
on her older sister for financial support, who had once had
an abortion, and contracted a sexually transmitted disease,
who had taught her nephew "the filthiest song'' and hated
her brother-in-law because he had learned of her licentious
behavior and dutifully reported it to his wife.

In contrast to the Ambrusko sisters, Fred was "a financial
planner'' who sold insurance, taught law courses at local col-

leges and to law enforcement officers. "Fred is a worker. He gets up early, gets home late. He puts in long hours."

The drug dealers the former Atlanta lawyer represented were well known in Atlanta and ran "very well-known, very successful nightclubs" that catered to Atlanta's judges and politicians, Froelich said. They knew Atlanta Hawks basketball star Dominique Wilkins and Deion Sanders, who played for both the Atlanta Braves and the Atlanta Falcons. Some had acquired letters of recommendation from prominent lawyers and politicians. In addition to Fred, they had also turned to one of the city's more prestigious law firms for advice. "My client didn't know" they were criminals, Froelich protested.

In fact, federal prosecutors had targeted Fred because his clients were black men, Froelich insisted to jurors raised in a state where federal marshals and federal, not state, judges had accompanied the formal end of segregation. But Froelich was undeterred. "The Atlanta bar is very cliquish," he said. "Lawyers in Atlanta did not like to go into the suburbs representing black people. He did. His clientele is a mostly black clientele."

That was why Fred had staked Eddie Lawrence in a chain of businesses that would service Atlanta's black neighborhoods, Froelich argued. As with his drug-dealer clients, Fred was also fooled by Lawrence, "the con men of con men" who hired Fred and then persuaded the lawyer he was not involved in a counterfeiting racket being investigated by the U.S. Secret Service, Froelich said. Once he learned that Eddie was "spending money and conning people all over the place," Fred had no choice but to take control of the company finances, warning Eddie that he would make a decision about the fate of the business after Thanksgiving.

Before he could do so, Sara was murdered. "Fred Tokars gets physically ill," Froelich told the jury. "He throws up. They had to call an ambulance."

Having lost his wife, Fred then became the victim of "the awesome power" of state and federal law enforcement authorities who decided he was a guilty man and gave sweetheart deals to his former business partner Eddie Lawrence and the drug dealers who were his clients. They, in turn, agreed to testify against him.

"My client doesn't know whether Eddie did it or why he did it," Froelich said. But Lawrence was there when Sara was killed, Froelich insisted, and the triggerman he hired, Curtis Rower, told police the truth when he said that the two had struggled over the gun, and that Lawrence pulled the trigger, firing the shot that took Sara's life.

"Mrs. Tokars recognized Eddie," Froelich insisted. "Eddie told Rower to shoot."

In jail and facing the death penalty for his crime, police offered Lawrence "the deal of the century," Froelich said as he held high a photo of Georgia's electric chair. "He doesn't ride the lightning if he can do one thing—give them Fred Tokars."

Responsible and generous, possessed of a good-hearted naiveté, Fred was everyone's victim, according to Froelich. It was Fred's own world view, and it was starkly at odds with reality.

Then Parker began his case against Fred and Mason—reconstructing for the jury the origins of the money-laundering conspiracy and the colorful criminal histories of the drug dealers with whom Fred established an uneasy but tenacious alliance. From the outset, the criminal enterprise was murderous.

Detroit homicide detectives took the witness stand first to tell the jury the spare details of Donte Snowdon's 1985 murder in Detroit and the arrest warrant they secured for Jessie Ferguson, a warrant that caused Ferguson and his partner, Julius Cline, to flee to Atlanta.

Police also recounted the 1990 murder of a witness to Snowdon's death who warned police five months before he was killed that Ferguson was trying to frighten him into recanting. Finally, the officers told the jury of the murder of Cline himself, executed in the driveway of his mother's home on the seventh anniversary of Snowdon's murder by a professional who dumped the stolen Georgia gun, wiped clean of fingerprints, in a nearby alley.

No one at the heart of Parker's broad conspiracy had any reservation about eliminating witnesses.

Ferguson was the first drug dealer to testify. He wore the hard expression of a man who killed easily and without conscience. He choked only one time, as he told the jury how he learned of Cline's murder in Detroit, the first and only time he would register genuine emotion. In a dispassionate, slurred baritone, he told of meeting Mason in a nightclub soon after arriving in Atlanta.

"I was looking for something to put money into to sustain a decent lifestyle," he told the jury. Mason soon ingratiated himself with Ferguson and Cline, and Ferguson explained how Mason came to be both a front man and a bank for the two drug dealers. Mason managed the clubs they financed with drug money. Mason secured as much as fifty thousand dollars in cash for them in a closet safe at his Buckhead condominium. Cline and Ferguson, in turn, gave Mason gifts and cash loans, including money to buy a Jaguar.

Mason wouldn't look at Ferguson as he testified. But as he sat at the defense table with his lawyers, he was the visible link between Fred and the Detroit drug traders—the front man with a semblance of legitimacy, the bridge between the drug dealers and the lawyer.

Ferguson was one of a procession of drug dealers, counterfeiters, criminals, and hangers-on who took the stand in Birmingham that month to testify in the drained, toneless voices of the perennially confined about the splashy neon nightclubs built with drug money that Mason and Tokars legitimized, about a club manager who couldn't handle money but was an eager recipient of it, and a white lawyer who busily formed corporations, arranged legal deals, and diligently importuned them to wash their cash through his Caribbean enterprises. Among them were would-be law enforcement officers, a succession of Mason's former lovers, and Atlanta businessmen who had accepted worthless promissory notes in lieu of payment for clubs that they eventually suspected had been built on corrupt foundations. Millions of dollars in drug money from the sale of tons of cocaine allowed them all to masquerade as entrepreneurs who displayed with ostentatious flair the trappings of wealth, the elegant apartments, the designer jewelry, the Mercedeses, BMWs, and Jags. The money gave them access to Atlanta city council members, county prosecutors, judges, lawyers, police, professional athletes, music producers, and Hollywood stars who gravitated to nightclubs that were numbered among the finest in the city.

Dominique Wilkins, now a center forward for the L.A. Clippers, drifted through, trailing an entourage of television cameras to tell the jury that he severed his relationship with the nightclub, Dominique's 21, after receiving word that Julius Cline sold cocaine.

"Basically, my brother told me that he heard some illegal activities was going on in the club as far as drugs. I just didn't want my name associated with that," said the star basketball player, who had played for the Atlanta Hawks. "He said Julius Cline was one of the guys that he heard was suspected of, you know, dealing drugs or whatever they were doing."

Wilkins said after his lawyer notified Cline and Mason that he was pulling his name off the club, "They called me and said I needed to come and get my stuff. They had set it all outside."

Deion Sanders, now a Cincinnati Red, took the stand to talk about his decision to lend his name to the nightclub Dominique had abandoned. "My name was just on the club. Really, I wasn't concerned about how it was being run," he said.

Like Dominique, he had given little thought to the deal before he signed it. "Really, it was just exposure at the time. I mean, it was a nice nightclub, exposure, plus you were just receiving a royalty off the top of it just for the use of your name."

Mason and Cline's lieutenant, Willie Harris, Sanders acknowledged, "were friends. I mean, if I seen them out, I seen them out." He also knew Cline from occasional games of pickup basketball at the gym.

Sanders said he had talked with Harris after Harris was arrested for trafficking in cocaine. "We didn't go into that," he said. "It was just, 'Hi, Willie. How are you? Hope you get out.' And that's it."

"At that time I was young and naive. And now I wouldn't do the same thing. I wouldn't make the same mistake twice," the ball player vowed.

The athletes' star power was self-evident. During his cross-examination, Froelich asked Wilkins for an autograph for a fellow lawyer's son. When Sanders, a diamond stud adorning one earlobe, testified, Mason's lawyer, Millie Geckler, gushed, "Mr. Sanders, I follow your career closely. I'm a fan of yours, and I'm a fan of the Falcons and of the Braves."

But those light asides failed to obscure the cumulative weight of the testimony or the names that resurfaced as each witness stepped into the sterile courtroom and swore to tell the truth.

Mason and Cline. Mason and Tokars. Tokars and Cline. The names kept surfacing in tandem with Atlanta's most flamboyant and significant clubs—the VIP, the Parrot, the Phoenix, Dominique's and Deion's 21 Club, Zazu's, Traxx, Diamonds and Pearls.

But there were warning signs, particularly for a former prosecutor who specialized in tax law and held an advanced accounting degree. Federal and state withholding taxes weren't paid. Liquor license fees weren't paid. Promissory notes were ignored. Creditors weren't reimbursed. Several partners, prominent among them Wilkins and Jim Killeen, abruptly severed ties with joint ventures that included Mason and Cline. Rumors persisted that the clubs were rooted in drug money and that their chief financiers and the managers they hired were drug dealers. The troubled histories they were willing to acknowledge hinted at even darker crimes. And the drug dealers who shuffled to the witness stand in Birmingham, while streetwise, were clearly unsophisticated about managing or hiding money. They carried guns and too much cash. They bought luxury cars, designer clothes, furs, and diamond jewelry for which they paid with rolls of bills they carried in their pockets. They hid away the bulk of their earnings in boxes, in closets and storage warehouses. For a lawyer with Fred's background and experience, the telltale signs should have been all but impossible to ignore.

That, of course, was Parker's point. Fred had knowingly descended into the underworld of crime. That downward spiral began when Fred resigned from the Fulton County district attorney's office in favor of an independent practice in office space he shared with Murray Silver, a lawyer whose name seemed to surface every few years in connection with prominent federal tax evasion investigations. Fred chose to ally himself with Silver. He chose to represent Ed Joiner, a notorious and charming confidence man, in Joiner's legal battles with the Internal Revenue Service while Joiner was engaged in a vast, highly questionable real estate scheme on the Caribbean island of Antigua. He began delving into the arcane complexities of offshore banking. He compiled his own money-laundering manual, and a newsletter he billed as ''the world's only confidential tax haven newsletter/magazine.'' He also began soliciting Silver to recommend him to Silver's drug-dealer clientele.

''He said they come across a lot of cash, and he said that most of the ones that he knew were stupid, that they really did not know what to do with the money after they made it with the exception of buying big cars and gold necklaces,'' Silver told the jury. ''When he handed me his booklet, I said to him that, frankly speaking, I didn't want anything to do with the I.R.S., and since this appeared to me to be some kind of a scheme to deposit large sums of money offshore, that I felt like that would invite the I.R.S. sooner or later to come into the thing. He said he was not concerned about the I.R.S. for the simple reason that he was not going to leave a paper trail. 'Without that trail,' he said, 'they cannot follow me. They can't find me, and they can't find the money.' ''

The prosecution called Eddie Lawrence on the trial's sixteenth day. Surrounded by federal marshals, Eddie took the witness stand, a small man with a thin moustache in a steel-blue suit. He was then twenty-nine and he had been jailed for more than a year.

Fred's defense lawyers objected to the marshals' presence, saying their courtroom watch tacitly served to underscore Lawrence's testimony by suggesting his court appearance had endangered him. In answer to Parker's careful questions, Eddie told the jury how he came to meet Fred Tokars, to join him in a business partnership, and, ultimately, to arrange the murder of his wife. When Parker asked Eddie to identify his former partner, Fred refused to look at him.

From the outset, Parker established that Lawrence was a criminal when he first consulted Fred Tokars. He was a thief, a sometime drug dealer, a counterfeiter, and Tokars knew it because Eddie had told him.

Nonetheless, the attorney chose to finance Eddie in a joint business venture. That joint partnership was established to launder drug money, Lawrence explained. "I knew a lot of drug dealers."

Eddie's testimony resonated with the testimony of other witnesses, criminals who were, like him, Fred's clients. The scheme Fred devised, Lawrence said, was to establish a business "where we could take drug money and buy houses, fix them up and sell them, and we would launder money that way." In every transaction, Fred would act as both an attorney and an accountant. Eddie would be the front man for drug dealers with criminal records. His businesses offered a legitimate explanation for the dealers' cash profits. Fred was "somewhat of a money broker," Eddie explained. "He would house money." Using a bank in the Caribbean islands, he could, for a fee, arrange the delivery of money with which he was entrusted through an electronic network of wire transfers.

Eddie said his job was to recruit drug dealers at the city nightclubs they frequented to "invest" a minimum of ten thousand dollars.

It was a logical, clean description of a complex and illegal financial fraud that Eddie, who had no more than a year of college, would have been hard pressed to devise on his own. And it dovetailed with Silver's description of Fred's entry into the realm of offshore banking and his solicitation, years before he met Eddie, of Silver's drug-dealer clientele.

Parker's questions showed the jury how Fred had legitimized Eddie, renting and furnishing his suite of offices, investing more than seventy thousand dollars in its operation, buying advertising space in the Atlanta *Black Pages*. He introduced Eddie to Atlanta City Council President Marvin Arrington at a campaign fund-raiser at Arrington's home and to Georgia Supreme Court Justice Leah Sears.

But Fred also let Eddie know he was someone to be reckoned with in the neon underworld of nightclubs, drugs, and dirty money. He invited Eddie to accompany him to Diamonds and Pearls where he introduced Eddie to Julius Cline,

Al Brown, Andre Willis, Willie Harris, and James Mason as
he confided that Cline was a drug dealer, Mason one of the
clients for whom he laundered money, and that drug money
had been used to renovate the club.

Eddie had first met Sara when Fred asked him to renovate
a downstairs bath, three months before Fred set in motion the
plot to kill her. In a muted, civil tone, Eddie talked about the
murder as if it were another business deal. In late July or
early August 1992, "He asked me if I would kill somebody,"
Eddie said. A month later, Fred elaborated. He wanted Eddie
to kill his wife before she could divorce him. At a succession
of lunches and dinners, Fred began to pressure Eddie, insisting that Sara must be eliminated.

"All she wanted from my understanding was the house and
the money in the bank," Eddie said. But Fred insisted that
"he had worked too hard; he went to school at night, and she
never did anything. All she ever did was spend his money,
and he wasn't going to give it to her. He would kill her first."

By November, Fred had grown angry at Eddie's reluctance
to follow through, and threatened to end their partnership and
strip Eddie of the companies he had bankrolled. As Eddie
recounted the story of how he came to hire Curtis Rower and
the bald details of how Sara came to die, her sister, Mary
Bennett, clapped her hand to her mouth in shock.

Eddie knew the certain answers to questions that had con-
founded Sara's family since her death, answers Fred provided
at a final meeting at the lawyer's downtown office less than
eight hours before Sara was killed. "He told me that he had
just called her; she was on her way back from Florida; she
should be in around eight or nine o'clock; and he was on his
way to Alabama; that the security system was broken; and
that the sliding glass door in the kitchen would be unlocked."

In Eddie's version of the murder, he remained a passive
and somewhat distant observer who watched and waited and
abandoned Sara to her fate. As he sat in his pickup, parked
in the drive of an unlighted, incomplete subdivision waiting
for Rower to return, he spotted Sara's 4-Runner.

"I observed the jeep just driving off the road into a field.
I didn't exactly expect that, but I observed it slow down, and
it just drove off the side of the road, and he jumped out."

No mention of the vehicle pulling to the side of Powers Road, no mention of it idling there for several minutes before it accelerated sharply left, barreled across the road and leapt into the unlighted field. No suggestion that Eddie had left his own truck to find out why Rower was idling on a main thoroughfare in a car he should have stolen from his victim.

As Eddie outlined his own instructions to Cornbread Rower, Fred removed his glasses and began wiping at his eyes. He blinked hard, biting his lip as if to summon tears. Before Eddie completed his testimony, Fred was blowing his nose with a handkerchief and wiping his mouth. He may have wanted observers to believe he was moved by a description of murder so devoid of emotion. But he appeared, instead, to be playing to the jury.

Meanwhile, Eddie marched on, through a brief call to Fred after Sara's death, when he learned his benefactor was leaving for Florida without arranging to pay him for the murder; his own arrest; his futile protestations of innocence; and finally, the plea agreement with the government to sidestep a death sentence.

For months, Eddie said dully, "I actually felt that I would die before I would testify against Fred Tokars. Then I feared for my safety, and I wanted to let him know that I was not going to change my story and testify against him."

"Now, did you also want the money?" Parker asked.

"Well, yes."

As Parker completed the prosecution's examination, Sara's sister, Mary, rushed helplessly to the courtroom door, her eyes welling with tears as she choked on the bare horror of a death planned so dispassionately and carried out so easily. But the U.S. marshals had locked the courtroom door. There she stood, trapped in the swirl of people who had never known her sister or suffered such a brutal loss. The helpless agony was plain on her stricken face at a tragedy trivialized by the casual congeniality and banter of the strangers she stood waiting to escape.

Then it was defense lawyer Bobby Lee Cook's turn.

Cook, then sixty-seven, had during his forty-five-year career acquired the legendary status of a folk hero among southern trial lawyers. He was born in the north Georgia mountains ten miles south of Summerville and raised on a small, impoverished farm during the Great Depression. After serving a stint in the U.S. Navy at the end of World War II and studying law at Vanderbilt University, he opened his Summerville practice in 1949.

Some said that, as a young lawyer, he would stand outside the county jail on Saturday nights shouting, "Anybody need a lawyer?" and, to those who replied in the affirmative, "What's your mama's phone number?"

His temper was as legendary as his legal prowess. Walker County residents said that, as a young man, Cook was "a rounder" who carried a baseball bat with him into town on Saturday nights, drawing ragged crowds who trailed him just to see who he would fight. In later years, he cultivated the antique courtesy and broad, melodious speech of the landed gentry that he peppered with casual profanities when he wished to emphasize a point. A white goatee softened a belligerent chin. The sandy hair of his lost youth, now faded to loamy gray, hung shaggy and uneven over the back of his jacket collar. But his eyes remained sharp as a hawk's behind his wire bifocals. He liked to say he was "just another country lawyer," and there were those, despite official denials from Hollywood, who insisted that he was the model for Andy Griffith's milk-swilling, hot-dog eating Atlanta lawyer, "Matlock." But Cook was far more shrewd, far more cosmopolitan, and far more eccentric than Griffith's rumpled character. He appreciated old books, fine wines, and elegant gardens. He had waltzed at presidential inaugurations and on New Year's in Vienna. For years, he chauffeured from courthouse to courthouse in a Silver Shadow Rolls Royce. He and his wife had acquired a parrot whose large ornate cage dominated a living room lined with leather books and graced by an Italian marble fireplace he had acquired from a ruined villa. When entertaining, Cook would cheerfully bellow, "Say bye-bye, Popo," at the brilliantly plumed, eccentric bird he insisted would live for decades after he and all his company had perished.

Although his grandfatherly appearance and courtly manners initially might lull or charm witnesses, they shed their guard at their peril. For Cook was renowned as a lethal master of the art of cross-examination. "Eviscerate" was the word law-yers who had faced Cook chose to describe his way with opposing witnesses. The moral outrage implicit in perhaps his most frequently asked question—"Now, that was a lie, wasn't it?"—had successfully stripped away the credibility of scores of witnesses who had brokered deals with prose-cutors in return for their testimony. Cook hated government informants with a singular passion he reserved for liars and traitors. They were, by their very nature, untrustworthy op-portunists to whom truth was as irrelevant as salvation. Cook was personally offended whenever prosecutors relied on such individuals to make their case. It was an unseemly shortcut that circumvented honest investigation and implicitly violated a defendant's constitutional rights to due process and a fair trial. He went after them with a rare vengeance, evoking a similar outrage in jurors so successfully that he had won ac-quittals in nearly 90 percent of his cases—a formidable rec-ord.

From the trial's outset, the Summerville lawyer had pro-nounced that by the time he finished with Eddie, "Even his mama will know he's a liar." But Eddie was prepared for his questions and, more important, for his high, oratorical style. He had been warned that Cook would pounce on inconsisten-cies, blowing them into lies and falsehoods as he stained Eddie with the broad brush of moral outrage. Eddie's lawyers, Bruce Harvey and Mark Spix, had squeezed into the court-room's narrow benches that morning, watching their client like nervous parents at a recital. They believed he was telling the truth; that Fred, as Eddie's mentor, had coolly instigated and orchestrated the crime, intending to use and then discard Eddie as easily as he had discarded Sara.

Parker had met with Lawrence and Spix four days before he took the stand. Together they had reviewed the summaries of his debriefings with authorities the previous August.

"I'm not going to defend you," Parker warned him. "You're going to have to take the heat. Don't look at me to take care of you. You can take care of you by telling the truth. But I'm not defending your conduct."

Eddie was concerned about his image. He had arranged Sara's murder. He was a liar, a thief, a petty criminal. But he didn't want to look bad. His lawyers sought to give him the confidence to tell the ugly truth.

"It's over," Harvey told him. "It's irrelevant how you look. Cook's whole purpose is to make you look bad. The best thing you can do is answer the questions."

"Take your hits," Spix told him. "Concede what you have to concede."

Harvey warned Eddie not to think about the answers, that Cook would make hash of a crafted, carefully worded, "weasely" response. "I was confident that if Eddie would answer the absolute truth without thinking, the answer was going to be correct," he said. "I told him the absolute, one hundred percent truth was the best answer. It was unambiguous. You would never get screwed up. You would never get caught in a lie."

Cook began his cross-examination politely enough. He introduced himself, saying, "If I ask you any question that you do not understand, if you will tell me so, I will try to rephrase it, okay?"

Cook always began that way, lulling his witnesses into a false sense of security with his introductory gentility. Eddie wasn't beguiled.

Cook moved easily from innocuous questions drawn from Eddie's resume to questions that had an edge, questions intended to peel back the rind of pretense to reveal a lie.

"Were you successful?"

"Well, not exactly, no. I wasn't that successful." It was a a truthful answer, but certainly not the image of a successful entrepreneur that Eddie coveted. Fear, nerves, and the knowledge that his life was at stake kept him from the bluff, inflated answers he might normally have offered.

"You were just barely making a living?" Cook inquired innocently.

"I really wasn't making a living."

"You wouldn't have been making as much as fifteen to twenty thousand dollars a year?"

"About that much, yeah."

"And you were trying to be honest, weren't you?"

"Sometimes." Eddie was cautious.

"You were trying to be honest with the people that you

dealt with to build up what you perceived to be a reputation in the business where you could do something for yourself, isn't that correct?'' It was a setup question.

"Yes."

Cook handed Eddie a 1990 application for a mortgage that Eddie had signed after stating he made four thousand dollars a month, about forty-eight thousand a year. He singled out the wage statement.

"That would have been a lie, wouldn't it?" he demanded in a booming voice that grounded on the word "lie."

"Most definitely, it is a lie."

"And you had no problem with that, did you?" Cook sneered.

"I did it. I did do it. I'll admit I did it," Eddie replied.

Cook then led Eddie through a series of questions about how he came to meet and hire Fred before segueing into Eddie's testimony before the federal grand jury.

"When you testified before the federal grand jury, you took the same oath and held up your hand and said that you would swear to tell the truth, the whole truth and nothing but the truth so help you God, didn't you?" Cook demanded.

"Yes."

"And everything you told the federal grand jury was the truth, wasn't it?"

"To the best of my knowledge, yes."

Cook triumphantly waved a transcript of Eddie's grand jury testimony and waded into inconsistencies between what Eddie had testified to the previous August and that morning. Time frames. Dollar amounts. Conversations. Turns of phrase. Everything was subject to Cook's scathing scrutiny. But he couldn't shake Eddie's equanimity.

When Cook challenged his memory, Eddie offered, "From time to time things I might not remember today, something may trigger it. And I might not remember now, but I can remember later on. And sometimes I don't remember everything."

When the lawyer scorned Eddie's account, he replied, "I'm very nervous now. I was very nervous, then. And a lot of time, I don't remember everything. I'm not saying that it is not true, but I have forgotten certain things, and then, when I went home, I might have thought about it.''

Occasionally, Eddie admitted he had been mistaken.

Cook's high rhetoric and moral sermonizing were ineffective in the face of Eddie's open admissions of wrongdoing. The inconsistencies he read from the grand jury transcripts like verses of the Gospel could be explained as simple misunderstandings or an uncertain memory that didn't rise to the level of words such as "falsehood" and "lie" that Cook flung at Eddie and the jury. Neither did the lawyer's occasional folksy turns of phrase, with which he had disarmed other witnesses to their detriment, appeal to or impress a streetwise black man nearly forty years his junior.

When Cook pressed him on a minor turn of phrase and Eddie tried cheekily to counter him, admitting only that "it is a strong possibility" that he had said what was printed in the transcript, Cook answered him in a mocking tone, "Sort of like it is pretty strong if you find a catfish in milk, sort of like finding a catfish in milk, that's pretty strong circumstantial evidence?''

"I don't understand what you are saying," Eddie replied.

They were from different worlds and different sensibilities. And the moral outrage that might resonate if Cook were defending a truly innocent man, or a man who had been threatened or manipulated into crime, collapsed when one looked at Fred—a former prosecutor, a former judge, an officer of the court, a well-to-do attorney—as he sat scribbling busily on a yellow legal pad, passing notes and whispering relentlessly with members of his legal team, and emoting shamelessly for the jury as prosecutors methodically unveiled his cruel and calculating hypocrisies.

But such questions were merely prelude, designed to unmask Eddie as a dissembler and a chronic liar who couldn't recognize the truth or distinguish it from his own self-serving fiction. Where Cook hammered Eddie was on the details of his final meeting with Fred at the lawyer's downtown Atlanta office to confirm and validate the murder plot.

No one could corroborate that final meeting, and if Cook could convince the jury that Eddie simply fabricated it to suck Fred into the maelstrom, then his entire story was suspect.

Cook demanded to know how Eddie could have walked past the guards without registering in a supposedly secure building; how he rode an elevator to Fred's office without the key he insisted was required to operate the elevator on weekends; why Tokars signed in but not out; who the blonde woman was who had ridden the elevator to the lobby with him and Fred when they left the building. Fred's lawyers would build their defense on witnesses who insisted that the building was too secure for Eddie's story to ring true.

Laced throughout Cook's cross-examination were the echoes of Fred's own, far more innocent version of his partnership with Eddie.

"You told him you owned several houses, that you were in the real estate business, and that you were building in the construction business and wanted to make something of yourself, didn't you?" Cook suggested. "And you asked him if he would be willing to help you and to get you into some joint venture to where you could build yourself up in the world and do something. And he told you after some several weeks that he would be glad to think about it and do something about it, that you seemed to be a pretty nice fellow, and you seemed to be pretty intelligent, and you just needed a little refinement."

But, Cook demanded sharply, "You were flim-flamming people in the real estate business back then?"

"I would not consider it a flim-flam," Eddie said in one of the few instances where he truly dissembled. "I would consider it that what I had planned did not go the way I planned it."

As Cook led Eddie one more time through the maze of small but inevitable events that ended in Sara's murder, he elucidated an alternate version drawn from Curtis Rower's own account to police, one that placed Eddie just outside of Sara's car window and made him a participant in the slaying.

Sara's car had "slowed down and then it made a certain quick left turn and it turned off the road into a field," Eddie insisted.

"You didn't go up to the jeep?" Cook demanded.

"No."

"Mrs. Tokars didn't see you?"

"No."

"Isn't it a fact that she did see you?" Cook looked at Eddie sharply.

"No," Eddie protested. "That is most definitely not a fact."

"That's what Mr. Rower said," Cook said deliberately.

"Yes."

"And that she recognized you and that was when you grabbed the gun and she was shot, isn't that correct?"

"That's completely false," Eddie was scared but adamant.

"That didn't happen?"

"No. That didn't happen."

Cook wanted the jury to believe that it did.

And so it went, a grueling cross-examination that straddled two days at the heart of the trial. Eddie withstood it well. Too nervous to be surly, too fearful to be cocky, he illuminated Fred as a willing associate of criminals and gave an account of Sara's murder that both he and the prosecutors who had cut deals with him could live with. Jurors would insist after the trial that they didn't believe him. But they did believe that Fred had arranged the murder of his wife. And Eddie Lawrence was the only one who could ever link Fred irrevocably to her damnable death.

It was during Eddie's cross-examination that Bobby Lee Cook surprised the jury with the news that the Cobb County police detectives who had investigated Sara's murder had inked a movie deal eight months before Fred was arrested and a month before Rower and Lawrence were indicted.

The information was contained in two cagey references Cook made as he questioned Eddie. "Did you know that these two detectives who seek to be movie stars had signed a movie contract?" he asked insolently.

"No," Eddie replied, but the question was intended for the jury, not for him.

On Sunday, March thirteenth, three days before Eddie took the stand, Cobb County District Attorney Tom Charron had called Buddy Parker privately with the explosive news. Parker had notified the defense the following day.

"We were all just burying our heads in our hands and saying, 'Oh, my God, oh, my God. How could they? I can't believe they did it,' '' Katherine Monahan recalled. "We couldn't believe it because they had worked so hard and been so cooperative. We really felt that they believed in the case, that they believed Fred did it, and they really wanted him convicted, and that they were good cops. And we were just stunned."

But after the initial shock, "We came to the conclusion that it wasn't really going to hurt our case that much because they weren't the main investigators. They had done the investigation on the murder only. Our federal agents had done the rest."

The detectives' superiors first learned of the deal on March third, while lawyers were still selecting the jury for the federal trial. That day, Pat Banks and Ron Hunton had gone to Pete Fenton, a lawyer and the Cobb County Police Department's deputy director, to ask if they could begin supplying a Hollywood movie production company with information about themselves and the biggest case of their careers. Aghast, Fenton had accompanied the duo to a meeting with Public Safety Director Robert Hightower. At that meeting, Hightower first learned that the detectives had optioned their exclusive rights on January 25, 1993, in a deal that could earn them each as much as one hundred thousand dollars if a movie of Sara's murder were made.

Like many of the players whose names surfaced publicly during the early days of the Tokars murder investigation, Hunton and Banks were inundated with calls from Hollywood producers who casually promised fees six times the detectives' annual salaries in return for their cooperation. On the advice of Banks's girlfriend, a former New York City police officer who knew a detective who had signed a similar deal, the duo asked the William Morris Agency to act as their agent.

But the detectives went to great lengths to prevent the deal from becoming public. They gave Banks's girlfriend legal authority to sign the contract on their behalf and included a confidentiality clause. Although they did consult Fenton about the deal, they skirted the chain of command to do so, insisting later that they "did not want to flaunt this in front of the guys

we have to work with," many of whom were also working
on the case.

Confronted by Hightower with a breach of ethics that so
clearly tainted their objectivity and threatened to derail Fred
Tokars's prosecution, the detectives initially denied accepting
any money when they signed. But when Hightower reviewed
the contract March tenth, Banks and Hunton admitted that
each had accepted $4,500 to secure the option for a year.
When Hightower suspended them with pay and launched an
internal investigation, the detectives argued that Fenton had
reviewed the contract before they signed it and given them
his blessing. Fenton, in turn, insisted that he had never seen
the actual contract. Nor was he aware that money had been
offered or changed hands.

An infuriated Hightower instantly suspended the detectives
and launched an internal affairs investigation of their conduct.
"On a scale of one to ten for stupidity, it's a fifteen," Hightower angrily told reporters.

By the time that Cook asked Eddie his insolent question
about a movie deal in which the government's star witness
had played no part, the revelation of the secret Hollywood
contract had already rocked the trial. "Here we have two
detectives investigating a murder case in which they have a
financial interest. Unbelievable. Incredible," Froelich had
sputtered two days before Eddie took the stand, certain now
that the literary spin of the detective's investigation had dictated Fred's arrest. The defense lawyer's suspicions were bolstered by the contract the detectives initially signed which
protected their identities "until after the trial of Sara Tokars's
husband," a passage the detectives had corrected to read,
"Sara Tokars's murderer."

But in truth, the defense was jubilant. Fred and his lawyers
were certain that the deal tainted not only the detectives but
also Eddie Lawrence, who had told them what they wanted
most to hear. While Parker grimly insisted that the deal had
little practical effect on the federal case, the defense clearly
thought otherwise. They jettisoned their worried gravity for a
bluff joviality. Before court convened, Fred moved among
them with an ill-concealed elation as they joked and pounded

reporters on the back with the boisterous mirth of a scoring athlete.

Froelich couldn't contain his jubilation. "There was an economic motive for the two detectives who were driving the murder case," he trumpeted. "There was an economic motive for them to do what they did." And they did it, he vowed, in cooperation with Sara's family.

When Parker called Cobb Detective Ron Hunton to the stand on March twenty-third to introduce the evasive statements Fred had made to Cobb police in the weeks immediately following Sara's death, Bobby Lee Cook stepped to the podium again.

"We've never met before, have we, Mr. Hunton?" he asked solicitously.

"No, sir." Hunton smiled nervously. "But your reputation precedes you."

Cook was not amused. In a voice laden with distaste, he answered, "Yours does, too, Mr. Hunton."

It was a scarring cross-examination. Cook, in high dudgeon, whipped Hunton for what the defense lawyer implied were apparent lapses in the detective's investigation after first demanding, "You have to be mighty careful in checking out everything don't you? You really have to dot your *i*'s and cross your *t*'s and follow every lead and check with every witness and every informant and try to find out as much as you can and arrive at a conclusion with absolute accuracy, don't you?"

Nothing escaped Cook's scrutiny or scorn. He was, by turns, scathing, sarcastic, outrageous, and rude. Many of the questions he raised had logical or harmless explanations. But Hunton—stung by the uproar over the movie deal, an internal affairs investigation, and his suspension from the police department—was too wary. He couldn't remember details of a case in which he had wholeheartedly invested himself, deflected too many questions by deferring to his partner, and was unnecessarily noncommittal. He surely resented Cook for defending a man that Hunton truly believed had slaughtered his wife.

For months, a snapshot of an innocent Sara and her two children had been taped on the wall in the tiny, concrete cubbyhole where he and Banks worked. He had breathed the case, inhaling it like smoke. He had pursued it as diligently as he knew how, and it had plagued his fitful dreams. But in the face of Cook's insinuating cross, Hunton sounded churlish and inept. Which, of course, was Cook's intent. He wanted the jury to believe that Hunton was a deceptive and greedy man, that his blunders and bad judgment were both intentional and sinister, that cash down, the seductive lure of wealth, and that alone, had led to Fred's arrest. The movie deal, the fact that the detectives had sought to conceal their involvement, and their willingness to lie about it sank what credibility Hunton had like a stone.

"You have lied to Mr. Hightower about this, haven't you?" Cook demanded.

"Yes, sir."

"You have lied to Bob Hightower, the man who runs your department, haven't you?" the defense lawyer bellowed.

"And you also agreed that you would turn over files, did you not, investigative files relative to the murder case against Mr. Tokars which you had agreed to sell at a time when he had not even been indicted? Tell this court and jury how you have the prerogative, being a public officer sworn to uphold the law, to sell the investigative materials on a murder case such as this?" Cook shouted.

"We were not going to sell the materials to this case," Hunton protested. "We were selling our life stories concerning this case. That's all we were going to do."

"You weren't interested in the money, anyway, were you?" Cook spat.

"No, sir, but I'm not a dummy," Hunton said hotly. "I didn't take a vow of poverty."

"You're not a dummy," Cook's baritone voice was heavy with disgust. "And you're a liar, too, aren't you?"

For the second time, a Hollywood movie deal had cracked the credibility of prosecution witnesses. For the second time, the promise of easy money would end in ignominy. Within a month, while the federal jury was still deliberating, Banks and Hunton were fired, just as WXIA-TV reporter Dean Phillips had been the previous year after admitting under oath that he had been negotiating a deal with Hollywood and prosecution witnesses. Pete Fenton quietly resigned.

The testimony of the police detective was tangential to the prosecution's case. But police interviews with Fred and Curtis Rower were part of a narrative through which Parker told a story of Fred's descent from a "white knight" prosecutor into corruption and violence. Then, one by one, he called Sara's family members to the stand to tell the story of her marriage, her death, and, afterwards, her husband's inexplicable behavior. They took the witness stand bereft, bitter, and bewildered, their terrible grief still agonizingly raw. They told the jury how Fred solicited money from friends and family for his Caribbean investments; his panicked desperation after Sara's death as he confided he was hiding money from the I.R.S., his determination to avoid police because he feared that scrutiny of his businesses would land him in jail for tax evasion, and his tearful admission that he had taken money from drug dealers to invest in Atlanta clubs.

Dr. Ambrusko swore that Fred knew what time Sara would arrive home from Florida the night she was killed because he had called just as she and the children were pulling down the drive.

"They left at twelve forty-five p.m.," he said, "and as they were leaving, the telephone was ringing. It was Fred. He wanted to know if Sara had already left, or when she was planning on leaving, and I told him they just pulled out of the driveway, and they were on their way home."

Before the prosecution rested, the elderly surgeon told the jury about the four questions he had posed to his son-in-law that might point to Sara's killer: "Who else might have known what time they were going to get home? Who knew you weren't going to be home? Who knew the door didn't work? Who knew that the burglar alarm was off?"

The answer, in every case, was Fred.

Taken together, their testimony suggested not only a pattern of criminal behavior, but a motive for murder. Froelich had to neutralize them. During the defense team's case, the scrappy lawyer set out to pummel their credibility by suggesting that they, too, had made a secret movie deal, and that they, too, were motivated, not by a desire to bring their sister's killer to justice, but by greed.

Sara's sister Therese bore the brunt of his attack.

Sara was barely buried before Hollywood producers had overwhelmed the family with insistent overtures. Therese had assumed responsibility for handling the barrage of calls. Dazed and grieving, she found that anything associated with Sara's death was simply too painful to contemplate and had asked a lawyer friend to act as a buffer and advise her informally. She responded, not for money because no amount of money could ever assuage Sara's loss, but out of a sense of responsibility to her dead sister and her family. Any money would go, not to her own family, but to Sara's children.

"My concern was to try to get a sense of how important it was to each of these companies that Sara be represented with the kind of dignity that I thought she deserved," she told the jury. "I tried to get a sense from them of how important it was to them that Sara's story be told accurately."

Froelich didn't believe her. He was abrupt and patronizing as he thumbed through a sheaf of letters and model agreements forwarded to her by Hollywood production companies and queried her as to whom she met, how much money was offered, the nature of the conversations she had and whether she consulted with her sisters about inking a deal.

"No sir," Therese replied. "My whole objective was to try to protect my family from these people."

But Froelich pounced on a letter from the entertainment company that had secured the police detectives' rights, claiming that the Ambrusko family had, in fact, cut a deal with the same firm. But Therese, a San Francisco contracts lawyer, denied that any agreement was ever reached, and none of the documents that Froelich held out for the jury's inspection were signed. Therese said she became aware nearly a year before the federal trial that firm representatives were asserting that an agreement was in place.

"They called me and said they were concerned that the option period was running," she said. "And I said, 'How could it be running if we don't have an agreement?' " Therese said she formally terminated negotiations after she learned that, once family members sold their rights, they would have no control over how Sara's life was portrayed.

Froelich insisted that Therese's letter formally withdrawing from negotiations was simply a ruse to sidestep any appearance of impropriety after her father and sisters were subpoenaed as federal witnesses.

Therese insisted she only wanted to stop a movie from being made "because I was afraid it would trivialize what was done to Sara. My concern was that Sara and the boys be treated with the dignity and the humanity that they deserved. I was concerned that a Hollywood movie company could make a movie about Sara without knowing her."

So Froelich called Skip Chasey, the senior vice president of the Hollywood entertainment firm, to testify. The lawyer then elicited from him the assertion, based on a cryptic note Chasey had scribbled on the back of a phone message, that a deal was, in fact, in place, despite the lack of a signed contract. "I was told that she wanted to send me a letter saying that we didn't have a deal, but that she didn't really mean it, and that, in fact, we still had a deal," Chasey said.

Froelich never explained why he thought that a Hollywood executive in stiff competition to acquire the rights for a movie ABC had already agreed to air had less motive to lie to a jury than Sara's oldest sister. Chasey, he insisted adamantly, "had no dog in this fight."

Therese, on the other hand, "misled the federal court," Froelich asserted later. "She lied on the stand about a movie deal, and we proved it. No one is harassing the Ambruskos. I'm trying to defend a client and get the truth out."

"Skip Chasey can think whatever he wants to think," the Ambruskos' lawyer, Dwight Davis, countered as he fumed over Froelich's continuing attacks on the family and his public willingness to call them liars long after the trial was over. "They didn't want a movie deal. They wanted their sister back."

Left unsaid was another motive that could have shaped the defense obsession with a movie deal. In the weeks preceding the federal trial, Fred himself had solicited an entertainment lawyer to make overtures on his behalf to Hollywood. By then, Fred had informed his lawyers that he was running short of cash and had no capital from which to draw. He thought if he could sell his rights, he could earn some funds for his defense, Froelich acknowledged later. "That's a totally different story than when a witness contacts Hollywood," he insisted.

But Fred was a witness. On March twenty-eighth, he took the stand to testify on his own behalf. Instead, he helped to secure his eventual conviction.

For weeks, his lawyers had coached him on his demeanor, seeking to evoke from Fred sincerity and a sense of puzzlement and loss that would convince a jury he was an innocent man—a victim poorly used by the criminal justice system, the federal government, police, and his wife's family. To that end, Fred could appear neither arrogant nor petulant. He could not afford to challenge or spar with the federal prosecutor who was his chief accuser. His lawyers felt they had little choice but to allow Fred to testify to color the spin of a procession of prosecution witnesses who suggested Fred was a shrewd and arrogant criminal who cared about only two things—making money and not getting caught. Credibility was the aim. Fred had to sound like a reasonable, respectable man.

And for most of his testimony as he answered the questions of his attorney, Jerry Froelich, Fred sounded self-assured, if indignant. "Absolutely not," he would answer hotly whenever Froelich asked if he had ever laundered drug money, washed funds through offshore Caribbean corporations or Atlanta nightclubs, advised drug dealers on how to manage, and legitimize, their illegal drug profits, cheated on his income taxes, or told anyone that he had. "Absolutely not," he asserted when Froelich asked if he had ever discussed killing his wife with Eddie Lawrence.

Sara was the one in the nightclub business, the one working for an Atlanta nightclub operator when they met. Murray Silver was the one who introduced him to offshore banking, and named and owned the island corporations that Sara had uncovered in 1989. His former clients, criminal defendants who had testified against him, had all been enraged by the legitimate legal advice he had tendered.

If men like James Mason and Eddie Lawrence were criminals, they had fooled him utterly. Mason had offered references from Atlanta's city hall, from a Tennessee congressman, an Atlanta entertainment lawyer, a radio program director, and the city court clerk who frequented Mason's nightclubs and whom Fred knew as a political operator. A client who worked for a bonding company was willing to vouch for Eddie Lawrence. He knew little of drug dealers such as Cline and Brown, having met them less than an honest handful of times.

The nightclubs for which he had occasionally handled legal matters "were all well-known clubs being attended by the elite of Atlanta," he explained. "People who went there that I met liked the clubs. They were always talked about, and I never saw any illegal activities. They were never talked about as being associated with any illegal activity. The police went to the bars, judges went to the bars, lawyers, doctors."

He had loaned Eddie Lawrence money because "I saw it as an entry into the black business in southwest Atlanta. It was a unique opportunity. He sounded like he had a good plan. The plan made sense to me. The concept was good, and I thought it would be a way I could get some business out of the black community in Atlanta."

He indirectly attached to Eddie a motive to kill Sara, if one assumed revenge was the intent. Fred explained that Eddie "was not a money man. He couldn't manage his money." By November 23, 1992, Fred said he had taken away Eddie's company checkbook, closed his accounts at two building supply stores, and informed him that he was sending a team of accountants to audit the companies he had financed immediately after the Thanksgiving holiday.

He insisted that, following Sara's murder, he had cooperated with police. "Every question they asked me I answered, and I told them I would give them every file they needed." He was thoroughly rehearsed. He had an answer for everything.

But he couldn't resist a petulant dig at Sara's family. Her sister, Joni Ambrusko, had acquired a set of professional family photos Sara had commissioned for Christmas, and Fred insisted that Joni "had destroyed all the negatives that had any pictures with me in it."

The night Eddie Lawrence was arrested, the Ambruskos

"started to scream at me," he complained. "All of Sara's sisters, her parents. They were just vicious. They were just brutal. I was threatened. John Ambrusko threatened to have me killed."

Fred said he had attempted suicide the day following Lawrence's arrest after his two sons had insisted on going to Busch Gardens with their aunts, uncles, and cousins. "I felt I was losing the last thing that I had," he told the jury as his lip quivered and his voice began to crack. "I couldn't explain to them what was going on, and I had lost Sara. I had lost my law practice. I had been driven out of Atlanta, and all of a sudden Rick and Mike were like saying, 'I want to be with them,' and so I felt like I was by myself." As Fred read his suicide note to the jury, he choked on his own self-pity, his voice broke, and he began to cry.

But to believe that Fred was telling the truth on the stand that day, one had to discount the testimony of nearly two dozen witnesses—among them six members of Sara's extended family; Fred's own clients, business partners, and associates; several lawyers, police, and federal agents. Independently motivated, at times not even aware of each others' existence, yet they had all united in a single, vast conspiracy, inflamed by the media, to frame him.

Parker never thought that Fred's lawyers would allow him to take the witness stand. He had far too many personal liabilities and far too many things that he could never hope to explain with any satisfaction. After watching Fred all morning as he denied any wrongdoing, heaped blame on others, and wept at his own misfortune, Parker was eager to reveal him as a man who indulged in lies, both large and small. He was determined to goad him into showing his true colors.

Fred's money-laundering manual, *Tax Havens and Offshore Investment Opportunities*, was just one example of how practiced a liar he was. He had plagiarized and stolen the information in the manual from others, had he not? Parker demanded.

Fred had said just that. As Froelich had questioned him that morning, Fred, in an effort to distance himself from the manual, had acknowledged that he had plagiarized the material. Now, he responded hotly, "First off, it's not a money-

laundering manual, and secondly, I had permission from the
people to go ahead and use that material to put together the
manual.''

Parker began reading to the jury, like a schoolmaster at a
lecture, an excerpt from the manual that sounded as if Fred
were soliciting criminals.

> Criminals of every type, each with the aim of illegal earnings
> and escape from prosecution, they are all haunted by the same
> fears, by the same sleepless nights until they discover tax
> havenry can solve the problems that plague them most. They
> discover that past experience of being denied the opportunities
> to enjoy their ill-gotten gains are not as insoluble as they once
> thought. Being prevented from investing in gainful busi-
> nesses, from purchasing automobiles, real estate, personal
> property, because the tax man demands an explanation of the
> source of the funds is now for many no more than a small
> inconvenience. This small minority of outside-the-law indi-
> viduals has constant need for legal money, money they can
> spend without fear of unpleasantness resulting. They require
> a means of turning their illegal revenues into acceptable, legal
> money. Those that engage in this practice refer to the act as
> laundering. Unable to share the facilities of offshore banks
> with the honest element, criminals have quickly come to the
> conclusion that laundering and other illegal activities are best
> kept from the light of day. Thus, the underworld never seeks
> to affiliate with offshore bank owners of integrity, but, in-
> stead, chooses to operate alone or in connection with other
> criminals when conducting the affairs of an offshore bank.

''I borrowed them from another manual,'' he repeated sullenly after Parker finished. ''Murray Silver told me to write
it.''

Next, Parker lured Fred into name-dropping by asking him
how he had become a judge. Only too happy to explain, Fred
looked directly at the jury, and offered, ''I was appointed by
Mayor Andrew Young. Andy Young was the United Nations
ambassador under Jimmy Carter. He walked with Martin Luther King back in the sixties in the civil rights movement. He
appointed me to my position.''

"How well do you know Andy Young?" Parker asked disingenuously.

"Fairly well. I mean, you know, I would go to his house during campaign functions," Fred replied.

Then, Parker won an admission from Fred that, to secure that judgeship, he had engaged in yet another deception. He had rented an empty apartment in Buckhead, and used the address to acquire a Atlanta driver's license and car tags, although he shared the house with his wife and children in another county outside the city.

"I feel as though my residence was in Fulton County at the time," he protested, "although I lived in Cobb County, and everyone knew about it, and if anyone had asked me about it, I would have disclosed the fact that I lived in Marietta."

"Are these matters you discussed with your wife?" Parker asked.

"She knew about them," Fred hedged.

"She knew about your interest in Atlanta politics, and about your interest in becoming a judge on a higher court?" Parker demanded.

"I assume she did," Fred was clearly irritated.

"Did she or did she not, sir?" Parker thundered. "Did you talk with her about your interest in getting another judgeship?"

"I can't recall a conversation where I talked about it with her, but I am sure that she knew," Fred answered smartly.

"How are you sure she knew?"

"Because," Fred insisted, "we lived together, and, you know, we talked about things. I mean, she was around me."

Parker had just succeeded in showing the jury that if Sara feared her husband's political and judicial connections could help him wrench away her children in the event of a divorce, she just might have had good reason. Parker then elicited from Fred an admission that in 1989 his wife had hired a private detective through whom she learned her husband was seeing another woman.

"I wouldn't describe it as an affair," Fred said, "but I had a relationship with her."

"I believe you describe it in your interview on December

sixth as a fling,'' Parker spat the word triumphantly at Fred.

"Whatever you want to call it,'' Fred said petulantly. "I didn't spend an awful lot of time with her. I'm ashamed of it, and I feel guilty about it, but I never thought of marrying her, and I didn't think of it as an affair.''

But with that fine distinction, what support Fred may have had among the jurors began visibly eroding. One female juror cast a knowing glance at another woman behind her, leaned back in her chair, and whispered something behind her hand as a third juror, who would later become the foreman, crossed his arms firmly over his chest and leaned back in his seat with a look of quiet disgust.

They knew him now, this lawyer who could excuse adultery by saying it didn't count because he never intended to leave his wife for his mistress. He was like all those other lawyers who had taken money for honest work and then had tricked them, their parents, their children, or their friends with slick words and easy morals. He was a shyster, who hid the truth in legalisms, who drowned honesty in innuendo and misdirection.

"Didn't you threaten Mrs. Tokars that if she went forward with a divorce you would do whatever you could to keep custody of the children?'' Parker demanded triumphantly.

"Not only did I never threaten her with that, but I would never do that,'' Tokars answered angrily. "I work sixty or seventy hours a week, Mr. Parker. There was no way that I could have taken care of children on my own, and there is no way that any divorce judge would have taken Rick and Mike away from Sara. I would never have asked for it, and it never could have happened in any state or in any county.''

But he also didn't think that having a girlfriend on the side was the same as having an affair.

Interspersed with personal questions about the state of his marriage when Sara was murdered, Parker goaded Fred into verbal jousts, winning reluctant admissions that he had inflated his own resume; sparring about notations in Fred's own business calendars that linked him irrevocably to the drug dealers he claimed he knew only in passing; and luring the lawyer into lengthy explanations of the mechanics of setting up shell corporations, the fine details of offshore banking, and a debate over Caribbean bank secrecy laws that made such enterprises so easy to conceal. Fred couldn't help himself. He preened his knowledge like some exotic bird, unaware that he was offering clear proof that he knew far more about such matters than he had previously suggested. Yes, he acknowledged, he had established several bank accounts under aliases in the Bahamas.

"It wasn't to conceal my use of the accounts," he protested. "It was to conceal the fact that I owned the corporations."

Parker showed him the documents Sara had smuggled from his safe. His voice rang with contempt: "Isn't it true that in the fall of 1992 you learned again about your wife, Sara Tokars's desire to divorce you? Isn't it true, sir, that she did go down to your office in September 1992 to work on your accounts? Isn't it true that she did not share your bedroom, that you and she did not have sexual relations during 1992? You knew in 1992 that she learned something at your law office, did she not?"

"No, she didn't want to divorce me then," Fred protested. "She wasn't at my law office working. There was nothing there to learn that would have hurt me, and that simply didn't happen."

"Half of Atlanta," he said, knew about the grand jury investigation of Diamonds and Pearls.

Parker then proceeded to shred Fred's suggestion that Sara's murder may have been motivated by Lawrence's desire for revenge. If that was the case, why hadn't Fred given Eddie's name to police? Why hadn't he mentioned the souring partnership?

"They never asked me any followup questions," Fred answered, as if, somehow, that justified withholding information that might lead to Sara's killer. "Not one time did they ask me for any documents related to any of these companies." If they had only asked, he would have told them what they needed to know.

It was as if the investigation was some sort of game. If one asked the right question, played the right card, only then would the answer be forthcoming. What mattered was who was smarter, who was more shrewd. Finding a killer never entered the equation. That, of course, was the kindest interpretation of Fred's testimony. Clearly, by covering for Lawrence, he was only protecting himself.

Even the motives that Fred insisted had led him to try to take his own life were hollow, Parker suggested.

"You explained to the media and to the people who watched that your attempted suicide was because you had lost your lifestyle," he said.

"Everywhere I went, the media and the press followed me, and they wouldn't leave me alone," Fred insisted. "And I felt like I was then losing my kids to the Ambruskos, and that's what I considered to be my life or my lifestyle. And I was losing it, and I was begging the press to leave me alone. I couldn't bring my kids to Atlanta because I couldn't expose them to that, and, yes, if you want to say that that's a bad word to use, or the wrong word to use, then that's up to you, but to me, that's what I meant when I said it."

"The truth is that the Ambruskos were the ones who were taking care of the children after the death of your wife Sara and not yourself, isn't that true?" Parker fairly shouted.

"I needed help with them because I was used to working full time, and I wasn't used to raising children," Fred protested.

In fact, Parker asserted triumphantly, it was Fred who had been willing to barter the children for $750,000, and Fred, not the Ambruskos, who had signed a contract with an entertainment lawyer and was seeking to sell his own rights to Hollywood.

"There were two things that the Ambruskos wanted more than anything in the world," Fred replied. "They wanted custody of my children, and they wanted the movie deal. And I fought them tooth and nail."

In fact, what the family wanted was what they couldn't have, what neither insurance nor a movie deal could buy. They wanted Sara back.

On Maundy Thursday, Parker stood before the jury to tell them the story of Fredric Tokars in one seamless narrative—who he was and why he must be found guilty. The date and his reliance on Dante for his closing had struck him, for he was telling the jury about another man's descent into hell—

one who never made the redemptive journey back.

Fred's tiny, wizened mother, dressed in black, sat in a pew directly behind her middle child, a son on either side of her. Across the aisle, Sara's six sisters, most of them also dressed in black, sat surrounded by their mother, father, husbands and boyfriends, and the family lawyers. Only Gretchen Schaeffer, Sara's older sister and a hospice nurse, wore white, a large cross dangling from her neck. They gripped each other's hands fiercely, bowed their heads, and, once more, prayed for Sara.

The crowd had spilled over into the judge's chambers where Parker's mother and his younger sister, both attorneys, sat with the aging parents of Parker's childhood friend, whom he had lost to the ravages of heroin.

Parker offered the jury a simple, clean explanation for the tedious weeks spent wading through corporate records, calendars, liquor licenses, and financial transactions. And as he pieced them together like a puzzle, it grew clear that every action had a reason, that every crime was another step down in Fred's descent to evil.

"This case is one of greed and violence," he said quietly. "And it surrounds an enterprise, a commercial activity, an illegal activity; an activity involving drugs, cocaine; an activity involving wealth, money, cash derived from the sale of cocaine, kilos of cocaine. There is a need to conceal how that cash is generated because you don't want people to know you are out there dealing drugs, because, if they know, if they find out, they may report you to the police, you may get caught, and you may go to jail for the rest of your life."

For that reason, he said, the drug dealers who had testified in Birmingham and others like them "need professionals. They need lawyers. They need accountants. They need businessmen to help conceal that wealth. This effort is described in simple terms as money laundering."

As an assistant district attorney, Fred Tokars had once prosecuted men like that, Parker said, as his sonorous bass echoed through the courtroom. By 1988, he was soliciting them. "Mr. Tokars said all these drug dealers, they are just a bunch of dummies. They are stupid. They know how to make a lot of money, but they don't know how to make investments.

"Mr. Tokars went on to recruit that drug money and drug dealers, and he did so because he opened those bank accounts at the Gulf Union Bank in the Bahamas," Parker's voice rose in outrage.

"And the only record that the government has of those bank accounts, ladies and gentlemen, has come from the materials that Sara Tokars copied. Were it not for Sara Tokars copying this material, there would be no record. The government never would have found those accounts and their existence were it not for this material and the notations in Fred Tokars's own handwriting in the calendars seized from his house."

Tokars tried to hide how much he earned, and how much he reported to the I.R.S., from his wife, Parker said. Even though he was married, and Sara wasn't working, he filed a separate tax return. "He kept from her the money he had. He hid from her the money in these accounts."

But, Parker reminded the jury, "She copied them. She copied parts of his diary reflecting meetings with his lover, and she turned them over to her sister, Krissy, and she said to her, 'If anything ever happens to me, take these to the police.'

"And ladies and gentlemen, I will tell you why Sara Tokars had a premonition of something happening to her. Because it was in August 1989 that Fred Tokars took out two additional life insurance policies on the life of Sara Tokars. On August 24, 1989, he took out a five-hundred-thousand-dollar policy, and on August 28, 1989 he took out a million-dollar policy. Now, if you are Sara Tokars, and you and your husband are having fights, and you want to divorce him, and he has threatened to keep the children if you try to divorce him, and all of a sudden he increased the insurance on your life by $1.5 million, don't you think that something bad may happen to you at some time in the future? And that's why she said to Krissy Ambrusko, 'If anything ever happens to me, turn these over to the police.' She had a premonition."

Three years later, that premonition was fulfilled, Parker explained. "Eddie Lawrence testified that Fred Tokars approached him and said, 'I want you to kill my wife. She's going to divorce me. She's going to take everything I have.' And Eddie Lawrence said that, finally, Fred Tokars threatened that if he, Eddie Lawrence, didn't do it, he, Fred Tokars, would destroy Eddie Lawrence. And could Fred Tokars do it? Destroy him?'' Parker bellowed. ''Absolutely! Absolutely!

''Eddie Lawrence was the one who had been dressed up to look like a sheep, who had been dressed up to look like an up-and-coming businessman in the black community, when, in fact, he was absolutely worthless at doing business. He was a con man. He cheated people, and Fred Tokars knew all of this, and he threatened Eddie Lawrence to take away from him something Eddie Lawrence had never had in his life, which was some possible degree of respect from some people.''

Sara was murdered ''as a direct result and a direct consequence of the conduct of Fredric W. Tokars,'' the prosecutor's voice rang through the silent court. ''Why was she killed? Something happened. Something happened by mid-September 1992 when he was no longer willing to allow her to divorce him, when he no longer could control her with his threats. Sara had been down to his office and worked on his accounts.

''She has been down to his office. She has discovered something new,'' Parker explained. ''She has discovered the fact that Al Brown has been arrested, the fact that the grand jury is investigating. She knew he was taking money from his clients. She knew they were drug dealers. She knew he was not reporting it on his income tax return.

''Sara Tokars,'' Parker ended, ''was a ticking time bomb.''

After a break, it was Froelich's turn in an argument he laced with a rare personal bitterness toward Sara's family and the government and a nearly apoplectic incredulity about the charges against Fred that he had carried throughout the trial. What emerged in Froelich's outraged defense was a theme also based on greed, incompetence, and a rush to judgment that had made Fred Tokars a victim.

''Mr. Parker said this case was about greed, violence, and activities that no one wanted to be discovered or disclosed,'' he said. ''He forgot a few things. He forgot about lies, about perjury, movie deals, detectives who don't do their job, and people who hear what they want to hear.''

But, he said as he pointed to Fred sitting impassively at the defense table watching him, the case was really about "how this man became the target of everybody, how the media hounded him, how everybody hounded him, how he lost his wife, he lost a career, and, as of now, he has lost the two children.

"You've seen greed here. You've seen movie deals, people wanting to say and do things to be in the movies. You know the camera can be as seductive as any drug, and that's what's going on here.

"Doesn't it get to you?" the lawyer demanded bitterly, his voice rising to a furious pitch. "Don't you say, 'Where is the evidence?' What are we talking about here? What is going on here?

"What do they have? They have nothing. They have absolutely nothing. Do you think the object of this exercise from the day the media jumped on this was, 'How do we get Fred Tokars?' Do you think he had a chance, a real fair chance in this case? Is this the way you would want an investigation run? Do you want police officers that will take the stand and lie, that will within thirty or forty days of the death of Sara Tokars, eight or nine months before Fred Tokars is arrested, go out and sign a contract for the trial of Fred Tokars? Are you insane? Are we insane here?"

In reality, it was Fred who was conned, Froelich said. "He, too, got conned by Lawrence. I submit to you that if Eddie Lawrence and Fred Tokars were involved in this murder, when Eddie Lawrence got arrested in Cobb County with all this publicity, what do you think the most natural reaction for him to do would have been?"

Froelich answered his own question. "Wait a minute. I'll give you the big guy. I'll give you Fred Tokars."

Instead, Froelich asserted, Lawrence waited for eight months before he talked. "And you know why?" he bellowed. "Because he didn't have the information yet. He didn't have the documents to construct the story."

Only after Eddie was given copies of other witnesses' statements to police by his lawyers did he step forward to accuse Fred, Froelich said. "Until he got those documents, he didn't have the facts to construct a story.

"Lock your doors, ladies and gentlemen. Eddie Lawrence is coming. He's going to be back out."

As for the government's theory that Fred had Sara killed to prevent her from revealing that he was evading taxes, Froelich derisively dismissed it. "There's no proof of it," he said. "According to the government, Fred told others, after the death of Sara, that he was involved in hiding money and income tax evasion. Now, how bright is it to kill one person and then create five other witnesses? It doesn't make sense."

What does make sense, he told the jury, was that Sara's family decided Fred was guilty.

"The underpinning of this is rotten. You are in the United States. We have a system where we are supposed to have integrity. You don't start out saying, 'I want this person and how do we get him?' You don't start out by lying. You don't start out by taking liars and putting them on the stand.

"That turns the world upside down. That turns the process from, 'Who did it?' to 'We believe this guy did it, and let's get him.' I don't think you will ever experience anything like this again in your life."

In closing, Froelich reminded the jury of Fred's suicide attempt that he had made the day after Eddie was arrested in one final plea for acquittal.

"Ladies and gentlemen, when you commit suicide, you know you are going to die, and you want the Lord and the world to know you went with a clean soul and a pure heart. So, if you have done something wrong, what do you do? You apologize and you tell the world. You say, 'I'm sorry I killed my wife. I was involved in murder. Forgive me.'

"That's not what Tokars said. Read the note. He said, 'The press killed me. The media killed me. No one would stand by me but my mother. My children left me.' Read that, and that will give you a feeling of what happened in this case. It will give you a feeling of the true Fred Tokars, and why he is innocent."

Then it was Parker's turn once more. This time, he must convince the jury that Fred was a killer, even though his wife's murder was no longer part of the indictment. For if jurors truly believed Fred had ordered Sara's execution, they would believe that he did it to conceal the illegal ways in which he had acquired his wealth, and find him guilty on all counts.

"Almost six hundred years ago, a man wrote a poem that has been recognized in western culture as one of the great works of literature," he began. "His name was Dante Alighieri. It was called *The Divine Comedy*. It was based upon a journey into hell, of the rise from hell, and then the eventual ascension into heaven. With regard to the Inferno, it was stated that malice is the sin most hated, and the aim of malice is to injure others whether by fraud or violence. Malice is the sin most hated.

"But Dante also alluded to one of the greater sins in lower hell," Parker said as he told the ancient story. "It was the sin of the hypocrite. You know what a hypocrite is? A hypocrite is a wolf in sheep's clothing. A hypocrite is a human being who portrays to be something good when they are really bad. And it was written that there, at this location, here the hyocrites are weighted down by great leaden robes. They walk eternally around and around a narrow track. The robes are brilliantly gilded on the outside, and are shaped like a monk's habit, for the hypocrite's outward appearance shines but brightly and passes for holiness, but under that show lies the terrible weight of his deceit which the soul must bear through all eternity.

"And that is so the case for Fred Tokars."

The rangy prosecutor with the commanding presence now moved to a large poster, entitled "The Image." On it, was a silhouette of a bespectacled Tokars at its center and the question, "Who is Fred Tokars?" Surrounding the silhouette were photos—of Sara and the boys under the heading, "Family Man"; Fred on the bench in his judicial robes under a second heading, "Judge and Political Supporter"; his tax return under a third heading, "Successful Attorney and Businessman"; and a news article he had authored under the heading, "Money-laundering Expert."

"Mr. Tokars has structured his life so that many people would see the gilded robes, the image of Fred Tokars as the money-laundering expert, the publications of how lawyers can help drug dealers launder money, the image of Fred Tokars as the successful attorney and businessman filing a form with the I.R.S. reporting income of $339,699, the image of Fred Tokars as a judge and a political supporter, the image of Fred Tokars as a family man,'' Parker said as he pointed out each photo.

"But underneath those gilded robes is the reality, the reality of who Fred Tokars was and is."

Parker suddenly ripped away the title to reveal the words, "The Reality" and pulled away the first photo, a copy of the news article Fred had published in the *Atlanta Business Chronicle*, to expose the title page of the money-laundering manual Fred had authored. "The hypocrisy of a money launderer," Parker read in a ringing voice. "He provided investment opportunities for drug dealers in offshore accounts."

He tore away Fred's tax return to reveal a photo of brick kilos of cocaine. "The hypocrisy of a racketeer," he boomed. "He collected cash from clients which he did not report to the I.R.S. Those were his own words."

He snatched away the photo of Fred in his judicial robes. Beneath it were the sinister photos of Julius Cline, pistol in hand, and Al Brown. "The hypocrisy of an aider and abetter of drug traffickers," Parker said accusingly. "Shell corporations used as a front to launder—in his words—'scumbags'' drug money."

Parker paused before he pulled away the photo of Sara. Then he uncovered the final piece in Fred's vast puzzle of deceit—the words, "$1.75 million in insurance."

"The hypocrisy of a murderer," the prosecutor pronounced, his voice resonating in the courtroom with the anger of an archangel. "And you know what? It was easy for Fred Tokars to make that decision to shut up Sara before she could disclose what she knew because there was $1.75 million in life insurance on her life. And he was greedy just like James Mason is greedy, just like Al Brown is greedy, just like Julius Cline is greedy. He is a wolf, and he is sitting over there."

Parker's deep voice cracked with emotion as he pointed an accusing finger at Fred. "He did it. He set it in motion. He unleashed the wolf in Eddie Lawrence. He unleashed the wolf in Curtis Rower. He is a wolf in sheep's clothing, and you know it. Wolves in sheep's clothing, they were masquerading and parading in our society as pillars of the community. And this is why we have so many problems in dealing with drugs. This is why we cannot educate our children to have respect, because members of the community who are pillars are aiding and abetting the sales of this product that is destroying our communities, whether they are in public housing or whether they are in upscale neighborhoods.

"He has violated the laws of ages. Thou shalt not covet. Thou shalt not kill. He has violated the law of the United States. What this case demands is justice. Justice must be done."

Finally, the prosecutor appealed to the jurors' Alabama heritage, reminding them of Birmingham's steel mill history and the enormous stone statue of Vulcan, the Roman god of fire, standing high on Red Mountain overlooking the city.

"You are not unlike Vulcan," he challenged them. "You are the forgers of a verdict. You must take from this courtroom he evidence in the record, the testimony from the witnesses, the inferences from the circumstances, and you must bring back to this community true verdicts, verdicts that can withstand the scrutiny, the close scrutiny that all will occasion upon it. I urge you to bring back and to forge true verdicts hard as steel. Make these verdicts verdicts that will speak the truth."

As the jury filed from the courtroom, Sara's sisters bowed their heads and wept.

The jury began deliberating on Good Friday. They set aside their deliberations for Easter, then resumed again on Monday, wading through a myriad of documents and testimony both technical and highly emotional. On Friday, April eighth, they returned their verdict. Guilty of participating in a criminal enterprise that transported, distributed, and sold cocaine; invested proceeds from illegal drug sales in Atlanta nightclubs; and protected its members from arrest and prosecution with kidnapping torture and murder. Guilty of conspiring to distribute cocaine. Guilty of money laundering. Guilty of causing the kidnapping and robbery of Sara Tokars. Guilty of placing interstate phone calls to arrange her murder.

Said one juror after the trial ended and Fred had been led away in chains, "It couldn't have been anyone else."

"Sara had a hand in this," her sister Gretchen said fer-

vently after her sister Mary thanked ''this brave jury'' for
their verdict. ''She couldn't fight in life, but in death, I'm
sure she had a hand in this.''

The documents that showed that Fred had hidden money
in the islands were Sara's legacy, an echo of her voice that,
in the end, had helped convict her killer.

Whenever her lost family had wondered what to do, ''We
would ask ourselves, 'What would Sara do?' '' Gretchen said,
''and she has never let us down. For the first time in a year,
we finally feel safe.''

Wracked with sobs, Sara's younger sister Joni said the verdict had fulfilled a vow the family had made. ''We all felt so
bad we weren't there to help her, to protect her,'' she said.
''We made a vow to Sara, we'd find out who murdered her.

''I can't look at Fred. It's all so sick. We'll never be happy
again.''

Nineteen

The Twelfth Juror

TWO YEARS AFTER SARA'S MURDER, CURTIS ROWER STILL strode through Ricky Tokars's haunted dreams.

He was the dark, featureless man, sullied by shadow, who skulked in empty rooms, behind every tree and bush, and at the edges of the night. He sucked at sleep. His signature was spattered blood on glass.

Try as he might, Ricky, now nearly eight, couldn't escape his mother's killer.

"I wish I could die," he would sob inconsolably. "My mom was killed. I can't get the bad thoughts out of my head. I keep praying for the bad thoughts to go away, but it doesn't work. I have a horrible life."

At night, as his aunts sought to comfort the quaking child, he would reenact the final moments of his mother's life.

"There's a burglar outside in the bushes," he would cry.

"Oh, no, Ricky," his youngest aunts and his grandparents sought to reassure him. "There's no one there."

But the child was adamant. "Yes, yes, he's there. He's probably waiting for us to fall asleep, and he'll murder me and Mike."

"Oh, God, no, Ricky. We won't let anyone hurt you or Mike. We have a burglar alarm and shatterproof glass. No one can get in."

"But he's there," Ricky would insist, his voice tinged with

421

a rising panic. "And he'll shoot the lock and come in and murder me before the police get here."

"Do you want us to send Krissy outside to make sure no one is there?" his aunt, Joni Ambrusko, asked one night in desperation.

"Okay," the child whispered hesitantly. But as soon as Krissy left the room, he was stricken with a more desperate terror. "No! No!" he screamed. "Don't let Krissy go out. The man will be there, and he'll grab her."

He threw one of his own small arms around his neck, placed his right forefinger to his temple as if it were a loaded gun, and fired.

"And he'll shoot her head against the glass, and there will be blood all over, all over me."

"Will it ever go away?" Ricky's aunts would desperately ask the child's psychologists.

"We don't know," they were told. "Probably not."

Late at night, and through the early morning hours, Joni would find herself keeping watch over her small nephews' fitful and uneasy sleep, so that, if they awoke, they would find her in the soft darkness of their rooms instead of the shadow of the man who had murdered their mother while they watched. When Ricky would wake and come padding to her side, whispering, "I'm scared, Joni. I had a nightmare," she would assure him, "You're going to be okay," as she walked him gently back to bed.

"But I'm scared, Joni."

"Don't worry," she always promised. "I'll stay here all night."

"Joni," he asked one night, his eyes welling with tears. "Do you think I'm brave?"

She hugged him. "Yes, Ricky. I think you're the bravest person I know."

During those bleak, endless months, Joni assumed her nephew's dreams. They coiled about her like wraiths, evil images so vivid she contemplated suicide to escape them. Her marriage to a Navy fighter pilot, only four months old when Sara was murdered, collapsed under the weight of Joni's terrible grief, her unshakable determination to find her murdered sister's killers, and her single-minded dedication to Sara's small boys. Late one night, in the exhausted calm that followed one of Ricky's bouts with terror, she wrote:

> *I can hear my sister calmly begging for her boys' lives*
> *to be spared. I can see her gripping the steering wheel.*
> *I know her scream. I see her head exploding, and her*
> *little body being thrust into the air at impact. I know*
> *she was praying. Now, since November 29, no matter*
> *what I do or how I try, whenever I'm alone, I can't*
> *escape the horror. I'm in the truck with Sara, in the*
> *dark, and I'm holding her, holding her head up trying*
> *to stop the blood and I pray for help, pray for a second*
> *chance. And I look outside the window of the 4-Runner,*
> *and I see the days going by, life going on. People are*
> *shopping or planning their holidays or going to base-*
> *ball games, but here in the truck, it's always dark. No*
> *matter what I do or how I try, I can't get out.*
>
> *The horror of what Sara went through that night is*
> *so visible, so conquering, so crushing, it is inescapable.*
> *The evilness of a planned, premeditated execution of*
> *my sister is so demonic it haunts us every day, every*
> *night. And now, when I look at my once joyous, vibrant,*
> *loving family, I see only destruction and devastation.*

"The night my sister was murdered, we were all killed." Such was the legacy of Sara's terrible death.

The Tokars children couldn't talk about their mother. If Mike, then six, overheard someone mention Sara's name, he would place his hands over his ears, crying, as he begged his aunts not to speak of her.

Or he would pack his belongings in his backpack, telling his grandfather as he did so, "I have to go looking for my mom."

"I can only ask if I can go with him," Dr. Ambrusko said. A man once hale who had now grown frail with grief, he would enclose in his slender surgeon's fingers the small hand of the sturdy but bereft six-year-old.

"Together we walk down the street in silence and neither of us knows where to go or what to do. I have held a heart in my hand many times in surgery and known exactly what to do to heal it, yet this little heart is terminally broken."

Dr. Ambrusko's own health and his wife's were broken by Sara's murder. Gripped by a paralyzing sorrow that weighted every breath, Phyllis Ambrusko faded to a dazed shadow, a woman who buried her laughter with her middle daughter. Barren of hope, drained of will, she lost herself in prayers.

Grief and a formidable depression stripped seventy-five pounds from Dr. Ambrusko's frame. He suffered a stroke. His heart grew weak. For months, the piano he had played since his girls were small sat silent. Late at night, a daughter might stumble on him standing silently in front of Sara's portrait, shoulders bowed and hands clasped as he whispered silent prayers for his dead daughter. As a Buffalo surgeon, he had saved hundreds of lives. As a father, he was haunted by his failure to save Sara's.

His savings drained by the unanticipated costs of raising his grandsons and legal fees associated with Fred's decision to sue the family, Dr. Ambrusko, now eighty-two, was forced to return to work as a surgical consultant at Manatee Memorial Hospital.

"Throughout my life, I have always felt that, no matter what challenge or obstacle I faced, I would somehow be able to figure out how to handle it," he said. "I'm eighty-two years old and for the very first time in my life, I face problems and shoulder worries and responsibilities that even the experts are unable to tell me how to handle."

In fact, Sara's sisters and their husbands spent their savings and slid hopelessly into debt to support their nephews as they defended themselves in court against Fred's civil lawsuits and the often virulent attacks of his defense lawyers. Everyone contributed what they could. Sara's oldest sister, a San Francisco lawyer, and her husband spent their savings and borrowed one hundred thousand dollars to help pay the heavy financial costs that grew from her sister's murder.

"I don't know how I will pay it back," she said.

But it was the attacks on her family following Sara's death that scored Therese Ambrusko's life with doubts—about God, about the courts, and the law that was her profession. "I'm desperate to believe in heaven," she said the summer after Fred was convicted. "I have to believe that Sara is okay. I cling to that, but I am scared she's not, and that I'll never see her again.''

The criminal justice system that permitted her surviving family to be publicly savaged in the name of due process now sickened her. Her faith that the courts, that could never restore Sara to her family, would still administer justice dissolved.

''When we had a memorial service for Sara with other family members and friends, Fred's lawyer said we did it for fame,'' she said. ''My family members and I have been called to testify at many hearings and the federal trial. Each time, Fred's lawyers attack us. I don't understand how they can be so cruel or why they do it. I worry that my elderly parents, especially my father who has a heart condition, won't be able to take the attacks.''

But it was her own guilt that most devastated her. Therese and her younger sisters flogged themselves as if they, somehow, had allowed Sara's murder to happen; that if they had paid more attention, been less trusting and more astute they could have prevented it. It made no difference that they had no way of knowing, had no reason to believe that their sister's life was forfeit and her husband was a killer.

As Therese drove to work each day, she would talk to Sara, begging God to take care of her and grant some solace to her family. She berated herself, ''Why didn't I do something to make it possible for her to feel that she could leave? I will never feel that I cherished her enough, and now I must live with the knowledge that I will never have the chance.''

The holidays that Sara had always loved and the traditions she perpetuated even after her sisters were grown and gone were now a source of wrenching pain. Sara's murder robbed them of joy. Sparklers on the Fourth. The crown of flowers, a present from the girls, that Phyllis Ambrusko wore every Mother's Day. Thanksgiving, a holiday now stripped of warmth and colored by a killer.

''Every birthday,'' Therese said, ''I have to confront the fact that I am still alive and Sara is dead, and I can never understand or accept that.''

Karen, too, was stricken with guilt. As children's graduations, anniversaries, and the other celebrations that mark a life rolled by, Karen came to believe that she didn't deserve to find joy in such simple pleasures that death denied her sister. When she looked in the mirror she saw Sara's death mask in its dim reflection. When she placed her hand on the doorknob, she felt the hand of her sister's killer.

"It feels like we were banished to the moon," wrote Gretchen Schaeffer, the second sister. "We look down to the earth and see people scurrying about day after day, living their lives. We wish we could come back, but we cannot. I have lost all faith in everything I was raised to believe in."

That was why Sara's sisters sought the death penalty for her killers. That was why they believed so deeply that not only Fred but Curtis Rower and Eddie Lawrence all deserved to die.

They gagged on the knowledge that the men who had callously stripped Sara of her life, although imprisoned, received medical care if they were sick or injured, were served three meals a day, watched television, saw their mothers, kicked drugs, found God, learned a trade.

"Long before they begin to suffer for their horrendous crimes, Sara will have crumbled into dust and been forgotten by most who have been touched by her tragedy," Gretchen said. "She will become just another name in brass letters on a cold, marble wall. But on the twenty-ninth day of every month, for the rest of my life, flowers of every color and fragrance will mark her place in splendor."

But as the second anniversary of Sara's murder circled, people began to find the Ambruskos' grief unseemly or, worse yet, staged and artificial. Such anguish made those who had never shared it uncomfortable. "Why don't they just get over it?" they would murmur. "Why don't they just get on with their lives?"

There was no artifice in the Ambrusko sisters' haunted grief. They didn't cry on command. The cameras pursued them. They weren't orchestrating a verdict; they were keeping a vigil, as they were certain Sara would have done for them. "How could we not?" Karen asked.

"We don't think about it," Krissy said. "We just do it."

Nor was there any respite from the interminable string of hearings and trials attached to Sara's killers. Subpoenaed as witnesses, pummeled on the witness stand, exposed time and again to the final grim details of Sara's life, her sisters remained flayed and raw with grief.

And every other Monday, fear still dialed the phone. Every other Monday, Fred, by permission of the court, was allowed to call his two small sons to talk.

After Fred's arrest, a Florida judge had allowed him to remain in communication with his sons. Although Ricky was certain his father had been arrested, no matter what police had told him, Fred insisted he was working with the F.B.I. to find Sara's killer. The Ambrusko family frowned on the bald lie, but kept silent before Fred's federal trial. Once he was sentenced to life without parole, they sat the boys down and explained to them that police and prosecutors had proved to a judge and jury that their father had orchestrated their kidnapping and their mother's execution.

The boys' psychologists had urged the Ambruskos to tell the children months before. But the Ambruskos waited out of their own broad sense of fair play, even while Fred's lawyers scoffed at any suggestion that the family would do anything but use the children for their own financial gain. When Gretchen, who as a nurse had told dozens of families their loved ones were dying, told her nephews about their father, they accepted an explanation that they had intuited long before. They had never been close to their father. He had always been a cold, remote, and largely absent figure in their lives. They didn't love him. They were afraid of him.

Yet, Fred still called his children. On those alternate Mondays, when the telephone would ring at the appointed time, the children would beg their aunt not to take the call. They refused to talk to their father, the man who had so nonchalantly surrendered them to a murderer and swaddled their small lives in fear.

"No, no," they would plead in desperation when their aunts would tell them Fred was on the phone. The sisters never forced Sara's sons to take their father's calls, a decision with which the children's psychologists concurred.

"Why would Sara want Rick and Mike to talk to a murderer?" Krissy demanded. "It's like putting your child on the phone with Charles Manson."

And on those nights that followed their father's calls, even if weeks had passed between them, any progress the boys had made toward normalcy would recede, and their sleep would once more be swamped with terror. Ricky would beg his aunts or grandparents to stay with him while he showered or stand outside the bathroom door while he relieved himself. They would resume their practice of carrying pagers when they left the house. If Ricky succumbed to his brutal fears that they, too, would be killed, he could reach them anywhere so they could reassure him they were safe and still alive.

Ricky always knew he was a witness against Curtis Rower, the man who had confessed to slaughtering his mother. He knew that Cobb County District Attorney Tom Charron was counting on him to testify. In fact, Ricky wanted to testify because, he told his aunts, he could finally help his mother. That dark night his mother died, he had done nothing but sit helplessly watching.

"I wasn't brave that night," he confided to Krissy. "I left my mother."

To win a murder conviction and a death penalty verdict, Charron needed Ricky's testimony. Although the child had never been able to identify Rower and didn't recognize him in a lineup, his version of his mother's murder differed significantly from Rower's, providing critical detail that no other witness could offer. With his mother dead and his four-year-old brother Mike half-asleep in the back seat, Ricky was the only eyewitness to the crime. He was the only one who could say with certainty that he and his family were kidnapped and that his mother was robbed of her purse before she was shot. He was the only one who could contradict Rower's insistent statement that Sara was killed by accident after he and Eddie Lawrence wrestled over the gun in the back seat of the car.

"No, no, no, no," Ricky had told Detective Pat Banks in June 1993. "There wasn't another bad guy."

All were critical elements of three of the four charges against Rower—robbery, kidnapping, felony murder. Ricky's eyewitness account bolstered the testimony of Eddie Lawrence, who had told police that Rower told him he had kidnapped Sara and robbed her of her purse before he killed her. And Eddie's testimony was tainted by his deal and his own role in Sara's death.

Nor would Ricky be testifying against his father by taking the stand in Rower's trial. Rower had told police he knew only that he was to kill Eddie's lawyer's wife. He didn't know until after the murder that the man who had hired him was a man named Fred, a man he learned by watching television was surnamed Tokars.

In fact, Ricky's younger brother, Mike, also wanted desperately to testify in court, pleading with his aunts that he, too, wanted to help his mother. He was disconsolate when they explained there was nothing he could tell the jury because he had been asleep.

But Cobb County Superior Court Judge George Kreeger was convinced that putting Ricky on the witness stand and asking him to relive his mother's death as he faced his mother's killer in a courtroom could irreparably harm the child. Knowing that Charron was adamant that Ricky testify, Kreeger consulted quietly with colleagues who were juvenile judges. What they told him about the damage to children who had testified against their parents in court only strengthened Kreeger's conviction that Ricky should not take the stand.

In fact, several Georgia psychologists publicly suggested what Ricky's own psychologist had already privately told the family. Many children who testify in court draw courage from the experience because they have finally been able to do something to help. Children, like adults, are often swallowed by an irrational fear that they somehow allowed a terrible crime to happen, that they are responsible for the damage that ensued. Although he was only six when he witnessed his mother's murder, Ricky still believed he should have saved her. True, he would relive his mother's shotgun slaying if called to testify. But those stark, bloody images already rode his dreams. By testifying, he was finally able to fight back.

Charron said children who have witnessed crimes, including their own abuse, are often called to testify. "They see that their testimony is being taken seriously, and adults are held responsible for their actions," he said.

But Kreeger didn't believe it. He wanted no part of a trial that forced an eight-year-old boy to face his mother's killer and testify in a death penalty case linked so closely to his father. After moving Rower's trial two hours east to Appling

to counter the effects of pretrial publicity, he let it be known
that he favored a quick and civil end to the matter. He wanted
the district attorney to accept a plea. When Charron refused,
Kreeger announced that he would comment publicly about
Charron's determination to call Ricky to the stand.

Before jury *voir dire* began, Kreeger stated in open court:
"I just wanted to make the observation that this case is a real
tragedy, and I think it would be a second tragedy if we had
to have an eight-year-old child in here to testify, and I just
think the case should be resolved and could be resolved in
the best interest of those children without that necessity."

The plea on the table was three sentences of life without
parole. Rower's lawyer, Edwin Marger, had made the offer
the day after Rower was arrested and, blowsy from cocaine
and weed, had confessed to Sara's murder. Charron had summarily rejected it, but it had remained on the table for more
than two years as Rower's only real hope of skidding off
Death Row.

Rower had been in custody twelve hours when his father
first met with Marger at a fast food restaurant north of Atlanta
that sat beneath a giant, fiery red, beaked landmark known as
"The Big Chicken." Albert Rower explained that his son had
been arrested for murder, and that the district attorney was
seeking the death penalty. Marger cited his normal fee for a
death penalty case, one hundred thousand dollars to $125,000.
The senior Rower blanched. He told the lawyer that maybe
he could afford five thousand. Marger took the case. Rower
didn't know it, but he had just hired the former lawyer for
Haitian President for Life Jean-Claude "Papa Doc" Duvalier.
He had also hired a defense lawyer, who unlike many of his
colleagues, believed that, in some cases, the death penalty was
appropriate.

Born in New York, raised in Miami, and addicted to the
azure intrigue of the Caribbean, Marger had first caught Duvalier's eye at the dictator's inauguration as *"Presidente en
Vie"* at the Basilique in Port-au-Prince in 1959.

Bright, observant and ruthless, the dictator had singled
Marger out amid the urgent press of bodies packed into the
cathedral as one of the few who didn't succumb to the clois-
ter's spiraling temperatures and swampy heat. Many in atten-

dance that day were overcome by heat exhaustion. Yet
Duvalier himself, dressed nattily in a tuxedo and top hat,
never broke a sweat. And Marger, his face a round moon in
the pool of faces, seemed capable, in the sweltering throng,
of a discipline the dictator both cultivated and admired. "I
withstood the heat very well," Marger explained.

Within days, Marger was invited to the palace. During the
next eight years, he became one of the dictator's trusted ad-
visers on matters of international law regarding Haiti's often
angry relationship with the United States.

Marger has always been circumspect about the finer details
of his career. By the time he settled in Haiti, he had storefront
offices in Miami and in the only four-star hotel in the Do-
minican Republic. Through his Santo Domingo office, which
housed one of the few teletype machines on the island, drifted
foreign correspondents covering Cuba and the turbulent Caribbean, covert agents, mercenaries, businessmen, military
men, and government officials. Marger, a rotund man with
merry eyes and a perpetually quizzical air, opened his office
to all of them. In those revolutionary years of brigades and
rebellions when Communism was consuming Cuba, Marger
was a shrewd and sociable man.

He said he arrived in Haiti in 1959 "by accident" and
settled in Port au Prince simply because "I fell in love with
it." He maintained his law offices in Miami and in Santo
Domingo but attached himself to a Haitian newspaper where
he was credentialed as a foreign correspondent. As Duvalier's
adviser, Marger befriended Haiti's generals, its colonels, its
power brokers, and its ruling class. Yet he was a familiar of
the street beggars who greeted him as he made his way
through the squalid back streets of the island's capital city.
He acquired a house with a grand staircase and five servants
from a general who had fallen out of favor. His children
roamed the countryside on horses, and the peasants brought
them safely home at night.

But in 1967, the relationship ended as suddenly as it began.
Duvalier called Marger to the palace. "Ed, it's time to go,"
he told the lawyer.

"When would you like me to leave, your excellency?"
Marger asked.

"A month," Duvalier said. Eight years of political intimacy were dismissed as casually as dust.

There were those who whispered that, during those Caribbean years, Marger, a former cryptographer with the U.S. Army Corps, was one of the C.I.A.'s covert operatives. Marger denied it, insisting that his decision to hire U.S. Representative Bob Barr, then one of the Company's South American analysts, was his closest connection to the C.I.A. Marger said he hired Barr, who had recently graduated from law school, because "I had a lot of business in Latin America. He came to me highly recommended."

A year after he left Haiti, Marger surfaced in Charleston as a supervisor with the U.S. Office of Economic Opportunity, overseeing Lyndon Johnson's War on Poverty programs in eight southern states and "going into places nobody wanted us and making friends." He had acquired a DC-5 Aero Commander in Haiti, and he would fly into the rural South, a New York Jew who would post guards around the plane and then disarm suspicious locals with his blunt but approachable manner and perpetual air of sardonic amusement.

Eventually he made his way to the tiny town of Jasper in the north Georgia mountains, much the same way as he had found himself in Haiti. There, on Main Street in a rural town two hours north of Atlanta, he opened an office in one of the town's original buildings. "I got lost," he shrugged when asked how he came to land so far from home and from the Caribbean. "In my practice, all you need is a hat and a telephone."

By the time Marger met Curtis Rower's father on December 23, 1992, he cheerily insisted, "I'm just a country lawyer"—a plump, elvish man with a salty goatee and photos of guerrillas on his study walls, a man who favored red suspenders and a Panama hat he wore rakishly over a thinning cascade of unruly gray curls.

When Marger first met Rower, the twenty-two-year-old had been in police custody nearly twelve hours, a crack addict tumbling off a brutal high, a black man held in one of metropolitan Atlanta's whiter counties for the murder of a white suburban housewife. By the time Marger met with him there was little the lawyer could do. Rower had already waived his right to counsel and given a legal, lengthy confession to police.

"Who's got Tom Charron's phone number?" Marger asked.

That night, Marger offered the Cobb County district attorney his deal. Rower would trade a plea that would lock him up forever for his life.

"No," Charron informed Marger. "I'm not going to do it."

Tom Charron had been a zealous advocate for the death penalty since his election as Georgia's youngest district attorney and Cobb County's first Republican, in a year that former Georgia Governor Jimmy Carter led the Democratic party to the White House.

But despite the circumstances of his election, Charron was far too political to be a maverick. He was a man of bluff charm and surface grace who, when asked why he was a prosecutor, answered, "I've always loved to be in politics."

As a prosecutor, he said he had married his two loves, politics and the law. But in conversation, at least, politics came first. A graduate of a defunct night law school in Atlanta, Charron had been in practice little more than a year when he ran for district attorney in 1976. He had been in public office ever since.

Politics had always dictated Charron's wholesale pursuit of the death penalty against anyone whose crimes, according to Georgia's law, were Death Row calling cards. In twenty years as a district attorney, he had sent a dozen men to Death Row, more than any other prosecutor in the state. But he had lost just as many death cases in the penalty phase, unable to convince juries that the men they had convicted of murder, men who had killed with "an abandoned and malignant heart," now deserved to die. Those losses never seemed to rattle Charron's outwardly cool demeanor. "It is a decision the citizens should make, not a judge and not the prosecuting attorney," he said whenever a jury sentenced a killer to life instead of to Death Row. If a jury rejected his demands for death, so be it. He was so matter-of-fact, so nearly nonchalant about it all, which only infuriated a defense bar that quickly labeled him an indiscriminate deathmonger.

But then there was the murder of Sara Tokars. "If this isn't a death penalty case," Charron asked, "then what is? If I don't seek the death penalty in this case, how can I justify seeking the death penalty in any other case?"

Not only had Rower confessed, he had left behind a trail of witnesses for whom he had outlined the murder plot and described the cold details of Sara's actual death. Charron scoffed at arguments that he simply ought to accept the plea and save the county the cost of transferring and trying Rower's case in another jurisdiction scores of miles from Atlanta.

"If economics becomes a factor, then you're placing a dollar amount on justice," he said. "And the only winner is the defendant."

By the time Rower was indicted, Charron had witnessed two executions, determined that, only by witnessing them, he could ask a jury honestly to sentence a killer to die. For him, the two electrocutions in the sanitized pallor of a small room with a single glass window and a square wood chair the size of a throne was neither a spectacle nor a horror show. It was efficient, with a certain bureacratic dignity. Death, unlike the crime scene photos that crossed Charron's desk, was bloodless and nearly imperceptible. Justice was done. No more. No less. His murder victims had experienced far worse before they died. He had left the death chamber's anteroom without a twinge of conscience or remorse.

Ed Marger insisted that Rower never intended to kill Sara and that her death, in the end, was the sad result of a struggle and a shot accidentally fired.

"Curtis's attitude was always, 'Look, I'm guilty. I'm willing to be punished, but I don't want to die,' " Marger said. "He's a very unusual guy. He admitted to almost everything. He wanted to know how he could help."

He also prospered in jail. Forced into abstinence, Rower kicked his drug habit, ate three balanced meals a day, and began working out. He gained weight. He lost his glassy stare.

But no matter what Marger said, Assistant U.S. Attorney Katherine Monahan, who had assisted Parker in the Tokars prosecution, didn't believe that Rower ever encountered remorse or guilt after killing Sara. Conscience, if he had one, left him largely alone. A year before his trial, when Marger's

deal was still on the table, Monahan had interviewed Rower
in a Cobb County jail cell. He repulsed her.

"He didn't have any concept of what he had done," she
said. "Yeah, he's sorry. But sorry he got caught, sorry he's
sitting in jail, sorry he's exposed to the death penalty. He
could care less about the Tokars children. And he didn't have
much to say about Sara. I was so repulsed I didn't even want
to be in the same room with him."

He was so matter-of-fact as he talked about kidnapping
Sara and her children, as if he were recounting a trip to the
store. "He didn't even know Tokars," Monahan said. "He
didn't know why they were up there killing this woman. He
didn't care. He just wanted the money."

Rower seemed decidedly cheerful that day as she sat in a
holding cell with him. A young mother with a new baby,
Monahan felt herself sinking into a helpless depression as she
listened to him talk about Sara's murder as if it were some
unavoidable accident. As a county prosecutor, hired on Fred
Tokars's recommendation, she had inhaled those random,
ruthless, senseless killings like cigarette-stained air. But when
she became a federal prosecutor she had left that poisonous
smoke of violence.

"I was sitting in the same room with the man who killed
Sara Tokars, and I truly believe that he killed her intentionally," she said. "He didn't care whether he did it in front of
those kids. He probably didn't care about the lives of those
children. He hopped out of a moving car, and they rolled on.
I talked to him about it, and I knew he was lying."

There was no struggle over the gun. "That was his one
excuse, his one shot at not getting the death penalty," she
said. " 'I didn't really mean to do it. Don't execute me. I did
it, but it was an accident.' There's no way I'll ever believe
that."

But it was the story to which Rower stubbornly clung and
which Marger had no choice but to embrace.

When Rower's trial began on February 27, 1995, the criminal trial of former football star O. J. Simpson for the murders
of Ronald Goldman and Simpson's wife, Nicole, was still in
progress in Los Angeles, and racism on the part of L.A. police
had already bubbled ominously to the surface. But the L.A.

jury had not yet handed down the acquittal that so fiercely polarized the country along a racial fault line. Yet, three thousand miles away, Marger and his cocounsel, David Simpson, were seeking a like-minded jury to hear the death case against Rower, a jury that might be particularly susceptible to the argument that Rower was simply a pawn of a white lawyer and a patsy of white police.

To that end, the two defense lawyers asked juror after juror if they had decided whether or not media broadcasts and accounts of the trial had persuaded them that O. J. Simpson was a killer. Were they following the L.A. trial? Had they joined in any ad-hoc discussions or offered any off-the-cuff analysis? Was there too much publicity surrounding the double murder in Brentwood? Did the criminal justice system, in fact, treat whites better than blacks? Would they have the strength of character to stand by their verdict, even if every other juror disagreed? Laced through those questions was the reminder that, in this trial, a black man once more "was accused of crimes against a white lady."

Some of the jurors Rower's defense lawyers questioned said they weren't interested, and that Simpson was "old news." Others had avidly watched the Simpson trial. None admitted having an opinion as to O. J.'s ultimate innocence or guilt.

"I absolutely cannot tell you right now whether I think he's guilty or innocent. I can't tell," said one white woman who was subsequently seated as a juror. "I think there's been a lot of media hype, and I don't really think it's fair to judge it on the basis of the media."

Charron's questions reflected his single-minded approach to the trial. Largely limited to the death penalty, they were designed to weed out those members of the jury pool who opposed or were troubled by it. Charron sought jurors who could firmly sentence a man to death.

On February 27, 1995 the lawyers struck the jury. Seated in the jury box were eight men and four women: nine whites and three blacks; two black men and a single, young black woman. It was, by and large, an educated jury, drawn to the tiny town of Appling from a county that included Augusta, one of Georgia's larger cities. Many held supervisory positions. Several had military backgrounds.

There was a physical plant supervisor from the Veterans Administration Hospital in Augusta, a graduate of Georgia Military College and a Naval Reserve veteran who was a chemical plant operator for Westinghouse, a subcontractor at the Savannah River nuclear plant. Joining them were the special projects officer for the director of Georgia Military College's School of Computer Science and a computer systems administrator for a cutting tool manufacturer. Rounding out the jury were a recent college graduate with a political science degree who was living at home and managing a fast-food restaurant while she contemplated law school; a landscaper who lived with his parents and whose father was a retired military police officer; a pipe fitter at a chemical company whose uncle had been murdered; an auto mechanic at an Augusta dealership; a registered nurse supervisor; and a teacher of deaf children.

The twelfth and final juror was a man named Henry Parks. Parks, then thirty-one, was a computer systems programmer-analyst for an Augusta firm that provided maintenance and technical support to one of the city's large chemical companies. He was a captain in the U.S. Army Reserve and, while on active duty, had been a platoon leader. He was married with two children, ages four and six, the same age as the Tokars boys at the time of the murder. He was a religious man, a junior deacon and Bible School superintendent at the Baptist church his family attended.

He was also one of the few African-American men in the jury pool. Asked on a jury questionnaire whether he would like to serve as a juror, he penned an answer that reflected an attitude grown dusty with disuse in the self-centered decades that followed Watergate and the Viet Nam War. "It is my civic duty to serve."

Charron's first question to Parks concerned the death penalty. "Could you equally and fairly consider the death penalty, as well as life imprisonment, in reaching your verdict?" he asked.

"Yes, I think so," Parks answered. "Even though I have

not heard the case, I think that is a possibility, yes. I do feel like I can fairly consider a death penalty."

Unlike many of the other jurors, Parks answered Charron's questions at some length. His answers sounded rational, reasoned, and intelligent. As Charron sought to gauge whether the death penalty was really a reasonable option for a religious, African-American man who would be asked to pass judgment on another, younger black man, Parks assuaged any doubts the prosecutor might have entertained.

"I think it basically depends on the circumstances and the fact that it was proven in a court of law," he answered. "And you're right. There are religious people that say you can never determine that a person is guilty. They have their own views, and I have mine. The same God that says, 'Thou shalt not kill,' also says 'Obey the laws of the land.' And if the law dictates that capital punishment is necessary, then you have to submit to the laws of the land."

"And you don't feel that if the death penalty was appropriate, that would clash with any of your religious or moral beliefs?" Charron asked.

"Personally, I do not," Parks responded.

But Charron wasn't through. "The victim in the case, Mrs. Tokars, was a white lady," he continued. "Her children were white. The fact that the defendant is an African-American and the victims were white in this case, would that have any bearing on whether you fairly consider the evidence in this case?"

"Personally, I don't think it has any bearing whatsoever," Parks said. "They are individuals, and I will consider the situation as individuals."

The impact of O. J. Simpson's ongoing murder trial in Los Angeles and the legacy of the Rodney King beating in L.A. in 1992, that also spawned racial disturbances in the streets of Atlanta, shaped Charron's next questions. Parks was, after all, a black man, and racism on the part of white L.A. police officers had fomented angry national debate about the arrests of both King and Simpson. Charron wanted to make sure he didn't choose for Rower's jury a man who might seek to nullify the laws and clear Rower simply because he was the black victim of a white society.

"From anything you have experienced in your life, Mr.

Parks, or anything you may have read or heard on television do you have any negative feelings about law enforcement?''

"I do not," Parks said. "Not in general. I believe in the law, and I believe in the system."

"And do you feel the court system as it acts now is fair to all persons, including minorities, as well as Caucasians?''

"That I cannot adequately answer because I have not seen it all," Parks demurred. "I haven't experienced it.

"Based on," he paused, then stumbled. "You have seen some for, you seen some against." He paused again. "I think you have to make a decision based on what you see here. I have never before been a juror. I've only seen the movies and this kind of stuff so, you know, I really can't answer, you know, how things were in the past. But I can say, based on my personal experience, I do feel that it is fair. It's a fair system."

"And you believe in the system?"

"I believe in the system. Yes, I do.''

But Parks's disjoint and somewhat awkward answer about the basic fairness of the criminal justice system, following his smooth replies to the prosecutor's previous questions, would, in retrospect, prove telling. It signaled either an eagerness to please the lawyers who questioned him or a subtle lapse in candor.

Before Marger began questioning Parks, he clearly signaled him as to what he was seeking in a juror. "One of the things that the defense is attempting to ascertain is whether or not a prospective juror comes into the court in any way with a prejudice, with a bias, with an opinion that will hurt the defendant," he explained.

In that context, state prosecutors became an ominous "them." "They're asking for the death penalty. They want the death penalty," Marger intoned. "We're asking that death not be given, and we don't want it to be given, so, in all honesty, we're probably looking for jurors who would not give the death penalty, and we want to know where we stand."

But Marger didn't pursue with Parks his feelings about the death penalty. Instead, he sought, as Charron had, to learn whether Parks had ever faced racial prejudice.

While in the U.S. Army Reserve, Marger asked, "Did you get the same type of obedience from blacks and whites?"

"Yes, I'd say so, yes," Parks answered.

"Were you treated the way that you would expect to be treated from both races?"

"I would say yes."

"In your personal life, have you ever personally been subjected to discrimination of any kind?"

Parks's answer was oblique. "I think to say that I have not would probably be naive, but I try to avoid situations," he answered carefully. "I think my personality is one that will allow me to avoid situations like that most of the time. Sometimes you're in situations that you cannot avoid, and I think that, for the most part, that I would probably say yes, I probably have sometime."

Most black men living in the South, when confronted with that question, were far less circumspect. Nearly everyone had at least one story of how skin color had made them an object of suspicion or contempt. If Parks had not experienced such bias, he was a notable exception.

Marger needed to make certain that Parks's careful answers didn't mask a man who held other African-American men to his own high standards of behavior. He wanted, instead, a man who would be sympathetic to the argument that Rower's guilt was somehow mitigated by his color and his deprived, impoverished childhood. "Would you, as an African-American man, hold it against Curtis Rower, an African-American man, because he had done something for which you are even considering the death penalty?" he asked. "Would you consider that was an affront to you or such an intrusion onto your life that you could not give him a fair and impartial hearing to life and death?"

"I do not," Parks answered firmly. "As I stated before, I look at individuals. I'm a man of individuals, and that's how I will consider this, as an individual."

Like Charron, Marger also asked Parks to elaborate on his religious beliefs. But while Charron wanted to ascertain whether Parks could truly pass judgment on another man rather than relegate that decision to God alone, Marger wanted to know whether Parks believed in the Old Testament adage, "an eye for an eye."

Parks's answer was thoughtful, but one that might have given Charron pause in his quest for jurors who would impose a death penalty.

"If we are going to talk about religion, under the law that was the way it was—an eye for an eye and a tooth for a tooth," Parks replied. "But I am a Christian first and foremost, and all those things have been done away. So now we no longer consider an eye for an eye, but instead of doing evil for evil, you combat evil with good. And that is the principle that I stand by, and I do believe that."

He was exactly the kind of juror that Marger sought, a forgiving one. "Will you give my client a fair trial if you're selected as a juror?" he asked.

"You can bet he will receive a fair trial," Parks answered emphatically.

When the jury was struck, Parks became the twelfth juror. By then, Charron had exhausted all his strikes. By then, even if something subtle in Parks's answers, something a little less than genuine had teased at the edges of Charron's legal sensibilities, he couldn't have prevented Parks from taking a seat in the jury box. But Charron was not a subtle man. He was more apt to challenge jurors who acknowledged openly that they had faced discrimination than one who sidestepped, however awkwardly, a similar admission. He never challenged Parks, and, if he had, a challenge more than likely would have failed. As the trial began, neither the veteran prosecutor of two dozen death penalty cases nor defense lawyers had any inkling of the pivotal role in Rower's fate that Parks eventually would play.

Even though the massive publicity surrounding Sara Tokars's murder, the arrests of Rower and Lawrence, and Fred Tokars's federal trial had largely bypassed Columbia County where Rower was on trial, as a precautionary measure, Judge Kreeger sequestered the jury. It was not something he wanted to do and, in truth, he had hoped to avoid it. The expense of boarding jurors for the month-long trial aside, sequestration was a massive invasion of privacy. The jury became virtual, if well-tended, prisoners. They could not travel about freely.

Everything they read and everything they watched on television was closely monitored. They were watched constantly by bailiffs. Time with their families was strictly limited. And they were forbidden to discuss the one thing that now dominated their lives—the trial. The courtroom, and that alone, became their world so that nothing else might sway them—not facts that weren't in evidence, not others' suppositions or opinions, nothing that wasn't already approved and packaged by the court.

Once more before opening arguments, Marger offered to allow Rower to plead guilty to the charges. His client, Marger argued, had authorized the offer "to protect the children." But Rower clearly intended to spare himself. The testimony of a tearful, terrified child could unleash such savage emotions that the jury might willingly, even eagerly, send Rower to the chair.

Charron roundly rejected Marger's overture.

There were legal reasons to be sure. The Georgia law establishing life without parole as a sentencing option in death penalty cases was barely two years old. It had never been challenged, and it remained unclear whether a defense lawyer could actually strike a plea bargain for a defendant that imposed a harsher penalty than he might otherwise face.

"This is not a case in which life without parole is an option," Charron said, "and the state will not agree to it."

But more than that, the Rower trial was Charron's first shot at Fredric Tokars. Upstaged by federal prosecutors, Charron had chafed for more than a year to go to trial in the most highly publicized case in Cobb County's history. Nor did he intend to allow Rower to sidestep the death penalty with a plea bargain that rubber-stamped the drug addict's own less damaging version of Sara's murder. Charron believed in the death penalty. His constituency believed in the death penalty. He was not about to bargain with a drug addict from an Atlanta housing project who had violated one of Cobb County's tranquil neighborhoods to kidnap and murder a housewife in front of her small children. Such a crime was a reckless affront to everything that Charron represented. If he accepted a plea, criminals from Atlanta's impoverished sprawl of abandoned neighborhoods might well begin looking northward to Cobb

County as fresh territory to plunder. Nor would Charron agree to Marger's offer to forgo a jury trial in exchange for a guilty plea and proceed directly to sentencing, which in Georgia death penalty cases also required a unanimous jury verdict.

To sentence Rower to die, the jury would have to disregard the killer's assertion that Sara's murder was "an accidental shooting as a result of a struggle with codefendant Eddie Lawrence," Charron argued.

Ricky Tokars, the prosecutor said, was "the only eyewitness who can testify that there was no struggle over a gun."

Without a trial, "the state is at a disadvantage in attempting to show to the jury that, in fact, the defendant's statement is incredible and that his account of what happened out there might not have happened," Charron insisted.

"This child is an eyewitness to a kidnapping and a murder and an armed robbery of his mother, and this child's testimony is going to be clearly and starkly different than the defendant's rendition of what happened that night. In order for this jury to fairly determine the proper punishment in this case, they're going to have to get beyond that one difference in the case—whether it was an accidental struggle over a gun and a shooting, or an intentional, premeditated, execution murder-for-hire, and for those reasons the state will not agree to life without parole."

And so, Rower's murder trial began.

That afternoon, as Charron made his opening statement to the jury, it was clear that Fred Tokars, as well as Curtis Rower, was on trial.

Rower was one of a trio of conspirators, Charron told the jury. "Eddie Lawrence has pled guilty to one count of murder and has received a life sentence for his testimony," Charron told the jury. "You will not hear and you will not see the name of the third coconspirator in this case, Fred Tokars, who is an attorney-at-law and a part-time judge in Atlanta, and who is the husband of Sara Ambrusko Tokars and the father of young Rick and Mike. Fred Tokars is indicted on the same charges, and his case is still pending.

"Fred set this whole series of actions in motion. Eddie Charles Lawrence—who is the middle man and business partner of Fred Tokars, who was pressured and persuaded by Fred

Tokars—because of friendship and business relationships and, yes, the lure of money—procured the hit man.

"That hit man, that person who murdered Sara Tokars for money or for the promise of money is sitting right over there today. Curtis Alfonso Rower."

It was Rower who agreed to kill Sara for five thousand dollars. It was Rower who strolled out of the house where he was staying on the night Sara was killed, dressed in dark clothes and carrying a sawed-off shotgun. It was Rower who entered the empty Tokars's home through an unlocked sliding glass door to wait for Sara to return. It was Rower she saw as she opened the kitchen door, a stranger with a shotgun who hustled her back into her car with her two sons and ordered her to drive. And it was Rower who pulled the trigger of that gun when she defied him later and refused to turn into an unlighted subdivision.

But it was Fred and Eddie whom Charron spoke about the most. It was Fred's plot to kill Sara and not Rower's willingness to carry it out that occupied him. He didn't tell the jury that Rower was a member of a robbing crew or that he had cultivated a reputation as a killer. He didn't tell the jury that Rower, not Lawrence, had acquired the gun. He didn't tell them that forensic evidence bolstered Ricky's statements that Rower and Lawrence never struggled over the gun or that its firing was accidental. He didn't tell them that after Sara's murder, Rower jubilantly proclaimed, "I did it!" and used her stolen money to celebrate by buying drugs and beer. He didn't tell them that, after the murder, Rower fretted only about getting paid for the hit.

In the end, that decision to emphasize Fred's role in Sara's murder rather than Rower's cold-blooded willingness to carry it out may have cost Charron dearly. By doing so, he unwittingly bolstered Marger's contention that Rower was not so much a killer as he was a patsy.

Marger began with Rower's confession, his highly detailed account of Sara's murder. It was a troublesome document for the defense because it outlined a malignant murder-for-hire. Its only saving grace was Rower's insistence that, in the end, even though he had agreed to kill Sara for money, he had pulled the trigger by accident.

That much was true, Marger told the jury, because Rower had made the statement after his grandmother had told him, "Tell them the truth." In that context, Fred Tokars's sinister motives were irrelevant because "Fred Tokars was completely unknown to him.

"The person he did know, however, for a fairly short period of time," Marger continued, "was a man by the name of Eddie Lawrence—a man who is a manipulator, a man that took advantage of the very many people he met. And he knew how to deal with people of the type that you're going to find Curtis Rower to be."

Curtis Rower, he said, was victimized by his environment, victimized by his poverty, and victimized by Eddie Lawrence. "The evidence will show that Curtis Rower was an addict, that he could be bought very cheap, that the only thing that he was interested in in life was getting more cocaine, and that he was probably the most easily swayed person they could find.

"The evidence will show that Curtis was not a hit man nor had ever been. The evidence will show that Curtis was looking for a little more cocaine. Once Eddie Lawrence was introduced to Curtis Rower, he started manipulating him. He gave him money to buy cocaine. He took him to places to buy cocaine, and Curtis used it and used it up until the day that Sara Tokars was killed. He used it up until the day that he was arrested. And he had used it the night before his arrest."

His confession, Marger argued, "was the truth as best he knew it. There were almost no details left out. He had no time to plan a statement."

And afterwards, the lawyer insisted, "Curtis Rower showed a tremendous amount of remorse, attempted to tell everybody how he felt about the children, about what he had done. You will find that for two years and four months or so Curtis Rower has always attempted to cooperate, always attempted to show remorse, always did what was right considering the part that he had in killing Sara Tokars."

Rower, of course, had made no such statements. His lawyer, Edwin Marger, had made them all on his behalf.

What Marger did next may well have changed the entire

outcome of the trial. He began arguing the law to a jury that didn't understand it.

"Curtis Rower never, not from the first day, has said that he has not been implicated and been the one who was involved with *felony* murder," Marger said. "The question that will come to mind is the question of malice. Was this a *malice* murder? That doesn't mean, nor will the evidence show, that he's any less culpable because it was not malice murder.

"The evidence will show that Curtis Rower, if anything, was a dupe. No evidence will show you that Curtis Rower did not involve himself in felony murder. The question that will be presented in the evidence is what really happened and was this premeditated."

It was Marger's first attempt to distinguish between the charges of malice murder and felony murder that Curtis Rower faced. Under Georgia law, a person committed malice murder if he or she killed deliberately "with malice aforethought," without provocation, and with "an abandoned and malignant heart." Murder-for-hire clearly fit the bill. But a killer could make a decision to murder another in the instant before death and still be guilty of malice murder.

Felony murder was one that occurred during the commission of another felony crime such as robbery, burglary, kidnapping, or rape. It could, and generally did, encompass malice murder. But it also included a murder that occurred by accident of circumstance during the commission of another crime.

Both felony murder and malice murder were punishable by death. But Marger knew that, if Rower was convicted only of felony murder, he had a chance to persuade the jury during the sentencing trial that Sara's murder was an accident. If Rower did not intend to kill her, he should not be sentenced to die.

"This case is not a question for the jury as to whether he's guilty or not of having kidnapped Sara Tokars," Marger continued. "He wanted to plead guilty the first day, and he still tells you that he is guilty of the kidnapping of Sara Tokars. He is guilty of taking her in the car, and he is guilty of having been in the car with the shotgun in his hand when she was killed.

"But as Curtis will tell you, what he was trying to do was get the five thousand dollars, that he never murdered anybody, he never intended to murder anybody. What he was trying to do is see if he could get the money and buy some more cocaine."

Marger bypassed Rower's purchase of the shotgun and his willingness to ride to Cobb County with Eddie and enter the Tokars's home alone. By the time Sara Tokars arrived, all Rower wanted to do was go back to Atlanta, Marger argued. He may have kidnapped her, but he didn't kidnap the children. Sara, not Rower, told Ricky to get back in the car. Rower didn't know the younger child was still sleeping in the back seat. When Sara stopped the car on Powers Road, "Eddie Lawrence pulls up behind, he opens the left rear door of the car, and he grabs for the gun. At that time, the gun, which is being held at the barrel by Mr. Lawrence, swings around. Lawrence goes out the door. The gun swings back around, the door closes, or not quite closes, and the gun goes off."

It was a novel theory, except for one problem. Ricky Tokars would say it never happened. Still, Marger had to sow that seed of doubt in the jurors' minds, whether or not it ever flowered.

Now, Marger tried to make Rower's confession into something more noble instead of what it was—a bare admission by a drug addict who made his living as a robber in a city where too many people turned to drugs and guns, certain they would die by the time they turned twenty-five.

"We are going to show you a series of events that happened that have to lead you to believe that something is wrong with the system," Marger concluded. "Yes, he is guilty of murder. He is guilty of the kidnapping of Sara Tokars. But he is not guilty of doing it with malice. He never intended to kill her, but he did. The fact that he is sorry does not bring back Sara Tokars. The fact that he's sorry does not, in any way, make the children a new mother. But he's done what he can. He presents himself to you in that light, and we hope that, when this case is terminated, that you will, in fact, find him guilty, but you will not find him guilty of malice murder."

It was that legal distinction, between malice and felony murder, that ultimately saved Curtis Rower's life.

The first prosecution witness was Sara's oldest son, Ricky Tokars. He had been six when his mother was killed in front of him. Now he was eight, a sweet-faced child with light brown hair styled in a crewcut reminiscent of the fifties.

Because Ricky had never been able to identify Rower in a lineup, Marger had asked if Rower could be absent from the courtroom so as not to frighten the child. Fearing that the Ambrusko family might seek to coach or otherwise influence him, Marger also asked that Ricky's grandparents and his aunts remain outside the courtroom while the child testified. "I think they are an undue influence on his testimony," he said.

Charron objected strenuously. "If anything, it would give comfort to that child if his family members are there with him," the prosecutor said. "Nor will there be any effort by family members to try to influence what this child may say on the stand. If anything, it would make it less traumatic if the family members were there."

And so they stayed, allowed into the old courtroom with the names of the county's war dead on the walls but relegated to the back rows so that their grief, their mourning black, their quiet prayers would not be apparent to the jury.

Ricky embodied their despair.

When Ricky bravely took the witness stand in Appling for the first and only time, he was living with his maternal grandparents, his aunt, Joni Ambrusko, and his younger brother, Mike, in Florida. He was in the second grade, and he played baseball, he said stoutly.

"Do you know what an oath is?" Charron asked him after he elicited some background information from the child.

"To tell the truth," Ricky answered.

"And what happens if you don't tell the truth?"

"I'll probably get grounded," he answered sturdily.

"And you're going to tell all of the truth here today?"

"Yes."

"And you understood when you raised your right hand and placed your left hand on the Bible, that that was an oath?"

"Yes."

"And that you are to tell the truth?"

"Yes."

The antique courtroom with its high, wide windows and brass chandeliers seemed suddenly cavernous as Charron began to lead the child delicately back in time to 1992 and a return trip from a Thanksgiving holiday in Florida that ended with his mother's murder.

"Do you remember the morning that you left, Rick, to come back to Marietta?"

"Yes."

"And before you left had you packed the car up with your mother and Mike?"

"Yes." A ragged breath caught in the child's throat. Tears trickled down his face.

"Are you a little nervous?"

Ricky nodded, gulped. His small voice steadied as he told the prosecutor about eating Sunday brunch that final day, the long drive home, about pulling into the garage and following his mother up the small stairwell to the kitchen door. Tears streaked his flushed face and he wiped his eyes furiously as he wrestled with the dark angel that was his memory.

"What happened when you went to the door, Rick?" Charron asked gently.

"I think she opened it, or the bad guy opened it, and then he said, 'Everybody get in the car. Give me all your money, and nobody will get hurt.' I was standing next to my mom."

As he described the gunman at the door, Ricky's voice was steady. But as he began describing "the pirate gun" the stranger held, he gasped for air and began furiously rubbing away more tears. Yet, the child resolutely continued to testify. The bad guy had kicked his dog. Jake had run away. He and his mother had both climbed back in the car. Mike was still asleep. The bad guy sat in back. His mom had given him her purse. He had said, "Drive."

"I accidentally, like my elbow, like it sort of rolled down the window a little bit, and he said, 'Put the window back up now,' " Ricky said.

"Was your mom scared?" Charron asked.

The child began to cry in earnest. "Yes," he said in a small, miserable voice. "She kept on driving. And the man goes, 'Turn here,' and my mom goes, 'Is it okay if I just drop you off here because I'm in shock, I'm so scared?' ''

"And what did the man say?" Charron asked.

Ricky twisted his hands helplessly. "Don't fuck with me," he repeated in a delicate voice.

"And what did your mom say?"

"I'm not trying to fuck with you."

"And what were you doing Rick?"

"I was just sitting there."

"And what happened after your mom said that back to the man?"

In his bell-like voice, the child answered simply, "He shot the gun."

Ricky rubbed his eyes with his small fists as if he could erase that bare, brutal memory. He told the jury he had watched through the windshield as the car barreled through a ditch and into a field.

"And what happened to your mom after you heard the shot?"

"She was dead."

"Where was the man with the gun?"

"He stayed in the car a couple of seconds, and then he started running."

"Did you ever see anybody else but that one man?"

"No."

"And when this man got in the jeep with you, was there anybody else in the jeep other than you and Mike and your mom and the man?"

"No."

"Did you ever see any other person other than that man in the car?"

"No," Ricky answered seriously. "But I think I saw like a light. It could have been another car's light going on, or it could have been our car light, but as soon as I got there I think I saw it, and it turned off."

"Some headlights in front of you?" Charron asked.

"Yes," the child answered. "Well, it wasn't in front of me. It was like sort of to the right."

Ricky didn't know it, but the car lights he spotted were close to where Lawrence had parked his pickup to wait for

Rower. Rower had seen them, too, realizing at that moment that Eddie Lawrence had not abandoned him after all.

"Did you see anybody?" Charron asked. "Did anybody run up to your car at that point when you were stopped on the side of the road?"

"No."

"Did anybody open the back left door while the man was sitting in the back?"

"No."

"At the point that the man fired the gun, was anybody else leaning in the car or there in the car with you and Mike and your mom and the man with the gun?"

"No."

"What did you do next?" the prosecutor asked.

Once more, the child's face crumpled in agony. "I sort of seed if my mom was still awake or if she was dead." His voice broke. "I woke my brother up. I told him, 'We have to go get help.'"

As Ricky told the jury how he turned off the ignition as his mother had taught him, woke his younger brother, and pulled him from the car, he uttered a single, strangled sob.

"We went to go get help." Tears bathed his face. His voice quivered. "I knocked on the door. I said, 'You've got to help us. Our mom got shot.'"

"And then did the police come?"

"Yes."

"And did you tell your story then to the police that night?"

"Yes."

"Thank you, Ricky. That's all I have."

In the break that followed, Ricky's family enveloped him. By then, the little boy was drawing deep, ragged breaths and wiping away relentless tears as they whispered encouragement to him.

Joni spoke encouragingly to her nephew, "It's going great. It's almost over. Are you okay? It's almost over."

Dwight Davis, the family lawyer, calmly advised the child about the cross-examination to come: "Just talk to him. Just tell him the truth." It was the advice Sara's family had always given to her children.

After the break, Gordon Billheimer, one of Rower's law-

yers, stood up to cross-examine Ricky. The defense team had
hired a child psychologist to advise them. Marger's own
daughter was Ricky's age, and he certainly wanted to protect
the boy from a scathing cross-examination. At the same time,
he wanted to be certain that none of Rower's lawyers alien-
ated the jury. Yet, they had to raise serious questions about
the child's testimony if they were to convince the jury that
Rower's account of Sara's murder wasn't simply one more
lie. Billheimer first had to establish a tenuous trust between
him and the boy.

"Will you do me a favor?" he asked. "This is kind of
scary for me, too, so if you get scared, and you want to have
a glass of water or you want to talk with your family or
someone you just tell me and the judge and we'll let you do
it, okay, because I'm very proud and pleased to meet you.
You're a very brave young man. You just do the best you
can."

Billheimer clearly wanted to set the nervous child at ease.
But he was also sending a strong message to the jury that
Rower's lawyers wanted to protect the boy, even though their
goal was to insinuate that his testimony had been intentionally
shaped by police and by his family to reflect Eddie
Lawrence's version of Sara's death rather than Rower's less
culpable one.

It would work far beyond his expectations.

Billheimer began by asking Ricky to identify "some of the
nice people that are back here who have come to help you
today."

Ricky earnestly complied. There were his aunts Gretchen,
Karen, Krissy, and Joni; an uncle and Krissy's fiancé; his
grandmother; his cousin Derek, his cousin Mary; the family
lawyers. Two pews full of family watching him. As he named
them, Ricky began to cry.

"Ricky," Billheimer asked gently. "I need you to tell me
some things that happened that night the best you can remember. I know you're doing your best, and again, if you get
scared just let me know, and we'll stop." He began asking
Ricky about the different police officers he had met that night,
who they were and what he had told them. If the child ever
knew, he didn't remember any of the officers' names, except

for Detective Pat Banks, and he only remembered Banks's first name. He remembered having talked to them, but, two years and five formal statements later, the eight-year-old couldn't remember exactly what he had said when he was six. But Ricky was a smart child who wanted desperately to do well, and finally to help his mother. By then, he also knew there were apparent errors in those statements, errors that troubled him because they contradicted what, two years later, he remembered.

He had discovered those discrepancies innocently, although it would not be perceived that way. As a matter of practice, lawyers have always asked witnesses to review their previous statements before testifying, to refresh their memory months or years later and to guard against contradictions that could be used to discredit them. There is nothing sinister in the practice, although in court both defense lawyers and prosecutors often seek to make it seem so. So, before Ricky testified, Joni Ambrusko had read to the child statements he had given to police during a nine-month interval that followed Sara's murder.

Ever the worrier, now steeled to anticipate the worst, Joni had fretted that, if she did so, she might later be accused of unduly influencing Ricky to parrot only what his mother's family wanted him to say. She held no illusions now that truth was a defense or that anyone's good reputation or good intentions were sacrosanct in a criminal court of law. Worried, she had consulted with Charron and the family's own lawyers. They had all encouraged her to read Ricky's statements to the child as long as she refrained from telling him what to say or do beyond simply urging him to tell the truth as he remembered it.

It was Ricky who had first discovered what he said were mistakes in the statements his aunt read to him. Although a police officer had noted that Sara had screamed and shoved Ricky to the floorboard just before she was shot, Ricky didn't remember it. He was also troubled by one statement which suggested that, as Rower took them hostage, his mother had screamed and their dog had run away. Jake had run away, Ricky insisted, only after Rower had kicked him in the throat.

"What do I do, Aunt Joni?" he had asked desperately.

"Just tell them the truth as you remember it," his aunt had reassured him.

Now, as Billheimer questioned him, Ricky seemed eager to explain that conversation and how he had identified the errors. Instead, his terse explanation made it sound as if his aunt had coached him, that she had pointed out the errors to him.

"When you talked to these police officers, were you trying to tell them the truth?" Billheimer asked. "You did the best job you could?"

"Well, I guess I was sort of shaky, then," Ricky answered, "and my Aunt Joni read with me some of the things, and I made some mistakes, but otherwise I tried."

"What mistakes did you make?"

Ricky pointed to the errors he had earlier identified for his aunt. "Like I said that my dog ran, but the man kicked my dog, and then he ran," he said.

"And your Aunt Joni told you that, pointed that mistake out to you?" Billheimer was quietly jubilant.

"No," Ricky explained. "I pointed that mistake out to myself, but when she was reading it to me."

"Well, when did she read it to you?" Billheimer asked.

"A couple of days before the trial."

"You're a good student in school," Billheimer continued. "Could you have read those things yourself?"

"Well, there's some big words that I couldn't understand," Ricky countered, "but probably, yes."

Billheimer now began to pick apart the child's formal police statements. Ricky didn't fully understand what he was asking. When the lawyer asked him if he knew what a "statement" was, the boy responded, "I learned about it in school. It's a sentence, right?"

By then, Ricky was flagging with fatigue. He rested his head on a small hand as Billheimer continued with his gentle but relentless questions. There would be no break for the child now, not while the lawyer could continue to suggest he had been coached.

Ricky insisted he had no memory of his mother shoving him to the floor of the car in the instant before she was killed. Billheimer needed for the jury to believe that it had happened.

Without such a movement, the defense theory of how a struggle over the shotgun between Rower and Lawrence could have happened and not been witnessed by the child dissipated, contradicted by the forensic evidence still to come.

But although Ricky was tired, he wasn't pliant.

"Do you remember telling one of the officers in the ambulance that your mom had pushed you down to the floorboard of the car?" the lawyer asked.

"No."

"You don't remember saying that?"

"No."

"You don't remember your mother doing that?"

"No."

Billheimer tried another approach.

"You spent a lot of time with your mom, didn't you? You did lots of stuff with your mom?"

Fresh tears began trickling down the boy's face.

"Yes."

"She was a great mom, wasn't she?"

"Yes."

"She would never ever want anything bad to happen to you, would she?"

"No." Ricky's voice cracked with emotion.

"Now," Billheimer paused, "do you remember now whether or not she pushed you down onto the floorboard of the car?"

But Ricky was resolute. He had been told to tell the truth, and he intended to do just that.

"No, she didn't."

"Well," in his effort to persuade the child, Billheimer's suggestion now included not only Ricky's mother, but police. "If the police officer came in and said he remembered you saying it that night, do you think you would have remembered better then or better today?"

"No," Ricky was adamant. "Because she didn't push me down."

"Well, would you have told the police officer that that night if it wasn't true?"

"Well, maybe because I was sort of shaky," Ricky explained honestly. "It just happened, and I was real scared."

"Well, do you think you remembered better then or better now?" Billheimer pressed the child.

"What do you mean?" Ricky asked.

"Well, I'm getting kind of old, so when I try to remember stuff that happened when I was a kid, I have trouble doing it sometimes," Billheimer explained avuncularly, "and maybe if I had written it down in a diary back then, I'd remember it better if I had looked at my diary."

"Yeah," Ricky answered. Then, in a spontaneous analogy that reflected the indelible impressions of his own boyish heart he answered, "You know how the first time you hit a home run, you always remember that, don't you?"

There were those in the courtroom that day so convinced that the Ambrusko sisters had coached the boy that they were certain Ricky's home run analogy was also scripted. No child, they insisted, could have made such a comparison on his own. But, listening to Ricky in the courtroom that day, Eddie Lawrence's lawyer, Mark Spix, knew better. Spix was a ball player, a catcher on an amateur baseball team, and an agent for other, younger ballplayers still dreaming of the major leagues. More than three decades had passed but Spix still remembered the first homerun he had ever hit, the slant of the sun, the smell of the grass, the arc the ball made as it soared over a roof and fell to earth in a nearby field. As clear as yesterday, as certain as tomorrow. One might argue that Ricky's memories had shifted in the two years since he had witnessed his mother's murder. But Spix knew that Ricky was telling the truth.

But Billheimer was one of those who believed the child had been coached. Now he asked Ricky a grueling series of repetitive questions that placed a subtle spin on what the boy had already told the jury.

"Think back when you and your Aunt Joni were going over these statements a few days ago and you were looking for these mistakes. Were there any other mistakes that you made?"

"There were a couple of other ones, but I don't remember them."

"Did you and your Aunt Joni talk about whether there were any other men there that night?"

"Yes."

"What did you and your Aunt Joni say?"

"Well," the child responded, "I said there weren't any other men there that I saw."

"Do you know why that's important, Ricky?" Billheimer asked.

"Well, it's because I think that the man that did that to my mommy, or that other guy, was saying that they fought over the gun, and it accidentally went off, right?"

"Right," the lawyer said. "That other man's name was Eddie Lawrence, right?"

Ricky was amenable. "Yes."

"He was the other bad guy?" Billheimer suggested.

"Uh-hmmm."

Billheimer was fighting for the jury now. It didn't much matter that Ricky's statements remained consistent. Billheimer was going to flag every question, every answer with a reminder that the child had reviewed his testimony with his aunt. Billheimer wanted the jury to believe that Joni Ambrusko, not Ricky himself, had pointed out inconsistencies in earlier statements and steered him toward her truth, a truth that would surely end in Curtis Rower's execution.

"Now did you and your Aunt Joni a couple of days ago talk about the statements where you said there may have been some other people there?"

"Not in the car or anything, no," Ricky answered.

"But you don't remember talking with your Aunt Joni about your statement where you said there were other people there," Billheimer was insistent now.

"Yes, I do remember talking about it with her," Ricky said. "She was asking me a couple of questions, like did you see any other men or anything, and I said no."

"Is that when she told you why it was important, because of the story the other man told?" the lawyer prodded the child.

"Yes," Ricky answered.

"Do you remember any other questions Aunt Joni asked you?"

"Yes, but it wasn't really about that. She was asking me

my five times tables," he answered innocently. He had been trying to finish his homework.

By then, Ricky was wearing out. His answers faded to acquiescent, nearly inaudible murmurs. He agreed amicably with each of Billheimer's leading questions. Yet, he never buckled as Billheimer attempted again to coax the child into saying he had seen two bad men, not one, inside his mother's car.

"There was only one bad man in the car," the child insisted.

"And your Aunt Joni wanted you to say that, didn't she?" Billheimer demanded.

"No," Ricky answered firmly.

But, by then, two people critical to Rower's fate were convinced that Joni Ambrusko had coached the boy. One of them was the twelfth juror, Henry Parks. The other was Cobb County Superior Court Judge George Kreeger. Already unhappy that the child had been called as a witness in his courtroom to testify against a killer he didn't know and couldn't recognize, Kreeger's heart quietly hardened against a family he now believed had manipulated the child, and by extension, himself. Their tears whenever they heard the grim recitation of Sara's death now seemed rehearsed, intended to sway the jury. Their flight from the courtroom whenever rage and grief became too much for them appeared, not as an effort to abide by his order forbidding the display of visible emotion, but as an orchestrated strategy through which the jury might divine Rower's guilt. His sense of fair play was offended, and while it might never affect the actual outcome of the trial, Sara's sisters, in turn, came to believe that Kreeger didn't like them, had no sympathy for their plight or their tremendous loss, and held them personally responsible for his sojourn in Appling. They detected daggers in his admonitions from the bench, and came to believe that he resented their right to cry for justice on behalf of their sister. He helped round out the circle of their disillusionment with the criminal justice system as their fight to prosecute Sara's killers slowly became "a war we couldn't win."

That night, despite Kreeger's utter belief that testifying would damage him, Ricky Tokars snagged a rare, peaceful sleep from the Charybdis of his nightmares. "He looked just like Sara used to look," Krissy said. "The covers were pulled up to his chin, and his cheek was resting on his hand." Sleep, for once, had soothed his worried frown. "He could finally do something," his aunt said. "He could finally help."

For the next week, a procession of crack addicts, hoodlums, criminals, and runaways paraded to the witness stand to tell the sordid story of the casual plot to kill Sara for money. They were Rower's family, his friends, his fourteen-year-old squeeze who was both handmaiden and house servant to Rower and his cousins, the outlaw who sold stolen guns from an apartment in an Atlanta public housing development. All of them knew Eddie Lawrence. All of them knew he had hired Rower to kill a Cobb County white woman. To them, it was no more than a "sweet lick" discussed as casually as a supper menu by the soulless, wide-eyed, and somewhat bored young man now watching them from the defense table. Somewhere along the line, in the stricken neighborhoods and public housing projects where they sweated out their lives, murder had become banal, undertaken with as little thought as lacing up one's shoes.

Other than Rower's companions, the cast of characters was largely familiar to the grieving Ambruskos. Eddie Lawrence, escorted by federal marshals and guarded by S.W.A.T. teams on the courthouse roof, swept in and out of Appling to testify against the man he had hired but never paid to pull the trigger. The police detectives, tainted now by their movie deal and their dismissal from the Cobb Police Department. Rower, himself, taped at his own bond hearing confessing the cruel, abrupt details of Sara's death.

Only when the crime scene technicians and forensic investigators testified did the sisters voluntarily leave the courtroom, incapable of viewing along with the jury the blood-soaked images of their sister's damaged corpse or the ghastly pallor of a face now blank in death.

In truth, there was no place for them to hide in the tiny courthouse with its central hall where lawyers, journalists, witnesses, Fred Tokars's mother, and Rower's parents mingled with grim camaraderie. There, in the old hall, amid the mutter of conversations broken by barks of laughter, they huddled miserably in corners, curled on the floor by the old iron radiators, circled like worried doves about their frail and aging parents, isolated in their grief and a rising anger that Sara had been largely forgotten.

Among the investigators who pieced together the bitter crime scene was Dr. Joseph Burton, a forensic pathologist who was the chief medical examiner for six metropolitan Atlanta counties.

Burton was a fair, meticulous scientist who prized truth above partisan lawyering. His expertise was formidable, and he had built a respected, national reputation on his methodical medical investigations and a tradition of presenting the unvarnished facts of a case. He believed that a jury required all the facts in order to convict, and he steadfastly refused to interpret the evidence to reflect a prevailing theory of innocence or guilt.

With a face as chiseled as a Caesar's on an ancient coin, Burton radiated a clear and confident authority when he testified. Juries both understood and trusted him as he explained to them his scrupulous crime scene reconstructions.

But his refusal to compromise or spin the results of his investigations, and his willingness to testify as a witness for both the defense and the prosecution had made him controversial among prosecutors who believed that a medical examiner and his staff were tools of the government whose only responsibility was to help them win. Burton's testimony had once so angered a prosecutor in a suburban county north of Atlanta that the lawyer had derisively dubbed him ''Lyin' Joe''—a sneer that others echoed whenever Burton failed to twist the evidence to accomodate their theories.

Burton's testimony in Curtis Rower's trial provided the defense with two things they eventually exploited to counter Ricky Tokars's testimony.

The position of Sara's body as she died suggested that she may have been shoving her older son to the floor when she was shot, just as he had told police that fatal night. Ricky no longer remembered it, but, according to Burton, Sara was leaning forward in the car, her upper body angled downward toward the front passenger seat where her small son huddled.

The barrel of the shotgun was between four inches and a

foot from her head as it discharged. But the back door, as well as the car windows, was closed or nearly so, Burton said. The pattern of spattered blood did not allow for a door open far enough to admit a man seeking to grab for the shotgun.

"Could that blood have gotten there in that condition had the door been open and someone leaning in?" Charron asked the medical examiner.

"I don't think so," Burton responded. "I think if an adult person had the door open enough to be leaning in, it would create too much of an angle at the door so that the blood pattern we see on the glass wouldn't be continuous with the pattern we see on the roof."

Yet, the defense managed to turn that damaging testimony to their advantage by securing a cautious answer to one especially murky question.

Praising Burton as "the finest expert" in crime reconstruction, the study of blood spatters and forensic pathology "not only in the state of Georgia but in the United States," Marger posed his own alternate scenario.

"There's a person in the door of the car struggling for a gun held by the person who is in the car," he said. "Immediately before the gun goes off, the person that's on the outside—who has his hand inside the car or part of his body—goes outside the door, the door cracks, doesn't close all the way, but cracks. The person, having come away from the physical holding of the gun, spins around and the gun goes off.

"Is that consistent with anything you've said?"

"Are you saying the person in the car still has the gun that goes off?" Burton asked.

"The person's arm with the gun is being held," Marger said. For him to argue that Lawrence was at fault and that Rower never intended to shoot Sara, Lawrence's hand needed to remain on the gun. "But he's pulled away from the other person."

What Marger was really asking was whether Lawrence could have slipped just outside the car door but maintained his grip on Rower's arm as Rower fell backward with the shotgun in his hand, losing his grip on the gun hammer and causing the gun to fire.

Burton answered cautiously. He had already explained that the car door was either completely closed or merely cracked. "If you get the door closed good enough, closed fast enough to be fully closed in that scenario it would still satisfy the forensic evidence," he said.

A nearly closed door clearly wouldn't allow space for an arm. And if Rower fell backwards, how could Lawrence—a small man—physically maintain a grip on Rower without pushing his way noticeably into the car's interior where Ricky would see him? But Charron never attempted to clarify the matter before Burton stepped down from the witness stand that day. And Burton's cautious answer in response to Marger's garbled question stood as an apparent and uncontested concession in the mind of the twelfth juror, Henry Parks.

Sara's family wore mourning colors to closing arguments on the day the case was given to the jury. What nobody knew then was that closing arguments would make no difference. The outcome of the case had already been determined by a quiet but remarkably recalcitrant man who had already decided that everyone was lying—prosecutors, witnesses, and defense lawyers alike—and that Curtis Rower, not Sara Tokars, was the victim.

Sara's family had moved from benches at the back of the courtroom to one at the front where they were face-to-face with her killer. They clutched each other's hands as Marger—in a pewter suit accented with his trademark red suspenders—told the jury that Curtis Rower was, in fact, a guilty man who had made "a full and complete confession.

"He told police he was guilty. He's trying to tell the family, 'I did it. I can't take it back. I'm sorry,' " Marger said. "He is guilty of felony murder and there is no question about it. A lady who absolutely had no right to be deprived of her life was killed. It's wrong."

But, he argued, Rower lived in a world apart, "in a subculture in a country of great bounties where people cheat, they steal, they lie, they take drugs. That's what this case is all about."

Because he was "a better class of criminal," Eddie Lawrence was able to cut a deal to save his life after "he seduced my client into committing a crime he otherwise would not have done." Rower, he said, was manipulated by men with more brains, more money and far more at stake. Yet Rower never intended for Sara to die. And what happened in those few critical seconds in a dark car on Powers Road is "the main aria" to the tragic opera that was Sara's death, Marger said.

"Eddie Lawrence opens the door to that car. At that moment, he is recognized by Sara Tokars. She screams. She turns around. She knows something is going to happen. She pushes the child down. Eddie Lawrence reaches in and grabs the gun by the barrel. When he reaches in for the gun, Curtis is, at this point, pulling back. If Eddie is pulling and Curtis Rower is pulling the other way, Eddie's hand slips off the gun, and Eddie goes out the door. Rower swings to the right, his hand is on top of the seat, he falls down. His feet go up."

Marger suddenly threw himself to the floor like a sack of flour and began waving his own feet in the air. "The gun went off with his feet in the air," he shouted as if he had just discovered gold. "Did he accidentally discharge that gun? Yes. He was committing felony murder."

But, he argued, "they have failed to show that my client maliciously killed that woman.

"In all the years I've practiced law, I've never sat here and asked a jury to convict my client," he finished. "No one will ever forgive me for saying this, but bring back a verdict of guilty of felony murder against my client."

The magnitude of that astonishing statement still permeated the courtroom as Charron strolled confidently to the podium. "You know Curtis Rower didn't accidentally discharge that gun," he told the jury. "He wasn't struggling with a sawed-off shotgun in the car door that could not have been opened." Sara's murder was no accident. After planning the murder for weeks, Rower had laughed while scrubbing her blood off his shoes.

"This is a cold-blooded execution-for-hire," Charron said deliberately. "Nothing more. Nothing less." Ricky Tokars was the only living witness. And they, he pointed at the defense emphatically, "want you to believe that as Ricky was pushed down, Eddie Lawrence leaned in, and he didn't see a thing."

But Ricky's testimony was clear. There was only one killer. He had told police and the jury, "A black man shot my mom."

If there had really been a struggle in the car, "Don't you think Sara would have floored that vehicle and tried to get the hell out?" Charron demanded.

"Curtis needed the money and would do anything for it." If he never intended to kill Sara why did he brag about it to his friends and relatives, Charron asked. Why did he order Sara to turn down a little used road where he had already agreed to meet Eddie? Why was the gun loaded and why had he cocked the hammer back?

"It's supposed to happen," he thundered.

Sure, he acknowledged, "Eddie Lawrence got a deal. I gave Eddie Lawrence a deal because Eddie Lawrence was the only one who could get to the mastermind who set this deal in motion. That person was Fred Tokars."

Eddie, in turn, implicated "the triggerman and the person who is going to benefit the most . . . the most culpable people in a murder.

"Sara Tokars," he said, "only wanted to be a mother, a housewife, a loving sister. . . . She doesn't understand her husband wants her murdered. That five thousand dollars is what her life is worth. Imagine what she was going through in that terrifying two miles. In one last act of trying to protect her children, her brains were blown out."

He pointed an accusing finger at Rower, who slouched non-chalantly in his chair. "Where are you ever going to find more malice, more premeditation, a more cold-blooded, abandoned, and malignant heart than you see here today?"

As the jury and observers filed quietly from the courtroom, Sara's family remained behind, struggling for breath in a rising tide of tears.

It wasn't long before it became clear that the jury was in trouble. Their deliberations had begun amicably enough. The twelfth juror—Henry Parks, a bespectacled, African-American computer analyst, a fervent church-goer with a wife and two small children—volunteered to be the jury foreman.

He had always been polite, he had paid attention during the six-day trial. The remaining eleven jurors were happy to elect him by acclamation.

Moments after he became foreman, Parks made a stunning announcement. He would never vote to convict Rower of murder. Moreover, he wanted to acquit Rower of robbing Sara Tokars although Rower had admitted doing so, and friends had testified that he spent the money on drugs. Rower couldn't be guilty of armed robbery, Parks argued, because Sara Tokars was already dead when he took her purse, and you can't rob a dead woman. Nor was Rower guilty of kidnapping either of Sara's children because Sara, not Rower, ordered Ricky to climb back into the car, and Mike didn't know he was being kidnapped because he was asleep.

In fact, Parks informed his eleven colleagues—all of whom believed that Rower was guilty of malice murder, felony murder, armed robbery, and three counts of kidnapping—he believed none of the evidence and none of the witnesses, dismissing the testimony of experts and eyewitnesses alike as lies, fakery, or overly rehearsed. He completely discounted Ricky Tokars's testimony, insisting that the child had been coached so thoroughly that he was merely a prosecution puppet.

Rower, on the other hand, was a victim of his poor upbringing. The jurors who believed him guilty simply didn't understand his culture. Parks's own deep religious beliefs had sprung from his own impoverished childhood, one juror offered later. Rower, Parks insisted, "was just confessing because he was there" the night Sara was murdered. And later, "He was the only one to show remorse."

That afternoon, the jury sent an unsigned note to the judge.

"For the life sentence Mr. Rower received," it read, "is there any possibility for parole in the future?" Rower, of course, had not even been convicted. Kreeger reconvened court to inform the jury that they were not to consider a sentence. They were only to determine Rower's innocence or guilt.

Some time later, another note, signed not by Parks but by another juror, was delivered to the judge.

"If we finish tomorrow will we be permitted to see family and friends Sunday?" it plaintively said.

Twenty-four hours later, a note to the judge suggested that the jury, possibly perplexed by Marger's demand for a verdict of felony murder and Charron's equal insistence on a malice murder verdict, had stumbled over the law. Dated March 4, 1995, it read:

Dear Judge,

We the jury would like the written formal definition of the following:
  1. felony murder
  2. malice murder
  3. armed robery [sic]
  4. legal dictionar [sic], *if possible*

[signed] *Forman* [sic] *of the Jury Henry Parks*

Kreeger reconvened court, then read again for the jury the legal definitions included in his initial charge. The jury trooped back upstairs to deliberate. But Parks again stumbled over the definition of malice murder. The jury sent Kreeger another note.

Dear Judge,

We the jury would like to receive the definition for felony murder and malice murder again.

[signed] Jury forman [sic] Henry Parks

Again, Kreeger reconvened court and read the legal definitions the jury had requested. This time, when Parks returned to the jury room, he angrily accused Kreeger of omitting part of the definition when he had read it to the jury the first time. Kreeger, Parks insisted, "was trying to trick me."

Nor did the twelfth juror like Rower's lawyers. Parks said

he was outraged that Marger would tell the jury to convict Rower of felony murder. He didn't believe Rower was guilty of robbery, didn't believe that one could rob a dead woman. If the murder didn't occur in tandem with the robbery, then Rower should be absolved of felony murder, Parks told his dismayed colleagues.

The other jurors tried desperately to reason with Parks. They reminded him again that Rower had confessed. But Parks was adamant. Rower shouldn't have to take the rap alone. Fred Tokars and Eddie Lawrence were just as, if not more, culpable. As angry as he was at Rower's lawyers, as inadequate as he believed they had been, he still believed their theory that Lawrence, not Rower, fired the shot that killed Sara Tokars. Lawrence, not Rower, should have been sentenced to death, he argued. He was angry that Lawrence had received a less harsh sentence and had never been sentenced on either the robbery or kidnapping charges. Curtis had been the victim of manipulators.

"God has brought me to this conclusion," he said.

The other jurors reminded Parks that Ricky Tokars had always said that only one man kidnapped his family and was in the car that night. Eleven of them believed the child. But Parks insisted that he had been coached. His testimony was not credible.

Parks also dismissed the testimony of Dr. Burton and his reconstruction of the crime scene, saying dismissively, "He doesn't know any more than I do about what happened in that truck." In fact, Parks insisted, "I know more about what happened in that car."

Finally, Parks simply refused to look at or listen to the evidence. He ignored the other jurors as they reread the transcript of Rower's confession. He sang gospel songs to drown out their arguments. He exercised his prerogative as foreman and refused to send out notes from other jurors begging the judge for some relief. When one juror accused him of having some hidden agenda, he stared at her and refused to answer. Another frustrated juror decided he was simply ignorant. Five came to believe that Parks's decision was motivated by his race.

On Monday, March sixth, the jury sent a fifth note to the judge.

Dear Judge,

We the jury would like to know the following:
1. *Can we use expert testimony as evidence?*
2. *We would also like to hear the definition of felony murder again.*
3. *There is still some debate as to whether or not an undecided verdict on one count will dismiss all the other indictments as well.*

[signed] Jury Forman [sic] Henry Parks

At midday, the jury finally notified the judge they had a verdict. Although Parks still steadfastly refused to find Rower guilty of murder, he had finally acquiesced and agreed to find him guilty of robbery and kidnapping. But when Kreeger read it, he rejected it. Beside the murder counts, the jury had written the word, "Undecided." When Kreeger ordered the jury to continue their deliberations, one juror left the courtroom in tears. Within the hour, one juror—her blood pressure soaring—had been rushed by ambulance to the hospital. A second juror also required medical attention. Kreeger dismissed the jury for the day, then sharply ordered Charron to settle the case. When Charron interrupted the judge, an angry Kreeger rebuked him from the bench. "I'm talking," he barked. "I'm not asking you for any comment at all. What I'm saying, based on these questions, is it's time for the state and the family and the defense attorneys to sit down and try to resolve this case. This is the point, I think, that causes you to need to go sit down and talk, and you haven't been listening."

"Not a chance," Charron tersely told the media after he left the courtroom.

On Tuesday morning, Parks made a serious concession. He wouldn't tell his fellow jurors why, but he said he would agree to find Rower guilty of felony murder. Another note reflected the shifting winds of jury opinion.

Dear Judge,

We the jury would like to know if we have control over the sentencing of felony and/or malice murder?

[signed] Jury Forman [sic] Henry Parks

Kreeger again sent back word that they were not to consider Rower's sentence, only his guilt or innocence. But by then the jury was so angry and so polarized that none of them were willing to accept a verdict of felony murder as a legitimate compromise. Either they would all find Rower guilty of both felony and malice murder or there would be no verdict. At midday, the jury sent down a final note, penned by another juror:

We are in agreement on counts 2–5. We cannot reach agreement on count 1, nor do we believe we will reach agreement. Therefore, we are deadlocked 11–1.

Kreeger refused to declare a mistrial. In remarks pointedly directed at Sara's family, Kreeger continued bluntly, ''I think some people need to use some common sense because of the additional arrangements of this case that could be made that would be a lot more satisfactory to the state than what may come out of this jury. I just think some common sense needs to be applied, and some people need to review their positions and represent their clients.''

Rather than replace a juror for failing to deliberate, Kreeger was demanding that Charron accept the plea the judge had advocated all along—life without parole. But neither Charron nor Sara's family would buckle. Having listened in abject horror to the descriptions of Sara's murder, Sara's sisters were fervent in their belief that Rower's life was forfeit.

Once more locked in the jury room, the deliberations grew so maddening that Rower, guarded by deputies a floor below, could hear the jurors shouting at Parks. When Kreeger was informed of that development, he reconvened the court to declare a mistrial.

As Parks left the courthouse that afternoon, he said only, "God's will has been done."

A day later, he insisted, "I did what was right in the sight of God and the state of Georgia. It was God who helped me make the decision of what I knew to be true."

He brushed away the complaints of other jurors by saying, "I know that I did what I was supposed to do. I can say I did my best."

Other jurors said later that Parks alone refused to consider the evidence in the case, relying instead on his own instincts and religious conviction. The computer analyst insisted that his religious beliefs "allowed me to convict on the evidence and charges and not emotion."

In Parks's own mind, he alone was the keeper of the flame of truth. "The truth will last forever, and a lie just for a short while. I can say I did my best. I would have done it for Curtis Rower or anyone else. It was just the evidence. It didn't have anything to do with race or age."

And Charron, having watched a single juror nullify a killer's confession and a verdict, could only shrug: "There I go again. I guess it's just my jinx."

Twenty

All About Winning

FRED TOKARS WOULD DIE IN PRISON. THAT WAS CERTAIN. What remained in question was whether old age or the state would kill him.

Three years of living isolated and imprisoned in a little-used wing of the Cobb County Detention Center awaiting trial for Sara's murder and a verdict that could finish his life had worried away the flesh from Fred's gangly frame. His hair had grown wild as weeds. Scored by dark tracks his fingers had plowed, it flowed carelessly back from a broad forehead and dangled in viney curls along his jaw. In his infrequent court appearances he seemed like some half-mad composer or a bedeviled scientist who had sold civility and his soul.

Perhaps his gaunt appearance was the apparition of a guilty conscience. His lawyers would insist it rose from the despair of an innocent man.

It was not an image that Bobby Lee Cook wanted to defend in the northwest Georgia mountains where the trial had been moved to escape the publicity that had saturated metropolitan Atlanta. But neither did Cook want to defend the image of the slick, officious lawyer who had sought to spar with Assistant U.S. Attorney Buddy Parker on a witness stand in Birmingham, and who sat at the defense table scribbling copious notes on a succession of legal pads as if he were his lawyers' equal.

Such an image might well convince a Walker County jury drawn from the mountains of northwest Georgia—where people were notoriously independent thinkers suspicious of city lawyers, the government, and the law—that Fred Tokars was a guilty man. In fact, some were already leery of the notoriety they feared might tarnish their county.

"We don't really want this trial here," one woman said during an angry telephone call to the court. "And if it is, we want to hang him."

But Cook was a shrewd and wily man. He knew this county and its citizens like the back roads of his hands. For fifty years, as he ascended into legend, he had steadfastly maintained his practice just ten miles south of the Walker County Courthouse where he tried his first case and where a photo of his daughter, the first and only woman judge elected by the county, now hung among Cook's former colleagues behind the judge's bench on the courtroom wall.

Larger than life, now cloaked in legend, a dirt farmer's son who had become a wealthy landowner, Bobby Lee was still comfortable on Walker County's dirt roads and in its small cafes. And in that mountain county still largely ignored by the Atlanta and Chattanooga media, Bobby Lee knew that word-of-mouth was still the foremost, fastest, and most influential form of communication. He was determined, even before the jury pool convened, to suggest to the good citizens of Walker County that Fred Tokars was a polite, sadly maligned, and harmless man. He was someone's shy, bespectacled younger brother; an earnest, bookish uncle; a neighbor's gullible son who had worked hard putting himself through school and building a career until he simply got mixed up with the wrong people.

Sara and her fate may have been the heart of the LaFayette trial. But from the start, it was a trial more for and about men—Fred, his lawyers, the prosecuting attorney, Eddie Lawrence. And because of that, there were larger issues of ego and personality, of principle and old rivalries at play on the third floor of the old sandstone courthouse anchored by parking lots and pear trees. Women—Sara, her sisters, her friends—were vilified or patronized, dismissed or forgotten.

The trial wasn't so much about them or justice. It was about winning.

When Cobb County deputies delivered Fred to the Walker County jail the week the trial began, Bobby Lee escorted his client to the beauty salon on the town square where the avuncular lawyer joked and flirted as the nervous stylist cut away Fred's unruly brown locks, transforming him from eerie hermit to a gawky boy-child. And as she snipped and trimmed, Fred chatted engagingly with her about his mother and his children, the minor triumphs and escapades that would resonate and be remembered. He never mentioned that he was doing life in prison.

That visit to a salon on the square was just one element of Cook's strategy. The lawyer also stripped Fred of his three-piece suit and yellow legal pads. Unlike the federal trial in Birmingham, this jury would know who the lawyers were and that Fred wasn't one of them. He was, instead, just an everyday joe like them, or their neighbors, or their mamas' other sons. He wouldn't look like someone who would launder drug money, or engage in financial chicanery, or represent drug dealers that sold poison to their children and made the cities uninhabitable, or have his wife slaughtered in front of her babies.

Fred was never Bobby Lee's kind of lawyer, and Summerville's favorite son wasn't going to tarnish his own legal reputation defending him as one. For one thing, Fred wasn't very good at his trade. He cheated, misled, and overbilled his clients. He consorted with them. He intermingled his clients' legal and extralegal business with his own. He just wasn't that smart. And Bobby Lee wasn't defending that. He was defending Fred against the rot at the heart of the criminal justice system—the government informant. He was defending Fred against Eddie Lawrence.

From the first day that Fred appeared in court to face the Walker County jury pool he dressed as if he were a casual observer. At Bobby Lee's behest, he had surrendered his tailored charcoal gray and navy pinstripe suits for a button-down Oxford shirt, open at the collar, khaki slacks, and a V-neck sweater. In fact, he had a six-pack of sweaters, one for every trial day of the week, indistinguishable and undistinguished except for hue. As he took his seat at the defense table every morning, arrayed in canary yellow or kelly green or powder blue or burgundy, Fred lacked only a pocket pen protector to complete the image of a harmless, gullible, somewhat awkward and bewildered man. Bobby Lee Cook had reined him in, like some vicious, headstrong gelding. Fred was no longer in control. The jury soon would know, if they didn't already, that in this town, in this county, in this trial, Bobby Lee Cook was running the show.

For Cook, it was a grudge match. Three years earlier in Birmingham, his cross-examination of Eddie Lawrence had failed to convince a jury that there was any reasonable doubt as to Fred's guilt. Bobby Lee's patrician carriage, his moral outrage, his stentorian pronouncements that Eddie was a liar had failed to rattle Fred's former business partner and conspirator in Sara's death. He had never been able to crack Eddie's streetwise urban facade so incongruous with the lawyer's high rhetorical style, or rattle him sufficiently under oath. It was, in fact, one of the rare times that Bobby Lee had stepped away from a witness stand without a trophy head.

He had spent the intervening three years preparing for a rematch. "I'll show you we've never had a bigger liar in north Georgia," he pronounced to news reporters at Susie's Sunset Cafe.

He was a little more crude after he shoved away the remains of his lunch and huddled with a cluster of men at a large table where he held court daily like a feudal lord. "When I get finished with him, you won't be able to drive a ten-penny nail up his ass with a fifty-pound hammer," he bragged.

But there was more to that pronouncement than simply one more shot at a witness who had seemingly bested him in a courtroom arena. When the Tokars trial finally opened in LaFayette, Bobby Lee was also belligerently challenging age and infirmity. Seven months earlier, he had been hospitalized for quintuple bypass surgery on a heart he must have surely assumed would always remain as sinewy and tough as his lawyering. Fred's murder trial had been postponed while he recuperated, an expansive, driven and creative man suddenly forced by health and circumstance to rest for much of the day and trade decades of inhaling tobacco smoke like an elixir for the slick, stale flavor of a now unlit cigar.

He would never admit that the massive surgery had weakened him, even as those who had watched him for years in Georgia courtrooms now saw the strenuous demands of a trial sap at his physical stamina and suck the color from his chiseled visage. Bobby Lee would turn seventy at the end of the trial's first month. "I have everything I want," he growled at an impromptu public party in his honor. But he no longer had his youth.

More than age and a second shot at Eddie Lawrence were at stake in this murder trial. In its mirror was the dim reflection of a far older trial, another sensational Cobb County murder—the dual slaying of Warren and Rosina Matthews, both prominent pathologists, that had played out nearly three decades earlier. Cook had taken the case on appeal and won a stunning reversal by irrevocably tainting the prosecution's case. To obtain what they said were details of the murder, police had hypnotized a prostitute who claimed to have participated. Once she was in that highly suggestive state, investigators had extracted information that conformed to their theory of the crime. Her testimony—tainted by lies, hypnosis, and sexual relations she had entertained with two police detectives—was so questionable in its ultimate truth that a federal judge ruled that Cobb authorities, in their zeal to solve the case, had utterly trampled the defendants' right to a fair trial.

To Bobby Lee, the manipulation laced throughout the Matthews case violated every basic right the U.S. Constitution guaranteed. It smelled of star chambers and inquisitions, lynchings and witch hunts where women were deemed innocent only if they drowned.

His ardent defense in the Matthews case vaulted Cook into the ranks of the nation's foremost defense lawyers, fired into iron his distrust of government informants and coconspirators as witnesses, and cost then Cobb County District Attorney Buddy Darden his job. Tom Charron, one year out of a night law school, had sailed into office as the new district attorney on a platform that excoriated Darden for losing the case. But Charron wasn't really a reformer. Under his tutelage, Cobb

County criminal cases were routinely buttressed by the blowsy confessions of informants, collaborators, and jailhouse snitches.

Moreover, Charron was politically ambitious, a fledgling Republican who sought diligently to erode the state's traditional Democratic influence in the counties arcing north of Atlanta. Bobby Lee, on the other hand, was a formidable Democrat, a former state legislator who contributed royally to Democratic campaign coffers, who revered Jimmy Carter as the finest president in the country's modern history, and who had torn away the veils of deceit shrouding the Bush administration's secret money funnels to Iraq by the Atlanta branch of an Italian bank—money that built a war engine for Saddam Hussein and eventually sucked America into the Gulf War.

No, Bobby Lee Cook did not like Republicans. Nor did he trust Charron's lieutenant, Jack Mallard, a lawyer nicknamed "Blood" for his ruthless prosecutions. Mallard had prosecuted Wayne Williams in 1981 and convinced a jury to convict him as the perpetrator of the notorious Atlanta child murders. A decade after Williams was convicted, Cook had challenged that conviction after learning that Mallard and the Fulton County district attorney's office had withheld from the defense relevant although unsubstantiated information that the Ku Klux Klan, rather than Williams, might have executed the child slayings to foment an Atlanta race war.

In the Tokars case, Bobby Lee faced Charron and Mallard again. The Summerville lawyer trusted neither of them, reviled their politics, and vilified the raw opportunism and the cunning with which he thought they bartered justice.

To help him, Bobby Lee had enlisted Marietta lawyer Jimmy Berry, a veteran of more than two dozen Georgia death penalty cases who, in many ways, was the Cobb district attorney's alter ego. Where Charron was one of the county's increasingly populous northern interlopers, Berry was a native who still spoke in the rich, loamy drawl of the Georgia piedmont, a man with a neighborly manner that immediately set at ease anyone who met him; a man as solid as earth with the rugged, square features of one who might have drawn his living, not from office work, but from the soil and sun.

He possessed a wry, leprauchaun's smile and a self-deprecating sense of humor. Yet he was a formidable adversary in a courtroom. In more than two dozen death penalty trials, he had never lost a man to the hard corridors of Death Row, except for one who insisted on representing himself. Berry, who had acted only as a legal adviser, had locked that case in appeals for years. Juries had acquitted ten of his capital defendants. He was, Charron admitted, the lawyer who had bested him in court more than any other lawyer in the county.

Berry, like Charron and Jerry Froelich, had also earned his law degree in night school. He had devoted the first five years of his legal career to real estate law. But in 1978, after defending the relative of an employee in a county murder case, he surrendered his real estate practice for the less certain, more grueling, ambiguous work of criminal defense where not every man is innocent, not every woman wrongly accused. Berry wasn't a courtroom brawler. Yet, he acknowledged, he was addicted to the heady draughts of adrenaline that sluiced through every trial. "I love to try cases," he said. "It pumps me up. It makes me feel I'm alive."

Ego also surely played a role, he reflected. "If you ever talk to a defense lawyer, and he tells you he doesn't have an ego, he's a liar. You've got to have a little bit of an ego. You've got to want to win."

But Berry also was a death penalty warrior, battling a punishment that violated his moral code and taunted God. "I think it's kind of strange that you can have a law against killing people, yet the state can kill people," he said. "I don't think we teach our children anything positive by saying that."

He abhorred the notion that prosecutors could withhold information from the defense in making their case to a jury. "I think the district attorney's office is there for one particular purpose. That is to present all the evidence," he said. "He shouldn't care whether the case is won or lost. He should present all the evidence. If you're looking at justice and truth, then you want a jury to have all the information. Why not give it to them? Why pick and choose?"

Berry wasn't one of the true believers, at least at first, who swore that Fred was innocent. He just wanted to save his life.

But Ed Moriarity, the newest member of Fred's high-caliber defense team, was convinced that the media, the police, and Sara's family had wrongly hounded Fred into a prison cell. Moriarity was the partner of Wyoming lawyer Gerry Spence. The two men—Spence the son of a chemist and a teacher, and Moriarity, a scrappy miner's son, had built their reputations winning some of the nation's most notorious civil suits. After a nuclear power plant worker named Karen Silkwood, contaminated with plutonium, died in a suspicious automobile accident en route to a meeting with a *New York Times* reporter, Spence and Moriarity sued the Kerr-McGhee Nuclear Corp.—the power company that employed Silkwood—on behalf of her family. They won $10 million. In 1993 they successfully defended white separatist Randy Weaver after U.S. marshals killed his fourteen-year-old son and the F.B.I. surrounded his family's home on Ruby Ridge near Bonner's Mill, Idaho. During the seige, F.B.I. snipers killed Weaver's wife as she held their baby in her arms and later wounded Weaver. After a federal jury acquitted Weaver, Spence sued the government, winning a $3 million settlement.

But while Spence might play the giant slayer and rage and roar in an open court, Eddie Moriarity—modest, self-effacing, unfailingly loyal, quick to anger only if he felt ignored—was always his diligent, more circumspect other half. "I'd just as soon others have the notoriety," he said. "I do the inside work, and Gerry gets the glory."

When Moriarity joined the Tokars case, he was, he said, simply buying back his soul.

Moriarity had undertaken the case *pro bono*. And it was, in truth, a form of penance for prosecuting and securing the 1985 execution of a drug dealer who had once fancied himself the leader of a criminal syndicate that would eventually control Wyoming.

Mark Hopkinson had gone to the gas chamber at Wyoming State Penitentiary in Rawlins cursing Spence and Moriarity for securing the four murder convictions that cost him his life. Three of the victims were Spence's best friends—a Wyoming lawyer, his wife, and fifteen-year-old son. They had died in 1979 when their house was blown apart with dynamite, an execution Hopkinson had ordered from his federal prison cell. The investigation languished until Spence and Moriarity, at the request of the victims' surviving son, accepted commissions as special prosecutors.

At the time, "We did not know where the investigation would lead," Moriarity said. "We did not know it would be a capital offense. Neither Gerry nor I were trying to do it as a death penalty case."

Fingered by the man whom he had hired to plant the dynamite, then convicted of three counts of murder, Hopkinson became one of only two men put to death in Wyoming in the last forty years.

Although Spence resigned his prosecutor's commission after Hopkinson's conviction, and later asked that his sentence be commuted, Moriarity doggedly and successfully fought Hopkinson's appeals, even as it gnawed at him to do so. "I've never been in favor of the death penalty," he said. "I've always been a criminal defense attorney.

"But when you sign up for something, you have to do it no matter whether you believe in it or not," he said. "I had signed on to do a job. No matter what my personal feelings were, I had a duty to uphold the law.

"I, Ed Moriarity, don't have the authority to circumvent the statute. It does not mean I will ever do it again. In hindsight, if there was one thing in life I could change, it would be that."

Profoundly disturbed by Hopkinson's 1992 execution and the role they played in it, even though they knew him as a guilty man, Moriarity and Spence vowed after his death to accept, *pro bono*, one death penalty case a year.

"I was going to try to give back, to save lives in death penalty cases," Moriarity explained. The one proviso: "It had to be a life worth saving." His intention: to work a case on behalf of somebody who really couldn't pay anything, "some poor kid with no family."

Fred Tokars fit none of those criteria. Fred, in fact, was shopping for another hotshot lawyer who could be persuaded to work for him for free. In the months that followed his Birmingham conviction, Fred had in private bitterly derided Jerry Froelich, Froelich's defense of him, his competence, and the entire trial strategy in which he, himself, had played no small part. In Fred's mind, he was once more a victim—this time of his own defense team, he told his mother in bilious telephone calls from prison. His lawyers were imbeciles, incompetents. Blaming Eddie for Sara's death wasn't sufficient. They should have blamed Sara. They should have blamed the drug dealers and the killers he had counseled who never paid their bills. They should have blamed Al Brown.

Fred's federal trial had taken a physical toll on Froelich. In its aftermath, he was hospitalized with a thyroid condition so grave he spent days in intensive care and more than a month recuperating. He nearly died. Yet, Fred told his mother snidely, he thought Froelich was "just faking it."

By the middle of 1994, Fred had solicited civil and criminal services from an even dozen lawyers either in his defense, in soliciting his own book or movie deal, or in suing the Ambruskos for Sara's insurance money and custody of the children. He had racked up nearly seven hundred thousand dollars in legal fees. He had paid a little more than half, the bulk of it—$275,000—to Bobby Lee Cook, to defend him in La-Fayette, not in federal court. Froelich, to whom he had paid a little less than eighty thousand, had swallowed another two hundred thousand in fees and expenses.

Almost everyone else, most of them among the cream of lawyerdom in Florida and Georgia, were working for free. Fred had paid nothing to Berry, who had joined the team in 1994, nor to Atlanta lawyer Jay Strongwater, who had sat at the defense table throughout Fred's federal trial, penned some of the defense team's more cogent legal arguments in U.S. District Court and authored an appeal that had piqued the interest of federal appeals court judges in Atlanta. Instead, Fred had sought to have himself declared indigent.

But a Cobb County superior court judge had demurred. "There are some people who would be happy just to have Bobby Lee Cook," Cobb Superior Court Judge Watson White had said archly from the bench at a hearing where Fred insisted he had no more than four hundred dollars left in two small bank accounts. "You should have thought of that when you were a suspect."

Moriarity and his daughter, Michelle, who had recently established a practice in metropolitan Atlanta, would eventually bring that total to fourteen.

So need wasn't an issue for Fred, even though it was a death penalty case. Neither was competence of counsel, for the lawyers who represented him in Birmingham and who were defending him against the death penalty in LaFayette were among the finest in the state.

In fact, Moriarity rejected the first overture on Fred's behalf, made by his former fraternity brother from the University of Miami. But Alan Bell, now attached to a ventilator as he struggled to survive a grim allergic reaction to what he called environmental poisoning, persisted. Old friends, both lawyers, alike in too many ways to count, Bell saw each of them as trapped in similar prisons, Fred in a cell and Bell in a weak and sickly body that had confined him for more than two years to a bed. He wrote again to Moriarity and Spence.

The letters, accompanied by court transcripts, appalled Moriarity's sensibilities. Fresh from the Weaver case, the sweeping but separate conspiracies alleged both by federal and state grand juries incited his own deep distrust of government. His partner had once suggested he was "cophating." But Moriarity didn't hate police or federal agents as a category. He despised those officers who, in his eyes, shirked their duty, drank too much coffee, cut too many corners. He was a meticulous, precise, and extraordinarily logical man. The truth, not the devil, was in the fine details. And, after reviewing transcripts, reports, interviews, and physical evidence, Moriarity couldn't find enough independent verification, enough unbiased corroboration to convince him that Fred had been righteously convicted.

"After months of reviewing the facts, I honestly believed Fred Tokars didn't have anything to do with the murder of his wife, Sara," Moriarity said firmly. "I don't believe Fred Tokars was involved in any money laundering either." Instead, the Wyoming lawyer held, "Fred was stupid in a lot of ways for being a man as smart as he is. A lot of people as smart as Fred Tokars don't have a lot of common sense about people they associate with."

But Moriarity's image of Fred went beyond that of a gullible dupe of street-smart kids like Eddie Lawrence and the criminals who were Fred's clients. Without any corroborating evidence, he would say earnestly, "I don't have a doubt in my mind that Fred loved Sara, although they had some marital problems.

"Fred should not have been involved in extramarital affairs," he offered somewhat apologetically. "But, if you follow the state's theory, Fred was an adulterer; therefore he was a murderer."

Moriarity wasn't buying it. What was missing from Fred's adulterous liaisons, he said, was some palpable feeling, some emotional connection that would have made adultery a motive for murder. The $1.75 million in insurance, he said, was simply "a good investment" by a knowledgeable and frugal lawyer who was also an insurance agent.

Moriarity, with his excruciating attention to detail, became "the glue that holds the team together," Jimmy Berry would say during the LaFayette trial's opening rounds. "Bobby Lee is the general. Jerry is the wild man." And as for himself, Berry said wryly, "I guess I'm the silver-tongued devil."

Berry's first responsibility was to interview the jury pool from which the lawyers would eventually choose a jury. All of them were questioned individually as they sat alone in the jury box in the old courtroom, answering personal questions about their jobs, their families, and their beliefs, about whom they knew, or what they may have heard. Many of them had never been in a courtroom before. Few, if any, had ever been placed under oath, or taken a seat in a jury box or on a witness stand. They were nervous, intimidated, skittish, occasionally combative. Berry approached each one as if he were gentling a high-strung horse. He eased into his questions, leaning against the podium as if it were a back fence—an unpretentious, careful man whose speech remained colored with the inflections of the rural South.

"There are no right or wrong answers," he would reassure them with a grin as he coaxed from them the details of their lives. They liked him instinctively, these plain, hardworking, earthbound jurors who saw in him a reflection of themselves. More than that, they trusted him. He wasn't there to trick or embarrass, intimidate or condemn them. He had no ax to grind.

For three weeks, as Berry questioned more than one hundred jurors, coaxing and cajoling from them clues that might sway the outcome of the trial, the lawyer individually befriended them. In doing so, he became their compass point, a reliable star by which they could map their way.

By contrast, Charron approached the jury with the hale, hearty tones of the perennial backslapper. He was, after all, a politician. But his bluff, expansive style in this instance lacked Berry's warmth, his simple, deferential grace. And where Berry's questions were wide-ranging, Charron, once again, honed in on each potential juror's belief in and ultimate willingness to invoke the death penalty. His questions were posed to ferret out the faint of heart, those people too sentimental, too squeamish, too uncertain, or too forgiving to sentence a man to die.

For Charron, the stakes had gotten very high. More than four years after Sara's death, he had finally won his shot at prosecuting the man who had ordered her execution. He had chafed angrily as federal prosecutors usurped the spotlight in the aftermath of Fred's 1993 arrest in Florida. He had flexed his considerable political muscle as former president of the National Association of District Attorneys and quietly appealed to former colleague U.S. Attorney General Janet Reno to have Sara's murder removed as an element of the federal racketeering conspiracy so he could seek the death penalty unchallenged. He had turned to U.S. Senator Sam Nunn and U.S. Representative Buddy Darden, his old nemesis, for help in persuading Reno to delay the federal trial so the state trial could take precedence, a maneuver that had failed.

After Fred was sentenced to three federal terms of life without parole, there were those who argued that Charron simply ought to drop the matter and save the Cobb taxpayers money. Fred wasn't going anywhere. Why insist on putting him to death?

Charron had faced similar questions before Curtis Rower's trial. The editorial board of *The Atlanta Constitution* had echoed Judge Kreeger's stern recommendation to accept Rower's offer to plead to life without parole. But the stunning outcome of Curtis Rower's mistrial had not cost Charron politically. Instead, Charron's constituents returned him to his fourth term in office with a wider majority than ever less than three months before Fred's murder trial began.

Charron, however, had been stung by the Rower verdict. In its aftermath he backed a bill in the Georgia General Assembly that, if it had passed, would have eliminated the requirement for a unanimous jury verdict during the sentencing phase of a death penalty trial. Civil rights activists angrily labeled it "the Rower amendment." If Charron wasn't actually stacking the deck against his two most notorious suspect killers, Fred and Rower, he was certainly making a run at rearranging it.

It was during the long, tedious days of jury selection that Sara's sisters began their sad pilgrimages to LaFayette. At first, they came mostly in pairs, or small clutches of three or four—Therese from California, Joni from Florida, Mary from New Jersey, Krissy from the Atlanta suburb of Woodstock.

Defense lawyers had once again succeeded in banning them from the courtroom, even before the jury was selected. In a sweeping motion, former magistrate James Bodiford, now a Cobb County Superior court judge, had banned all witnesses from the courtroom from the opening day of jury selection—before any testimony was ever offered—through the entire trial. The ban was total and absolute, even after a witness testifying had been released from subpoena. Prosecutors had subpoenaed three of Sara's sisters and her father to testify. The defense issued subpoenas for the remaining sisters, Sara's mother, and her first cousin, Mary Rose Taylor. For a second time, they would not be permitted in a courtroom to watch the case take shape against their former brother-in-law.

Still, Sara's sisters were drawn to the courthouse on the square where they lingered helplessly in the corridors, keeping their haunting vigil for their sister because, Krissy explained, "That's what Sara would do if it were one of us."

By now, they were also afraid—of Fred, of his lawyers, of doing or saying anything that could be misconstrued or used to bludgeon them on the witness stand or postpone once more the awful, protracted wait for justice that had bled their lives for four miserable years.

By January 1997, when the LaFayette trial began, the Ambrusko sisters wanted to tell the agonizing story of their grief, of their fight to find and prosecute their sister's killer, of their sacrifices to save her sons. They wanted to talk about their sister, they wanted to counter the sneering accusations that Fred's lawyers made so easily or with such relish.

The enforced silence—that sprang both from their role as witnesses and from the civil battle to secure Sara's insurance, not for Fred and his lawyers but for Rick and Mike—had scarred them badly. They could do nothing to counter the scathing allegations of greed that Fred's lawyers made against them or deflect the suggestive attacks that scalded their character.

"I sometimes wonder which is worse, and how can anything ever be worse than Sara's murder?" Joni worried, as she clustered with her sisters in a basement room three floors below the courtroom.

"And yet, what these lawyers did to our family. A day doesn't go by without my saying, 'Is this legal?' "

They didn't understand why the case had evolved into a personal vendetta against them; why—after the federal trial—the details of how Fred had betrayed Sara and his children and shamelessly used their family still remained in question; or how anyone could believe that they had done anything other than what they thought was right.

They already knew what they would face once they stepped inside the courtroom as witnesses. Jerry Froelich, angry, bitter, and caustic, had warned the family's attorney during a conference over the insurance money, "Tell the family to go to Tom Charron and tell Tom to drop the case. Fred will be in jail for the rest of his life. Drop the charges, and, if you do, we'll settle the insurance and put it in trust for the boys. If you don't, we're dragging you through the mud. It will be bloody. And it's going to be on Court TV."

"Terrorized. That's the word," Krissy said. "Fred and his lawyers used Rick and Mike to terrorize us. Once we came into the system, they continued to terrorize us. They made us feel like criminals. If your sister was murdered, how could you not want to be at her trial?"

Yet they maintained their steadfast silence, unwilling to say anything that might cost them dearly on the witness stand, or cause a judge once more to postpone the trial. They still hoped for justice, although they worried helplessly that they might eventually face another hung jury, as unconvinced as they were certain of Fred Tokars's guilt.

The lawyers spent twelve days striking a jury. But the issue that preoccupied them most was the explosive debate over whether Ricky Tokars would testify for the prosecution in his father's death penalty trial. He was now ten, a serious young man with a heart as wide as the ballfields on which he excelled as a pitcher, a child old beyond his years who, despite his own terrors, had assumed the role of knight protector of his younger brother, his grandmother, and his aunts. On the playgrounds and ballfields of Bradenton, he zealously guarded Mike. At home, he was the first to offer his arm to his tiny, increasingly frail grandmother. When he found an aunt in tears over some memory of his mother, he would dole out boyish hugs and reassurances until he coaxed a smile. Since learning that a jury had convicted his father of arranging his mother's death, he had refused to speak to him. And, according to his aunts, Ricky was prepared to testify in a trial that might end his father's life because he wanted justice for his mother and because he would never feel safe as long as his father was alive.

The profound psychological implications attached to Ricky's testimony, and the role it might play in ending his father's life, genuinely disturbed Jerry Froelich. He had no children of his own but had spent hours talking with his own sisters and in-laws about their children, soaking in their fierce outrage that anyone would expose a child to the poisonous possibility of playing a role in his own father's execution. It strengthened Froelich's fierce belief that Sara's family was willing to do anything, and sacrifice anyone, to secure Fred's death. Unaware of Ricky's terror whenever his father called or fears perpetuated by the knowledge that his father had arranged his mother's murder and his sons' kidnapping from a distance, Froelich was certain that money, not a desperate hunger to feel safe in a now blood-soaked world, drove Sara's family to champion Ricky's testimony.

Froelich's anger, and that of his co-counsel, spilled out in impassioned pretrial motions where he argued,

For the past four-plus years this family has done nothing but pursue the death of Fred Tokars, the father of Rick and Mike Tokars. They have pursued this goal with the help of the Cobb County District Attorney and the media. They have allowed their hatred of Fred Tokars to blind them to the damage that will be done to Rick Tokars if he is once again forced to testify.

In fact, the Ambrusko family "stands to benefit financially if Fred Tokars is convicted," Froelich wrote, citing the civil battle over Sara's death benefits and the family's aborted negotiations to sell their rights to Hollywood.

This case is different from all others before it because Rick Tokars is now being forced, as a minor, to testify against his father in a death penalty action. Will Mr. Charron and the Ambrusko family be able to go back and correct the harm when Ricky learns that he testified against his father in a trial if his father got the death penalty? If the brutal and violent death of his mother had a detrimental effect on Ricky, what will be the long-term psychological effects of testifying against his father if it later results in his death?

But if Fred's defense lawyers were truly outraged that Sara's family would encourage Ricky to testify, they were also afraid of what the child might say. They had never interviewed Fred's older son, saying that Fred had forbidden them from doing so and from calling Ricky as a defense witness. By now, they also knew that Fred no longer talked with his sons by telephone. They couldn't predict with any certainty what Ricky might say if he were asked whether his father should die. They didn't know Ricky believed that justice for his mother now required his father's life. But they certainly knew that if the child were to testify there was a very real risk he might make some similarly damning statement to a jury.

The defense was also seeking desperately to allay the raw emotional impact of the child's agonizing testimony, fearing that it might thoroughly bias the jury against Fred, despite the outcome of the Rower trial. They had rejected repeated offers from Charron to excuse Ricky from testifying and substitute his videotaped testimony, including his lengthy cross-examination, from the Rower trial. Ricky should not be allowed to testify because recollection of his mother's murder was coached and he had no independent recollection of the facts, they argued. They refused to relinquish their right to question him in front of a Walker County jury. "We think he has relevant information," Froelich said. What that information was, he wouldn't say.

In a pretrial hearing after the jury was struck, Fred interjected himself into the proceedings and abruptly ended the debate. Midway through Froelich's rising, angry argument, Fred suddenly beckoned his lawyer to the defense table. The lawyers abruptly recessed. When they returned, Froelich notified the judge that Fred did not want his son to testify. They would agree to read Ricky's previous testimony in the Rower trial to the jury. They would not agree to show them the videotaped testimony, to hear Ricky's voice as it broke on his mother's name, to see his tear-stained face or watch him as he fought to smother his sobs.

Fred's lawyers insisted that Fred was simply sparing his child. Prosecutors and Sara's family were certain he was only sparing himself.

On the trial's thirteenth day, Tom Charron lifted his lanky frame from a padded chair he and his staff had imported from Cobb County, strolled to the jury box, and began telling Sara's story to a rural, largely blue-collar jury that knew little of the arcane world of money laundering and offshore corporations, or the seamier underbelly of Atlanta where drug deals, prostitution, and violence flourished. Before they were chosen, few had heard of Sara's murder. Those who had knew none of the details of her husband's Birmingham trial. Now, after more than four years of waiting, it was finally Charron's turn to convince them Fred Tokars was a guilty man.

The narrative was a simple one, illustrated by a large photo of a smiling Sara with her two boys—the one her sisters had distributed at her funeral. By now the story was also a familiar one to nearly everyone present in the courtroom but the jury. The end of a Thanksgiving holiday with family. A woman alone with her two children in tow, returning home in the dark after a long drive, confronted by a killer on her kitchen stairs. How she pleaded with him not to hurt her or her children. One juror began to cry.

Awful in its simplicity, the story rolled to its conclusion, carried by Charron's easy bass. A terrifying journey down a dark road. Sara's refusal to turn into an empty cul-de-sac. The shot that killed her, blood splattered on the windshield and her children. How the two boys resolutely plodded across a cold, black field for help that was too late. Fred wouldn't look at the jury. Head slightly bowed, he centered his gaze on the defense table's polished surface as Charron recounted how police began unraveling the corrupt conspiracy arching behind Sara's death—Curtis Rower, the hit man, the murderer, the man with the "pirate gun"; Eddie Lawrence, a criminal who hired Fred Tokars to represent him and then became his business partner; and Fred, the lawyer, the accountant, the "purported tax expert" who lectured law enforcement authorities on white-collar crime, who introduced his young protégé to a state supreme court justice and a city council president even as his marriage slid into disrepair.

Fred was secretive, controlling, a man unwilling to honor his marriage vows who denied his wife a divorce, threatened to separate her from her children, and insured her life for an extraordinary $1.75 million when their union foundered. And, as he was sucked into the whirlpool of a federal racketeering investigation, Fred finally arranged Sara's death.

"It is a case that the evidence will show you deals with ambition, blind ambition of the defendant wanting to exercise his political power and control people," Charron told the jury. "It is a case of greed and more and more wealth."

More than that, he finished, "It is a case of betrayal—the betrayal of a marriage and a family and the oath of a husband; betrayal of the security of love and the dedication of a father; betrayal of the promise of fidelity and the love of a husband; betrayal of his profession and his oath as a lawyer.

"We will prove the evidence in a road map that will ultimately lead to his guilt."

As Charron took his seat, Jimmy Berry stood up, faced the jury, and rested his hands gently on Fred's shoulders. "This is Fredric William Tokars," he said. "He is the one charged in this indictment."

In the slow, disarming drawl that was his trademark, Berry now began to woo the jury with his easy candor, drawing on the weeks he had spent quietly questioning them in the hollow courtroom, gentling and befriending them even as he persuaded them he was someone they could trust. They already liked him. Now Berry wanted the jury to believe him, too.

"I know you," he said, as, once more, he leaned against the podium as if he were a neighbor. "You know me because I talked with you a lot during *voir dire.* Bobby Lee," he gestured deferentially to the county's nearly native son, "is known world wide. He is an asset to the community, and you should be proud to have him as a neighbor."

The jury should trust him, too.

But then, they were special, Berry said, singled out because they would listen, because they would be fair.

"Let me tell you right now Fred Tokars is not guilty," Berry said with all the sincerity he could muster. "The state is not going to be able to prove to you beyond a reasonable doubt that he committed this crime."

Jimmy unveiled a photo, a smiling, tan and windblown Fred standing on a brilliant beach, his waist encircled by his beaming wife in a blissful portrait drawn from the dawn of their relationship. "This is another story," he said. And the sordid accusations, Berry insisted, that had brought Fred Tokars to this day and place derived, not from an array of evidence that cumulatively damned him but from the untrustworthy account of a single man seeking only to save himself, "a man the evidence is going to show you is a murderer, a kidnapper, a drug seller, a liar, a perjurer, a counterfeiter, a con man of ultimate degree, a man with no honor." A man named Eddie Lawrence.

"This incredible lie that Eddie Lawrence has told is fed by jailhouse snitches and by people who had an interest in the case and a biased opinion," Berry said.

"You're going to find out how Eddie formulates a con," he promised. "He's going to con police, the D.A., the Ambrusko family. And if you're not careful, he's going to con you."

Fred was not some sinister manipulator, Berry told the jury. He was, in fact, a victim—a smart but gullible man who chose his friends and his business associates badly, a man who was easily duped. It was Eddie, not Fred, who was a friend of the drug dealers who ran the city's nightclubs. It was Eddie—with less than a year of college—not Fred, the lawyer and accountant, who designed their chain of interlocking businesses as a money laundry. It was Eddie, not Fred, who had Sara killed after he learned that Fred had placed those businesses in a trust for his wife and then stripped Eddie of his company checkbook and his credit line.

But if revenge drove Eddie to kill Sara, a desire to silence Fred, his lawyer, as a possible witness against him also motivated drug dealer Al Brown, Berry told the jury.

Prosecutors had been barred by the judge from mentioning Fred's previous federal conviction in the racketeering enterprise that had also included Brown. Now Berry skated tauntingly close to that hidden conviction, suggesting that Brown was so angry with Fred for urging him to enter a guilty plea after his 1992 arrest that he hired a disgruntled Lawrence to kill, not Fred, but Sara.

No one ever investigated that possibility, Berry said, because the two lead detectives cut a movie deal that depended on Fred's conviction; because the media had decided Fred was guilty; and because Sara's family wanted the couple's children for their own.

It was a fanciful distortion of the facts that, to be credible, required both a conspiratorial frame of mind and a judicially enforced silence about the parallel federal investigation that had ended in Fred's conviction. Not in the four years since Sara's death had Fred ever suggested that Brown and Eddie plotted to murder his wife to exact some form of freak revenge.

But Berry was not deterred. "This whole investigation is tainted from the beginning," he said. "It's tainted by the family. It's tainted by the police. It's tainted by the media. Fred Tokars is a scapegoat in this case. And what a terrible tragedy this whole case is. A beautiful woman is killed by Eddie Lawrence and Curtis Rower. What would be a terrible tragedy, as well, is if Fred Tokars is convicted of something that he did not do.''

The prosecution's first witness was Sara's younger sister Joni. By calling her first, Charron was conjuring a living image of the wife and mother who could not bear witness against the man who killed her.

Three of Sara's sisters and their cousin, Mary Rose Taylor, would eventually take the witness stand, their testimony bolstered by Sara's friends and her father in a rising accusatory chorus.

Tom Charron would lay the foundations of his case upon their testimony—that their sister was miserable in her marriage; that Fred as a husband was an angry tyrant who neglected and misused Sara and the children; that, over time, Sara became as wary as a beaten child who, timid and unsure, still pressed for an escape; that she finally found "the goods" that might persuade her husband to release her and the children even as the federal money laundering investigation threatened to engulf him.

But Charron would leave the sisters largely to fend for themselves on the witness stand against the strident and insinuating cross-examinations of Fred's lawyers, just as he had during weeks of pretrial hearings in 1994, and as Buddy Parker had during Fred's federal racketeering trial that same year. Charron didn't want to appear as if he were hiding something from the jury, so he rarely objected to the harsh examinations of defense lawyers who pummeled the sisters with questions designed to erode their public character and, thus, their legitimacy as witnesses. They became fair game in a televised, public hunt for reasonable doubt while the prosecution, for the most part, allowed the distortions artfully suggested by Fred's defense lawyers to stand uncorrected. Sara's sisters wanted to fight back, to explain, to clear the air and clarify the record. But the rules of court barred them from doing so. They were allowed only to answer the questions asked of them. They were honorable women, and they suffered as their integrity was tarnished to save a chameleon of a man who now appeared weak, weepy, and largely incapable of the evil deed ascribed to him.

When Therese escorted Joni to the courtroom door that first

day, she said, "I felt like I had delivered my sister to the monsters. I gave my sister a hug. I felt like I was delivering my sister to be brutalized just like Sara."

The defense objected strenuously to the testimony of Sara's family and confidants who recounted her sour marital history; her growing terror of a husband who swung between tyranny to neglect; and suggestions that, during the last few months of her life, she might have become a palpable threat.

"We didn't know we were trying a divorce case," Berry groused while Cook dismissed the testimony as "rubbish the state is throwing before the jury to have a prejudicial effect."

But Sara's desire for a divorce was significant. Eddie Lawrence had always insisted that Fred wanted Sara killed because she intended to divorce him. Divorced, the lawyer would be ineligible to collect on the insurance that secured Sara's life. Divorced, she was free to testify against him before a federal grand jury in an investigation that lent credibility to her hesitant allegations of money laundering and her knowledge of their cash-only household.

Even as Fred's attorneys excoriated Charron for what they indignantly described as character assassination, they engaged in similar tactics worthy of the bitterest divorce. In artful statements only thinly disguised as questions, they subtly but surely distorted and undermined Sara's character, as if she were so undesirable and selfish a spouse that Fred would certainly have let her leave with the children and without a protest if she had really wanted to divorce him.

To counter assertions by Sara's friends and family that her husband used the family purse strings to control and manipulate his wife, defense lawyers insinuated that Sara was, instead, a wastrel in a tawdry profession, a spoiled woman irresponsible with money who, before her marriage, owned a Mercedes and sank thousands of dollars into debt. She, not Fred, was the player, who, as a nightclub marketer, had become friends with Atlanta athletes and had hired women, including her own sister, to model swimsuits and designer lingerie. She had drawn her husband into the business by introducing him to her friends and bosses. After she quit her job to stay at home, they suggested without proof that she eagerly indulged in spending sprees with her husband's hard-

earned money. She had a four-hundred dollar weekly allowance, a maid, an expensive car. The house was full of toys.
There were televisions and VCRs in the car and in her children's rooms. Her sons went to private school. Fred, they
insisted, paid the bills, the tuition, and the mortgage. "Someone who gets four hundred dollars a week might be able to
buy whatever she wants to buy," Froelich pointedly suggested to the rural jury, some of whose annual incomes barely
approached that figure.

Said Jimmy Berry, "She wasn't wanting for anything."
And, if it wasn't a perfect marriage, if Fred did indulge in an
occasional affair, who knew what drew people to each other
and what kept them together? Sara, Berry said, was more than
likely happy, despite what her embittered sisters said.

And, if every request for clothes or money was a weary
battle, a tug-of-war for control, Froelich, the bachelor, insisted
that, eventually, Fred always gave in to his wife's requests.
That she had to fight for it, in his mind, was simply beside
the point.

Those who knew Fred saw his hand in the attacks on Sara,
in the defense lawyers' attempts to characterize Fred as the
generous one and his in-laws as the villains who manipulated
Sara into seeking a divorce she never wanted and never intended to pursue. If sentenced to die, Fred would go to the
chair, they said, not proclaiming his innocence but asserting,
instead, that he wasn't a cheapskate.

But the mockeries of Sara as a loose spender were jarred
into perspective when prosecutors called Patricia Williams to
the witness stand, the first of two prostitutes with whom Fred
allegedly consorted, to testify. Fred may have given Sara an
allowance of four hundred dollars a week, but he easily spent
that much money and more trolling Atlanta for illicit sexual
gratification.

As Williams slipped into the courtroom to take the soft-
spoken oath, she didn't look like a tramp. She looked like
someone's wayward daughter. She was a tall woman with
delicate features, short brown curly hair, her voice laden with
the rolling cadences of the rural South. As she entered the
courtroom, Fred removed the dark-rimmed glasses he always
wore and laid them carefully on the defense table.

When she testified, Williams was doing time in a Georgia prison for violating her parole. Until she was imprisoned, she had never quite kicked an addiction that compelled her to buy and use cocaine and had led to her conviction for possessing illegal drugs. For twenty of her thirty-four years, Williams had been a prostitute. On Saturday, September 26, 1992— just two months before Sara's death—a man she swore was Fred Tokars had picked her up in the downtown hotel district just around the corner from his office. She was flushed from dancing, and he had paid her a single hundred-dollar-bill for a three-minute "date" in the back of the limousine he had hired for the occasion and promised to drop her off at a Buckhead dance club twenty minutes away. He told her he had "a dance business."

"I told him I had been a stripper and I could help him with his dance business," she said.

He was wearing a coat and tie at the time, Williams said as she identified Fred in the courtroom as the man she had serviced so expediently. The only difference was that when she had first met him he was wearing glasses with dark frames. He was one of perhaps a thousand men she did business with that year. But she remembered him because it was her thirtieth birthday and because the questions he asked her had made her mouth oily with fear.

He had asked her first if she did drugs. Afraid she might have to fight him for her fee if he thought she were an addict, she denied it. He told her she looked as if she was a user. And if she was, he persisted, did she know any drug dealers who might be willing to kill his wife.

"That kind of scared me," she recalled. "I asked him, 'Why? Is it because your wife is not satisfying you in bed?' "

No, he answered, his wife was divorcing him, she knew too much, and he had too much to lose.

"After he made that statement," she told the jury, "I was ready to get out of the car."

Three months later, in jail in Cobb County and falling off an extended high, she said she recognized Fred on television the night that Curtis Rower and Eddie Lawrence were arrested. She saw images of Sara's sisters begging anyone with information to come forward.

Williams said she called her mother first "and told her what I knew." Then, she said, "I gave the officers a note that I knew something about it.

"I told them I didn't want part of any reward, I didn't want help with my sentence," she said. "The reason I was telling this was because I'm a mother, I have four children, and if anything happened to one of mine and if someone knew something . . . I would ask that they have it in their heart to come and tell someone," she said.

Even under cross-examination, Williams sounded credible. Her replies were soft-spoken and reasonable. She loved her children. She was turning her life around. Jimmy Berry couldn't crack her. And when he pushed her to reveal where her children were staying, she slid into a panic so genuine that it lent credence to her statements that the thought of Sara's children had caused her to step forward. She clearly wanted to protect them from either real or imagined harm, and she certainly didn't want a suspected killer knowing where they were.

Her identification of Fred never wavered. "When somebody asks me something as significant as killing his wife," she said, "I would take a second look."

Three days later, a second prostitute who had engaged in a far more expensive liaison with Fred Tokars took the stand. Dion Fearon was a small, slender black woman with large, sleepy eyes and, despite a white bonnet that resembled a pilgrim's, the demeanor of a coiled rattler. Extradited as a material witness from her home in North Hollywood, California, where she ran an "adult entertainment" business, she flew to Georgia accompanied by a burly bodyguard who sat just outside the courtroom as she testified. Until Sara's murder, she had been a dancer at an Atlanta strip club, an employee of Lawrence Industries, and, briefly, Eddie's girlfriend. She had also been Fred's paramour.

Fearon said she had engaged in three separate sexual liaisons with Fred, each one costing him around eight hundred dollars—twice the weekly allowance he doled out grudgingly to his wife. During one three-hour tryst at a $150 room at the Ritz-Carlton near his office, he had confided that he intended to have his "nosey" wife "taken care of." Eddie Lawrence would do it, Fred told her, because Eddie owed him money.

She was sullen but straightforward as she answered Berry's cautious questions. She was a woman who knew far more than she said on the witness stand about Fred and Eddie's partnership and business practices that dallied at the edges of illegality.

Fred had bragged to her about insurance fraud schemes and laundering dirty drug money. He had confided that Eddie was a front man for their companies so the firms would qualify for minority small business loans and contracts. With her in mind, he had incorporated Executive Entertainment, Inc.

"I wouldn't exactly call it dating," she said of her short-lived relationship with Lawrence, although she acknowledged that, at one time, he had suggested that they marry. She preferred her occasional liaisons with Fred, which cost the lawyer $2,500. "I wouldn't exactly call it paying me," Fearon insisted as she explained how Fred had stiffed her for the Ritz-Carlton hotel room and bar tab.

Her very presence tainted the defense even as it bolstered the testimony of Sara's friends and sisters that Fred was a faithless and fickle man. She wasn't in jail, had signed no movie deal, and had been forced to testify against her will. She had no motive for tarnishing Fred. And she was dangerous when cornered. Berry hustled her off the stand as quickly as he could.

"She could have hurt us bad," he acknowledged ruefully after she was gone.

But Charron was playing a risky game. During Fred's Birmingham trial in 1994, Assistant U.S. Attorney Buddy Parker had decided not to call Williams or Fearon to the witness stand, fearing, in part, that because they were prostitutes their testimony might be summarily dismissed as no more than convenient lies. Surrounding Eddie Lawrence with such questionable corroboration, by inference, reinforced defense allegations that his testimony was just one more sweet deal.

Charron had no such compunction. Buoyed by the surprisingly powerful impact that Williams and Fearon made, he called two more prison inmates to the witness stand to testify that Fred had approached them seeking a hired killer.

The most surly and uncooperative inmate was a former

Tokars client named Reynaldo Victorine, a killer from the Virgin Islands identified by federal authorities as the suspected ring leader of a Caribbean drug trafficking gang that frequently indulged in murder to protect its illegal operations.

Convicted in 1991 of an Atlanta murder, Victorine had hired Fred in 1992 to handle his appeal. He insisted to authorities that he had paid the lawyer the exorbitant sum of fifty thousand dollars in cash and money orders—twenty thousand for Fred and thirty thousand that the lawyer assured him would buy the goodwill of a sitting judge who would make certain Victorine's murder conviction was reversed.

On the surface, it was easy enough to dismiss Victorine's claims as those of a disgruntled client who had demanded a refund after he lost his appeal. And Victorine was, at best, a sullen witness with a nearly indecipherable island patois who had given a statement to police only after they told him Fred had named him as a possible suspect in Sara's murder. By then, Fred had dropped the case but reimbursed Victorine for only a fraction of his fifty-thousand-dollar fee. Parker had refused to call Victorine as a witness, concerned that the defense might use his quarrel with Fred over money to suggest that Victorine had both means and motive to murder Sara.

Yet there was a disturbing resonance to Victorine's story. The killer had approached at least one more Atlanta defense attorney who had turned down the appeal because he knew that it would fail. The fee, whether it was fifty thousand dollars or only twenty thousand as Fred's lawyers insisted, was still extravagant. And anecdotes from his clientele suggested that Fred routinely inflated his own judicial role and hinted, without their knowledge, that his friendships with Andrew Young, Georgia Supreme Court Justice Leah Sears, and others enabled him to buy their influence. Such covert suggestions were outrageous and slanderous slurs on the character and integrity of the men and women who befriended him, more sinister because they were made in private to criminals to barter usurious legal fees.

Victorine had testified under oath at a series of marathon hearings in Cobb County in 1994. But by the time deputies escorted him to LaFayette in chains where he slouched on the witness stand like some glowering Buddha, Victorine had decided he would not testify, and refused to answer the lawyers' questions on the grounds that he might incriminate himself. Yet, prosecutors were so eager to read his previous testimony into the record that they insisted on calling him as a witness anyway. What that decision enabled the defense to do was suggest to the jury once again that prosecutors seeking to end Fred Tokars's life just might be willing to lie to a jury to obtain the verdict they wanted.

"Pardon my candor," Cook said to Cobb Superior Court Judge James Bodiford, "but this defendant is a bum. He looks like a bum. He walks like a bum. He is a bum."

He was also Cook's ideal and preferred form of fodder— a convicted felon, an unrepentant killer, a disgruntled liar. In two fractious hearings and, eventually, in front of the jury, he mocked and scorned Victorine even as he demanded, "What you told the detectives in this case was false, wasn't it? Isn't it true that the district attorney's office knows it's false? You're not worried about being incriminated, are you? The hell with the truth!"

To those questions and more, Victorine belligerently invoked the Fifth Amendment, utterly undermining what little credibility he might have claimed, until Cook finally sneered dismissively, "Thank you for your candor."

It was not the only time Cook openly questioned Charron's tactics. He and Berry were certain Patricia Williams had lied with the complicity of Charron and his legal staff. The two lawyers knew by rote the procedures of prosecutors who always reviewed prior statements with witnesses before they took the stand. Yet Williams had testified that she had neither read nor reviewed her 1992 statement to police with Assistant District Attorney Joan Bloom. Bloom had not corrected her while Williams was under oath, although she eventually acknowledged, outside the jury's presence, that Williams was mistaken.

Bobby Lee extracted that admission from Bloom again in open court, calling her to stand before the jury to testify that her own witness had, in fact, made several misleading statements.

"I did go over testimony with her. I talked to her before I

put her on the stand,'' Bloom said. Williams's statement to
the contrary ''was not true.''

But, she said, ''I honestly thought she was confused.''

''You didn't call it to the court's attention, did you?'' Cook
chided her. ''I did, didn't I?''

Charron would turn to one more felon to buttress Eddie
Lawrence's testimony, a convicted bank robber and diagnosed
schizophrenic who had twice before acted as a federal informant. His name was John Roberts, and he and Fred had
shared a prison cell while Fred was awaiting federal trial. Fred
had offered him ten thousand dollars to kill Eddie Lawrence.
He told the jury, ''Eddie was the star witness against him in
both cases and without his testimony there was no case
against him.''

In fact, a talkative Tokars had confessed to his cellmate
that he had his wife killed ''because he needed her life insurance to pay money he owed to a drug dealer''—seven
hundred thousand dollars that he was supposed to have laundered but that had somehow disappeared. Roberts said Fred
had told him, ''The crack heads weren't supposed to kill her
in front of the kids.''

What lent credibility to Roberts's statements were two
money orders that Norma Tokars, Fred's mother, sent to Roberts under an alias, and an uncanny explanation for Fred's
obsession with obtaining $750,000 of Sara's death benefits.

Roberts had no way of knowing that, since Sara's death,
Fred had for months repeatedly, at times almost frantically,
demanded $750,000 of Sara's death benefits from the Am-
brusko family. He was willing to kidnap and barter his sons
for the money. He adamantly refused to place more than $1
million in trust for the children. For months, he refused to
enroll the children in school or allow them to see a psychologist, telling the Ambrusko family, ''We need to get this insurance thing worked out.'' In letter after letter to the
Ambruskos's lawyers from his attorney, that $750,000 sum
surfaced as inviolate and utterly non-negotiable.

Roberts provided the explanation as to why.

''He said when he was acquitted, he would write a book
and movie about being accused of having his wife killed,''
said Roberts. ''Then he asked me, for book purposes, how

you would go about killing a person in prison.''

He said that Fred gave him addresses and telephone numbers of Lawrence's relatives who might know of Lawrence's whereabouts in the network of federal prisons strung across the country. ''He said he wanted me to write them down,'' Roberts recalled, ''because he didn't want anything in his handwriting. I didn't totally believe him, so I asked him for some good faith.''

That good faith manifested itself in two money orders, totaling $350, that Fred's mother purchased and sent to Roberts under an assumed name, that of his long-estranged sister.

Handwriting experts tied the money orders irrevocably to Norma Tokars after Roberts told police of the alleged murder-for-hire plot in 1994. Norma eventually admitted she had sent the money to pay Roberts for a $280 pair of sneakers for her son. She used an alias, she said, because Fred told her prison rules barred inmates from giving each other money. The brief note and the happy face she penned on the order were ''a joke,'' not a ruse, she said.

But the jury never heard the handwriting analysts testify or saw the fury of letters written by Fred's lawyer that reflected Fred's obsessive demands for $750,000. Instead, Charron allowed Roberts's testimony to stand virtually uncorroborated and thus vulnerable to the sharp, insinuating challenges of Fred's battery of lawyers.

Eddie Lawrence's credibility, when he took the stand against his former mentor midway through the trial, suffered a similar fate.

Following his testimony in Fred's federal trial, Eddie's innate cockiness had resurfaced. Warned that his testimony might be subject to an even harsher, more abrasive scrutiny the second time around, Eddie bragged, ''I can handle Bobby Lee.'' He was utterly unprepared for the battering to which he was subjected. He mounted the witness stand dressed in a navy pinstripe suit that was too short in the cuffs and too narrow across the shoulders, even for someone with Eddie's compact frame. Nonetheless, the contrast between Eddie and his former mentor was notable. Eddie was dressed as Fred had taught him, while Fred sat at the defense table in a dark green sweater, looking as awkward and harmless as a high school freshman.

Normally, Cook eased into a cross-examination, lulling his witness into a false self-confidence before he eviscerated him with the deftness of a surgeon. This time, Bobby Lee traded his legal scalpel for a sledgehammer.

With his first question, a minor discrepancy on Eddie's resume, the lawyer opened an unrelenting attack on Eddie laced with sarcasm, a sneering disgust, and utter contempt that lasted the better part of two days and led him to call Eddie a liar dozens of times.

"That's not the truth, is it?" he bellowed as Eddie attempted to answer his questions. "That's not what happened, is it? You're a liar. You've lied so much even you don't know when you're lying or telling the truth. Can you name anyone before five o'clock who can believe anything that you said? Why don't you tell the truth?"

The lawyer was combative and provocative as he cross-examined Eddie on the details of police statements based, not on tape-recorded conversations, but on notes of grueling interviews; on his grand jury testimony; on testimony he gave in two previous trials but had not reviewed in years. His tactics were calculated, intended to goad Eddie into qualifying his statements, or justifying rather than simply acknowledging his crimes; to stamp him as a cocky dissembler who couldn't keep his story straight; to lure him into a battle of wit and words with the lawyer that he would never win.

"You wouldn't have said anything like that because it would have been a big lie, and it would have hurt your conscience," the lawyer sneered whenever Eddie protested.

"You just made that up, didn't you? Sometimes, people lie when it's to their advantage and will help them. Sometimes people will lie when it's not to their advantage. And sometimes people will lie when they don't know they're lying. Which category do you fall into?"

As always, Cook punctuated his brutal cross-examination with questions that began with the artful phrase, "Don't you know," which preceded a sometimes highly imaginative interpretation of events. They were traps, statements masquerading as questions intended to lure Eddie into contradictions that would sabotage his testimony. Bobby Lee had employed the technique for decades, befuddling dozens of star witnesses until the thread of their testimony was lost in a briary tangle of missteps, misunderstandings, misinterpretation, and denial.

Lawrence was wary of such traps, having first been warned of them before he testified in Birmingham. But if he corrected the indignant lawyer for some perceived misstatement, Bobby Lee, his voice laced with a venomous incredulity, would answer, "Oh? That's not correct? What I just said is not correct? Oh, let's see if it is. Are you sure about that? Sure about that?

"Are you telling this court that I am attempting to defraud this court? Well, let's see if I can try to defraud the court again."

By the end of Eddie's first day on the witness stand, he was quivering with rage and fear. For those who knew the intimate details of the case, the discrepancies Bobby Lee Cook had sought to exploit were, for the most part, minor and easily explained.

But after Eddie confessed in 1993, police had failed to buttress his story with sufficient independent investigation of their own. Those witnesses who could corroborate significant aspects of Eddie's story, and who had testified against Fred during his federal trial, were never called to reiterate their testimony before the LaFayette jury. Drug dealers. Murray Silver, the lawyer with whom Fred had shared an office. The private detectives Sara had approached or hired. Although Charron had been more than willing to call prostitutes and prison inmates to testify, he dismissed the others, who had less serious credibility problems, as too tainted to testify. Nor did Charron rise to object as Bobby Lee's courtroom decorum vanished and he gleefully bludgeoned the state's star witness.

"I didn't want anyone to think I was protecting him," Charron said later in an answer that reflected his political rather than his legal sensibilities. To him, Eddie was a necessary but distasteful evil, and he wanted to be sure the jury and anyone watching the nationally televised proceedings knew it.

Eddie knew he had been abandoned. Bereft of his own lawyers, humiliated on the witness stand yet forced to hold

his temper and his tongue, left to sit in silence on the stand
during court breaks when everyone else was grabbing bottled
Cokes and coffee, Eddie simmered with resentment, glaring
at his former mentor as Fred smirked openly at the defense
table, unable to hide his pleasure at Eddie's discomfort. And
gradually, Eddie fell back on the glib, slick, evasive answers
of a low-rent flim-flam man. Which was exactly what Bobby
Lee intended.

"You're pretty slick, aren't you?" he demanded as Eddie
struggled to answer his aggressive questions. "When you get
through with all that double talk, answer this. Why don't you
come clean? I want you to stop lying to this jury."

And on it went. One man, a namesake, who had known
Bobby Lee for years and who came to the courtroom to
watch, offered, "What you see in the courtroom, that's as
much like the young Bobby Lee as you'll ever see." Aggressive, insolent, and eager for a fight.

"This," Bobby Lee said during one courtroom break, "is
more fun than I thought."

By Eddie's second day of testimony, Bobby Lee had in-
jected a subtle but ugly racial element into his questions, a
prejudicial edge normally at odds with the man himself. He
had ardently supported civil rights during a far darker era of
Georgia's history and had abandoned politics after a failed
run for U.S. Congress during which he had made an open bid
for segregationist votes.

"You don't like me, do you?" he hissed as Lawrence attempted for the second day to field the accusatory questions
lobbed at him.

"I don't like what you're doing," Eddie answered stoutly.

"I'm so sorry," the lawyer spat contemptuously as he
faced the all-white jury. "I'll let you put me in my place any
time you want to."

A short time later, the lawyer insisted on reading two utterly gratuitous portions of two letters Eddie had written from
jail in January 1993. "You asked whether or not I like white
ladies," Bobby Lee read as he flaunted the letter before the
jury. "I love everybody . . . [and] I like rap music, especially
'gangsta' rap."

"What," he sneered, "is 'gangsta' rap?"

In fact, Eddie had made Fred a dupe, the lawyer told the jury. Without prejudice, he had seen promise in a younger black man only to become an unwitting victim of Eddie's endless frauds.

"The fact is you have beat everybody you did business with," he insisted. "You're really a coward, aren't you? You're a coward."

Eddie's testimony was the climax of the trial. Yet the proceedings would shuffle drearily along for another month, dominated largely by Wyoming lawyer Ed Moriarity, who single-handedly slowed the trial's pace to an agonizing crawl. Enamored with minutia, less familiar with the case than the rest of Fred's legal team, an ardent death penalty foe, Moriarity grilled witnesses for hours, demanding information that often seemed marginal or irrelevant to the case. He was highly critical of investigators for not gathering evidence that other investigators still to come had actually collected and analyzed. To him, every detail was equally compelling, every fact as weighty as another.

"A man's life is at stake here," he replied angrily when questioned, even delicately, about why he asked one alarm technician to discuss the physics of dissipating steam, and a police detective whether he had traced the lot numbers of a Tootsie Roll found in the Tokars's home the night Sara was murdered. His own investigations were far more particular. Regardless of whether police had secured confessions in Sara's murder, Moriarity was adamant that they should have investigated far more thoroughly than they did.

Both Charron and Judge James Bodiford appeared loathe to curb the endless cross-examinations. Charron was, for the most part, unwilling to risk having the jury think he was hiding something from them by objecting. But Bodiford, presiding over his first trial as a newly elected superior court judge, seemed motivated by different sensibilities.

Bodiford had a boyish face and ruddy cheeks that gave him a charming look of perpetual embarrassment. When he was a young prosecutor, Charron had hired him as an assistant district attorney. But for the past dozen years, Bodiford had been a magistrate judge. In that role, he had been called upon to be a mediator more often than a referee in court. Eager to please, Bodiford was clearly more at ease with compromise, arbitration, and the amicable resolution of differences than he was with the control required to end the legal brawls that erupted throughout the Tokars murder trial. Governed by a basic sense of fairness, he sought as often as possible to forge unofficial compromises between the prosecution and defense. He was largely unsuccessful. For the courtroom had become a battlefield for defense lawyers who often took advantage of a judicial ruling only to object vehemently when the prosecution tried to follow suit.

The lawyers' bellicose and competing egos exasperated him. Under the unwinking eye of the television camera, defense lawyers, in particular, lectured Bodiford shamelessly—Bobby Lee in a patronizing, more patrician manner and Froelich like some neighborhood scold. More than once, Bodiford left the bench in a flurry of black robes to cool a hot temper he kept admirably in check.

"Bob, I'll have that other aspirin now," he told a bailiff after one particularly fractious exchange early in the trial—a request that quickly became a catch phrase among trial reporters whenever the proceedings ground to a stony halt.

And, as the trial stretched into its second month and winter faded to a cautious spring, the judge worried ceaselessly about the sequestered jury, locked away from their families, their conversations monitored, and accompanied by deputies wherever they went.

Largely confined to court and their motel, the jury had become visibly restive. Most of them stopped taking notes, and nearly all of them began to smoke. Whenever Moriarity rose to question a witness, their request for breaks became more frequent. They didn't like the Wyoming lawyer. They thought he was wasting their time and that he lacked good sense.

But Moriarity's tedious cross examinations had an unanticipated effect. As Fred's murder trial became mired in tedium and became the longest sequestered jury trial in Georgia history, the district attorney began urgently paring the list of more than two hundred witnesses he had intended to call, fearing that jurors would blame him for their predicament and retaliate by acquitting the man he had waited so long to convict. He and his staff began whispering worriedly in the halls about "the O. J. effect"—that a jury locked for so long away from families, friends, and their life would issue the most expedient verdict so they could just go home, much like the Los Angeles jury that acquitted O. J. Simpson did.

Every day, witnesses who had already appeared in federal court were sloughed from the list—witnesses who would have buttressed large chunks of Eddie Lawrence's confession to the jury, shored up the testimony of Sara's sisters, augmented and legitimized the now movie-soiled investigation conducted by Cobb police. Curtis Rower's confession. Murray Silver's flustered affirmation of Fred's fascination with offshore corporations and his first overtures as a tax shark who bragged that the I.R.S. boys were too stupid to catch him laundering money because he would leave no paper trail for them to follow. The private detective who confirmed that Fred was having an affair. The maid, who had witnessed Sara's will and who should have found Sara's body and made the murder plot complete. The federal agents who had investigated Fred and Eddie Lawrence. The prominent politicians to whom he had contributed so generously and whose names he bandied about so loosely. People who could unmask the lies of Fred's five-and-dime sweater sets as they traced the sinister downward spiral of his life.

What remained, outside of the technical reconstruction of the murder scene, was largely the testimony of criminals, buttressed by the women who loved Sara most and were most vulnerable to defense allegations of bias. Charron rested his case on the trial's forty-seventh day.

The defense called few witnesses of its own. Their strategy had always been to discredit Eddie Lawrence utterly and convince the jury—during lengthy, combative cross-examinations—that Fred was the innocent victim of some grand conspiracy among police, the media, the government, and the Ambrusko family. To further that notion, Fred had testified during his federal trial. In LaFayette, he confided to his jailers that he intended to testify again.

But, despite hints from his lawyers that Fred would tell the jury in his own words an alternative version of events, in the end, Fred remained judiciously silent, his clever arrogance, his air of self-importance, his contemptuous nature unceremoniously capped by the defense team's rueful acknowledgment that, if he took the stand, Fred just might talk himself onto Death Row.

Instead, they called Fred's alter ego to the stand, his younger brother, Andy, who strongly resembled Fred and who still looked to him with the open, undiscerning adoration of a puppy. As Fred beamed encouragingly at Andy, a collections officer in the credit department of a suburban building supply company, Andy recounted a childhood that paralleled Sara's own—a large family with siblings close in age, a father who was a doctor. Andy, who had dated Sara's younger sister, Karen, for more than two years, told the jury that he had always been close to the Ambrusko family.

When Sara met Fred in Atlanta, years after they had graduated from high school, "it was just kind of fate," Andy said. "I think they hit it off spectacularly right away. I think Fred was real happy." Sara was a divorcée. Fred "had had a few girlfriends in his past." They eloped, Andy said, because Sara's first marriage had not yet been annulled. "They wanted to get married immediately and not wait any longer."

Andy soon adopted the theme that had run through Fred's defense—that Fred was a devoted family man whose only fault was spending too many hours working to support a wife accustomed to living just a little too well.

"Fred wanted to make sure that Sara's lifestyle was similar to the lifestyle she had growing up. They lived very, very comfortably and had virtually everything they ever wanted. Fred was working very, very hard to do that to make her happy and make her very comfortable," Andy said. Every morning, his brother would rise at four o'clock, work in his basement study until nine, then depart for work where he remained until eight each night.

Sara "had a lot of possessions, a lot of clothes" for which her husband paid, Andy said. "Fred would make sure Rick and Mike had everything they needed." His brother, he explained, had imposed financial constraints on his spendthrift wife "to control her spending to a certain degree. She had a habit of running up a lot of money on charge cards."

Yet, he insisted, "They looked very happy. They communicated a lot. I saw a lot of respect. Fred always respected

Sara. She was a sharp lady. She spoke well. She was very beautiful.''

Andy went further than that. In his mind, his brother was as gentle a parent as Sara, whose family and friends had described her as a devoted Pied Piper among children.

Although his brother rose before his children and arrived home after they had been put to bed, ''Fred was as big a kid as they were. He'd get down on the floor, run around with them, play war with them.''

Sara's family ''loved Fred. He would make everybody laugh. He was so smart. He would offer to advise them.''

Congenial and eager to please, Andy explained the damaging insurance policies on his sister-in-law's life as simply a sound investment, ''He wanted to get a large insurance policy for him and Sara so that if anything happened, it would take care of them for the rest of their lives.''

Andy said he was honored when his brother asked him to serve as trustee of his will and his insurance policies. Sara, he said, didn't want the money placed in trust at all.

Missing from Andy's testimony was any description of the paternal and punitive nature of the trusts that limited Sara and her children to ten thousand dollars a year, gave Andy absolute authority, and placed heavy restrictions on its use, including a provision that decreed the money could not be used to pay the mortgage on the house.

Yet even Andy dropped an occasional inadvertent hint that all was not well in the Tokars's household. When asked to describe how his brother felt about Sara, he stumbled at one point. ''He seemed,'' he said and hesitated a heartbeat, ''I don't want to use the word jealous . . .'' He recovered quickly. ''He had a great deal of respect for her whole personality. He went to her for advice. He asked her advice on a lot of different issues.''

Noticeably missing from that description was any mention of love.

Fred's defense lawyers also looked to Andy to foster their contention that Fred had always cooperated with police and that his suicide attempt stemmed not from the capture of his coconspirator in his wife's murder plot but from his desolation at her death.

Fred, he said, "was helping the cops as much as he could. I didn't see anything other than cooperation." The police, he said, never questioned his own family, although he later acknowledged that no one ever contacted them on his brother's behalf.

When he saw Fred on Christmas Day at a Sarasota hospital recovering from his suicide attempt, "He was just a basket case," Andy recalled. "We've always been really close. We depend on each other a lot for confidence and spiritual things. I think seeing me really helped him a lot."

With that, he began reading the suicide note Fred had scrawled before he passed out from too many pills and too much alcohol. He choked with emotion as he read his brother's directive: "I want Andy to take care of my money. He is so strong and honest."

Tears streamed down his face as he read Fred's own explanation for his suicide attempt and his written insistence, "There are many people all over Atlanta who love me." Fred, too, began to cry—silent sobs that contorted a face running with great, sloppy tears. It was Fred at his most pitiable and self-pitying, and at his most genuine.

During his trial he had listened impassively to heart-rending descriptions of his elder son's nightmares in the wake of his mother's death, drinking coffee with studied disinterest while the jury remained outside the courtroom. He had remained unmoved as his wife's disembodied voice echoed through the courtroom in a brief, tape-recorded conversation with an alarm company on the day she was murdered.

On two other occasions, while the jury was seated—as his sons' teachers talked about the children, as a medical examiner described her horrendous wounds—Fred had cried, but only with great effort. He had summoned dry, quivering, airless sobs after first removing his glasses, then rapidly hyperventilating as he swiped at his nose and eyes with a large white handkerchief. They were performances, and he abandoned them for banter and cheap laughter as soon as he left the courtroom with his deputy escorts.

He had cried copiously only as he listened to a recording of his first interview with police within hours of Sara's death—an interview during which he sobbed uncontrollably in a stupor of alcohol, exhaustion, and shock even as he evaded detectives' delicate but persistent questions. This time, as he once more listened to his own words, he dissolved in a dismal image of public desolation. Once more, it was his own plight, not Sara's, that cracked his marble heart.

Andy was the last defense witness. After the jury left, Fred stood up to make his own plea to Judge Bodiford in an aggrieved tone that sought to justify and slip into the public record what he had declined to tell the jury himself. He had decided not to testify, he said, because Bodiford had refused to allow the jury to hear a single line from the suicide note stating he had taken a polygraph and passed.

The reliability of polygraphs remains circumspect and hotly debated. They are not allowed as evidence in court. Fred had taken a private polygraph examination arranged by his lawyers shortly after Sara's murder. Defense lawyers had never released the questions or allowed Fred to be polygraphed by an independent operator. Nor did they intend to do so now. But they argued vigorously that Fred had attempted suicide because no one believed him even though he passed the polygraph. Bodiford had dismissed the line as both unprovable and too self-serving.

Now Fred rose to admonish the judge. "Your Honor, I would like to testify in this case, but I feel like I can't because of your ruling on the suicide note. I didn't murder Sara. I was not involved in her murder. It's extremely important to tell the jury what was going on in my mind. I don't see how I can possibly take the stand and not tell the jury what was going on in my mind." He began to cry. He was being persecuted and, as always, it was somebody else's fault.

But Fred's own words and actions are what ultimately condemned him. His own prevaricating statements to police juxtaposed against the actions of his six-year-old son reflected the malice of an abandoned and malignant heart. He sat, head bowed, wearing a charcoal-gray sweater, as First Assistant Cobb County District Attorney Jack Mallard reminded the jury in his closing statement of Fred's stunning unconcern about his wife's safety, his attempts to shield Eddie Lawrence's name from the police, his deceptiveness, his chronic lack of candor.

"We're talking about a lawyer, a well-respected, influential lawyer," Mallard said, his voice sharp with the inflections of south Georgia. "We're talking about a former prosecutor and a judge knowledgeable about the law." Yet, with his wife's murder only hours old and knowing how critical those first hours were to solving it, "He gave a completely worthless interview from a police investigative standpoint because he had nothing to say." Mallard was outraged. "Contrast that to little Ricky Tokars, minutes after his mother's brains were blown out. He gave a description of the perpetrator, a description of the shotgun. He was giving an accurate account of what he had been through. Little six-year-old Ricky was able to cooperate with police. Were Tokars's words and actions consistent with innocence or with guilt?"

Eddie Lawrence, the prostitutes and drug dealers who had reluctantly paraded to the witness stand to testify against the Atlanta lawyer "are not my friends," Mallard said. "They're Fred Tokars's partners, business associates, and friends. And they're angels compared to someone who would hire a hit man to kill his wife in front of his two children."

It was left to Jimmy Berry to dissect the state's case against Fred Tokars and woo the jury into an acquittal. By then, Berry was convinced Fred was innocent of the crime, too naive to notice that Eddie Lawrence was a criminal but too clever to participate in such a haphazard murder plot. Yet, he ruefully acknowledged Fred's faults to the jury as he said apologetically, "This is not a popularity contest. We are not asking you to like Fred Tokars. We are not asking you to condone what Fred Tokars has done as far as adultery is concerned."

But, Berry was emphatic, "It's not about whether Fred had a bad marriage or Sara slept with the children. It's not about whether Fred had affairs." Instead, it was about Eddie Lawrence, the man who Berry insisted really murdered Sara— a counterfeiter, a liar, a drug dealer, a flim-flam artist, and a killer. Maybe Eddie was in business with the Detroit drug dealers whose names Berry had flung before the jury without telling them a federal jury had linked them to Fred in a criminal drug enterprise. Maybe, by killing Sara, they were sending a warning to Fred. Maybe Eddie was jealous of Fred for sleeping with a prostitute he wanted to marry. Maybe he was just a disgruntled business partner looking for revenge. "You aren't responsible," Berry told the jury softly, "for solving the mystery of Sara Tokars's death."

But it was Bobby Lee Cook in all his hoary majesty who drew the crowds to the Walker County courthouse that day. His mortality betrayed him, and he faced the courtroom audience and the television camera in the balcony more often than he faced the jury, as if he sensed that this argument for this acquittal might be among his last. It was the final roar of an ancient, raging lion being swept away by time.

A jury trial is "the taproot of America," he said, "the linchpin in the American system in which we cannot deprive a person of liberty or take away their money without ladies and gentlemen such as you.

"This is not just an important case for Fred Tokars. It is an important case for everyone. If the liberties and constitutional rights and fairness that the Constitution enshrouds in him are not protected, your rights will not be protected."

It was, for the most part, an older jury of his neighbors in that still sparsely populated county, one of the few that would absorb his references drawn from the Second World War: Anzio, Normandy, General George Patton's race across France.

Eddie Lawrence's testimony against Fred Tokars was a violation of those hard-won liberties, he said. Eddie Lawrence was the soiled anathema of constitutional due process.

"He's a liar, a cheat, and a scoundrel. If he said it was raining, I wouldn't get my coat and hat."

His voice rose from a rugged whisper to a roar as he bellowed at the prosecutors like a gale force wind. "That you could deprive somebody of liberty and maybe of life on the word of somebody so scurrilous gives me grave concern about being in the hallowed halls of justice."

But in the end, Bobby Lee's closing wasn't about Eddie. It wasn't about Fred. It certainly wasn't about Sara. It was about him. His creed, his nearly out-of-date and ideal belief in justice and liberty and patriotism, and his first reluctant farewell to the rigors of trial law.

"I've been doing what I'm doing almost fifty years," he said, in a soft, windy voice that echoed of an old pump organ.

"My wife says too long. The first case I tried in this great old courtroom was in 1950. I've seen a lot, a lot of sadness throughout this country to fill up this courtroom in tears.

"I apologize for getting violent. I apologize for getting excited. My daughter told me not to get excited. I have had five bypasses. I appreciate the fact that you are good citizens, good Americans. I have done my duty. I may have knocked and shoved and pushed. I have not cheated."

He paused. "You are not responsible for the consequences of the verdict. You are responsible for the truth of the verdict."

Bobby Lee took his seat as the jury filed out, then rose to greet a crush of spectators, his public, the salt of his earth.

The jury was out only ten hours. At 5 p.m. Saturday, they returned to court with a verdict. None of his defense lawyers had expected a verdict so quickly. They had convinced themselves that methodical jurors would deliberate through the weekend as they sifted through reams of documents and the testimony of seventy-five witnesses. Tom Charron strolled into the courtroom smiling.

The jury found Fred guilty of malice murder, a death penalty offense. As the verdict was pronounced, the former lawyer who had betrayed his wife and his profession bowed his head, closed his eyes, and cried. But the jury acquitted him of three other charges—murder during the commission of a felony, kidnapping, and robbery.

In reality, the verdict was a blow to prosecutors. They had failed to convince the jury that, regardless of whether Fred knew his wife would be kidnapped and robbed before she was brutally slain, he had masterminded the murder plot. He bore responsibility for every crime and consequence. But defense lawyers were the ones who appeared the most rattled and grim. Three of them now truly believed Fred was as gullible and innocent as Bobby Lee had wanted him to appear.

But the jury could never overlook or adequately explain the stunning $1.75 million for which Fred had insured Sara's life or find sufficient reason why Eddie Lawrence would orchestrate her shotgun slaying on his own. They had heard the taped statements in which Fred defended his business partner, had acknowledged the omission of Eddie's name in the list of suspects the lawyer gave police. If Eddie was as criminal a liar as Bobby Lee proclaimed, Fred should have named him as an embittered business partner who might carry an ugly grudge.

Yet, the jurors were fair-minded. And if they believed Eddie Lawrence, they had to believe that Fred had told him to kill Sara at the house, that he knew nothing of the kidnap, or Sara's final, terror-filled ride, or the robbery. They acquitted him of those charges and felony murder, believing that by hiring Curtis Rower instead of carrying out the plan himself, Eddie, and not Fred, was accountable for those crimes.

Only the jury knew that the verdict also represented a compromise with two older, retired jurors who had wanted to acquit Fred because they did not want to see him die.

"We have to regroup," was all Jimmy Berry could say as he stumbled down a rear stairwell from the third-floor courtroom after the jury was dismissed for the night. "We may have lost the battle, but we haven't lost the war."

At the jury's request, court reconvened the following day—a Sunday—at 8 a.m. to hear evidence on which jurors would rest their decision either to spare Fred's life or condemn him to execution. State law had prevented them until now from learning anything of Fred's federal conviction or his sentences to life without parole for his part in a vast drug conspiracy that included arranging Sara's kidnapping, her robbery, and murder. On Sunday, Tom Charron stood and read to them the thirty-page federal indictment. As the names of the Detroit drug dealers rang through the courtroom together with the litany of nightclubs that Fred incorporated; as the drug crimes, the assaults, the conspiracies, and Sara's kidnap and murder were enumerated; the effect on the jury was dramatic. They were visibly stunned, then angry. They recognized the names Al Brown, James Mason, and Julius Cline, which defense lawyers had flung at them as they sought to sully Eddie. They now heard Fred described as "the money launderer" for those sinister men. The defense had lied to them. They had issued a verdict that was more than fair only to find they had been misled.

There was more to come. For in the life or death phase of the trial, Sara's family and friends could finally go before the

jury and lay bare the raw agony of their loss. Eight of them—
a nephew, three sisters, her father, several friends and neighbors—for the first time told Sara's story and theirs. Derek
Schaeffer, a San Diego college student and Sara's nephew,
sobbed uncontrollably as he told the jury, "Along with the
death of Sara came the death of part of my soul. And all I
have left is the memories."

Heartrending in their stark simplicity, the stories introduced
Sara to the jury not as a thoughtless spendthrift or a somewhat
spoiled divorcée but as she truly was—a generous, genuine,
selfless woman devoted to her family and dedicated to her
friends, a woman most often found playing on the floor with
the children at family gatherings.

"She had so much love to give," Schaeffer said. "She
never went anywhere without a smile."

As each witness told how Sara's loss had scarred his or her
life, tears trickled down the faces of spectators and jurors
alike. Tokars himself caught a ragged breath and soon began
to cry.

"Sara found a way to continue to be the heartbeat of our
family," explained her sister Therese as tears threatened to
choke her into silence. "Whenever there was a crisis or a
reason to celebrate, Sara would pack the boys in the car and
be there for the crisis or plan the celebration, no matter what
it took." A mother's surgery. The return of Joni's husband,
a Navy fighter pilot, from the Persian Gulf. Her father's
seventy-fifth birthday.

"She was the angel of the neighborhood," said Patricia
Tatum Rhodes. "She was fun. She was light. She was sunshine. None of us will ever be the same."

Sunday's testimony surged through the quiet courtroom in
a rolling sea change that devastated the defense. Fred's attorneys caught the icy stares, saw the outrage and betrayal in
the jury's faces. They were seasoned lawyers, yet the change
in the jury shook them to their core. What had once seemed
improbable—that a jury would condemn a man to death on
the slurred word of Eddie Lawrence—now loomed as a
frightening likelihood.

They would present their own powerful counterdefense
when court reconvened two days later. And among those who

took the witness stand on Fred's behalf was his defense lawyer, Jerry Froelich, who crossed the line from advocate to
witness with alacrity.

The fight to acquit Fred Tokars had grown so personal that,
for weeks, Froelich had been threatening to testify, insisting
that no one knew the case as well as he did and no one could
counter better the testimony of prosecution witnesses.

"They read parts of the indictment that were not related to
Fred Tokars," Froelich insisted angrily. "There's no way I
could stand by, allowing such misleading testimony to go in."

It was Froelich at his most outrageous, and a serious gamble for the defense, who risked revelations under cross-
examination that might normally be shielded by
attorney-client privilege. Yet Froelich was right about one
thing. He did know the federal case better than Tom Charron.
So when Froelich gave the jury his own interpretation of
Fred's federal conviction, Charron failed to challenge several
bold mischaracterizations.

Froelich told the jury there was "no evidence Mr. Tokars
was ever involved in drug dealing or drugs" without mentioning the defense had fought successfully to exclude that
testimony from the federal trial. He also swore "there was
no evidence of money going offshore," ignoring the notations
in Fred's personal calendars regarding significant Caribbean
bank deposits and wire transfers, as well as the trail of bank
accounts and offshore corporations that Sara had once copied
from his safe. He also characterized Fred's money laundering
as the activities of an attorney who had set up corporations
for a fee. Finally, he told the jury that Fred's conviction included his wife's murder, although the murder-for-hire charge
had been stricken from the indictment.

Over Charron's outraged objections, Bodiford qualified
Froelich as an expert witness and allowed him to tell the jury
that Fred would never get out of federal prison, even though
the defense was still aggressively appealing Fred's federal
sentence.

But, Froelich told the jury disarmingly, "The Supreme
Court receives fifteen to twenty thousand appeals a year. I
think they rule on about a hundred."

Finally, Froelich insisted that Eddie Lawrence would never

serve out his life sentence in a Georgia prison because he was a protected federal witness. "In reality, the federal government will not allow him to go into a state institution," Froelich asserted. Eddie, he avowed, would be out in seven years, even though his federal sentence was for an even dozen. But Fred, he said, "will never be released from prison. He will have to die in prison."

If there were those on the jury who didn't want Fred to die yet couldn't abide the possibility of parole, Froelich had just handed them a reason to be merciful.

Then, for the first time since Sara's death, Fred's family stepped into the awkward, embarrassed spotlight to plead for the life of a brother and son. Jerome Tokars, the oldest brother and a physician working for the Centers for Disease Prevention and Control in Atlanta, had accompanied his mother to the courtroom. He had long been estranged from his younger brother for reasons that the few who knew would not divulge. Now he asked the jury to spare Fred for his mother's sake.

When his father died in 1990, Fred was the son to whom his mother turned for solace, Jerome told the jury. Norma Tokars had been "heartbroken, very upset as were we all," when Sara was murdered. She now volunteered at a Decatur church. She visited her imprisoned younger son every Saturday and Sunday. "She is always there," he said. "She rarely misses a day." She talked to Fred daily. If Fred were executed, his brother said, "It would be a devastation for my mother. She is very convinced he is innocent. She is very broken-hearted about this whole episode."

What effect would Fred's death have on him? "I am not sure I can find the right words," he answered. "For the last four years, we've been living a horror story with a sense of impending doom. . . . Execution is the worst thing I can imagine happening to me. The Fred Tokars I knew, and know, is a generous, decent person, and please, do not kill him." At the defense table, Fred began to weep.

After leaving the witness stand, Jerome escorted his tiny mother into the courtroom to testify. She had traded her sneakers and the casual attire she had worn to other trials, where she often sat reading or working crossword puzzles,

for a dark floral print and a black jacket. Her angular face
was set. Sara's sisters watched her coldly.

"I'm not okay," she told Fred's lawyer stiffly. She didn't
want to answer any questions. She wanted to read a statement.

"Please don't kill my son," she read in a tough, dry voice
of suppressed emotion. "I beg you to spare my son's life."

Losing her husband had been "terrifying and dreadful,"
she said. "In the weeks following my husband's death, I
would wake up lonely, anxious, and depressed. Every morning for weeks, I would dial Fred at 5 a.m. in Atlanta. He
would pick up the phone, and we would talk and talk. No son
showed more compassion and understanding and patience
than he did."

Fred's sons, she insisted, "were content and happy to be
with their dad. They slept in the same bed, squished together
with Fred in the middle. Clearly, I could see they loved one
another. To this day he writes them every day."

Since his incarceration, her son had begun to pray, she said.
"I haven't touched or hugged or held Fred in two-and-a-half
years. Our greeting is hands on the glass." Each time they
parted, he would signal her, "Be strong, and chin up," she
said. "I'll take that the rest of my life." It was a poignant
plea from a mother asking a jury that included at least two
women like her, a older widow and a retired nurse, to spare
her son's life for her sake rather than his own.

The Ambrusko sisters listened stonily, seething with the
bitter knowledge that they could never hug their sister again,
that, unlike Norma and her son, they could never see or talk
with Sara except in their prayers and dreams.

Fred's younger sister, Lisa Aydin, dissolved in tears soon
after she was sworn in as a witness. But like her oldest
brother, her memories of her brother reflected a family relationship far more distant than that of the Ambrusko sisters.
She described him as if he were a distant memory in a high
school year book, "a good blocker" on the football team, a
swim team member, "a real comedian."

When Lisa married an Iranian who was seeking permanent
residency and American citizenship, she had turned to her
brother for help. "He set us up with an immigration lawyer,"
she said. "We were really young and confused, and I knew

that Fred would help me. I didn't have any doubts."

At times, it sounded as if she was grasping for an elusive closeness that never quite materialized. Lisa told the jury that when her father was hospitalized during his final illness, her brother had bustled through the intensive care unit, shuffling papers officially and complaining, "Why isn't there a phone? I have to make some calls."

"It helped my dad recover," she said. "He was really proud of Fred."

Like her older brother, Lisa pleaded with the jury to spare her brother for her mother's sake. But the language of familial intimacy was as hard and awkward for her as it was for her brothers, Jerome and Andy. "I have to take care of two little girls," she told the jury when asked what would happen to her family if Fred were executed. "If anything happened to him, it would be really stressful. It would be hard to be happy."

Norma Tokars's plea would influence two women on the jury, women identified by the court observers who came daily and who knew them with the neighborly intimacy prevalent in a still small, southern town as "King James Christians." God was their backbone. Their beliefs were grounded in a New Testament that chided men and women for casting the first stone; the plain religion of church meetings and summer revivals that was grounded in forgiveness and redemption.

That was the hymnal chord to which the defense was building. Redemption even in confinement. The value of a human life to others, even one who had forfeited the life of his wife and laid bare with grief the lives of her children, her family and her friends.

Virginia Proctor had lived in Atlanta for nearly fifty years. She was Norma Tokars's neighbor, a nurse and a lay minister who had studied theology at Emory University. She began a correspondence with Fred after he was jailed for Sara's murder.

"I believe with all my heart this is a man who can be rehabilitated and still has a contribution he can make, whether in confinement or otherwise," she testified. "I so firmly feel that Fred, with the help of divine intervention, can reinvent his life and make a contribution, even though it may be in confinement.

"I feel very strongly in the sacredness of life. I am not convinced we really have the right or privilege to take a life."

That opposition to the death penalty should not have had an impact on jurors who had sworn before they were selected that they could administer the death penalty if it were warranted by the evidence and the law. But that simple statement and the calm, clear strength of her beliefs would resonate through the verdict.

From Proctor and from Hosea Batton, Fred's former supervisor at the National Cash Register Corporation, came the testimonials that Fred had found God and been saved.

Batton, a dedicated Christian, had begun trying to reach Fred in prison after he was sentenced to life without parole in Birmingham. "I was very interested in Fred's soul," he told the jury. "The Lord could do him an awful lot of good."

When Fred learned of Batton's overtures, he had called his former employer at home. "Guess what?" Batton's wife told her husband after she took the call. "Fred has been saved."

There were those in the courtroom that day who were certain that Fred's jailhouse conversion was just another ploy executed by a calculating man who had long since traded a conscience for expediency. For every inmate who found God, there were dozens more who saw a public conversion as a tool to win privileges or parole, to shorten their sentences or to escape Death Row. And in keeping with those more cynical professions of belief, Fred never admitted his sin, never showed remorse, and never sought absolution.

Instead, he nodded approvingly at Proctor's words. And as Batton testified, he once again began to gasp for breath and wipe his tearless eyes in yet another bid for sympathy.

"We just talked about his reading his Bible and praying," Batton said as he recounted his single visit with Fred. From that visit and a half-dozen telephone calls, Batton told the jury he was convinced that Fred's conversion was genuine.

"Fred had definitely had an experience with the Lord. I'm here to say that I believe Fred has made a change."

But it was Fred's former college fraternity brother, Alan Bell, whose testimony realized the Ambrusko sisters' deepest dread. Bell invoked Sara's sons in his plea to the jury to save his old friend's life.

Sucking oxygen from a portable tank, his body wracked by crippling chemical sensitivities that had forced him to live in virtual isolation, Bell told the jury, "I believe Ricky and Mikey are going to want to meet their father face to face, to talk to him, look at him, hear him, judge him, feel him and decide for themselves who he is and what he did. Give them the opportunity to do that."

Ricky, said Bell, would one day realize that his testimony against Curtis Rower had become evidence against his father. "Please don't put Ricky in a situation where he could be haunted and taunted for the rest of his life with guilt and the burden of thinking that his testimony helped to kill his father," he pleaded.

It was a powerful statement, the argument that the Ambrusko sisters had unsuccessfully urged Tom Charron to let them counter when they had testified about the impact of Sara's death. For the truth, they said, was that Rick and Mike were terrified of their father, a man they knew now had ordered their mother's murder and placed their own lives in jeopardy. The children's psychologists had said the execution of their father might ultimately relieve the boys' grave anxieties that Fred might also arrange their deaths as he had once arranged their mother's.

Ricky had already testified against the gunman who, as the child had watched, had stolen his mother's life. What the jury didn't know was that the boy, now ten, had been equally willing to take the stand once more—this time at the murder trial of a man he no longer accepted as his father. He had hand-picked the song that accompanied a video of Sara's life that the prosecution screened for the jury. And, as he had watched the grueling cross-examination of Detective Pat Banks on Court TV, Sara's elder child had demanded to call the cable network to vouch for Banks and tell reporters that defense lawyers' accounts of the boy's own statements to police were wrong.

Joni had worried for days that Fred would once more use the children, as he had during his marriage and after Sara's death. She sat helplessly in the courtroom and listened to Bell, knowing there was nothing she could do.

Outside, the pear petals blew from the trees as the rising dark of a thunderhead dimmed the filmy daylight filtering into the third-floor courtroom. As court adjourned and the courtroom was vacated by all the shadows, a sudden wild wind sucked out a window and opened the vaulted room to the warp of an angry rain.

It was left to Jimmy Berry, the jury's friend, to plead for Fred Tokars's life. He would build that argument on those witnesses who saw in Fred some lost reflection of their own salvation, who believed that he could be redeemed.

"Our religious upbringing is based on the belief in kindness and mercy and humanity and, above all, forgiveness," Berry said. "We have the ability in this country to forgive."

An eye for an eye and a tooth for a tooth was an unenlightened philosophy of vengeance that would leave a civilation toothless and blind. "You," he told the jury, "have the right and the authority to recommend mercy.

"We all feel for this family," he said, nodding at the Ambrusko sisters knotted in their stiff and terrifying silence as they stifled and swallowed their tears. "We all want this family to be well. But let me tell you something. Killing Fred Tokars is not going to make this family well. What's going to happen two years from now, five years from now, twenty years from now when these children want to talk to their father? They may want to embrace him. They may not. They may want to talk to him. They may not. But they won't have a choice. If you take the life of their father, they won't have a mother or a father. I don't care what a parent has done, there is a bond. Don't take away that bond. Don't take away the children's father, because maybe, somewhere down the road it may be very important for them to know their father.

"What would Sara want?" he concluded. "If executing Fred Tokars would have even more of an emotional impact on the children, I think that ought to be considered. I simply ask you to do this. I ask you to search your heart and soul. I ask you to find life in this case."

The Ambrusko women choked on the invocation of their sister's name. They had expected Fred's lawyers to urge mercy for his children's sake. But so abrupt and unanticipated was Berry's final question to the jury and his suggestion that Sara herself would have asked for her husband's life that Krissy and Karen abruptly fled the courtroom, gagging with revulsion and grief.

As Krissy retched in the bathroom, Karen struggled to swallow her sobs, whispering, "How could he do that?" over and over as she stood helplessly on the stairs.

In that instant, they hated Jimmy Berry for even uttering Sara's name. Mercy for the man responsible for the kidnap, the dark abandonment and utter terror of her sons? No. Sara would have been a lioness. Sara would have killed him herself.

"The most disgusting and sickening thing about all of this was that Jimmy Berry used Sara and Rick and Mike to save the life of that cold-blooded murderer," Krissy said angrily. "They are the three most innocent people, and he used them. And in doing that he spit on her grave."

In less than three hours, the jury decided Fred's fate. As they filed gravely into the courtroom for the final time, Norma Tokars sat silently with her eldest son, her head bowed to her knees. Defense lawyers looked as solemn as pallbearers. Jimmy Berry, dressed in the earth-green suits he favored, couldn't read the jury this time, didn't know what they might do but feared it. His heart sank as the jury entered. They were too grave. Several were near tears. At least one was crying. No one would look at Fred.

Dressed in a forest-green sweater and khakis, Fred alone appeared nonplussed, nodding to his family as he urged his mother in a stage whisper, "Be strong. Be strong."

Five of the Ambrusko sisters took their seats in the second row of the cavernous courtroom near the jury, clasped hands, bowed their heads, and once more prayed for their lost Sara. As the court clerk read the verdict, the weight of her words pressed as heavy and as suffocating as sand. Shoulders buckled. Heads drooped. Eyes closed as breaths were caught or sucked away.

Guilty of murder for hire. Guilty of murder for money. Guilty of a murder "outrageously and wantonly vile," a trip of terror that ended with a woman slain in front of her two children, a woman who in her final moment of life knew only she had not saved them. The jury affirmed every aggravating circumstance, any one of which would have been enough to send Fredric Tokars to the chair, a man with a malignant and abandoned heart whose crime Tom Charron called the reflection of an utterly corrupt, perverted, and immoral state of mind.

Everyone was certain now that the jury had condemned Fred to die. No one expected the clerk's next words. "We recommend that a life sentence be imposed."

The verdict broke the Ambrusko sisters utterly. Their belief in justice ruined, they strangled on bitter sobs. Joni bent double in her seat, her arms cradling her bowed head as she warded off the verdict like a blow. Mary's hand caught an audible gasp as it escaped her lips. She hugged herself, rocking in her seat like a devastated child. Karen faced the jury, tears streaming down her cheeks as she mouthed at several stricken jurors, "How could you do this?"

Several jurors cried in sympathy and frustration. By then, Fred was crying, too, mouthing the words, "I love you," to his dry-eyed mother and his stone-faced brother, hugging his lawyers whose own eyes glistened with unshed tears.

As they were individually polled, the jury held firm, although as each replied, several were virtually inaudible. After Bodiford pronounced the state's life sentence, Fred, surrounded by nearly a dozen sheriff's deputies and marshals, was hustled from the courtroom, speechless as a decr, clutching his legal folder to his breast with now cuffed hands.

Ten of the twelve jurors had wanted to condemn Fred to death. But two women, both health care professionals like Fred's mother, were adamant. One, a retired hospital coordinator, opposed death even before the jury began deliberations, despite pretrial assurances that she could sentence Fred to die if the circumstances warranted. The other woman, a retired nursing assistant, told reporters later, "After thirty-something years in the medical field trying to save lives, I couldn't take a life." She acknowledged that Fred was "a cold man." But, she said, "he could be generous when he wanted to. He loves his mother, and I believe he loves his sons. I think he has some good in him."

So ten jurors acquiesced, making what for some was a queasy compromise. But being forced to vote for life when they believed in death was far more palatable to the jurors who changed their minds and votes than forcing two women who were adamant for life to vote to execute a man. They could justify a life sentence, despite Fred's list of sins, because Eddie Lawrence would eventually be free and because another jury had failed even to convict Curtis Rower, the triggerman, of murder.

In the wide central corridor of the courthouse, Norma Tokars gratefully embraced the lanky, elder attorney who had helped to save her son. "I never believed that a Walker County jury would kill your son," Bobby Lee Cook reminded her. "I told you that."

With a small smile, she offered, "We are thankful for the verdict. Life is sweet," a tiny woman whose criminal son remained her anchor and whom two jurors much like her had refused to take from her.

But Sara's family was stunned. Hustled by the media from the small basement room where they had spent much of the trial's nine weeks, they couldn't stop the tears from falling or strip the anguish and the outrage from their voices.

"We are completely devastated," said Therese Ambrusko, the oldest sister and a lawyer who felt betrayed by her profession and her career. "We keep thinking Fred is going to wake up tomorrow morning, and Sara is not, and it's wrong." The trial was a travesty orchestrated by a system she no longer believed in or understood, she said. "The criminal justice system lets down the good people and saves the murderers. And I'm ashamed to be a part of it. They won. Justice was not served."

Epilogue

A War We Couldn't Win

"JUSTICE WAS DONE," RICKY TOKARS GRAVELY TOLD HIS aunt when he learned of his father's life sentence. "But not enough."

Sara's sons knew their father was a killer. That he could hand them over so easily to a deadly stranger still terrified them, even though he would now die in prison.

Death, Krissy Ambrusko said, "was the only right thing to do.

"We wanted so much to tell the kids they will be safe again," she said the day after Fred was hustled away by federal marshals. "Now, we don't know what we'll tell them. He's said to more than one person that it's because of us that he's in jail."

"We feel like he has a vendetta against us now," her older sister, Mary Bennett said.

And Joni worried, "We just don't know what he's capable of."

Sara's death had made them wary of the world. No fear could ever be dismissed again.

As the sisters separated for their homes in California, Florida, New Jersey, and New York, they clung to one hard reality—that, in the eyes of the law, Fred Tokars was now a killer. He had never admitted it, had sought with the insurance money and his sons to bargain it away. But Sara's family had

527

remained steadfast. They had held hands at Sara's crypt and vowed: "We will take care of Rick and Mike. And we will find your killer." They had finally kept faith with a sister they knew would have done the same for them.

After the murder trial ended, there were those who were quick to say it had all been just a waste of time and money, no more than an expensive political sail in the prevailing winds. But the Ambrusko sisters were adamant.

"It would have been horrifying for the family to know that Fred was doing time as a money launderer for drug dealers but, on paper at least, he would have gotten away with murder," Joni said. The cost of the trial should never outweigh justice, she insisted. "The good guys did not lose."

Fred's conviction as Sara's murderer wasn't the final legal battle associated with her death. But it was the pivot on which the other cases turned. Within six weeks of Fred's conviction, Curtis Rower had also strolled away from Death Row in exchange for a sentence of life without parole.

It galled Sara's family that he would not be tried again, that he would never face the death penalty and would never be executed for carrying out their sister's murder. They insisted they were still prepared to go forward, that Ricky was ready to testify, that they would once more see their character and their reputations strafed by opposing lawyers seeking to save their sister's killers.

"We were raised to believe the whole judicial system was a search for truth," Joni said bitterly. "And then we were forced into this four- or five-year war that had nothing to do with truth."

But, in the end, they swallowed like some foul, ill-tasting medicine the reality of the law. A mistrial forced by a rogue juror had already permitted Rower to sidestep a murder conviction once. Neither Fred, who masterminded the murder plot, nor Eddie Lawrence, who directed Rower like a deadly missile, had forfeited their lives. A jury would be hard-pressed to condemn Rower now, while those who set the plot in motion were given back their lives. Cobb County Superior Court Judge George Kreeger, who had long wanted Charron to accept Rower's guilty plea, had let the district attorney know in no uncertain terms that a Rower jury would be fully informed as to the fate of his coconspirators.

And if a jury decided not to send Rower to Death Row, the resulting life sentence would be parolable by law. Sara's family wanted to go to trial, wanted desperately to secure his death. But the old Georgia statute that governed Rower's sentence simply did not allow for life without parole. Reluctantly, the Ambruskos acquiesced. Tom Charron accepted the gunman's guilty plea and a sentence of life without parole.

However Sara's family refused to dignify the agreement with any kind of public seal that they approved of it or found it at all acceptable. On April 23, 1997 when Curtis Rower appeared before Kreeger a final time, no member of Sara's family was there. For the first time since her death, the Ambruskos were absent from a hearing.

In a statement their lawyer released after Rower was sentenced, the family announced, "We have completely lost faith that the criminal justice system will render the only just punishment, the death penalty. We now know that our search for a just punishment for Sara was a war we could not win."

By then, the Eleventh Circuit of the U.S. Court of Appeals had upheld Fred's federal racketeering and money-laundering convictions, and the U.S. Supreme Court had refused to hear the case. Fred's federal appeals were over. He would spend the remainder of his life in federal prison. He would never be paroled.

Once that federal conviction was affirmed, another Cobb County judge rejected Fred's claims to the insurance money that he had coveted since Sara's death. After nearly four years of litigation, Cobb County Superior Court Judge Dorothy Robinson awarded the Tokars boys the entire $1.75 million.

As soon as the state trial had ended, Fred had stopped calling or writing to his children. But he had continued to fight for the money derived from Sara's murder that rightly should have reverted to his sons. Even after his federal conviction, Fred's civil lawyers argued that he had not been found guilty of murder and so was entitled to the benefits. For Fred, the money had always been what drove him.

But those lawyers, too, soon tired of the legal game. There was nothing in it for them now, and although they initially appealed the judgment, they dropped it a short time later, leaving the way clear for Sara's children to bank the funds bought with their mother's blood.

And the Ambrusko family, after more than four years, began gathering the shattered pieces of their lives. They were battered. They were broke. And they were finally going home.

Through it all, they had kept their sister alive in her sons' wide hearts. When Ricky, a pitcher with the Manatee–Braden River Little League, struck out a string of batters to win a big league game, he told his aunts afterward, "I think I know how I struck out all those kids today. When I was walking to the pitcher's mound, I said a prayer to my mom. And I think she heard me."

For the sisters, it was a cherished step forward toward a normal life and a poignant tribute to their sister.

"We're going to take these kids to their baseball games, and we're going to cheer for them for Sara," Krissy vowed later. "We're going to take them to school, and go to Sunday mass. . . . We're going to be with them through the happy times and the sad times—for Sara. And we're going to try to give them a normal and happy life because that's what she wanted."

They promised they would be there for the Christmas plays where they would clap the loudest for Sara's sons because that's what Sara would have done. They would take them to the Statue of Liberty and the White House and remind them that their patriotic mother had taught them to sing "God Bless America" and "The Star-Spangled Banner" before she taught them "Twinkle, Twinkle, Little Star."

They would teach them to ski and teach them to pray.

"And if they're frightened," Joni vowed to her dead sister, "we'll comfort them. And when they are scared to forge ahead, we'll tell them how brave you were."

They would also continue their pilgrimages to the quiet, airy chapel north of Atlanta where Sara's crypt nestled near a wall of glass that caught and held the sun.

On a table below the crypt where her sisters had taped pictures of the Tokars boys lay a family photo, Mother's Day cards to "the World's Greatest Mom," and snapshots of her sons in baseball uniforms. Nearly hidden among a spray of pink roses, tiny pots of silken flowers, a teddy bear, a flag, and other small talismans of grief and loss, lay a note left by a friend.

Sara, it said. *They finally got him.*

Compelling True Crime Thrillers
From Avon Books

FATAL PHOTOGRAPHS
by Jack R. Nerad
79770-4/ $6.99 US/ $8.99 Can

CLUB FED
**A TRUE STORY OF LIFE, LIES, AND CRIME
IN THE FEDERAL WITNESS PROTECTION PROGRAM**
by George E. Taylor Jr. with Clifford C. Linedecker
79569-8/ $6.99 US/ $8.99 Can

FATAL MATCH
INSIDE THE MIND OF KILLER MILLIONAIRE JOHN DU PONT
by Bill Ordine and Ralph Vigoda
79105-6/ $6.99 US/ $8.99 Can

SECRETS NEVER LIE
**THE DEATH OF SARA TOKARS—
A SOUTHERN TRAGEDY OF MONEY, MURDER,
AND INNOCENCE BETRAYED**
by Robin McDonald
77752-5/ $6.99 US/ $8.99 Can

THE GOODFELLA TAPES
by George Anastasia
79637-6/ $5.99 US/ $7.99 Can

SPEED KILLS
by Arthur Jay Harris
71932-0/ $5.99 US/ $7.99 Can

14083

THE TRUTH ABOUT UFOs
from Kevin D. Randle, U.S.A.F., Retired

PROJECT MOON DUST
Beyond Roswell—Exposing the Government's Continuing
Covert UFO Investigations and Cover-Ups
80603-7/$6.99 US/$8.99 Can

CONSPIRACY OF SILENCE
79918-9/$6.99 US/$8.99 Can
What the public needs to know about the U.S. Government's
official investigations and cover-ups of modern UFO activity.

A HISTORY OF UFO CRASHES
77666-9/$5.99 US/$7.99 Can

co-authored with Donald R. Schmitt

UFO CRASH AT ROSWELL
76196-3/$6.99 US/$8.99 Can
The complete, uncensored and indisputable true story of
America's closest encounter.

THE TRUTH ABOUT
THE UFO CRASH AT ROSWELL
77803-3/$6.99 US/$8.99 Can

In a follow-up to their groundbreaking work, this volume
includes startling new evidence from previously
top-secret government reports and additional testimony from
eyewitnesses who finally stepped forward after years
of fear-induced silence.